Oxford Smart

# AQA GCSE CHEMISTRY
## for Combined Science: Trilogy

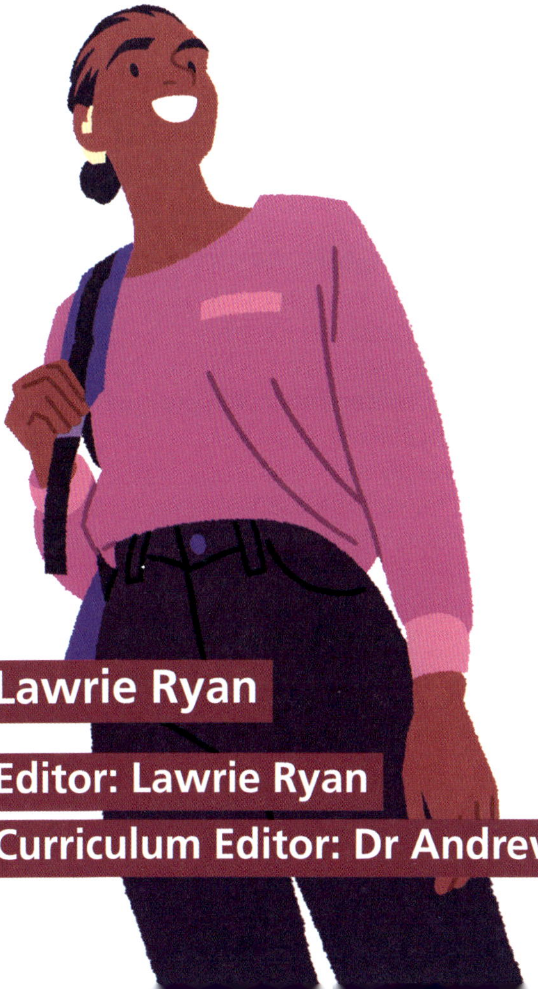

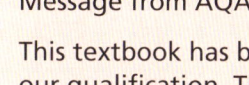

Message from AQA

This textbook has been approved by AQA for use with our qualification. This means that we have checked that it broadly covers the specification and we are satisfied with the overall quality. Full details of our approval process can be found on our website.

We approve textbooks because we know how important it is for teachers and students to have the right resources to support their teaching and learning. However, the publisher is ultimately responsible for the editorial control and quality of this book.

Please note that when teaching the AQA GCSE Combined Science: Trilogy course, you must refer to AQA's specification as your definitive source of information. While this book has been written to match the specification, it cannot provide complete coverage of every aspect of the course.

A wide range of other useful resources can be found on the relevant subject pages of our website: www.aqa.org.uk.

AQA material is reproduced by permission of AQA.

Lawrie Ryan

Editor: Lawrie Ryan

Curriculum Editor: Dr Andrew Chandler-Grevatt

# Contents

Required practicals iv
How to use this book v
Digital support on Kerboodle viii
Structure of assessment ix
Metacognition: Becoming an expert learner x

## 1 Atoms, bonding, and calculations 2

| C1 | **Atomic structure** | |
|---|---|---|
| C1.1 | Atoms | 4 |
| C1.2 | Chemical equations | 6 |
| C1.3 | Separating mixtures | 8 |
| C1.4 | Fractional distillation and paper chromatography | 10 |
| C1.5 | History of the atom | 12 |
| C1.6 | Structure of the atom | 14 |
| C1.7 | Ions, atoms, and isotopes | 16 |
| C1.8 | Electronic structures | 18 |
| C1 | Practice and Exam-style questions | 20 |

| C2 | **The Periodic Table** | |
|---|---|---|
| C2.1 | Development of the Periodic Table | 22 |
| C2.2 | Electronic structures and the Periodic Table | 24 |
| C2.3 | Group 1 – the alkali metals | 26 |
| C2.4 | Group 7 – the halogens | 28 |
| C2.5 | Explaining trends | 30 |
| C2 | Practice and Exam-style questions | 32 |

| C3 | **Structure and bonding** | |
|---|---|---|
| C3.1 | States of matter | 34 |
| C3.2 | Atoms into ions | 36 |
| C3.3 | Ionic bonding | 38 |
| C3.4 | Giant ionic structures | 40 |
| C3.5 | Covalent bonding | 42 |
| C3.6 | Structure of simple molecules | 44 |
| C3.7 | Giant covalent structures | 46 |
| C3.8 | Fullerenes and graphene | 48 |
| C3.9 | Bonding in metals | 50 |
| C3.10 | Giant metallic structures | 52 |
| C3 | Practice and Exam-style questions | 54 |

| C4 | **Chemical calculations** | |
|---|---|---|
| C4.1 | Relative masses and moles | 56 |
| C4.2 | Equations and calculations | 58 |
| C4.3 | From masses to balanced equations | 60 |
| C4.4 | Expressing concentrations | 62 |
| C4 | Practice and Exam-style questions | 64 |

## 2 Chemical reactions and energy changes 66

| C5 | **Chemical changes** | |
|---|---|---|
| C5.1 | The reactivity series | 68 |
| C5.2 | Displacement reactions | 70 |
| C5.3 | Extracting metals | 72 |
| C5.4 | Salts from metals | 74 |
| C5.5 | Salts from insoluble bases | 76 |
| C5.6 | Making more salts | 78 |
| C5.7 | Neutralisation and the pH scale | 80 |
| C5.8 | Strong and weak acids | 82 |
| C5 | Practice and Exam-style questions | 84 |

| C6 | **Electrolysis** | |
|---|---|---|
| C6.1 | Introduction to electrolysis | 86 |
| C6.2 | Changes at the electrodes | 88 |
| C6.3 | The extraction of aluminium | 90 |
| C6.4 | Electrolysis of aqueous solutions | 92 |
| C6 | Practice and Exam-style questions | 94 |

| C7 | **Energy changes** | |
|---|---|---|
| C7.1 | Exothermic and endothermic reactions | 96 |
| C7.2 | Using energy transfers from reactions | 98 |
| C7.3 | Reaction profiles | 100 |
| C7.4 | Bond energy calculations | 102 |
| C7 | Practice and Exam-style questions | 104 |

## 3 Rates, equilibrium, and organic chemistry 106

| C8 | **Rates and equilibrium** | |
|---|---|---|
| C8.1 | Rate of reaction | 108 |
| C8.2 | Collision theory and surface area | 110 |
| C8.3 | The effect of temperature | 112 |
| C8.4 | The effects of concentration and pressure | 114 |
| C8.5 | The effect of catalysts | 116 |
| C8.6 | Reversible reactions | 118 |
| C8.7 | Energy and reversible reactions | 120 |
| C8.8 | Dynamic equilibrium | 122 |
| C8.9 | Altering conditions | 124 |
| C8 | Practice and Exam-style questions | 126 |

| C9 | **Crude oil and fuels** | |
|---|---|---|
| C9.1 | Hydrocarbons | 128 |
| C9.2 | Fractional distillation of oil | 130 |

| C9.3 | Burning hydrocarbon fuels | 132 |
| C9.4 | Cracking hydrocarbons | 134 |
| C9 | Practice and Exam-style questions | 136 |

## 4 Analysis and the Earth's resources — 138

| C10 | **Chemical analysis** | |
| C10.1 | Pure substances and mixtures | 140 |
| C10.2 | Analysing chromatograms | 142 |
| C10.3 | Testing for gases | 144 |
| C10 | Practice and Exam-style questions | 146 |

| C11 | **The Earth's atmosphere** | |
| C11.1 | History of our atmosphere | 148 |
| C11.2 | Our evolving atmosphere | 150 |
| C11.3 | Greenhouse gases | 152 |
| C11.4 | Global climate change | 154 |
| C11.5 | Atmospheric pollutants | 156 |
| C11 | Practice and Exam-style questions | 158 |

| C12 | **The Earth's resources** | |
| C12.1 | Finite and renewable resources | 160 |
| C12.2 | Water safe to drink | 162 |
| C12.3 | Treating waste water | 164 |
| C12.4 | Extracting metals from ores | 166 |
| C12.5 | Life cycle assessments | 168 |
| C12.6 | Reduce, reuse, and recycle | 170 |
| C12 | Practice and Exam-style questions | 172 |

| Paper 1 questions | 174 |
| Paper 2 questions | 178 |

### Maths skills for Chemistry

| MS1 | Arithmetic and numerical computation | 180 |
| MS2 | Handling data | 186 |
| MS3 | Algebra | 190 |
| MS4 | Graphs | 193 |
| MS5 | Geometry and trigonometry | 196 |

**Working scientifically** — 198

Glossary — 205
Index — 209

Appendix 1: The Periodic Table — 214

# Required practicals

Practical work is a vital part of studying chemistry, helping to support and apply your scientific knowledge, and develop your investigative and practical skills. The chemistry part of your GCSE Combined Science: Trilogy course has six required practicals that you must carry out. Questions in your exams could draw on any of the knowledge and skills you have developed in carrying out these practicals. This could include planning an investigation, making predictions, measuring and analysing results, drawing graphs, and identifying patterns. You might also be asked about practicals that you have not done before but are similar to ones you have done.

A 'Required practical' feature box has been included in this student book for each of your required practicals. Further support is available on Kerboodle.

| | Required practical | Topic |
|---|---|---|
| 8 | **Making salts** Prepare with the appropriate apparatus and techniques, a pure, dry sample of a soluble salt from an insoluble carbonate or oxide. | C5.5 C5.6 |
| 9 | **Electrolysis** Investigate the electrolysis of different aqueous solutions using inert electrodes. | C6.4 |
| 10 | **Temperature changes** Use appropriate apparatus to investigate the variables that affect energy changes in reactions involving at least one solution. | C7.1 |
| 11 | **Rates of reaction** Investigate how changes in concentration affect rates of reactions using a method involving measuring the volume of a gas produced and a method involving a change in colour or turbidity. | C8.4 |
| 12 | **Chromatography** Use paper chromatography to find out the $R_f$ values of the dyes found in different food colourings. | C10.2 |
| 13 | **Water purification** Analyse and purify water from different sources, including pH, dissolved solids and distillation. | C12.2 |

# How to use this book

This book has been written by subject experts to match the 2016 specifications. It is packed full of features to help you prepare for your course and achieve the very best you can.

**Key words** are highlighted in the text. You can look them up in the glossary at the back of the book if you are not sure what they mean.

Many diagrams are as important for your understanding as the text, so make sure you revise them carefully.

### Synoptic link

Synoptic links show how the content of a topic links to other parts of the course. This will support you with the synoptic element of your assessment.

There are also links to the 'Maths skills for Chemistry' chapter, so you can develop your maths skills whilst you study.

### Study tip

Study tips give you hints and advice on the things you need to know and remember, and what to watch out for.

### Metacognition

Metacognition feature boxes give you handy revision-focused tips that are supported by cognitive science.

### Key points

Linking to the Learning objectives, the Key points boxes summarise what you should be able to do at the end of the topic. They can be used to help you with revision.

### Learning objectives

- Learning objectives at the start of each spread tell you the content that you will cover.
- Any objectives marked with the higher-tier icon H are only relevant to those who are sitting the higher-tier exams.

### Practical

Practicals are a great way for you to see the science in action for yourself. These boxes may be a simple introduction or reminder, or they may be the basis for a practical in the classroom. They will help your understanding of the course.

### Required practical

These practicals have important skills that you will need to be confident with for part of your assessment. Your teacher will give you additional information about tackling these practicals.

H

Anything in the higher-tier spreads and boxes must be learnt by those sitting the higher-tier exam. If you will be sitting the foundation tier, you will not be assessed on this content.

### Maths

This feature highlights and explains the key maths skills you need. There are also clear step-by-step worked examples.

### Summary questions

1 Each topic has summary questions. These questions give you the chance to test whether you have learnt and understood everything in the topic.
2 The questions start off easier and get harder, so that you can stretch yourself.
3 Any questions marked with the higher-tier icon H are for students sitting the higher-tier exams.

v

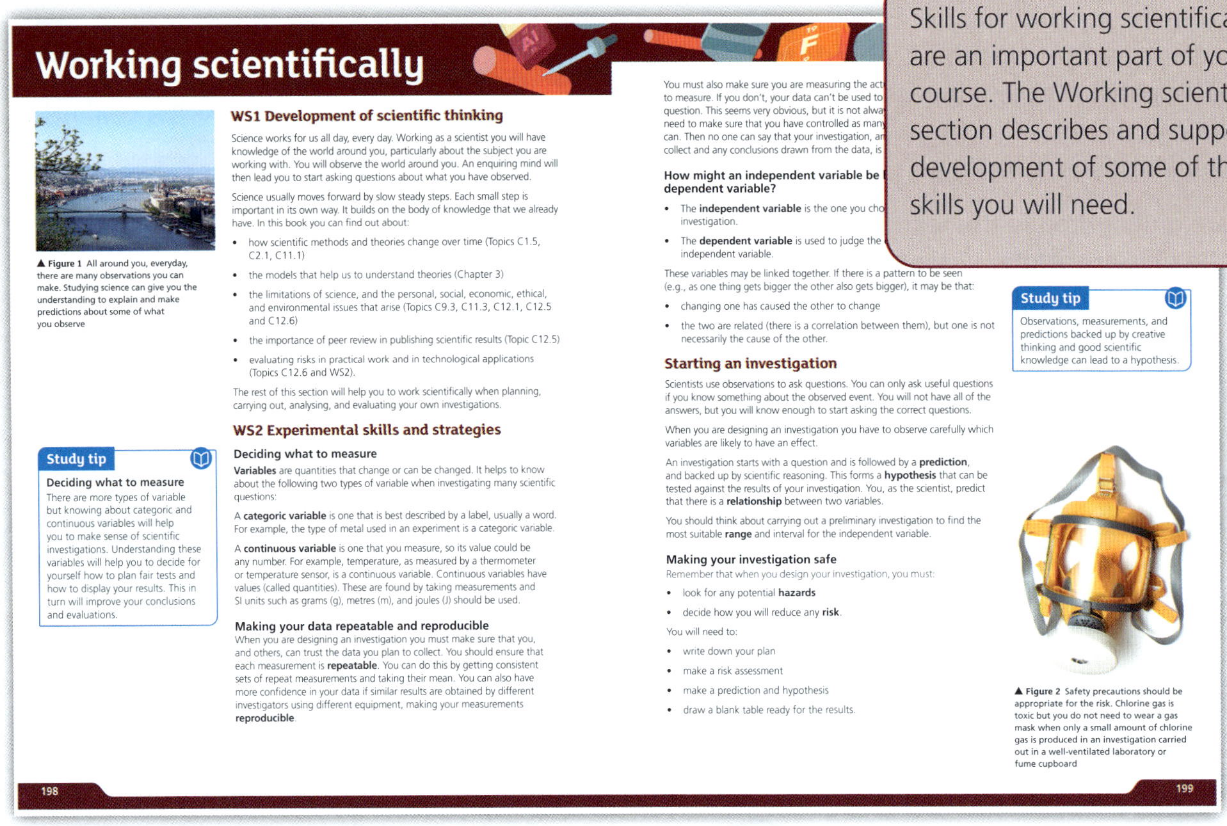

# Working scientifically

Skills for working scientifically are an important part of your course. The Working scientifically section describes and supports the development of some of the key skills you will need.

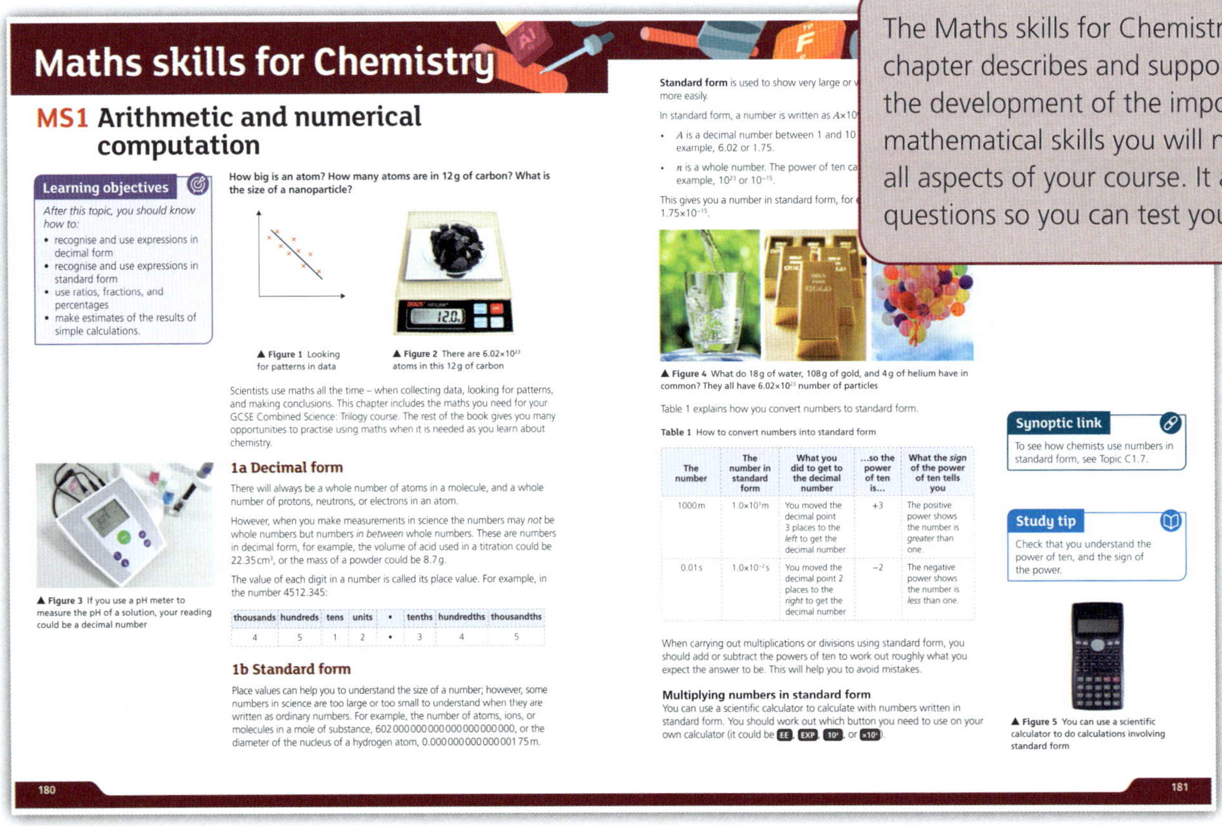

# Maths skills for Chemistry

## MS1 Arithmetic and numerical computation

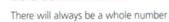

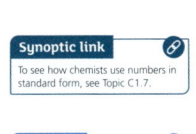

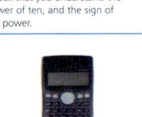

The Maths skills for Chemistry chapter describes and supports the development of the important mathematical skills you will need for all aspects of your course. It also has questions so you can test your skills.

The section openers include an introduction to the section, some retrieval questions to test your prior knowledge, and a chapter map to help you see where you are in the course.

# 1 Atoms, bonding, and calculations

Atoms are the chemical building blocks of our world. The Periodic Table organises these atoms and the elements they make in a way that helps us to make sense of the physical world. Chemists have evidence that atoms themselves are made up of a nucleus surrounded by electrons in different energy levels. Theories of the bonding between atoms explain how atoms are held together to make millions of different materials. Scientists use knowledge of structure and bonding to engineer new materials with properties designed for new uses in a range of technologies.

Chemists use their calculations from quantitative analysis to determine the formulae of compounds and the equations for reactions. They also use quantitative methods to determine the purity of chemical samples and to monitor the yield from chemical reactions. They can make sense of how different chemicals react together and can establish patterns to predict the behaviour of other chemicals.

1 What is the difference between an element a… compound?

2 What do we call the new substances made i… chemical reaction?

3 Define a mixture.

4 What is the general word for a liquid that ca… dissolve another substance?

5 What are the vertical columns in the Periodic Table called? — groups

6 Which state of matter has most space between its particles? — gas

7 Write a word equation for the reaction of magnesium with oxygen. — magnesium + oxygen → magnesium oxide

8 What is the relationship between the mass of all the reactants and the mass of all the products in a chemical reaction? — the mass of reactants and the mass of products are the same

9 In a chemical reaction between calcium and oxygen, name the product of the reaction. — calcium oxide

10 When hydrogen reacts with oxygen, the only product is water. If 4 g of hydrogen produces 36 g of water, what is the mass of oxygen that reacted? — 32 g

Put paper here

## Journey through GCSE Chemistry

YOU ARE HERE

**Atoms, bonding, and calculations**
C1 Atomic structure
C2 The Periodic Table
C3 Structure and bonding
C4 Chemical calculations

**Chemical reactions and energy changes**
C5 Chemical changes
C6 Electrolysis
C7 Energy changes

**Rates, equilibrium, and organic chemistry**
C8 Rates and equilibrium
C9 Crude oil and fuels

**Analysis and the Earth's resources**
C10 Chemical analysis
C11 The Earth's atmosphere
C12 The Earth's resources

2 3

At the end of every chapter there are Practice questions and Exam-style questions. The questions test your literacy, maths, and working scientifically skills, as well as your knowledge of the concepts in that chapter. The Exam-style questions can also call on knowledge from any of the previous chapters to help support the synoptic element of your assessment.

There are also further Exam-style questions at the end of the book to cover all of the content from your course.

# C1 Atomic structure

## Practice questions

1 a i Name the sub-atomic particles found in the nucleus of an atom. 1 MARK
ii What is the maximum number of electrons that can occupy each of the first two energy levels or shells? 1 MARK
b i Explain the overall charge on any atom. 3 MARKS
ii Describe how an atom can become an ion with a 2+ charge. Explain your answer. 2 MARKS
iii Define atomic number and mass number. 2 MARKS

2 a Define what the term mixture means to a scientist. 1 MARK
b Explain the differences between a mixture and a compound. 2 MARKS
c Name the technique you would use to separate and collect:
i hydrated copper(II) sulfate, $CuSO_4{\cdot}5H_2O$, from its aqueous solution 1 MARK
ii a precipitate of lead iodide from the solution formed when aqueous solutions of lead nitrate and sodium iodide are mixed 1 MARK
iii water from a solution of potassium chloride 1 MARK
iv ethanol from a mixture of water and ethanol. 1 MARK

3 Use the data in the table to answer the following questions:

| Chemical element | Melting point in °C | Boiling point in °C | Density in g/cm³ |
|---|---|---|---|
| bromine | −7 | 59 | 3.12 |
| caesium | 29 | 669 | 1.88 |
| fluorine | −220 | −188 | 0.00158 |
| strontium | 769 | 1384 | 2.6 |
| xenon | −112 | −108 | 0.0055 |

a Determine the physical state of each element in the table at 25 °C. 3 MARKS
b Name the element that exists as a liquid over the widest range of temperatures. 1 MARK
c Write the chemical symbol for atoms of each element in the table. 1 MARK
d Classify each element in the table as a metal or a non-metal. 1 MARK
e Write the electronic structure of:
i a fluorine atom 1 MARK
ii a fluoride ion, $F^-$. 1 MARK

4 This question is about some of the elements in the Periodic Table. You will need to use the Periodic Table to help you answer some parts of the question.
a Neon, Ne, is the 10th element in the Periodic Table.
i Is neon a metal or a non-metal? 1 MARK
ii Are there more metals or non-metals in the Periodic Table? 1 MARK
iii Give the number of protons a neon atom contains. 1 MARK
iv The mass number of a neon atom is 20. How many neutrons does it contain? 1 MARK
v Give the name and number of the group to which neon belongs. 1 MARK
vi Name two other elements in the same group as neon. 1 MARK
vii Write the electronic structure of a neon atom. 1 MARK
viii Describe what is special about the electronic structure of neon and the other elements in its group. 1 MARK
b The element radium, Ra, has 88 electrons.
i How many protons are in the nucleus of each radium atom? 1 MARK
ii How many electrons does a radium atom have in its highest energy level (outermost shell)? Give a reason for your answer. 1 MARK
iii Determine whether radium is a metal or a non-metal. 1 MARK
iv Radium's three most common isotopes are radium-224, radium-226, and radium-228. Describe the difference between the atomic structures of the three isotopes. 1 MARK
v Calcium is in the same group as radium. Its atomic number is 20. Write down its electronic structure. 1 MARK
vi Calcium forms 2+ ions in its compounds. Using the $^{40}Ca$ atom, determine the number of protons, neutrons, and electrons in a $Ca^{2+}$ ion. 1 MARK

5 Balance the following symbol equations:
a $Na + Cl_2 \rightarrow NaCl$ 1 MARK
b $Al + O_2 \rightarrow Al_2O_3$ 1 MARK
c $Fe_2O_3 + C \rightarrow Fe + CO_2$ 1 MARK
d $Al(OH)_3 \rightarrow Al_2O_3 + H_2O$ 1 MARK
e $Ba(NO_3)_2 \rightarrow BaO + NO_2 + O_2$ 1 MARK
f $C_4H_{10} + O_2 \rightarrow CO_2 + H_2O$ 1 MARK

## Exam-style questions

01 This question is about rock salt. Rock salt is a mixture of sand and salt.

01.1 A student followed the method to separate… salt into crystals of sand and crystals of salt…

**Step 1:** Add 25.0 g of rock salt to a beaker.

**Step 2:** Add 250 cm³ of water.

**Step 3:** Filter.

Suggest **one** improvement to Step 2 to get a better separation of rock salt and water.

01.2 **Figure 1** shows step 3 of the method.

**Figure 1**



What word best describes the salt solution i… **Figure 1**? Choose the correct answer.

A distillate C filtrate
B polymer D supernatant

01.3 Explain why the sand becomes the residue in **Figure 1**.

01.4 Describe how the student could produce dr… salt crystals from the salt solution in step 3.

01.5 The student produced 2.5 g of dry salt cryst… Suggest why the student could not have predicted the mass of dry salt crystals that would have been produced.

02 A student investigated green ink using chromatography. The student set up the apparatus as shown in **Figure 2**.

**Figure 2**



03.2 There are two isotopes of chlorine: $^{35}_{17}Cl$ and $^{37}_{17}Cl$. In terms of sub-atomic particles, describe the similarities and differences between these two isotopes of chlorine. 3 MARKS

03.3 Explain why both isotopes of chlorine have the same chemical properties. 2 MARKS

03.4 The relative atomic mass of chlorine is 35.5. Outline what this tells you about the abundance of the two isotopes. Explain your answer. 2 MARKS

20 21

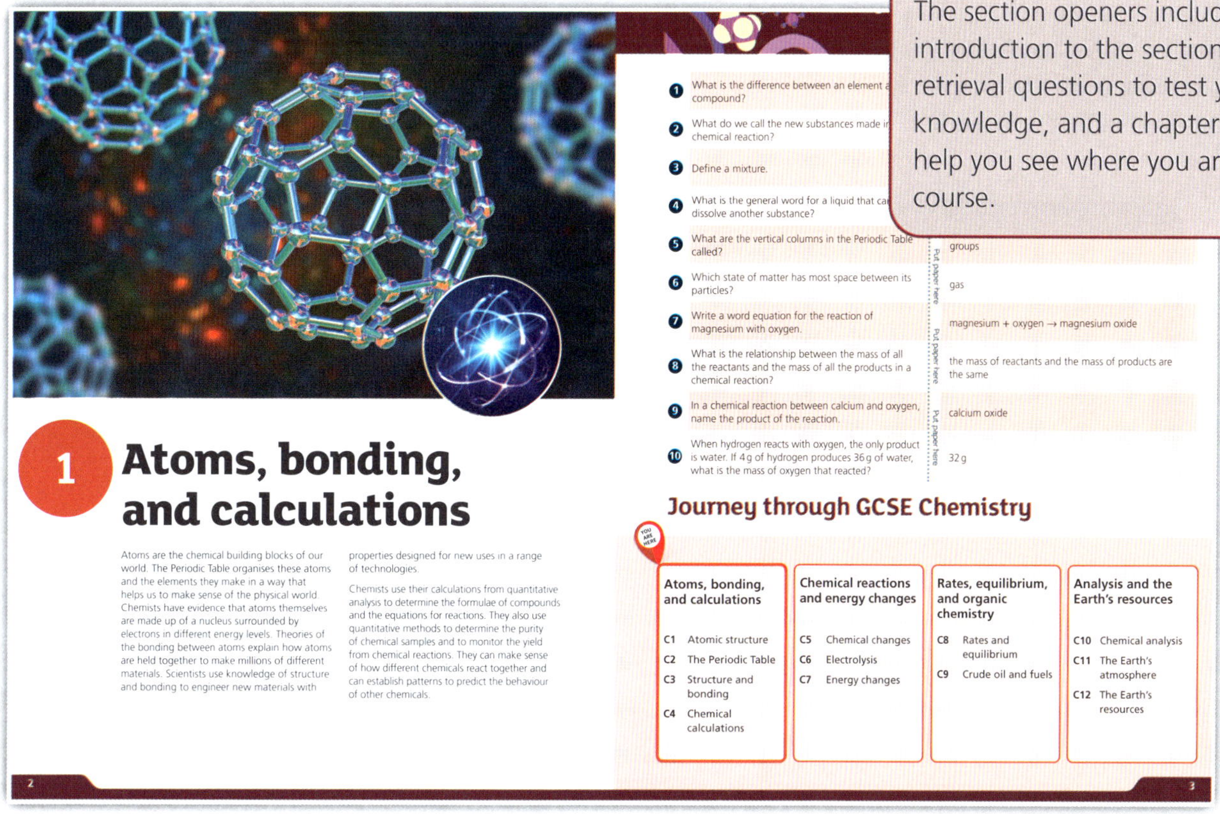

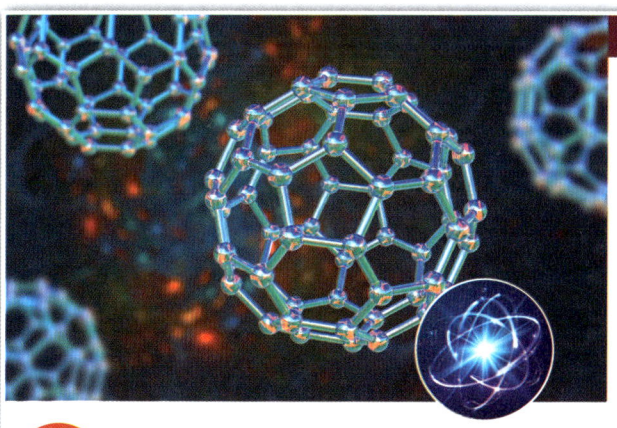

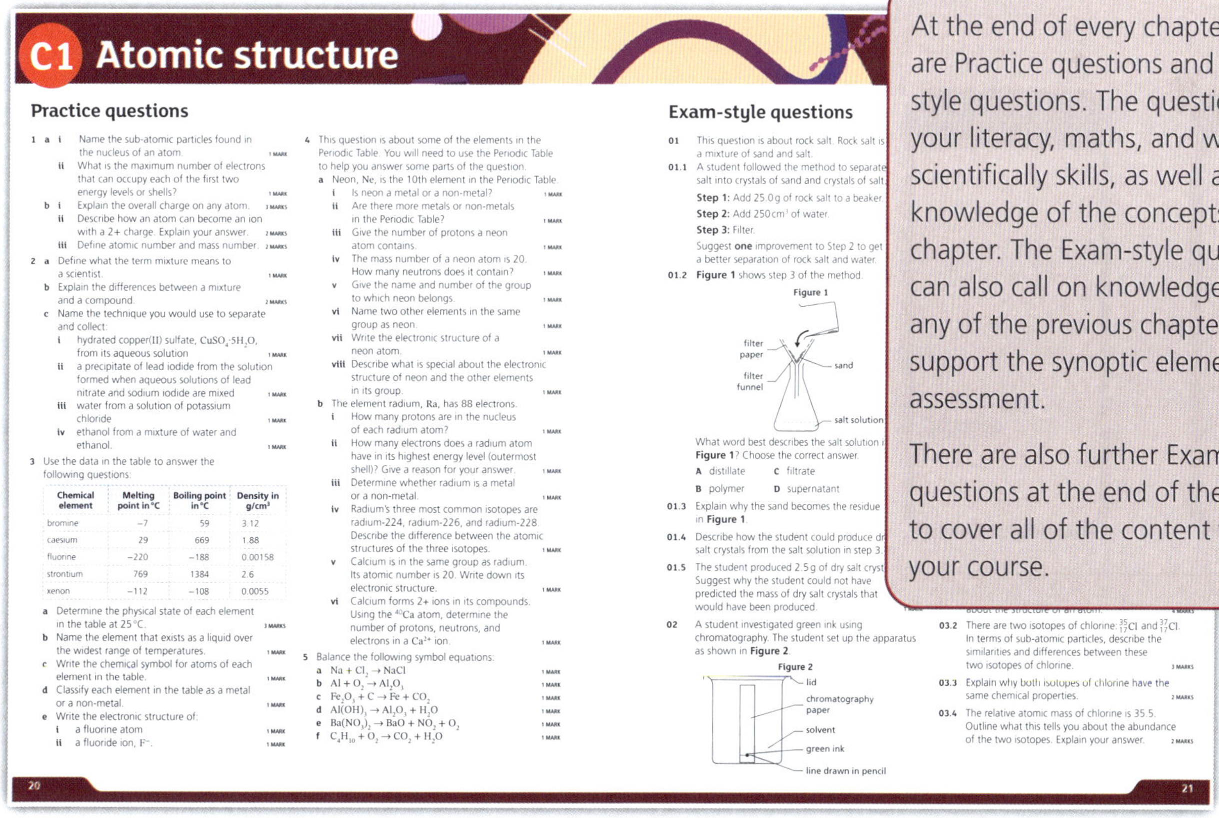

# Digital support on Kerboodle

This book is supported by Kerboodle, which provides digital support for AQA GCSE Combined Science: Trilogy. If your school subscribes to Kerboodle, you'll be able to access plenty of resources to help you with your studies and with revision.

**Learn anywhere** with onscreen access to student resources and a digital version of this book.

**Check what you know** with regular, low-stakes quizzes to test your knowledge and make sure it sticks.

**Keep motivated** with a variety of engaging content including knowledge organisers, interactive activities, quizzes, animations, and videos.

**Build your confidence** with adaptive technology that provides a personalised journey – take a quiz, receive results and feedback immediately as well as a next step to help you improve or take you further.

**Get personalised support** with intervention and extension assessments that are tailored to your strengths and weaknesses and keep you learning.

**Deepen understanding** with spaced repetition, where you are asked follow-up questions on completed topics at regular intervals to encourage retention and quick retrieval of knowledge.

# Structure of assessment

There will be two examination papers for GCSE Combined Science: Trilogy, which you will sit at the end of your course.

## Paper 1

This paper will test you on content from chapters C1 to C7 in this book. There are some Paper 1 practice questions at the back of the book.

| What's assessed | Time | Marks available | Percentage of GCSE |
|---|---|---|---|
| • Atomic structure and the Periodic Table<br>• Bonding, structure, and the properties of matter<br>• Quantitative chemistry<br>• Chemical changes<br>• Energy changes | 1 hour 15 minutes | 70 | 16.7% |

## Paper 2

This paper will test you on content from chapters C8 to C12 in this book. There are some Paper 2 practice questions at the back of the book.

| What's assessed | Time | Marks available | Percentage of GCSE |
|---|---|---|---|
| • The rate and extent of chemical change<br>• Organic chemistry<br>• Chemical analysis<br>• Chemistry of the atmosphere<br>• Using resources | 1 hour 15 minutes | 70 | 16.7% |

## Question types

Understanding how to approach exam questions will help you succeed in your exams. Both Paper 1 and Paper 2 include a mix of question types:

- Multiple-choice questions are answerable from a given set of answers.

- Structured questions are closed questions that ask for a single-word or single-choice answer. These can include completing sentences, linking boxes, or labelling diagrams.

- Closed short-answer questions can be answered with a single word or a short phrase. These might include naming or defining things, or stating a fact.

- Open-response questions have no answer options and ask you to think carefully about possible answers based on what you've learned. They include drawing diagrams, open short-answer questions, calculations, and extended-response questions.

Each question will show how many marks it is worth. Extended-response questions are worth up to six marks and will test your literacy skills as well as how well you answered the question. They may also require you to bring together ideas from two or more topics.

The practice questions in this book will introduce you to all these different question types.

Remember too that practical questions account for 15% of the total marks overall from both papers.

# Metacognition: Becoming an expert learner

## Learning objectives

*After this topic, you should know:*
- how to use the Plan, Monitor, and Evaluate cycle and apply it when completing unknown tasks
- evaluate common revision strategies to understand what, when, and why to use them.

Learning and revising GCSE Combined Science: Trilogy can sometimes feel overwhelming because you have to recall and apply a lot of complex knowledge. It is important to understand your own learning processes and make sure you are aware of a variety of strategies that are available to help.

### Understanding yourself as a learner

Expert learners have a good understanding of their own strengths and weaknesses. They are also able to approach new and unfamiliar tasks in a structured way. The Plan, Monitor, and Evaluate cycle is a structure you can follow to help you approach a new task like an expert learner. The example below shows the types of questions you should ask yourself when completing a new task.

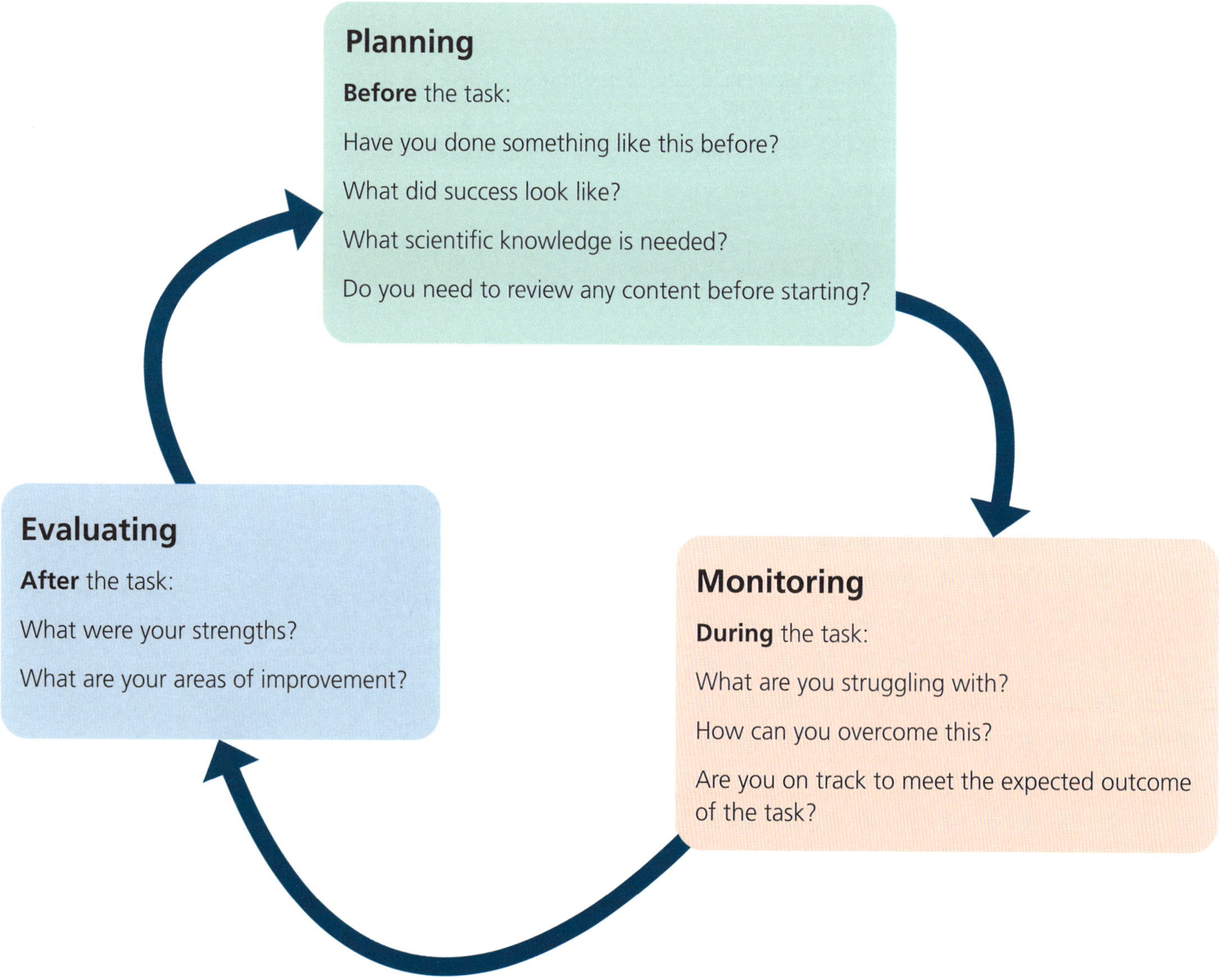

**Planning**

**Before** the task:

Have you done something like this before?

What did success look like?

What scientific knowledge is needed?

Do you need to review any content before starting?

**Monitoring**

**During** the task:

What are you struggling with?

How can you overcome this?

Are you on track to meet the expected outcome of the task?

**Evaluating**

**After** the task:

What were your strengths?

What are your areas of improvement?

▲ **Figure 1** The plan, monitor, and evaluate cycle

## Understanding effective revision strategies

Revision is an important part of the learning process. It is important to understand what effective strategies you have available, how and when you should use them, and why they are useful.

### Growing a question tree

**What**: A question tree is a type of flow chart that breaks down a complex procedure into manageable steps.

**When**: A question tree is best suited for breaking down steps of a required practical activity or a complex procedure like balancing a chemical equation.

**Why**: Procedures with many steps, like analysing the results from a required practical, need you to consider multiple things at the same time. A question tree simplifies this process. It also helps break it down so that you can revise it and apply it to new questions or tasks in the future.

**How**: Here is an example of a question tree that can be used to identify the products at the electrodes when conducting electrolysis of an aqueous solution.

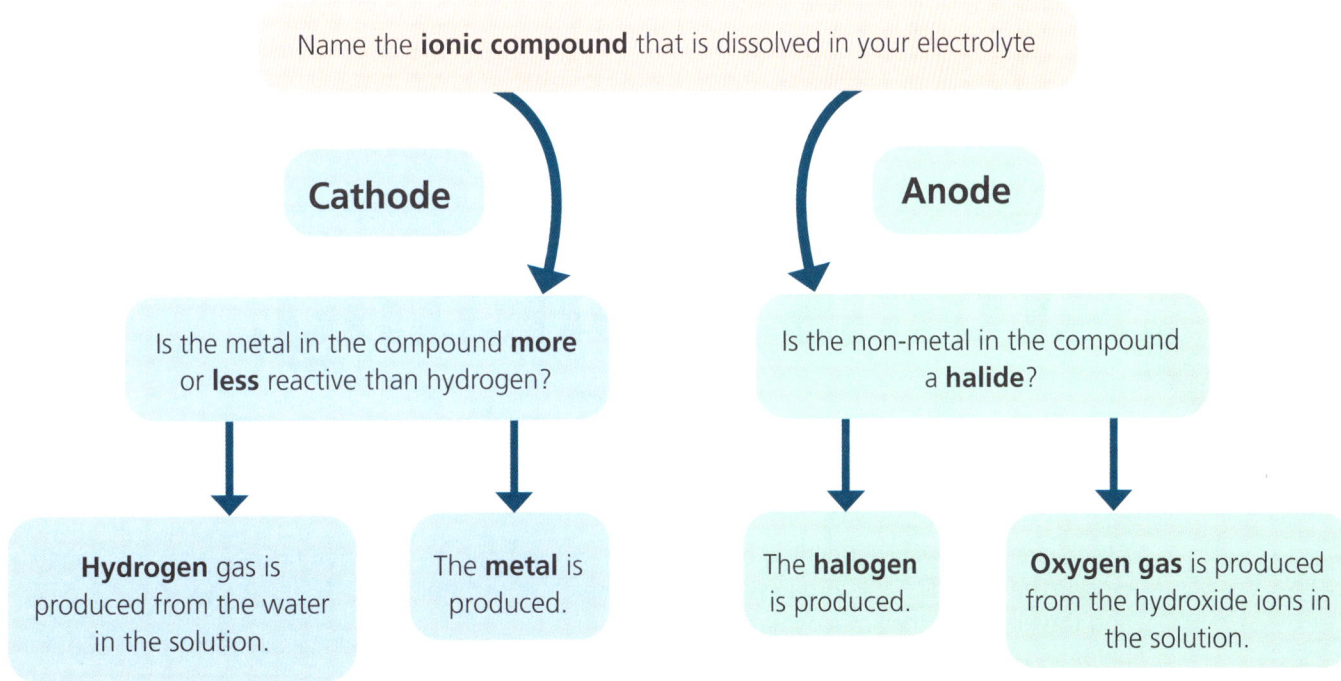

▲ **Figure 2** A question tree

### Summary question

The 'Making salts' required practical involves reacting an acid with a metal or an insoluble base, such as a metal oxide, metal hydroxide, or a metal carbonate.

1 Create your own question tree to simplify the steps of the practical.

*Hint: You need to be able to identify the reagents needed for a range of different salts.*

xi

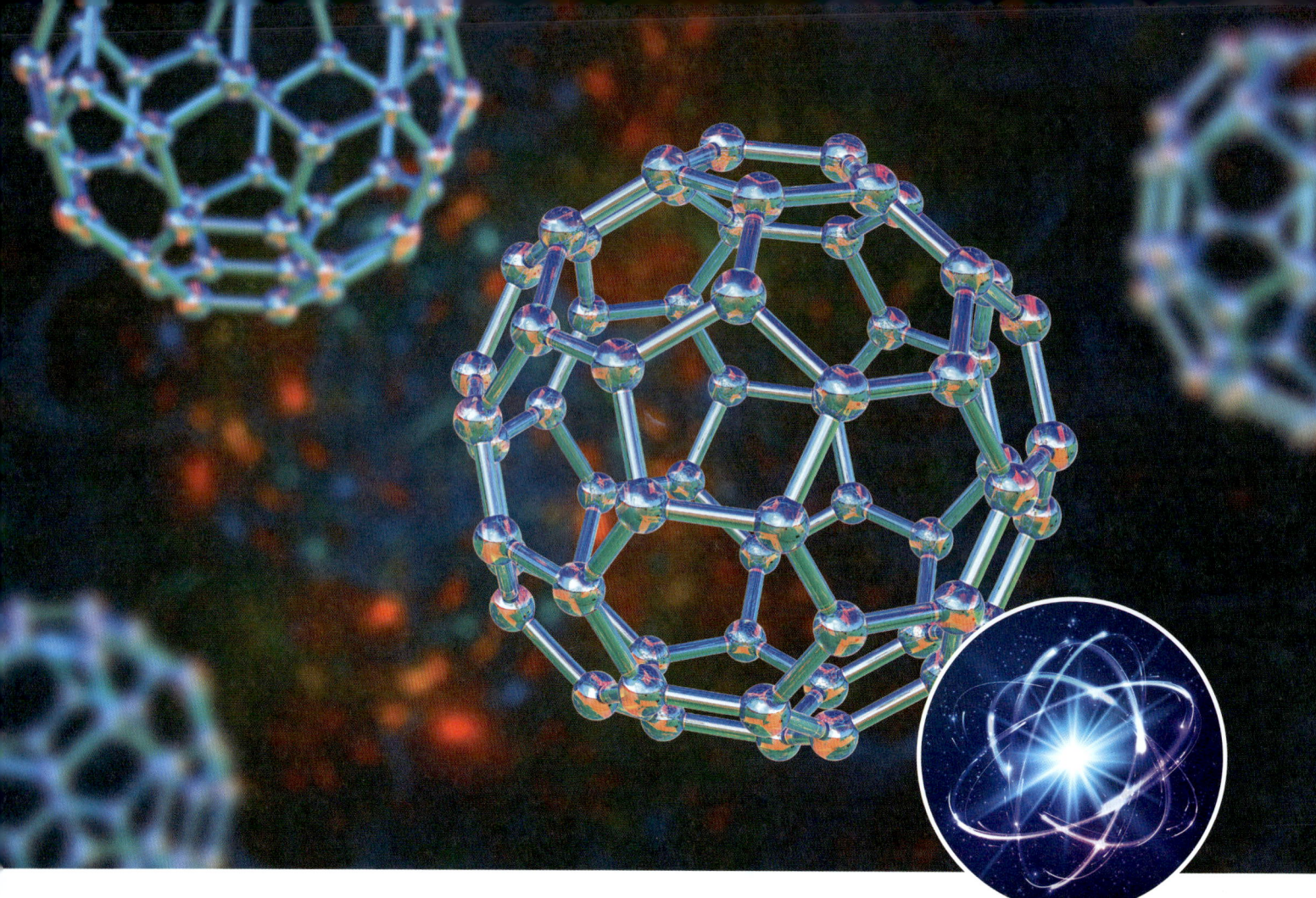

# 1 Atoms, bonding, and calculations

Atoms are the chemical building blocks of our world. The Periodic Table organises these atoms and the elements they make in a way that helps us to make sense of the physical world. Chemists have evidence that atoms themselves are made up of a nucleus surrounded by electrons in different energy levels. Theories of the bonding between atoms explain how atoms are held together to make millions of different materials. Scientists use knowledge of structure and bonding to engineer new materials with properties designed for new uses in a range of technologies.

Chemists use their calculations from quantitative analysis to determine the formulae of compounds and the equations for reactions. They also use quantitative methods to determine the purity of chemical samples and to monitor the yield from chemical reactions. They can make sense of how different chemicals react together and can establish patterns to predict the behaviour of other chemicals.

| | | |
|---|---|---|
| 1 | What is the difference between an element and a compound? | an element is made up of only one type of atom whereas a compound is made up of two or more types of atoms |
| 2 | What do we call the new substances made in a chemical reaction? | products |
| 3 | Define a mixture. | a mixture is made up of two or more substances that are not chemically combined together |
| 4 | What is the general word for a liquid that can dissolve another substance? | solvent |
| 5 | What are the vertical columns in the Periodic Table called? | groups |
| 6 | Which state of matter has most space between its particles? | gas |
| 7 | Write a word equation for the reaction of magnesium with oxygen. | magnesium + oxygen → magnesium oxide |
| 8 | What is the relationship between the mass of all the reactants and the mass of all the products in a chemical reaction? | the mass of reactants and the mass of products are the same |
| 9 | In a chemical reaction between calcium and oxygen, name the product of the reaction. | calcium oxide |
| 10 | When hydrogen reacts with oxygen, the only product is water. If 4 g of hydrogen produces 36 g of water, what is the mass of oxygen that reacted? | 32 g |

Put paper here

Put paper here

Put paper here

Put paper here

Put paper here

# Journey through GCSE Chemistry

YOU ARE HERE

**Atoms, bonding, and calculations**

- **C1** Atomic structure
- **C2** The Periodic Table
- **C3** Structure and bonding
- **C4** Chemical calculations

**Chemical reactions and energy changes**

- **C5** Chemical changes
- **C6** Electrolysis
- **C7** Energy changes

**Rates, equilibrium, and organic chemistry**

- **C8** Rates and equilibrium
- **C9** Crude oil and fuels

**Analysis and the Earth's resources**

- **C10** Chemical analysis
- **C11** The Earth's atmosphere
- **C12** The Earth's resources

# C1 Atomic structure

## C1.1 Atoms

### Learning objectives

*After this topic, you should know:*
- the definition of an element
- that each type of atom has a chemical symbol
- the basic structure of the Periodic Table
- the basic structure of an atom.

Millions of different substances have been catalogued by scientists.

All substances are made of tiny particles called **atoms**. There are about 100 different types of atoms found naturally on Earth. These can combine in a huge variety of ways, giving all those different substances.

A relatively small number of substances are made up of only one type of atom. These substances are called **elements**. An atom is the smallest part of an element that can exist. As there are only about 100 different types of atoms, there can only be 100 different elements.

Elements can have very different properties. Some elements such as silver, chromium, copper, and gold are shiny, solid metals (Figure 1). Other elements such as oxygen, nitrogen, argon, and chlorine are non-metals, and these examples are all gases at room temperature.

### Chemical symbols

The name used for an element in everyday life depends on the language being spoken. For example, the element sulfur is called 'schwefel' in German, 'baaruud' in Somali, and 'azufre' in Spanish. However, the world of science forms a global community, and scientists from many nations communicate with each other and publish their findings. So, it is important that there are symbols for elements that all nationalities can understand. These symbols are abbreviations of the elements' names, which are primarily in Latin or Greek, and sometimes Arabic or Persian. They are shown in the **Periodic Table** (Figure 2).

▲ **Figure 1** An element contains only one type of atom – in this case, gold

▲ **Figure 2** The Periodic Table shows the symbols for each type of atom

C1 Atomic structure

- The symbols in the Periodic Table represent atoms. For example, O represents an atom of oxygen and Na represents an atom of sodium.
- The elements in the Periodic Table are arranged in vertical columns, called **groups**. Each group contains elements with similar chemical properties.
- The 'staircase' drawn on the right of the Periodic Table in bold red is the dividing line between metals and non-metals.

## Atoms, elements, and compounds

Most of the substances you come across are not elements. They are made up of different types of atoms bonded together and are called **compounds**. Water is a compound made up of hydrogen and oxygen – Figure 3 shows its structure.

The compound water contains one oxygen atom and two hydrogen atoms. So, its chemical formula is written as $H_2O$. If there is no subscript number written after an atom's symbol in a chemical formula, it can be read as '1', that is, the ratio of H atoms : O atoms is 2 : 1.

Chemical bonds hold the atoms tightly together in compounds. Some compounds are made from just two types of atoms (e.g., water or carbon dioxide, $CO_2$). However, most compounds consist of more than two different types of atoms.

### Synoptic link

For more information on the Periodic Table of elements, see Topic C2.1.

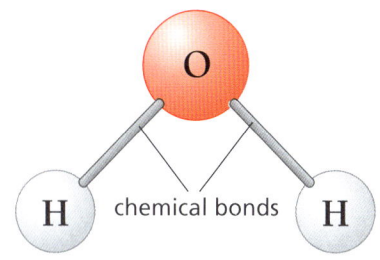

▲ **Figure 3** Water is an example of a compound. Chemical bonds hold the hydrogen and oxygen atoms together

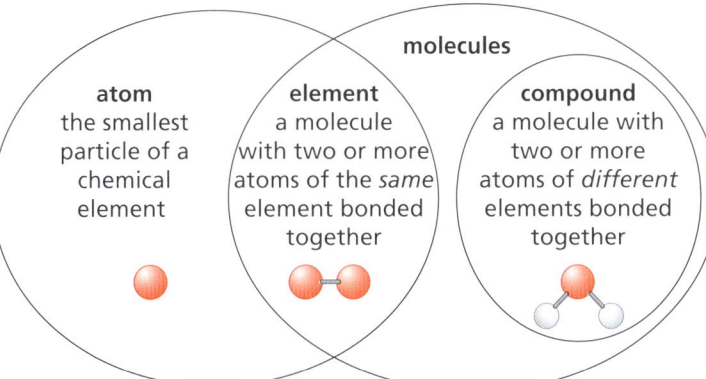

◀ **Figure 4** Atoms, elements, and compounds are all slightly different things. It's important to know the difference. For example, not all molecules are compounds – some of them are elements

The term **molecule** can be used to describe compounds, for example 'a molecule of water'. However, this term can also be used to describe when atoms of the same element bond together. For example, oxygen can exist as a molecule with the formula $O_2$ (Figure 4).

All atoms are made up of a tiny central **nucleus** with **electrons** orbiting around it (Figure 5).

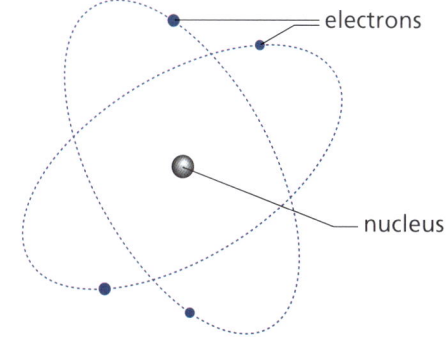

▲ **Figure 5** Each atom consists of a tiny nucleus surrounded by electrons

### Summary questions

1. Define the term 'element'. **1 MARK**
2. Draw diagrams to explain the difference between an element and a compound. **2 MARKS**
3. Describe the basic structure of an atom. **2 MARKS**
4. Explain what information can be deduced from the chemical formula of carbon dioxide, $CO_2$. **2 MARKS**

### Key points

- Elements contain only one type of atom. Each element is given a symbol, which are listed on the Periodic Table.
- Compounds contain more than one type of atom, and are given a chemical formula that tells us the ratio of different types of atoms.
- An atom has a tiny nucleus at its centre, surrounded by electrons.

# C1.2 Chemical equations

## Learning objectives

After this topic, you should know:
- what happens to the atoms in a chemical reaction
- how the mass of reactants compares with the mass of products in a chemical reaction
- why there can be an apparent loss or gain in mass during reactions involving gases in open containers
- how to write balanced symbol equations, including state symbols, to represent reactions.

Chemical equations show the **reactants** (the substances you start with) and the **products** (the new substances made) in a reaction.

You can represent the test for hydrogen gas using a **word equation**:

hydrogen + oxygen → water
(reactants)          (product)

In chemical reactions the atoms get rearranged. You can investigate what happens to the mass of reactants compared with mass of products by looking at the Practical box.

Using symbol equations helps you to see how much of each substance is involved in a reaction.

For example, calcium carbonate decomposes (breaks down) on heating. You can show the reaction using a symbol equation like this:

$$CaCO_3 \rightarrow CaO + CO_2$$

This equation is **balanced** – there is the same number of each type of atom on both sides of the equation. This is very important, because atoms cannot be created or destroyed in a chemical reaction. This also means that:

*The total mass of the products formed in a reaction is equal to the total mass of the reactants.*

This is called the **Law of conservation of mass**. In reactions involving gases, this law can appear to be broken when the reactions are carried out in open containers, such as test tubes and conical flasks, as some of the mass escapes a gas. Similarly, a piece of copper *increases* in mass when heated in air. The apparent extra mass comes from the oxygen gas that the copper reacts with to make copper oxide.

You can check if an equation is balanced by counting the number of each type of atom on either side of the equation. If the numbers are equal, then the equation is balanced.

## Adding state symbols

You can also add **state symbols** to a balanced symbol equation to give extra information. The state symbols used are (s) for solids, (l) for liquids, (g) for gases, and (aq) for substances dissolved in water, called **aqueous solutions**.

So the balanced symbol equation, including state symbols, for the decomposition of calcium carbonate is:

$$CaCO_3(s) \rightarrow CaO(s) + CO_2(g)$$

The balanced symbol equation for the reaction of hydrochloric acid and sodium hydroxide is:

$$HCl(aq) + NaOH(aq) \rightarrow NaCl(aq) + H_2O(l)$$

## Practical

**Conservation of mass in chemical reactions**

You will carry out three chemical reactions on a small scale, keeping the beakers on the balance throughout. Experiment 1 is a precipitation reaction, experiment 2 is an acid-alkali reaction, and experiment 3 is a displacement reaction.

- What observations show that a chemical reaction has taken place?
- Does the mass stay the same in each experiment?
- If there was a difference in mass, what reasons could there be for this?

Now plan an experiment involving measuring the mass of a chemical reaction where you think the mass would decrease during the reaction.

**Hint:** Think about the physical states of the reactants and products in the reaction.

**Safety:** Wear eye protection and wash your hands after the experiments.

# C1 Atomic structure

## Making an equation balance

In the case of hydrogen reacting with oxygen, it is not so easy to balance the equation. First, you write the formula of each reactant and product:

$$H_2 + O_2 \rightarrow H_2O$$

Counting the atoms on either side of the equation you see that there are:

**Reactants**  
2 H atoms, 2 O atoms

**Products**  
2 H atoms, 1 O atom

So, you need another oxygen atom on the product side of the equation. You cannot simply change the formula of $H_2O$ to $H_2O_2$. ($H_2O_2$ – hydrogen peroxide – is a bleaching agent, which is certainly not suitable to drink.) But you can have two water molecules in the reaction – this is shown as:

$$H_2 + O_2 \rightarrow 2H_2O$$

Counting the atoms on either side of the equation again, you get:

**Reactants**  
2 H atoms, 2 O atoms

**Products**  
4 H atoms, 2 O atoms

Although the oxygen atoms are balanced, you now need two more hydrogen atoms on the reactant side. You do this by putting '2' in front of $H_2$:

$$2H_2 + O_2 \rightarrow 2H_2O$$

Now the equation is balanced (Figure 1), and you have:

**Reactants**  
4 H atoms, 2 O atoms

**Products**  
4 H atoms, 2 O atoms

### Summary questions

1. Magnesium burns in oxygen with a bright white flame, forming an oxide as the only product.
   Write the word equation for this reaction. **1 MARK**

2. a Explain why all symbol equations must be balanced. **2 MARKS**
   b Balance the equation: $H_2 + Cl_2 \rightarrow HCl$ **1 MARK**

3. Balance these symbol equations:
   a $KNO_3 \rightarrow KNO_2 + O_2$ **1 MARK**
   b $Li + O_2 \rightarrow Li_2O$ **1 MARK**
   c $Fe + O_2 \rightarrow Fe_2O_3$ **1 MARK**
   d $Fe_2O_3 + CO \rightarrow Fe + CO_2$ **1 MARK**

4. Sodium metal, Na, reacts with water to form a solution of sodium hydroxide, NaOH, and gives off hydrogen gas, $H_2$. Write a balanced symbol equation, including state symbols, for this reaction. **2 MARKS**

5. A mass of 33.6 g of magnesium carbonate, $MgCO_3$, completely decomposed when it was heated. It made 16.0 g of magnesium oxide, MgO.
   a Calculate the mass of carbon dioxide, $CO_2$, produced in this reaction. **1 MARK**
   b Write a balanced symbol equation, including state symbols, to show the reaction in part **a**. **2 MARKS**

### Study tip

When balancing a chemical equation, you can NEVER change a chemical formula.

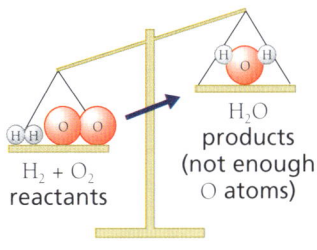
not balanced

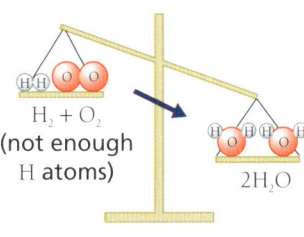
still not balanced!

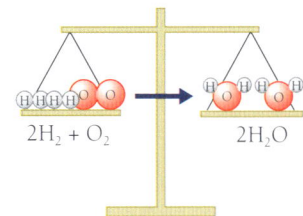
balanced at last!

▲ **Figure 1** Balancing an equation

### Key points

- No new atoms are ever created or destroyed in a chemical reaction: the total mass of reactants = the total mass of products.
- There is the same number of each type of atom on each side of a balanced symbol equation.
- You can include state symbols to give extra information in balanced symbol equations. These are (s) for solids, (l) for liquids, (g) for gases, and (aq) for aqueous solutions.

# C1.3 Separating mixtures

**Learning objectives**

After this topic, you should know:
- what a mixture is
- how to separate the components in a range of mixtures by:
  - filtration
  - crystallisation
  - simple distillation.

When analytical chemists working on forensic or medical investigations are given an unknown sample to identify, it is often a mixture of different substances.

*A mixture is made up of two or more substances (elements or compounds) that are not chemically combined together.*

Mixtures are different to chemical compounds. Look at Table 1.

**Table 1** The differences between compounds and mixtures

| Compounds | Mixtures |
| --- | --- |
| Compounds have a fixed composition (the ratio of elements present is always the same in any particular compound). | Mixtures have no fixed composition (the proportions vary depending on the amount of each substance mixed together). |
| Chemical reactions must be used to separate the elements in a compound. | The different elements or compounds in a mixture can be separated again more easily (by physical means using the differences in properties of each substance in the mixture). |
| There are chemical bonds between atoms of the different elements in a compound. | There are no chemical bonds between atoms of the different substances in a mixture. |

Before the substances in a mixture are identified, they are separated from each other. As it states in Table 1, you can use physical means to achieve the separation. The techniques available include:

- filtration
- crystallisation
- distillation
- chromatography (see Topic C1.4).

These separation techniques all rely on differences in the physical properties of the substances in the mixture. These could be different solubilities in a solvent or different boiling points.

## Filtration

The technique of **filtration** is used to separate substances that are insoluble in a particular solvent from those that are soluble in the same solvent. For example, you have probably tried to separate a mixture of sand and salt before in science lessons (Figure 1).

The sand that you collect on the filter paper (called the residue) can then be washed with distilled water to remove any salt solution left on it. The wet sand is finally dried in a warm oven to evaporate any water off and leave the pure, dry sand.

## Crystallisation

To obtain a sample of pure salt (sodium chloride, NaCl) from the salt solution following filtration, you would need to separate the salt in the solution (called the filtrate) from the water. You can do this by evaporating the water from the salt solution.

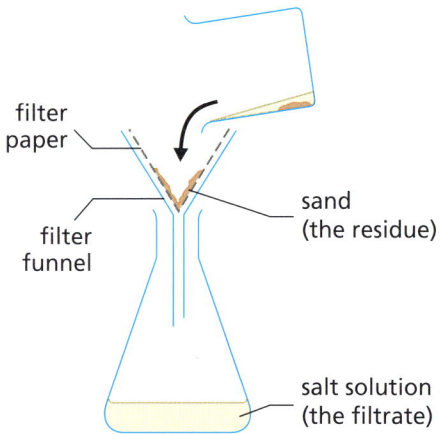

▲ **Figure 1** Filtering a mixture of sand, salt, and water in the lab. Make sure you keep the level of liquid below the top of the filter paper in the funnel. Otherwise residue can enter the filtrate collected

▲ **Figure 2** Filtering in the home – some people like filter coffee made from ground-up coffee beans. The solid bits that are insoluble in water get left on the filter paper as a residue

C1 Atomic structure

The best way to do this is by heating it in an evaporating dish on a water bath (Figure 3). Using a water bath is a gentler way of heating than heating the evaporating dish directly on a tripod and gauze.

Heating should be stopped when the solution is at the point of crystallisation. This is when small crystals first appear around the edge of the solution or when crystals appear in a drop of solution extracted from the dish with a glass rod. The rest of the water is then left to evaporate at room temperature to get a good sample of sodium chloride crystals. A flat-bottomed crystallisation dish or Petri dish can be used for this final step, to give a large surface area for the water to evaporate from.

## Distillation

Crystallisation separates a soluble solid from a solvent. However, sometimes you need to collect the solvent itself instead of just letting it evaporate off into the air. For example, some countries with a lack of fresh water sources purify seawater to obtain usable water. Distillation allows us to do this.

In simple distillation, a solution is heated and boiled to evaporate the solvent. The vapour given off then enters a condenser. This is an outer glass tube with water flowing through it that acts as a cooling 'jacket' around the inner glass tube from the flask. Here the hot vapour is cooled and condensed back into a liquid for collection in a receiving vessel (Figure 4). Any dissolved solids will remain in the heated flask.

▲ **Figure 3** Crystallising sodium chloride from its solution in water. If you heat the evaporating dish directly on the gauze there is a danger that all the water will be evaporated off, resulting in very hot salt spitting out of the dish

### Synoptic link

To find out more about crystallisation, see Topic C5.5.

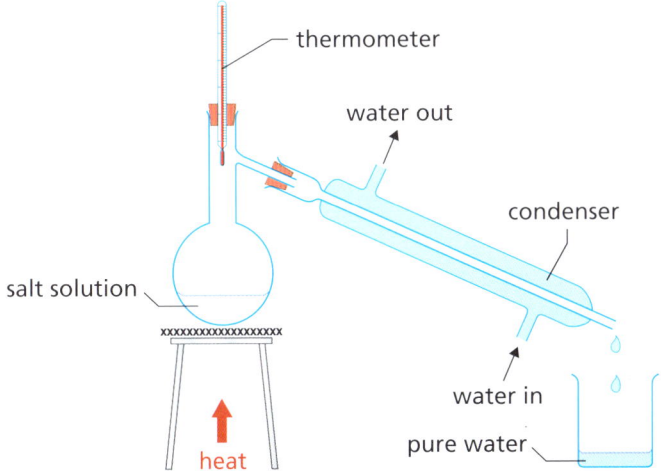

◀ **Figure 4** Distilling pure water from salt solution

### Summary questions

1   Define the term mixture. **2 MARKS**

2   Explain how the process of distillation can be used to remove dissolved impurities from a sample of water. **4 MARKS**

3   'A mixture has no fixed composition, whereas a compound has.' Explain what this means, using hydrogen, oxygen, and water to illustrate your answer. **3 MARKS**

4   Sulfur is soluble in the flammable liquid xylene but not in water. Sodium nitrate is soluble in water but not in xylene.
    Describe and explain two ways to safely separate a mixture of sulfur powder and sodium nitrate to collect pure samples of each solid. **6 MARKS**

### Key points

- A mixture is made up of two or more substances that are not chemically combined together.
- Mixtures can be separated by physical means, such as filtration, crystallisation, and simple distillation. (The physical separation techniques of fractional distillation and chromatography are discussed in Topic C1.4).

9

# C1.4 Fractional distillation and paper chromatography

## Learning objectives

After this topic, you should know:
- why fractional distillation is needed to separate some liquids
- how fractional distillation works
- how paper chromatography works.

## Fractional distillation

You saw how simple distillation works in Topic C1.3. Distillation can also be used to separate mixtures of miscible liquids, such as ethanol and water. The word miscible describes liquids that dissolve in each other, mixing completely. They do not form the separate layers seen in mixtures of immiscible liquids that have been allowed to settle, such as the oil and water layers in a salad dressing.

The miscible liquids will have different boiling points, so you can use this to distil off and collect the liquid with the lowest boiling point first.

However, it is difficult to get pure liquids from mixtures of liquids with similar boiling points by simple distillation, as both liquids give off vapour before they reach their actual boiling points. So to aid separation you can add a fractionating column to the apparatus for distillation (Figure 4 in Topic C1.3). This is usually a tall glass column filled with glass beads, which is fitted vertically on top of the flask being heated (Figure 1).

The vapours must pass over and between the glass beads in the fractionating column before they reach the condenser. The temperature in the fractionating column is highest at the bottom of the column, getting lower as the vapours rise and cool. The substance with the higher boiling point will condense more readily on the glass beads nearer the bottom of the column and drip back down into the flask beneath. The substance with the lower boiling point will continue rising and pass over into the condenser, where it is cool enough to turn back into the liquid state and be collected.

Fractional distillation is used to separate ethanol from a fermented mixture in the alcoholic spirits industry and in the use of ethanol as a **biofuel**.

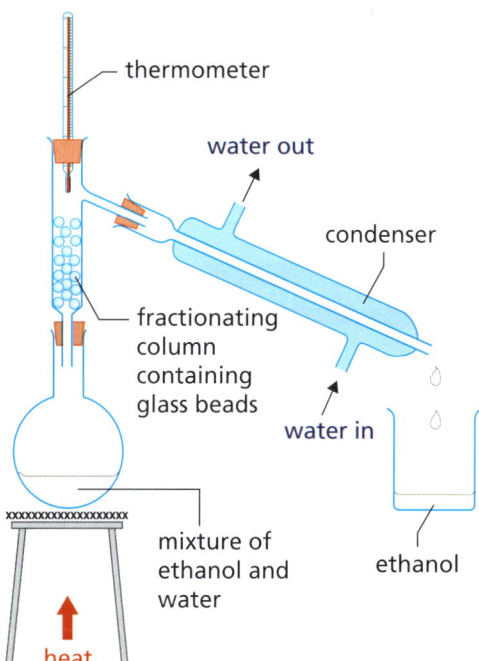

▲ Figure 1 The fractional distillation of the miscible liquids ethanol and water. The ethanol collected is flammable so it is important that the Bunsen flame is kept away from the ethanol collected in the beaker

## Carrying out paper chromatography

One technique that is used to separate (and identify) substances from mixtures in solution is paper **chromatography**. It works because some compounds in a mixture will dissolve better than others in the solvent chosen (Figure 3).

A capillary tube is used to dab a spot of the solution on a pencil line near the bottom of a sheet of absorbent chromatography paper. The paper is then placed standing in a solvent at the bottom of a beaker or tank. The solvent is allowed to soak up the paper, running through the spot of mixture.

The relative solubility in the solvent of the components making up the mixture determines how far they travel up the paper. The more soluble a substance is in the solvent, the further up the paper it is carried. Different solvents can be used to maximise separation. The solvent can be chosen from several possibilites, or two solvents can be used one after another.

## Synoptic link

One application of fractional distillation is in oil refineries – see Topic C9.2.

## Synoptic link

You can find out how you can use chromatography to identify substances in Topic C10.2.

C1 Atomic structure

## Practical

### Detecting dyes in food colourings

In this experiment you can make a chromatogram to analyse various food colourings.

Set up the experiment as shown in Figure 2 and Figure 3.

What can you deduce from your chromatography experiment?

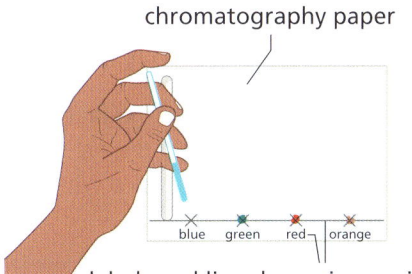

▲ **Figure 2** Setting up a chromatogram. Take care using the capillary tube as the glass is very thin

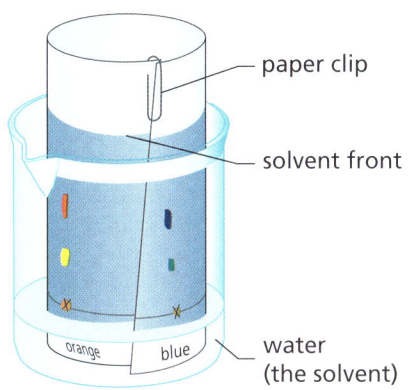

◀ **Figure 3** A chromatogram is the paper record of the separation. If the components of the mixture are not coloured, you can sometimes spray the chromatogram with a detecting agent that colours them

## Study tip

When doing the detecting food dyes experiment, make sure to use a pencil to draw the labels and lines, not a pen. Some pen inks are soluble in water so will dissolve or bleed up the paper too, which could make your results hard to read!

## Metacognition

Look back at your work on separating substances in this chapter.

Draw a table to summarise your work – with columns for the name of the separation technique, the type of substances you start with in the mixture, how the technique works, and a final column to evaluate effectiveness.

## Summary questions

1  a  Draw and label the apparatus you could use to separate a mixture of ethanol and water. **2 MARKS**
   b  Name this method of separation. **1 MARK**

2  a  Describe a method to separate the dyes in coloured inks. **4 MARKS**
   b  A paper chromatogram from a mixture of two substances, **A** and **B**, was obtained using a solvent of propanone. Substance **B** was found to travel further up the paper than substance **A**.
      What does this tell you about substances **A** and **B**? **1 MARK**

3  Explain why you would be able to collect a more concentrated sample of ethanol from a mixture of water and ethanol using the apparatus drawn in **1** than by using simple distillation. **4 MARKS**

4  Look at the boiling points of the three liquids in the table:

| Liquid | Boiling point in °C |
|---|---|
| water | 100 |
| ethanol | 78 |
| propanol | 97 |

A mixture was made by stirring together equal volumes of these three miscible liquids.

Evaluate the effectiveness of fractional distillation as a way of separating this mixture into the three pure liquids. **3 MARKS**

## Key points

- Fractional distillation is an effective way of separating miscible liquids, using a fractionating column. Separation is possible because of the different boiling points of the liquids in the mixture.
- Paper chromatography separates mixtures of substances dissolved in a solvent as they move up a piece of chromatography paper. The different substances are separated because of their different solubilities in the solvent used.

11

# C1.5 History of the atom

## Learning objectives

After this topic, you should know:
- how and why the atomic model has changed over time
- that scientific theories are revised or replaced by new ones in the light of new evidence.

## Early ideas about atoms

The ancient Greeks were the first to have ideas about particles and atoms. However, it was not until the early 1800s that these ideas became linked to strong experimental evidence when English scientist John Dalton put forward his ideas about atoms.

From his experiments, he suggested that substances were made up of atoms that were like tiny, hard spheres. He also suggested that each chemical element had its own atoms that differed from others in their mass. Dalton believed that these atoms could not be divided or split. They were the fundamental building blocks of nature.

In chemical reactions, he suggested that the atoms re-arranged themselves and combined with other atoms in new ways. In many ways, Dalton's ideas are still useful today. For example, they help to visualise elements, compounds, and molecules, as well as the models still used to describe the different arrangement and movement of particles in solids, liquids, and gases.

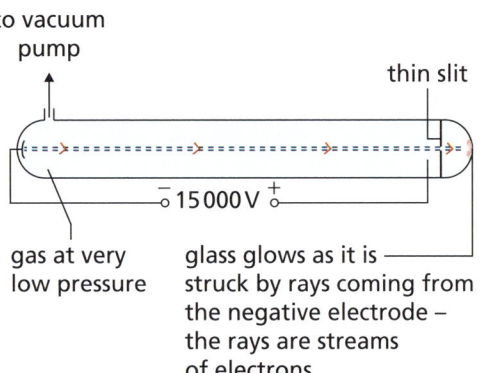

▲ **Figure 1** Thomson's experimental evidence for the existence of electrons

## Evidence for electrons in atoms

At the end of the 1800s, a British scientist called J.J. Thomson discovered the **electron**. This is a tiny, negatively charged particle that was found to have a mass about 2000 times smaller than the lightest atom. Thomson was experimenting by applying high voltages to gases at low pressure (Figure 1).

Thomson did experiments on the beams of particles. The particles were attracted to a positive charge, showing they must be negatively charged themselves. He called the tiny, negatively charged particles electrons. These electrons must have come from inside the atoms in the tube. So Dalton's idea that atoms could not be divided or split had to be revised.

Thomson proposed a different model for the atom. He said that the tiny negatively charged electrons must be embedded in a cloud of positive charge. He knew that atoms themselves carry no overall charge, so any charges in an atom must balance out. He imagined the electrons as the bits of plum in a plum-pudding (Figure 2).

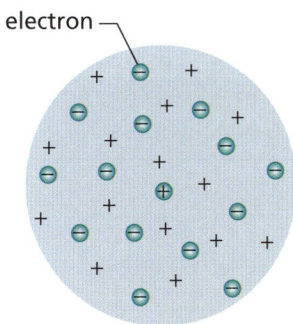

▲ **Figure 2** Thomson's 'plum-pudding' model of the atom

## Evidence for the nucleus

The next breakthrough in understanding the atom came about 10 years later. Geiger and Marsden were doing an experiment with radioactive particles. They were firing dense, positively charged particles (called alpha particles) at the thinnest piece of gold foil they could make (Figure 3). They expected the particles to pass straight through the gold atoms with their diffuse cloud of positive charge (as in Thomson's plum-pudding model). However, their results shocked them (Figure 3).

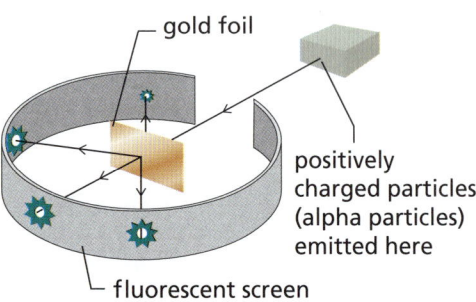

▲ **Figure 3** The alpha particle scattering experiment, carried out by Geiger and Marsden, which changed the 'plum-pudding' theory

# C1 Atomic structure

Their results were used to suggest a new model for the atom (Figure 4). Rutherford suggested that Thomson's atomic model was not possible. The positive charge must be concentrated at a tiny spot in the centre of the atom. Otherwise the large, positive particles fired at the foil could never be repelled back towards their source. It was proposed that the electrons must be orbiting around this **nucleus** (centre of the atom), which contains very dense positively charged **protons** (Figure 4).

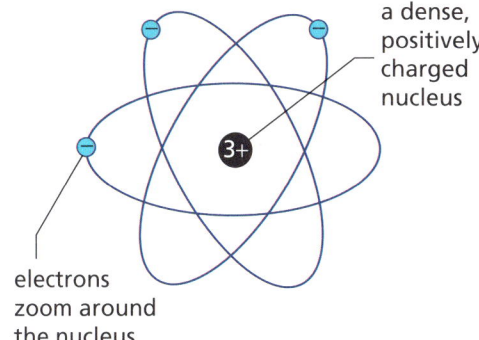

▲ Figure 4 Rutherford's nuclear model of the atom

## Evidence for electrons in shells (energy levels)

The next important development came in 1914, when Niels Bohr revised the atomic model again. He noticed that the light given out when atoms were heated only had specific amounts of energy.

He suggested that the electrons must be orbiting the nucleus at set distances, in certain fixed energy levels (or shells). The energy must be given out when excited electrons fall from a high energy level to a low energy level. Bohr matched his model to the energy values observed (Figure 5).

## Evidence for neutrons in the nucleus

Scientists at the time speculated that there were two types of sub-atomic particles inside the nucleus. They had evidence of protons but a second sub-atomic particle in the nucleus was also proposed to explain the missing mass that had been noticed in atoms. These **neutrons** must have no charge and have the same mass as a proton.

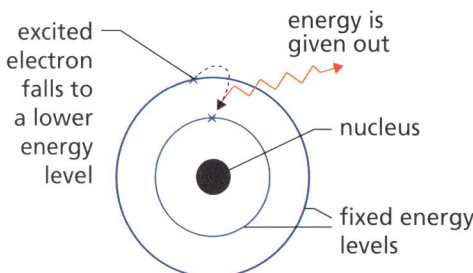

▲ Figure 5 Bohr's model of the atom

Because neutrons have no charge, it was very difficult to detect them in experiments. It was not until 1932 that James Chadwick did an experiment that could only be explained by the existence of neutrons.

## Summary timeline

| When? | What happened? |
|---|---|
| Early 1800s | John Dalton writes about atoms as tiny, hard spheres, and that each element has its own atoms |
| Late 1800s | J. J. Thomson discovers the electron and develops the 'plum-pudding' model |
| Early 1900s | Geiger and Marsden perform experiments that help Rutherford confirm the existence of protons and the nucleus |
| 1914 | Niels Bohr creates the Bohr model: electrons orbiting the nucleus at fixed distances |
| 1932 | James Chadwick proves the existence of neutrons |

### Summary questions

1. Name two scientists involved in work developing models of the atom. **2 MARKS**
2. Which sub-atomic particle did J.J. Thomson discover? **1 MARK**
3. Describe J.J. Thomson's 'plum-pudding' model of the atom. **2 MARKS**
4. Explain the difference between the plum-pudding model of the atom and the current nuclear model used at GCSE level. **2 MARKS**

### Key points

- Ideas about atoms have changed over time.
- New evidence has been gathered from the experiments of scientists who have used their model of the atom to explain their observations and calculations.
- Key ideas were proposed successively by Dalton, Thomson, Rutherford (following the Geiger Marsden experiment), Bohr, and Chadwick, before the development of the model of the atom you use at GCSE level today.

# C1.6 Structure of the atom

### Learning objectives

*After this topic, you should know:*
- the location, relative charge, and relative mass of the protons, neutrons, and electrons in an atom
- what the atomic number and mass number of an atom represent
- why atoms have no overall charge
- that atoms of a particular element have the same number of protons.

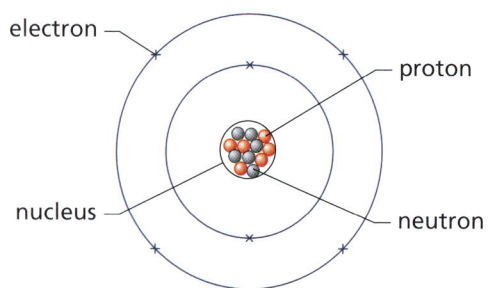

▲ **Figure 1** *Understanding the structure of an atom gives important clues to the way chemicals react together. This atom of carbon has six protons and six neutrons in its nucleus, and six electrons orbiting the nucleus. The protons are shown in red, and the neutrons in grey. Although the number of protons and electrons are always equal in an atom of an element, the number of neutrons can differ (but in this carbon atom they are the same)*

### Synoptic link

You can find out how to calculate the relative atomic mass of an element in Topic C4.1.

You have now seen how ideas about atoms have developed over time. At GCSE level, you use the model in which a very small nucleus is in the centre of every atom. This nucleus contains two types of sub-atomic particles, called **protons** and **neutrons**. A third type of sub-atomic particle orbits the nucleus. These very tiny particles are called **electrons**.

Protons have a positive charge. Neutrons have no charge, that is, they are neutral. So the nucleus itself has an overall positive charge. The electrons orbiting the nucleus are negatively charged. The relative charge on a proton is +1 and the relative charge on an electron is −1.

The mass of an atom is concentrated in its nucleus. A proton and a neutron each have the same mass. The electrons are so light that their mass can be ignored when working out the relative mass of atoms (Table 1).

**Table 1** *The relative charge and mass of sub-atomic particles*

| Type of sub-atomic particle | Relative charge | Relative mass |
|---|---|---|
| proton | +1 | 1 |
| neutron | 0 | 1 |
| electron | −1 | very small (it would take almost 2000 electrons to have the same mass as one proton or neutron) |

Because every atom contains equal numbers of protons and electrons, the positive and negative charges cancel out. So, there is no overall charge on any atom. For example, a carbon atom is neutral. It has six protons, so you know it must have six electrons (Figure 1).

## Atomic number

All the atoms of a particular element have the same number of protons. For example, all hydrogen atoms have one proton in their nucleus, all carbon atoms have six protons in their nucleus and all sodium atoms have 11 protons in their nucleus.

The number of protons in each atom of an element is called its **atomic number**.

The elements in the Periodic Table are arranged in order of their atomic number. If you are told that the atomic number of an element is eight, you can identify it using the Periodic Table. It will be the eighth element listed – oxygen. Knowing the atomic number of an element, you also know its number of electrons (as this will equal its number of protons). So, oxygen atoms have eight protons and eight electrons.

## Mass number

As you know, the protons and neutrons in an atom's nucleus make up nearly all of the mass of the atom.

The number of protons plus neutrons in the nucleus of an atom is called its **mass number**. A beryllium atom, Be, has four protons and five neutrons, so its mass number will be 4 + 5 = 9.

# C1 Atomic structure

Given the atomic number and mass number, you can work out how many protons, electrons, and neutrons are in an atom. For example, an argon atom has an atomic number of 18 and a mass number of 40.

- An atomic number of 18 means argon has 18 protons. Remember that atoms have an equal number of protons and electrons. So, argon also has 18 electrons.
- Argon's mass number is 40, so you know that: 18 (the number of protons) + the number of neutrons = 40
- Therefore, argon must have 22 neutrons (as 18 + 22 = 40).

You can summarise the last part of the calculation as:

number of neutrons = mass number − atomic number

## Study tip

In an atom, the number of protons is always equal to the number of electrons. You can find out the number of protons and electrons in an atom by looking up its atomic number in the Periodic Table.

## Maths

### Worked example

The metal lead, Pb, has an atomic number of 82 and a mass number of 207.
How many protons, neutrons, and electrons does an atom of lead contain?

### Solution

atomic number = number of protons, $p$
= number of electrons, $e$
= **82**

mass number = number of protons, $p$ + number of neutrons, $n$
= 207

So substituting in the value of $p$, you get:

$82 + n = 207$

You can rearrange the equation so that its subject (i.e., the quantity you want to find out) is $n$, by subtracting 82 from both sides of the equation:

$n = 207 − 82 = \mathbf{125}$

So, an atom of lead has **82 protons, 125 neutrons,** and **82 electrons**.

## Summary questions

1. Draw a table showing the location, relative charge, and relative mass of the three sub-atomic particles. **3 MARKS**
2. Explain why all atoms are neutral. **2 MARKS**
3. How many protons, electrons, and neutrons do the following atoms contain?
   a  A nitrogen atom, with atomic number 7 and mass number 14. **1 MARK**
   b  A uranium atom, with atomic number 92 and mass number 235. **1 MARK**
4. Using the Periodic Table, determine the number of each of the sub-atomic particles in the following elements:
   a  silver **1 MARK**
   b  potassium **1 MARK**

## Key points

- Atoms are made of protons, neutrons, and electrons.
- Protons have a relative charge of +1, and electrons have a relative charge of −1. Neutrons have no electrical charge. They are neutral.
- The relative masses of a proton and a neutron are both 1.
- Atoms contain an equal number of protons and electrons, so carry no overall charge.
- Atomic number = number of protons (= number of electrons).
- Mass number = number of protons + number of neutrons.
- Atoms of the same element have the same number of protons (and hence electrons) in their atoms.

15

# C1.7 Ions, atoms, and isotopes

## Learning objectives

*After this topic, you should know:*

- how to work out the number of protons, neutrons, and electrons in an ion
- how to represent an atom's atomic number and mass number
- how to estimate the size and scale of atoms, using SI units and the prefix 'nano'
- the definition of isotopes.

## Synoptic link

For more information about the formation of ions from atoms, see Topic C3.2.

## Maths

When dealing with very large or very small numbers, scientists use 'powers of ten' to express a number. For example, a distance of one million metres (1 000 000 m) is written as $1 \times 10^6$ m. One millionth of a metre is written as $1 \times 10^{-6}$ m (see Maths skills MS1b).

Using standard form, we can write the radius of an atom as $1 \times 10^{-10}$ m, or 0.1 nanometre (nm). Compare this to the approximate radius of its nucleus, which is about $1 \times 10^{-14}$ m. This shows what a small space is occupied by the nucleus of an atom, as its radius is less than $\frac{1}{10\,000}$ the radius of a single atom. Therefore, almost all of an atom is space, occupied by an atom's electrons.

## What is an ion?

You have seen that atoms are neutral because they have an equal number of protons (each carrying a positive charge) and electrons (each carrying a negative charge). However, sometimes atoms can lose or gain electrons, for example, when metals react with non-metals. If an atom gains one or more electrons, it gains an overall negative charge because it has more electrons than protons. You say that the atom has become a negative **ion**. If it loses one or more electrons, it becomes a positive ion because it has more protons than electrons.

**An ion is a charged atom (or group of atoms).**

Think about an oxygen atom. What happens when it gains two electrons? The atomic number of oxygen is 8, so the original oxygen atom has eight protons (8+) and eight electrons (8−). When it gains two electrons, there are still eight protons (8+) but now it has 10 electrons (10−). So, the overall charge on the negative ion formed is 2−. You write the formula of the ion as $O^{2-}$.

The $O^{2-}$ ion has 8 protons, 8 neutrons, and 10 electrons.

If a lithium atom loses one electron, it has two electrons (2−) and three protons (3+). Therefore, it forms a positive ion with a single positive charge, $Li^+$.

This $Li^+$ ion will have 3 protons, 4 neutrons, and 2 electrons.

## Representing the atomic number and mass number

You can show the atomic number and mass number of an atom like this:

| mass number | 12 | | 23 | |
|---|---|---|---|---|
| | | C (carbon) | | Na (sodium) |
| atomic number | 6 | | 11 | |

Given this information, you can work out the numbers of protons, neutrons, and electrons in an atom. The bottom number is its atomic number, giving you the number of protons (which equals the number of electrons). Then you can calculate the number of neutrons by subtracting its atomic number from its mass number (see Topic C1.6).

Sodium, $^{23}_{11}Na$, has an atomic number of 11 and its mass number is 23.

So, a sodium atom has 11 protons and 11 electrons, as well as (23 − 11) = 12 neutrons.

## The size of atoms

It has been estimated that a person has about 7 billion, billion, billion atoms in their body. That huge number is written as 7 followed by 27 zeros: 7 000 000 000 000 000 000 000 000 000 (in **standard form**, $7 \times 10^{27}$).

# C1 Atomic structure

You cannot see the atoms because each individual atom is incredibly small. An atom is about a tenth of a billionth of a metre across.

## Isotopes

Atoms of the same element always have the same number of protons. However, atoms of the same element but with different numbers of neutrons are called **isotopes**.

Isotopes always have the same atomic number but have different mass numbers. For example, two isotopes of carbon are $^{12}_{6}C$ (carbon-12) and $^{13}_{6}C$ (carbon-13). The carbon-12 isotope has six protons and six neutrons in the nucleus. The carbon-13 isotope has six protons and seven neutrons; that is, one more neutron than carbon-12.

Sometimes extra neutrons make the nucleus unstable, so it is radioactive. However, not all isotopes are radioactive – they are simply atoms of the same element that have different masses.

Different isotopes of an element have different *physical* properties. For example, they will have a different density. However, they always have the same *chemical* properties. This is because their reactions depend on their electronic structures. As their atoms will have the same number of protons and the same number of electrons, the electronic structure will be the same for all isotopes of an element.

For example, look at the three isotopes of hydrogen in Figure 2. Each has a different mass and tritium is radioactive. However, all have identical chemical properties; for example, they all react with oxygen to make water:

$$2H_2(g) + O_2(g) \rightarrow 2H_2O(l)$$

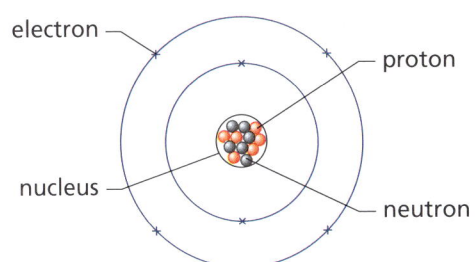

▲ **Figure 1** An atom of carbon

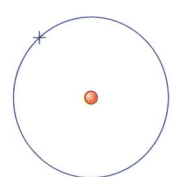

$^{1}_{1}H$ hydrogen (hydrogen-1)

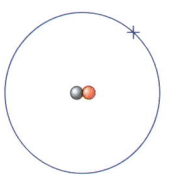

$^{2}_{1}H$ deuterium (hydrogen-2)

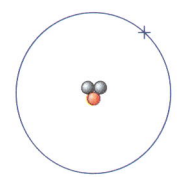

$^{3}_{1}H$ tritium (hydrogen-3)

▲ **Figure 2** The isotopes of hydrogen – they have identical chemical properties but different physical properties, such as density

## Summary questions

1. Define the term isotopes. **1 MARK**

2. Look at Figure 1. Which isotope of carbon is shown? **1 MARK**

3. Identify the number of protons, neutrons, and electrons there are in each of the following atoms:

   a $^{11}_{5}B$ **1 MARK**    c $^{24}_{12}Mg$ **1 MARK**    e $^{127}_{53}I$ **1 MARK**

   b $^{14}_{7}N$ **1 MARK**    d $^{37}_{17}Cl$ **1 MARK**

4. The atomic radius of a boron atom is $9 \times 10^{-11}$ m.
   a Give its atomic radius in nanometres. **1 MARK**
   b Calculate the approximate radius of its nucleus (in nm), given that it will be about one ten thousandth the radius of the boron atom. Give your answer in standard form. **1 MARK**

5. Identify the number of protons, neutrons, and electrons there are in each of the following ions:

   a $^{19}_{9}F^-$ **1 MARK**    c $^{39}_{19}K^+$ **1 MARK**

   b $^{31}_{15}P^{3-}$ **1 MARK**    d $^{27}_{13}Al^{3+}$ **1 MARK**

## Key points

- Atoms that gain electrons form negative ions. If atoms lose electrons, they form positive ions.
- You can represent the atomic number and mass number of an atom using the notation: $^{24}_{12}Mg$, where magnesium's atomic number is 12 and its mass number is 24.
- Isotopes are atoms of the same element with the same number of protons but different numbers of neutrons. They have identical chemical properties, but their physical properties, such as density, can differ.

17

# C1.8 Electronic structures

## Learning objectives

After this topic, you should know:
- how the electrons are arranged in an atom
- the electronic structures of the first 20 elements in the Periodic Table
- how to represent electronic structures in diagrams and by using numbers.

The model of the atom that you use at GCSE level has electrons arranged around the nucleus in **shells**, rather like the layers of an onion. Each shell represents a different energy level.

The lowest energy level is shown by the shell that is nearest to the nucleus. The electrons in an atom occupy the lowest available energy level (the available shell closest to the nucleus).

### Electron shell diagrams

An energy level (or shell) can only hold a certain number of electrons.

- The first, and lowest, energy level (nearest the nucleus) can hold up to two electrons.
- The second energy level can hold up to eight electrons.
- Once there are eight electrons in the third energy level, the fourth begins to fill up.

Beyond the first 20 elements in the Periodic Table the situation gets more complex. You only need to know the full arrangement of electrons in atoms of the first 20 elements.

▲ **Figure 1** A simple way of representing the arrangement of electrons in the energy levels (shells) of a sodium atom

You can draw diagrams to show the arrangement of electrons in an atom. For example, a sodium atom has an atomic number of 11 so it has 11 protons, which also means it has 11 electrons. Figure 1 shows how you can represent an atom of sodium.

To save drawing atoms all the time, you can write down the numbers of electrons in each energy level. This is called an **electronic structure**.

For example, the sodium atom in Figure 1 has an electronic structure of 2,8,1. You start at the lowest energy level (innermost or first shell), recording the numbers in each successive energy level or shell. The numbers of electrons in each shell are separated from each other by a comma.

Silicon, whose atoms have 14 electrons, is in Group 4 of the Periodic Table. It has the electronic structure 2,8,4. This represents two electrons in the lowest energy level (first shell), then eight in the next energy level, and four in its highest energy level (its outermost shell).

The best way to understand these arrangements is to look at the examples of standard notation in Figure 2.

### Electronic structure and the Periodic Table

Look at the elements in any one of the main groups of the Periodic Table. Their atoms will all have the same number of electrons in their highest energy level. These electrons are often called the outer electrons because they are in the outermost shell. Therefore, all the elements in Group 1 have one electron in their highest energy level (Figure 3).

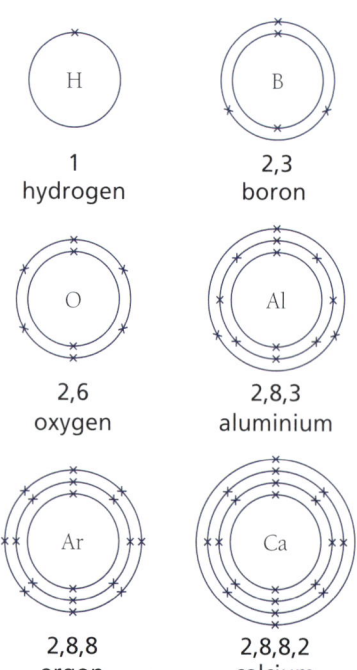

▲ **Figure 2** Once you know the pattern, you should be able to draw the energy levels (shells) and electrons in the atoms of any of the first 20 elements, when given their atomic number

# C1 Atomic structure

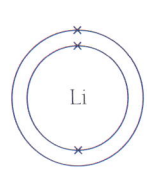 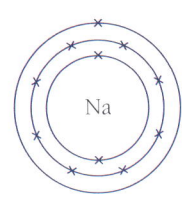 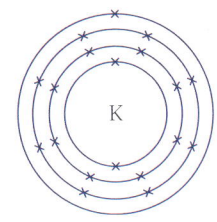

▲ **Figure 3** Lithium, sodium, and potassium are Group 1 elements, so all have one electron in their outermost shell. This makes them very reactive so always be careful when using them

The chemical properties of an element depend on how many electrons it has. The way an element reacts is determined by the number of electrons in its highest energy level (or outermost shell). So because the elements in a particular group all have the same number of electrons in their highest energy level, they all react in a similar way.

For example, when the Group 1 elements are added to water:

lithium + water → lithium hydroxide + hydrogen
sodium + water → sodium hydroxide + hydrogen
potassium + water → potassium hydroxide + hydrogen

The elements in Group 0 of the Periodic Table are called the **noble gases**. They are very unreactive elements. Their atoms all have a very stable arrangement of electrons with eight electrons in the outer shell, except for helium, which has two electrons in the outer shell.

## Summary questions

1  **a** Which shell represents the lowest energy level in an atom? **1 MARK**
   **b** How many electrons can each of the lowest two energy levels hold? **1 MARK**

2  **a** Write the electronic structure of potassium (atomic number 19). **1 MARK**
   **b** How many electrons does a potassium atom have in its highest energy level (outermost shell)? **1 MARK**

3  Using the Periodic Table, draw the arrangement of electrons in the following atoms and label each one with its electronic structure.
   **a** He   **1 MARK**   **c** Cl   **1 MARK**
   **b** Be   **1 MARK**   **d** Ar   **1 MARK**

4  State the name and symbol of the atom shown in Figure 4. **1 MARK**

5  **a** Why do the Group 1 metals all react in a similar way with oxygen? **1 MARK**
   **b** Write word equations for the reactions of lithium, sodium, and potassium with oxygen to form their oxides. **3 MARKS**
   **c** The Group 1 metals also react with chlorine gas, $Cl_2$, to form chlorides, such as lithium chloride, LiCl, and sodium chloride, NaCl.
   Write a balanced symbol equation for the reactions of lithium, Li, and sodium, Na, with chlorine gas (see Topic C1.2). **2 MARKS**

### Study tip

Make sure that you can draw the electronic structure of the atoms for all of the first 20 elements when given their atomic number or their position in the Periodic Table (which tells you the number of electrons).

### Synoptic link

For more information on the reactions of elements and their electronic structures, see Chapter C2.

### Metacognition

Reflect on your work on the structure of the atom in this chapter. Working in a pair, prepare a short test for one another to answer. Attempt each other's questions. Discuss your answers together when you finish. Make a note of any disagreements to sort out in a plenary session.

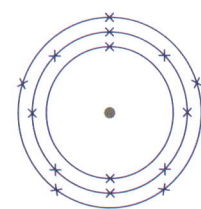

▲ **Figure 4**

### Key points

- The electrons in an atom are arranged in energy levels or shells.
- The lowest energy level (1st shell) can hold up to 2 electrons and the next energy level (2nd shell) can hold up 8 electrons. The 4th shell starts to fill after 8 electrons occupy the 3rd shell.
- The number of electrons in the outermost shell of an element's atoms determines the way in which that element reacts.

# C1 Atomic structure

## Practice questions

1. **a i** Name the sub-atomic particles found in the nucleus of an atom. *1 MARK*
   **ii** What is the maximum number of electrons that can occupy each of the first two energy levels or shells? *1 MARK*
   **b i** Explain the overall charge on any atom. *3 MARKS*
   **ii** Describe how an atom can become an ion with a 2+ charge. Explain your answer. *2 MARKS*
   **iii** Define atomic number and mass number. *2 MARKS*

2. **a** Define what the term mixture means to a scientist. *1 MARK*
   **b** Explain the differences between a mixture and a compound. *2 MARKS*
   **c** Name the technique you would use to separate and collect:
   **i** hydrated copper(II) sulfate, $CuSO_4 \cdot 5H_2O$, from its aqueous solution *1 MARK*
   **ii** a precipitate of lead iodide from the solution formed when aqueous solutions of lead nitrate and sodium iodide are mixed *1 MARK*
   **iii** water from a solution of potassium chloride *1 MARK*
   **iv** ethanol from a mixture of water and ethanol. *1 MARK*

3. Use the data in the table to answer the following questions:

| Chemical element | Melting point in °C | Boiling point in °C | Density in g/cm³ |
|---|---|---|---|
| bromine | −7 | 59 | 3.12 |
| caesium | 29 | 669 | 1.88 |
| fluorine | −220 | −188 | 0.00158 |
| strontium | 769 | 1384 | 2.6 |
| xenon | −112 | −108 | 0.0055 |

   **a** Determine the physical state of each element in the table at 25 °C. *3 MARKS*
   **b** Name the element that exists as a liquid over the widest range of temperatures. *1 MARK*
   **c** Write the chemical symbol for atoms of each element in the table. *1 MARK*
   **d** Classify each element in the table as a metal or a non-metal. *1 MARK*
   **e** Write the electronic structure of:
   **i** a fluorine atom *1 MARK*
   **ii** a fluoride ion, $F^-$. *1 MARK*

4. This question is about some of the elements in the Periodic Table. You will need to use the Periodic Table to help you answer some parts of the question.
   **a** Neon, Ne, is the 10th element in the Periodic Table.
   **i** Is neon a metal or a non-metal? *1 MARK*
   **ii** Are there more metals or non-metals in the Periodic Table? *1 MARK*
   **iii** Give the number of protons a neon atom contains. *1 MARK*
   **iv** The mass number of a neon atom is 20. How many neutrons does it contain? *1 MARK*
   **v** Give the name and number of the group to which neon belongs. *1 MARK*
   **vi** Name two other elements in the same group as neon. *1 MARK*
   **vii** Write the electronic structure of a neon atom. *1 MARK*
   **viii** Describe what is special about the electronic structure of neon and the other elements in its group. *1 MARK*
   **b** The element radium, Ra, has 88 electrons.
   **i** How many protons are in the nucleus of each radium atom? *1 MARK*
   **ii** How many electrons does a radium atom have in its highest energy level (outermost shell)? Give a reason for your answer. *1 MARK*
   **iii** Determine whether radium is a metal or a non-metal. *1 MARK*
   **iv** Radium's three most common isotopes are radium-224, radium-226, and radium-228. Describe the difference between the atomic structures of the three isotopes. *1 MARK*
   **v** Calcium is in the same group as radium. Its atomic number is 20. Write down its electronic structure. *1 MARK*
   **vi** Calcium forms 2+ ions in its compounds. Using the $^{40}Ca$ atom, determine the number of protons, neutrons, and electrons in a $Ca^{2+}$ ion. *1 MARK*

5. Balance the following symbol equations:
   **a** $Na + Cl_2 \rightarrow NaCl$ *1 MARK*
   **b** $Al + O_2 \rightarrow Al_2O_3$ *1 MARK*
   **c** $Fe_2O_3 + C \rightarrow Fe + CO_2$ *1 MARK*
   **d** $Al(OH)_3 \rightarrow Al_2O_3 + H_2O$ *1 MARK*
   **e** $Ba(NO_3)_2 \rightarrow BaO + NO_2 + O_2$ *1 MARK*
   **f** $C_4H_{10} + O_2 \rightarrow CO_2 + H_2O$ *1 MARK*

# Exam-style questions

**01** This question is about rock salt. Rock salt is a mixture of sand and salt.

**01.1** A student followed the method to separate rock salt into crystals of sand and crystals of salt.

**Step 1:** Add 25.0 g of rock salt to a beaker.

**Step 2:** Add 250 cm³ of water.

**Step 3:** Filter.

Suggest **one** improvement to Step 2 to get a better separation of rock salt and water. *1 MARK*

**01.2** **Figure 1** shows step 3 of the method.

Figure 1

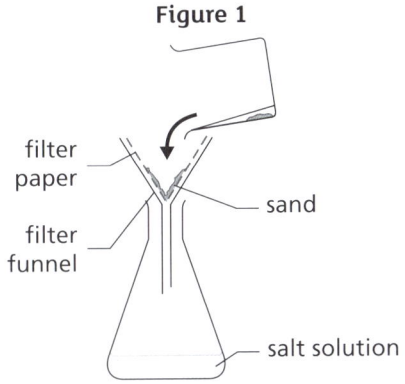

What word best describes the salt solution in **Figure 1**? Choose the correct answer.

A   distillate    C   filtrate
B   polymer       D   supernatant    *1 MARK*

**01.3** Explain why the sand becomes the residue in **Figure 1**. *2 MARKS*

**01.4** Describe how the student could produce dry salt crystals from the salt solution in step 3. *3 MARKS*

**01.5** The student produced 2.5 g of dry salt crystals. Suggest why the student could not have predicted the mass of dry salt crystals that would have been produced. *1 MARK*

**02** A student investigated green ink using chromatography. The student set up the apparatus as shown in **Figure 2**.

Figure 2

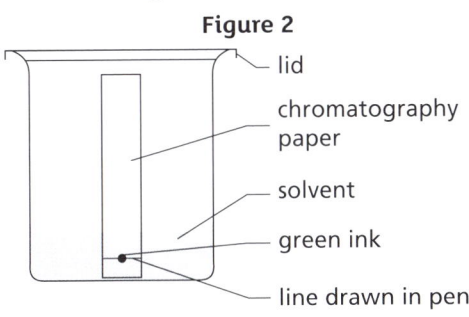

**02.1** Describe what would have happened if the student had set the apparatus up as shown in **Figure 2**. *2 MARKS*

**02.2** Explain why the line should be drawn in pencil and not in ink. *2 MARKS*

**02.3** Another student set up the apparatus correctly. The chromatogram produced is shown in **Figure 3**.

Figure 3 — yellow spot, blue spot

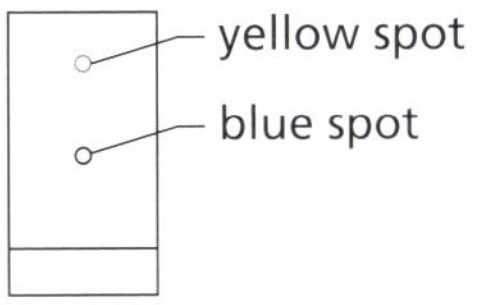

What does **Figure 3** tell you about green ink? *2 MARKS*

**02.4** Describe why the yellow dye moved further up the paper. *1 MARK*

**03** This question is about atoms.

**03.1** In the early 1900s, an experiment was done that caused scientists to change the model they used to describe atomic structure.

A very thin layer of gold foil was bombarded with alpha particles. Alpha particles are positively charged. **Figure 4** shows the results of the experiment.

Figure 4

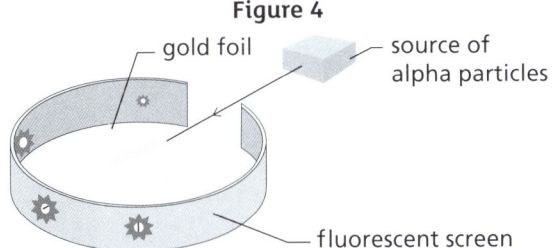

**Result 1** Very few alpha particles were repelled back towards the source of alpha particles.

**Result 2** Most of the alpha particles went straight through the gold foil.

Explain what Result 1 and Result 2 tell us about the structure of an atom. *4 MARKS*

**03.2** There are two isotopes of chlorine: $^{35}_{17}\text{Cl}$ and $^{37}_{17}\text{Cl}$. In terms of sub-atomic particles, describe the similarities and differences between these two isotopes of chlorine. *3 MARKS*

**03.3** Explain why both isotopes of chlorine have the same chemical properties. *2 MARKS*

**03.4** The relative atomic mass of chlorine is 35.5. Outline what this tells you about the abundance of the two isotopes. Explain your answer. *2 MARKS*

# C2 The Periodic Table

## C2.1 Development of the Periodic Table

### Learning objectives

*After this topic, you should know:*
- how the Periodic Table was developed over time
- how testing a prediction can support or refute a new scientific idea.

Imagine trying to understand the chemical elements:
- without knowing much about atoms
- with some chemical compounds mistakenly thought to be elements
- without knowing a complete list of the elements.

This is the task that faced scientists at the start of the 1800s.

During the 19th century, chemists were finding new elements almost every year. They were also trying very hard to find patterns in the behaviour of the elements. This would allow them to organise the elements and understand more about chemistry.

One of the first suggestions came from John Dalton. He arranged the elements in order of their atomic weights, which had been measured in various chemical reactions. In 1808 he published a table of elements in his book *A New System of Chemical Philosophy*.

▲ **Figure 1** Looking for patterns in the chemical elements in the early part of the 19th century was a bit like solving a crossword puzzle. Some answers were clear, as scientists did have some correctly identified elements. However, they only had a vague idea about others, as some compounds were wrongly thought to be elements. They did not even know the clues for other answers, as there were still undiscovered elements

▲ **Figure 2** Dalton and his table of elements

In 1864, British chemist John Newlands built on Dalton's ideas. Newlands also arranged the known elements in order of atomic weight but noticed that the properties of every eighth element seemed similar.

He produced a table showing his 'law of octaves' (Figure 3). However, he assumed that all the elements had been found. He did not consider the fact that chemists were still discovering new ones. So, he filled in his rows of eight elements, even though some of his elements were not similar at all. His table only really worked for the known elements up to calcium before the pattern broke down.

Other scientists ridiculed his ideas and refused to accept them.

C2 The Periodic Table

| H 1 | F 8 | Cl 15 | Co and Ni 22 | Br 29 | Pd 36 | I 42 | Pt and Ir 50 |
| Li 2 | Na 9 | K 16 | Cu 23 | Rb 30 | Ag 37 | Cs 44 | Os 51 |
| Be 3 | Mg 10 | Ca 17 | Zn 24 | Sr 31 | Cd 38 | Ba and V 45 | Hg 52 |
| B 4 | Al 11 | Cr 19 | Y 25 | Ce and La 33 | U 40 | Ta 46 | Tl 53 |
| C 5 | Si 12 | Ti 18 | In 26 | Zr 32 | Sn 39 | W 47 | Pb 54 |
| N 6 | P 13 | Mn 20 | As 27 | Bi and Mo 34 | Sb 41 | Nb 48 | Bi 55 |
| O 7 | S 14 | Fe 21 | Se 28 | Rh and Ru 35 | Te 43 | Au 49 | Th 56 |

▲ **Figure 3** Newlands and his table of octaves. Looking at Newlands' octaves, a fellow chemist commented that putting the elements in alphabetical order would probably produce just as many groups of elements with similar properties

## Mendeleev's breakthrough

In 1869, the Russian chemist Dmitri Mendeleev (Figure 4) solved the problem. At this time around 50 elements had been identified. Mendeleev arranged all of these in a table. He placed them in the order of their atomic weights. Then he arranged them so that a periodic (regularly occurring) pattern in their properties could be seen, but he did have his doubters.

Mendeleev also left gaps for elements that had not yet been discovered and then he used his table to predict what their properties should be. A few years later, new elements were discovered with properties that closely matched Mendeleev's predictions. Then there were not many doubts left that his table was a breakthrough in scientific understanding.

However, not all elements fitted in with Mendeleev's pattern. Some elements did not line up as expected from their atomic weights. Iodine and tellurium are an example. To keep the pattern, Mendeleev simply changed their order where necessary to keep the pattern going. This problem was a mystery for decades.

It was finally solved at the start of the 20th century when scientists began to find out more about the structure of the atom. Only then could they solve this issue of certain elements breaking the periodic pattern. They discovered that elements in the Periodic Table are arranged in order of their number of protons (their atomic number) and not their atomic weights. The existence of isotopes (with their different numbers of neutrons) accounted for the oddly heavy atomic weights of some elements.

▲ **Figure 4** Dmitri Mendeleev on a Russian stamp issued in his honour in 1969. He is remembered as the father of the modern Periodic Table. Using the table, chemists could now make sense of the chemical elements

### Key points

- The Periodic Table of elements developed as chemists tried to classify the elements. It arranges them in an order in which similar elements are grouped together in vertical columns.
- The Periodic Table is so named because of the regularly repeating patterns in the properties of elements.
- Mendeleev's Periodic Table left gaps for the unknown elements, which when discovered matched his predictions, and so his table was accepted by the scientific community.

## Summary questions

1. What data did Newlands and Mendeleev use to put the elements in order? **1 MARK**

2. **a** Look at the Periodic Table in Appendix 1. Name two elements, other than iodine and tellurium, which do not appear in order of their relative atomic masses. **2 MARKS**
   **b** Explain why this was a problem for Mendeleev and how it was eventually solved. **5 MARKS**

3. Explain how Mendeleev persuaded any doubters that his Periodic Table really was a useful tool for understanding the chemical elements. **3 MARKS**

23

# C2.2 Electronic structures and the Periodic Table

### Learning objectives

*After this topic, you should know:*
- how atomic structure is linked to the Periodic Table
- how metals and non-metals differ, including the electronic structures of their atoms and their positions in the Periodic Table
- why the noble gases are so unreactive.

### Synoptic link

You will see in Chapter C3 how an atom's outer electrons are transferred or shared when atoms react and combine with each other.

### Synoptic links

You first looked at the positions of metals and non-metals in the Periodic Table in Topic C1.1.

You also saw in Topic C1.7 how atoms can gain or lose electrons to form ions.

### Metacognition

Working online with a partner, find the boiling points of Group 0 elements – helium, neon, argon, krypton, xenon, and radon.

Plot the data on a graph to display the trend in the boiling points of the noble gases.

Did you find the negative numbers difficult to plot? Can you identify a pattern in the data?

The chemical elements are placed in order of their atomic (proton) number in the Periodic Table. This arranges the elements so that they line up in groups (vertical columns) with similar properties. There are eight main groups in the Periodic Table (Figure 1).

The Periodic Table also gives an important summary of the electronic structures of all the elements. Elements in the same group of the Periodic Table react in similar ways. This is because their atoms have the same number of electrons in the highest occupied energy level (outer shell).

**The group number in the Periodic Table tells you the number of electrons in the outermost shell (highest occupied energy level) of an atom.**

For example, all the atoms of Group 3 elements have three electrons in their outermost shell (highest energy level). Those in Group 6 have six electrons in their outermost shell.

## Metals, non-metals, and electronic structures

You will have studied the different properties of metals and non-metals before. The main difference is that metals conduct electricity, but non-metals are generally electrical insulators. Notable exceptions are some forms of carbon. In general, metals also have much higher melting and boiling points. Comparing solid examples, metals are ductile (can be drawn out into wires) and malleable (can be hammered into shapes without smashing), whereas non-metal solids are brittle.

The non-metal elements are found in the top right-hand corner of the Periodic Table (above the 'staircase' in Figure 1). The atoms of elements in Group 5, Group 6, and Group 7 can gain electrons when they react to form negative ions. The atoms of Group 5 elements tend to gain three electrons, those in Group 6 gain two electrons, and those in Group 7 gain one electron. These negatively charged ions then have the electronic structure of the noble gas at the end of their row (called a period). The number of protons does not change as the ions form.

The metal elements are found on the left-hand side and centre of the Periodic Table. When elements in Group 1, Group 2, or Group 3 react they tend to lose electrons and form positive ions. They attain the same electronic structure of the noble gas that is at the end of the period one row above them. Again, the number of protons does not change as the ions form.

## Group 0 – the noble gases

Look at the Group 0 noble gases, shaded brown and labelled in Figure 1. The atoms of noble gases have eight electrons in their outermost shell, making the atoms very stable. The exception is the first of the noble gases, helium. Helium has just two electrons, but this complete first shell is also a very stable electronic structure.

The stable electronic structure of the noble gases explains why they exist as single atoms. They are monatomic (single atom) gases. They have no tendency to react and modify their electronic structures by forming molecules. However, chemists have managed to make a few compounds of the larger noble gases. For example, the compounds $XeF_6$ and $XeO_4$ contain the most reactive non-metallic elements, fluorine and oxygen. As with many groups in the Periodic Table, there are trends in properties. For example, the boiling points of the noble gases get higher going down Group 0. Helium, at the top of the group, boils at –269 °C, whereas radon, at the bottom, boils at –62 °C.

## Study tip

Metals react by losing electrons. Non-metals react with metals by gaining electrons, but the noble gases are very unreactive due to their stable electronic structures.

Relative atomic mass / Atomic (proton) number: 1 H 1

| Period numbers | Group 1 | Group 2 | | | | | | | | | | | Group 3 | Group 4 | Group 5 | Group 6 | Group 7 | Group 0 |
|---|---|---|---|---|---|---|---|---|---|---|---|---|---|---|---|---|---|---|
| 1 | | | | | | | | | | | | | | | | | | 4 He 2 |
| 2 | 7 Li 3 | 9 Be 4 | | | | | | | | | | | 11 B 5 | 12 C 6 | 14 N 7 | 16 O 8 | 19 F 9 | 20 Ne 10 |
| 3 | 23 Na 11 | 24 Mg 12 | | | | | | | | | | | 27 Al 13 | 28 Si 14 | 31 P 15 | 32 S 16 | 35.5 Cl 17 | 40 Ar 18 |
| 4 | 39 K 19 | 40 Ca 20 | 45 Sc 21 | 48 Ti 22 | 51 V 23 | 52 Cr 24 | 55 Mn 25 | 56 Fe 26 | 59 Co 27 | 59 Ni 28 | 63.5 Cu 29 | 65 Zn 30 | 70 Ga 31 | 73 Ge 32 | 75 As 33 | 79 Se 34 | 80 Br 35 | 84 Kr 36 |
| 5 | 85 Rb 37 | 88 Sr 38 | 89 Y 39 | 91 Zr 40 | 93 Nb 41 | 96 Mo 42 | 98 Tc 43 | 101 Ru 44 | 103 Rh 45 | 106 Pd 46 | 108 Ag 47 | 112 Cd 48 | 115 In 49 | 119 Sn 50 | 122 Sb 51 | 128 Te 52 | 127 I 53 | 131 Xe 54 |
| 6 | 133 Cs 55 | 137 Ba 56 | 139 La 57 | 178 Hf 72 | 181 Ta 73 | 184 W 74 | 186 Re 75 | 190 Os 76 | 192 Ir 77 | 195 Pt 78 | 197 Au 79 | 201 Hg 80 | 204 Tl 81 | 207 Pb 82 | 209 Bi 83 | 209 Po 84 | 210 At 85 | 222 Rn 86 |
| 7 | 223 Fr 87 | 226 Ra 88 | 227 Ac 89 | | | | | | | | | | | | | | | |

Elements 58–71 and 90–118 (all metals) have been omitted

**Reactive metals** These metals react vigorously with other elements (like oxygen or chlorine), and with water. They are all soft – some of them can even be cut with a knife!

**Non-metals** These elements have low melting and boiling points, and many are liquids or gases at room temperature and pressure.

**Transition elements** This block between Group 2 and 3 contains the elements that most people think of when the word 'metal' is used. Examples are iron, nickel, silver, and gold. These metals are not usually very reactive – some, like silver and gold, are very unreactive.

**Noble gases** These (non-metal) elements are very unreactive, and it is very difficult to get them to combine with other elements.

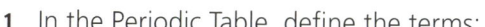

▲ **Figure 1** The modern Periodic Table. The elements are arranged in order of atomic number

## Summary questions

1. In the Periodic Table, define the terms:
   - **a** group (1 MARK)
   - **b** period. (1 MARK)
2. **a** How do the numbers of metal and non-metal elements compare with each other? Estimate an approximate percentage difference. (1 MARK)
   **b** Describe how the electronic structures of the atoms of a metallic element change when they react. (1 MARK)
3. Give the number of electrons that atoms of the following elements have in their highest energy level (outermost shell).
   - **a** beryllium, Be (1 MARK)
   - **b** boron, B (1 MARK)
   - **c** potassium, K (1 MARK)
   - **d** helium, He (1 MARK)
   - **e** argon, Ar (1 MARK)
   - **f** radium, Ra (1 MARK)
   - **g** radon, Rn (1 MARK)
   - **h** iodine, I. (1 MARK)
4. Suggest why the noble gases are so unreactive. (1 MARK)
5. Explain why elements in many groups of the Periodic Table have similar chemical properties. (1 MARK)

## Key points

- The atomic (proton) number of an element determines its position in the Periodic Table. The number of electrons in the outermost shell of an atom of an element determines its group number.
- The number of electrons in the outermost shell (highest energy level) of an atom of an element determines its chemical properties.
- The atoms of metals tend to lose electrons, whereas those of non-metals tend to gain electrons. The noble gases in Group 0 are unreactive because of their very stable electron structures.

# C2.3 Group 1 – the alkali metals

**Learning objectives**

After this topic, you should know:
- how the Group 1 elements behave
- how the properties of the Group 1 elements change going down the group.

The first group (Group 1), on the left-hand side of the Periodic Table, is called the **alkali metals** (Figure 1). This group consists of the metals lithium, Li, sodium, Na, potassium, K, rubidium, Rb, caesium, Cs, and francium, Fr.

## Properties of the alkali metals

All the alkali metals are very reactive. They must be stored in oil (Figure 2). This stops them reacting with oxygen in the air. Their reactivity increases as you go down the group. So, lithium is the least reactive alkali metal and francium is the most reactive.

All the alkali metals have a very low density compared with other metals. In fact, the densities of lithium, sodium, and potassium are all less than 1 g/cm³, so they float on water. The alkali metals are also all very soft and can be cut with a knife. They have a silvery, shiny surface when you first cut them. However, this quickly becomes dull as the metals react with oxygen in the air. This forms a layer of oxide on the shiny surface, for example:

sodium + oxygen → sodium oxide
$4Na(s)$ + $O_2(g)$ → $2Na_2O(s)$

In a gas jar of oxygen gas, hot alkali metals burn vigorously, forming a white smoke of their oxides.

The properties of this unusual group of metals are due to their electronic structure. The atoms of alkali metals all have one electron in their outermost shell (highest energy level). This gives them similar properties. It also makes them very reactive because they only need to lose one electron to get the stable electronic structure of a noble gas. They react with non-metals, losing their single outer electron. They form a metal ion carrying a 1+ charge, for example, $Na^+$ and $K^+$. They always form ionic compounds.

## Melting points and boiling points

The Group 1 metals melt and boil at relatively low temperatures for metals. Going down the group, the melting points and boiling points get lower and lower. In fact, caesium turns into a liquid at just 29 °C.

## Reaction with water

When you add lithium, sodium, or potassium to water, the metal floats on the water, moving around and fizzing. The fizzing happens because the metal reacts with the water to form hydrogen gas. Potassium reacts so vigorously with the water that the hydrogen produced ignites and burns with a lilac flame, coloured by the potassium ions formed in the reaction. The reaction between an alkali metal and water also produces a metal hydroxide. This is why they are called alkali metals. The hydroxides of the alkali metals are all soluble in water. The solution is colourless with a high pH. (**universal indicator** turns purple.)

sodium + water → sodium hydroxide + hydrogen
$2Na(s)$ + $2H_2O(l)$ → $2NaOH(aq)$ + $H_2(g)$
potassium + water → potassium hydroxide + hydrogen
$2K(s)$ + $2H_2O(l)$ → $2KOH(aq)$ + $H_2(g)$

| | |
|---|---|
| 7 | Li lithium 3 |
| 23 | Na sodium 11 |
| 39 | K potassium 19 |
| 85.5 | Rb rubidium 37 |
| 133 | Cs caesium 55 |
| (223) | Fr francium 87 |

▲ **Figure 1** The alkali metals (Group 1)

▲ **Figure 2** The alkali metals must be stored in oil

## C2 The Periodic Table

### Practical

**Reactions of alkali metals with water**

The reaction of the alkali metals with water can be demonstrated by dropping a small piece of the metal into a trough of water (Figure 3). This must be done with great care. The reactions are vigorous, releasing a large amount of energy. Hydrogen gas is also given off (Figure 4).

- Describe your observations in detail, including a word equation and balanced symbol equation for each alkali metal used.

▲ **Figure 3** Reacting alkali metals with water

**Safety:** This is a demonstration and must be carried out by a teacher. Wear eye protection when watching this demonstration.

## Other reactions

The alkali metals also react vigorously with non-metals such as chlorine gas. They produce metal chlorides, which are white solids. The metal chlorides all dissolve readily in water to form colourless solutions.

The reactions get more and more vigorous as you go down the group. That is because it becomes easier to lose the single electron in the outer shell to form ions with a 1+ charge:

sodium + chlorine → sodium chloride
$2Na(s) + Cl_2(g) → 2NaCl(s)$

They react in a similar way with fluorine, bromine, and iodine. All ionic compounds of the alkali metals and non-metals are white and dissolve easily in water. The solutions formed are all colourless.

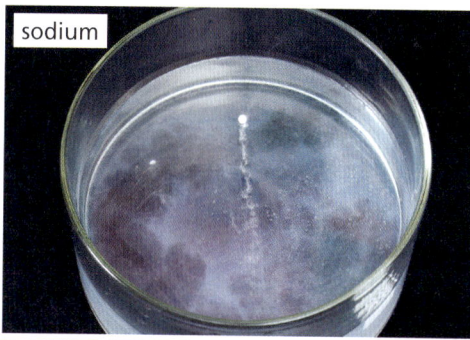

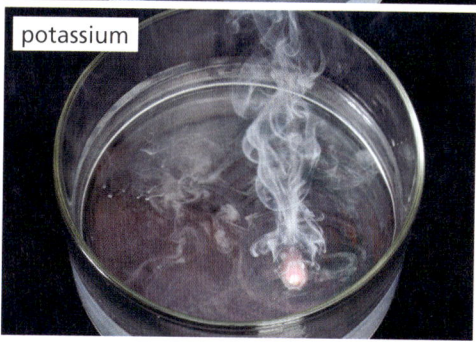

▲ **Figure 4** Lithium, sodium, and potassium reacting with water. The bottom photo shows the hydrogen produced burning with a lilac flame

### Summary questions

1. Write a word equation for the reaction of lithium with water. **1 MARK**
2. Describe the trend in the melting points of the alkali metals going down the group (as their atomic number increases). **1 MARK**
3. Explain why the alkali metals form ions with a 1+ charge. **3 MARKS**
4. Write a balanced symbol equation (including state symbols) and a description of the product formed for the reaction of caesium, Cs, with:
   a iodine **3 MARKS**   b bromine. **3 MARKS**
5. Caesium is near the bottom of Group 1 in the Periodic Table. Predict what would happen if it were dropped into water containing a little universal indicator solution. Include an explanation of your expected observations and a balanced symbol equation including state symbols in your answer. **6 MARKS**

### Key points

- The elements in Group 1 are called the alkali metals. Melting points and boiling points decrease going down the group. Reactivity increases going down the group.
- The alkali metals all react with water to produce hydrogen and an alkaline solution containing the metal hydroxide.
- They form 1+ ions in reactions to make ionic compounds. These are generally white and dissolve in water, giving colourless solutions.

27

# C2.4 Group 7 – the halogens

## Learning objectives

After this topic, you should know:
- how the Group 7 elements behave
- how the properties of the Group 7 elements change going down the group.

| 19<br>F<br>fluorine<br>9 |
|---|
| 35.5<br>Cl<br>chlorine<br>17 |
| 80<br>Br<br>bromine<br>35 |
| 127<br>I<br>iodine<br>53 |
| (210)<br>At<br>astatine<br>85 |

▲ Figure 1 The Group 7 elements

### Synoptic link

For further information on the bonding between non-metal atoms in substances, see Topic C3.5.

### Synoptic link

For further information on the bonding between non-metal ions and metal ions in substances, see Topic C3.2.

## Properties of the halogens

The Group 7 elements (Figure 1) are called the **halogens**. They are a group of toxic non-metals that have coloured vapours. They are classified as non-metals.

- They have low melting points and boiling points. Their melting points and boiling points increase going down the group (Table 1).
- They are poor conductors of heat and electricity.

As elements, the halogens all exist as molecules made up of pairs of atoms. These are called diatomic molecules. The atoms in each pair are joined to each other by a covalent bond.

**Table 1** The melting and boiling points of Group 7 halogens

| Group 7 halogen | F—F<br>$F_2$ | Cl—Cl<br>$Cl_2$ | Br—Br<br>$Br_2$ | I—I<br>$I_2$ |
|---|---|---|---|---|
| Melting point in °C | −220 | −101 | −7 | 114 |
| Boiling point in °C | −188 | −35 | 59 | 184 |

## Reactions of the halogens

The electronic structure of the halogens determines the way they react with other elements. They all have seven electrons in their outermost shell (highest energy level). So, they need to gain just one more electron to achieve the stable electronic structure of a noble gas. When they react with non-metals, they gain an extra electron by sharing a pair of electrons with another atom, for example, with hydrogen (Table 2).

**Table 2** The reactions of the halogens with hydrogen

| Equation | How the halogens react with hydrogen |
|---|---|
| $F_2(g) + H_2(g) \rightarrow 2HF(g)$ | explosive reaction, even at −200 °C and in the dark |
| $Cl_2(g) + H_2(g) \rightarrow 2HCl(g)$ | explosive reaction in sunlight, but slow in the dark |
| $Br_2(g) + H_2(g) \rightarrow 2HBr(g)$ | only react at over 300 °C in the presence of a platinum catalyst |
| $I_2(g) + H_2(g) \rightarrow 2HI(g)$ | only react at over 300 °C in the presence of a platinum catalyst (very slow, reversible) |

Table 2 shows the general trend that you find in Group 7 – the elements get less reactive going down the group.

The halogens also all react with metals to form ionic compounds. In this case, the halogen atoms gain a single electron to give them a stable arrangement of electrons. They form ions with a 1− charge, for example, $F^-$, $Cl^-$, and $Br^-$. Examples include sodium chloride, NaCl, and iron(III) bromide, $FeBr_3$.

C2 The Periodic Table

## Displacement reactions between halogens

You can carry out test-tube reactions to check the order of reactivity of the halogens, using the following rule:

**A more reactive halogen will displace a less reactive halogen from solutions of salts of the less reactive halogen.**

You use solutions of the halogens and their salts in water, for example, chlorine dissolved in water mixed with potassium bromide solution. The colour of the solution in the test tube after mixing will be due to the less reactive of the pair of halogens, which is left in solution as the aqueous molecule. For example, $Cl_2(aq)$ will be very pale green in solution, $Br_2(aq)$ will be yellow, whereas $I_2(aq)$ will be a darker red/brown colour.

### Synoptic link

For further information on the state symbols (s), (l), (g), and (aq) that are used in equations, see Topic C1.2.

### Practical

#### Displacement reactions

Add bromine water to potassium iodide solution in a test tube. Then try some other combinations of solutions of halogens and potassium halides.

- Record your results in a table and explain your observations.

**Safety:** Wear chemical splash-proof eye protection. Chlorine and bromine are toxic.

Bromine displaces iodide ions from solution because it is more reactive than iodine. Chlorine will displace both iodide ions and bromide ions.

So, chlorine will displace bromide ions, which form bromine molecules:

chlorine + potassium bromide → potassium chloride + bromine
$Cl_2(aq)$ + $2KBr(aq)$ → $2KCl(aq)$ + $Br_2(aq)$

Fluorine, the most reactive of the halogens, will displace all of the others. However, it reacts so violently with water that you cannot carry out reactions in aqueous solutions.

### Study tip

In Group 7, reactivity *decreases* as you go down the group. However, in Group 1, reactivity *increases* going down the group.

### Summary questions

1. In the Group 7 elements, identify the trend going down the group in:
   a. their melting points **1 MARK**
   b. their reactivity. **1 MARK**
2. a. Using the data in Table 1, determine the state of each Group 7 element at 20°C. **2 MARKS**
   b. What is the general name given to the Group 7 elements? **1 MARK**
3. a. Write the electronic structures of the ions in lithium fluoride, $Li^+F^-$. **2 MARKS**
   b. Describe how both the iodine and hydrogen atoms in hydrogen iodide, HI, manage to gain an electron. **1 MARK**
4. Write a balanced symbol equation, including state symbols, for the reaction of:
   a. sodium metal with iodine vapour **3 MARKS**
   b. chlorine water with sodium iodide solution. **3 MARKS**
5. Explain in detail what happens when a solution of bromine is mixed with sodium iodide solution. Include a balanced symbol equation with state symbols in your answer. **6 MARKS**

### Key points

- The halogens all form ions with a single negative charge in their ionic compounds with metals.
- The halogens form covalent compounds by sharing electrons with other non-metals.
- The reactivity of the halogens decreases going down the group. A more reactive halogen can displace a less reactive halogen from a solution of one of its salts.

# C2.5 Explaining trends

**Learning objectives**

After this topic, you should know:
- the trends in reactivity in Group 1 and Group 7
- how electronic structure can explain trends in reactivity in these groups.

As you saw in Topic C2.3, the Group 1 elements get more reactive going down the group, as shown in Figure 1.

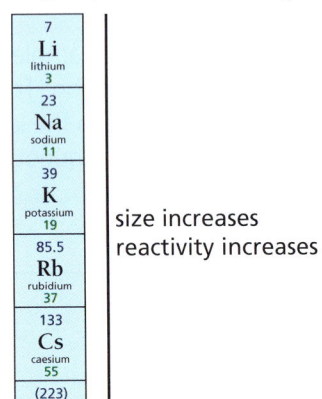

◀ **Figure 1** Group 1 atoms get more reactive as the atoms increase in size as you go down the group. This is because the distance between the outermost electron and the nucleus increases, so it's easier for the electron to be lost

The opposite trend is observed in the Group 7 elements (Topic C2.4), as shown in Figure 2.

You can explain these trends by looking at the electronic structures and how easily the atoms tend to lose or gain electrons in their reactions.

## Reactivity within groups

As you go down a group in the Periodic Table, the number of shells occupied by electrons increases by one extra electron shell per period. This means that the atoms become larger going down any group.

This has two effects:
- larger atoms lose electrons more easily going down a group
- larger atoms gain electrons less easily going down a group.

This happens because the outer electrons (which are negatively charged) are further away from the attractive force of the nucleus (which is positively charged because of its protons). Also, the inner shells of electrons 'screen' or 'shield' the outer electrons from the positive charge of the nucleus. You can see this effect with the alkali metals and the halogens. Remember that the atoms of alkali metals tend to lose electrons when they form chemical bonds. On the other hand, the atoms of the halogens tend to gain electrons.

## Explaining the trend in Group 1

Reactivity increases going down Group 1 because the atoms get larger so the single electron in the outermost shell (highest energy level) is attracted less strongly to the positive nucleus. The electrostatic attraction between the oppositely charged outer electron and the nucleus gets weaker because the distance between them increases.

The outer electron also experiences a shielding effect from the inner shells of electrons. This reduces the attraction between the outer electron and the nucleus.

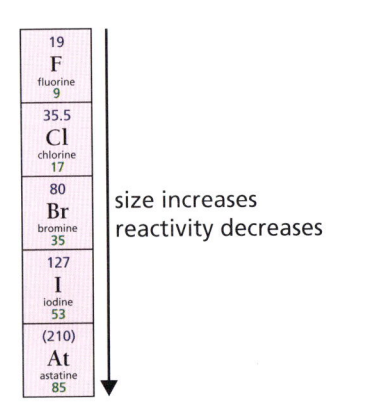

▲ **Figure 2** Group 7 atoms get less reactive as the atoms increase in size as you go down the group. This is because the distance between the outermost electron and the nucleus increases, so it's harder for the atom to gain an electron

C2 The Periodic Table

The size of the positive charge on the nucleus becomes larger as you go down a group, as more protons are present inside the nucleus. This suggests that the attraction for the outer electron should get stronger. However, the greater distance and the shielding effect of inner electrons outweigh the increasing nuclear charge. So, the change from Li to Li$^+$ takes more energy than Na changing to Na$^+$ (Figure 3).

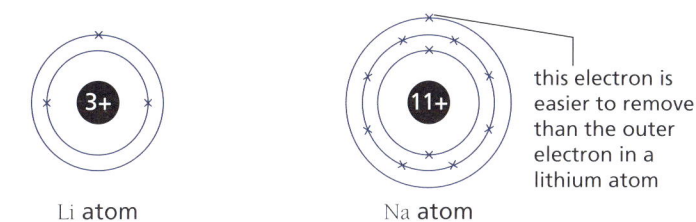

Li atom

Na atom — this electron is easier to remove than the outer electron in a lithium atom

▲ **Figure 3** Sodium's outer electron is further from the nuclear charge and is shielded by more inner shells of electrons than lithium's outer electron

Therefore, in Group 1, the outer electron gets easier to remove going down the group and the elements get more and more reactive.

## Explaining the trend in Group 7

Reactivity decreases going down Group 7. To explain this, you consider the same factors you looked at with the alkali metals:

- the size of the atom
- the shielding effect of inner electrons
- the nuclear charge.

When Group 7 elements react, their atoms gain an electron in their outermost shell (highest energy level). Going down the group, the outermost shell's electrons get further away from the attractive force of the nucleus, so it is harder to attract and gain an extra incoming electron.

The outer shell will also be shielded by more inner shells of electrons, again reducing the electrostatic attraction of the nucleus for an incoming electron.

The effect of the increased nuclear charge going down the group (which helps atoms gain an incoming electron) is outweighed by the effect of increased distance and shielding by more inner electrons. So, chlorine is less reactive than fluorine. The attraction for the incoming electron when F changes to F$^-$ is much greater than when Cl changes to Cl$^-$ (Figure 4).

an incoming electron experiences more attraction going into the outer shell of F compared with Cl

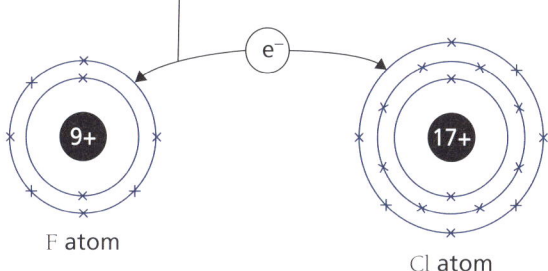

F atom          Cl atom

▲ **Figure 4** F forms F$^-$ more readily than Cl forms Cl$^-$

### Key points

- You can explain trends in reactivity as you go down a group in terms of the attraction between electrons in the outermost shell and the nucleus.
- This electrostatic attraction depends on several different factors:
  - the size of the atom
  - the shielding effect of inner electrons
  - the nuclear charge.
- It is easier for electrons to be lost for the larger atoms going down a group, and harder for them to be gained going down a group.

### Summary questions

1 Describe the trend in reactivity in:
   a  Group 1 *1 MARK*
   b  Group 7. *1 MARK*
2 Explain why potassium is more reactive than lithium. *4 MARKS*

3 Predict the difference in reactivity, giving reasons, seen in:
   a  Group 2, between magnesium and calcium *5 MARKS*
   b  Group 6, between oxygen and sulfur. *5 MARKS*

31

# C2 The Periodic Table

## Practice questions

1  a  Where in the Periodic Table do you find:
   i   the halogens? **1 MARK**
   ii  the noble gases? **1 MARK**
   iii the alkali metals? **1 MARK**
   iv  the transition elements? **1 MARK**
   b  In which groups would you find the four elements described below?
   i   This is a dense metal with a high melting point. It reacts only very slowly with water but will react when heated with steam. **1 MARK**
   ii  This is a metal that can be cut with a knife and is stored under oil. It reacts violently with water and forms ions with a 1+ charge. **1 MARK**
   iii This is a very unreactive, monatomic gas. **1 MARK**
   iv  This toxic gas is the most reactive of all the non-metallic elements. It forms ions with a 1– charge and will also form covalent compounds. **1 MARK**

2  Astatine, At, is a halogen whose atomic number is 85. It lies at the bottom of Group 7, beneath iodine, I.
   a  How many electrons occupy its outermost shell (highest energy level)? Explain how you worked out your answer. **2 MARKS**
   b  Predict the state of astatine at 20 °C. **1 MARK**
   c  For the compound sodium astatide, predict:
   i   its type of bonding **1 MARK**
   ii  its chemical formula **1 MARK**
   iii the word equation and the balanced symbol equation for its formation from its elements **3 MARKS**
   iv  whether or not you would see signs of a reaction if a solution of sodium astatide was mixed with chlorine water. Explain how you arrived at your answer. **2 MARKS**
   d  Place the halogens, including astatine, in order of reactivity, with the most reactive element first. **1 MARK**

3  Rubidium, Rb, is in Group 1 of the Periodic Table, lying directly beneath potassium, K.
   a  Predict the physical properties of rubidium, including its hardness, electrical conductivity, and melting point. **3 MARKS**
   b  i  Predict what the charge on a rubidium ion will be. **1 MARK**
   ii  Copy and complete the table below:

| Rubidium compound | Chemical formula |
|---|---|
| rubidium iodide | |
| rubidium fluoride | |
| rubidium hydroxide | |

   **3 MARKS**
   c  Write word equations and balanced symbol equations, including state symbols, for the following reactions:
   i   rubidium and water **4 MARKS**
   ii  rubidium and chlorine. **4 MARKS**
   d  Determine whether the reactions of rubidium in part **c** will be more or less vigorous than the same reactions using potassium. **1 MARK**

4  Group 0 is found as the last column in the Periodic Table, on the extreme right-hand side.
   a  What is the name commonly given to the elements in Group 0? **1 MARK**
   b  Write the name and symbol of the first four elements in Group 0. **2 MARKS**
   c  Explain which one of the first four elements in Group 0 is the odd one out in terms of the number of electrons in its outer shell. **3 MARKS**
   d  The Group 0 elements are found in trace amounts in the air. If air is gradually cooled down to extremely low temperatures, predict which of the first four elements would condense as a liquid first. Give a reason for your answer. **2 MARKS**

5  a  Explain how Dmitri Mendeleev used atomic weights to construct his Periodic Table. **2 MARKS**
   b  Explain how the scientific community were influenced to accept his Periodic Table. **6 MARKS**
   c  Explain why, in 1869, scientists could not explain why some pairs of elements in Mendeleev's Periodic Table appeared to be in the wrong order according to their atomic weights. **3 MARKS**

6  a  Explain how the atoms of metals and non-metals change when they react to form their ions, using magnesium as an example of a metallic element and oxygen as an example of a non-metallic element. **6 MARKS**
   b  Suggest how the radius of a metal ion compares with the radius of the metal atom it was made from. Give a reason for your suggestion. **2 MARKS**

# Exam-style questions

**01** Elements **A–G** are shown on the Periodic Table in **Figure 1**. **A–G** are not the symbols for the elements.

**Figure 1**

Choose one letter **A–G** to answer questions **01.1** to **01.6**.

**01.1** Which element is a very unreactive gas? **1 MARK**

**01.2** Which element is a metal that only forms 2+ ions? **1 MARK**

**01.3** Which element reacts explosively with water, forming an alkaline solution? **1 MARK**

**01.4** Which element has the atomic number 5? **1 MARK**

**01.5** Element **D** is in Group 7.

A solution of a Group 7 element will displace a less reactive Group 7 element from a solution of its salt. **Table 1** shows the colours of the solutions of some Group 7 elements and the solutions of sodium salts of some Group 7 elements.

**Table 1**

| Element | Colour of solution | Salt | Colour of solution |
|---|---|---|---|
| $Cl_2$ | colourless | NaCl | colourless |
| $Br_2$ | orange | NaBr | colourless |
| $I_2$ | brown | NaI | colourless |

Predict the colour changes, if any, which will be seen when the following solutions are mixed together. Explain your answers.

**a** chlorine solution and sodium bromide solution

**b** iodine solution and sodium chloride solution

**5 MARKS**

**02** This question is about Group 1 metals.
A teacher dropped a small piece of potassium into some water in a glass trough.

The equation for the reaction is shown below.

....... K(s) + ....... $H_2O$(l) → ....... KOH(aq) + ....... $H_2$(g)

**02.1** Balance the equation. **2 MARKS**

**02.2** Using the state symbols in the equation, outline **two** observations that you would expect to see when the potassium reacts with the water. Explain your answer. **4 MARKS**

**02.3** The teacher used a safety screen. Give one other safety precaution the teacher should take. **1 MARK**

**02.4** A few drops of universal indicator were put into the glass trough after the reaction. The universal indicator turned blue.

Why did the universal indicator turn blue? **2 MARKS**

**02.5** The list shows properties of metals.

Choose **two** properties that are typical of Group 1 metals.

**A** high density

**B** low density

**C** form compounds with a 1+ charge that dissolve in water forming colourless solutions

**D** form compounds that dissolve in water forming coloured solutions

**E** very hard **2 MARKS**

**02.6** The electronic structures of lithium and potassium are shown in **Figure 2**.

**Figure 2**

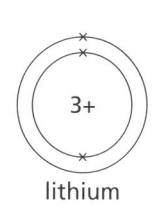

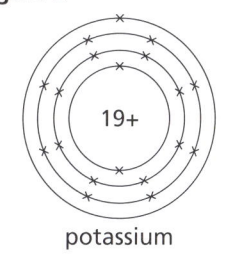

lithium    potassium

Why are lithium and potassium both in the same group of the Periodic Table? **1 MARK**

**02.7** Explain why lithium is less reactive than potassium. You should refer to **Figure 2** in your answer. **3 MARKS**

C2 The Periodic Table

33

# C3 Structure and bonding

## C3.1 States of matter

### Learning objectives

*After this topic, you should know:*

- that the melting and boiling points of a substance depend on the nature of its particles and the forces between the particles
- how to recognise that atoms themselves do not have the bulk properties of materials
- how to predict the states of substances at different temperatures, given appropriate data
- **H** the limitations of the particle theory.

**Figure 1** The three states of matter

- solid — particles vibrate
- liquid — particles slip and slide over each other
- gas — particles move very quickly in all directions; as the particles bash against the walls of the container, they exert a force that causes pressure

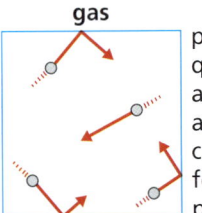

### Study tip

If a solid is heated and changes directly to a gas without melting (it does not pass through the liquid phase) the change of state is called sublimation.

From an early age, you can tell the differences between solids, liquids, and gases by using your senses. Later you learn that most substances can be classified as solids, liquids, or gases, and that these are called the three states of matter.

Solids have a fixed shape and volume. They cannot be compressed. Liquids have a fixed volume, but they can flow and change their shape. Liquids occupy just slightly more space than when solid (water and ice are exceptions). Gases have no fixed shape or volume. They can be compressed easily.

The **particle theory** is used to explain the properties of solids, liquids, and gases. It is based on the fact that all matter is made up of tiny particles, and describes:

- the movement of the particles
- the average distance between particles.

Look at the diagrams in Figure 1 that represent the three states of matter.

Each particle in a solid is touching its nearest neighbours and they remain in this fixed arrangement. They cannot move around but they do vibrate constantly.

The particles in a liquid are also very close together but they can move past each other. This results in a constantly changing arrangement of particles.

The particles in a gas have, on average, much more space between them. They can move around at high speeds in any direction. This means the particles have a random arrangement. The hotter the gas is, the faster the particles move. The pressure of a gas is caused by the particles colliding with the sides of the container. The more frequent and energetic the collisions, the higher the pressure of the gas. So, in a sealed container, the pressure of the gas increases as the temperature rises.

### Changing state

A solid turns into a liquid at its melting point. This is the same temperature at which the liquid freezes or solidifies back into the solid. The hotter a solid is, the faster its particles vibrate. Eventually, the vibrations will be so strong that the particles begin to break free from their neighbours. At this point, the solid starts to melt and become a liquid.

A liquid turns into a gas at its boiling point. The gas condenses back into the liquid at the same temperature. The hotter a liquid is, the faster its particles move around. As the temperature rises, more and more energy is transferred from the surroundings to the particles and more particles escape from the surface of the liquid. Its rate of evaporation increases. Eventually, the liquid boils and bubbles of gas rise and escape from within the liquid.

Change of state is a physical property and it is reversible. No new substances are formed in changes of state. For example, water molecules, $H_2O$, are the same in ice as they are in liquid water or in water vapour. It is just the

C3 Structure and bonding

movement and arrangement of the particles that differ and affect the properties of the substances at different temperatures, not any change in the particles themselves. Substances with higher melting points and boiling points have stronger forces acting between their particles.

## Energy transfers during changes of state

When you monitor the temperature of a solid as you heat it to beyond its melting point, the results are surprising. The temperature stops rising at the solid's melting point. It remains constant until all the solid has melted, and only then starts to rise again (Figure 2).

At its melting point, enough energy is transferred from the surroundings to the solid for the forces between the particles in the solid to break. This enables the particles to break away from their fixed positions in the solid and start moving around. Once all the solid has melted, the transfer of energy from the surroundings to the substance causes the temperature of the liquid to continue to rise as expected.

On the other hand, changes of state in which you cool down a substance involve particles becoming closer together, such as condensing and freezing (solidifying). The cooling stops at the boiling point and melting point when energy is transferred from the substance to the surroundings as stronger forces form between particles.

## Limitations of the particle model

The simple particle model assumes that particles are made up of solid spheres with no forces operating between them. This is useful when comparing the properties of solids, liquids, and gases. However, the particles that make up substances are atoms, molecules, or ions. They can vary in size from the small He atoms in helium gas to the polymer molecules in plastics, which can contain many thousands of atoms, and are not spherical. The interactions between neighbouring atoms, molecules, and ions can also distort their shapes. Atoms are mostly empty space, so real particles are not solid at all.

### Practical

#### Cooling curve

Heat a test tube of stearic acid clamped in a water bath until its temperature reaches about 75 °C. Then remove the test tube from the hot water and monitor the temperature as it falls. Plot or print off a graph of the results.

- What is the melting point of stearic acid?
- Explain the shape of the line on your graph.

**Safety:** Wear eye protection.

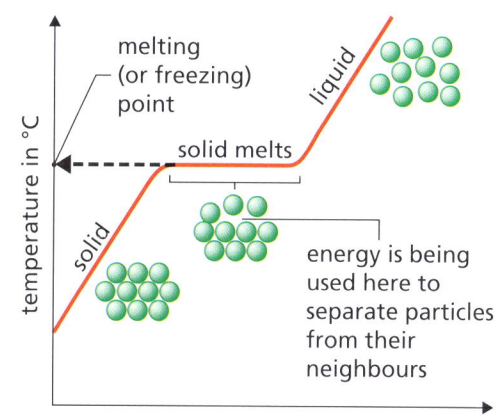

▲ Figure 2 The heating curve of a solid

### Key points

- The three states of matter are solids, liquids, and gases.
- The particles in a solid are packed together and vibrate around fixed positions. The particles in a liquid are close together but are free to move. The particles in a gas have lots of space between them and zoom around randomly.
- In melting and boiling, energy is transferred from the surroundings to the substance. In freezing and condensing, energy is transferred from the substance to the surroundings.
- The simple particle model of solids, liquids, and gases is useful but has its limitations.

## Summary questions

1. Use the particle model to draw a representation of how particles are arranged in the three states of matter. **3 MARKS**
2. Substance **Z** has a melting point of 35 °C and a boiling point of 120 °C. Give the physical state of substance **Z** at:
   a  20 °C  **1 MARK**   b  105 °C.  **1 MARK**
3. Explain why substances have different melting points. **2 MARKS**
4. Describe the changes that occur to the particles as a gas is cooled down to a temperature below its freezing point. **6 MARKS**
5. Using particle theory, predict how temperature and pressure affect the density of a fixed mass of gas. **6 MARKS**
6. Evaporation is the change of state that occurs when a liquid changes to a gas below its boiling point. You can investigate the factors that affect the rate of evaporation using a wet paper towel on a high-resolution electric balance.
   Plan an investigation into one factor that might affect the rate of evaporation of water from the paper towel. **5 MARKS**

35

# C3.2 Atoms into ions

### Learning objectives

*After this topic, you should know:*
- what a chemical compound is
- how elements form compounds
- how atoms can form either positive or negative ions
- how the elements in Group 1 bond with the elements in Group 7.

You already know that you can mix two substances together without either of them changing. For example, you can mix sand and copper sulfate together and then separate them again. No change will have taken place to the sand or the copper sulfate.

However, in chemical reactions the situation is very different. When the atoms of two or more elements react chemically, they make a compound.

**A compound contains two or more elements, which are chemically combined.**

The compound formed is different from the elements that it is made from, and you cannot get the elements back again easily. You can also react compounds together to form other compounds. However, the reaction of elements is easier to understand as a starting point.

The atoms of the noble gases, in Group 0 of the Periodic Table, have an arrangement of electrons that make them very stable and unreactive. However, most atoms do not have this electronic structure. When atoms react, they take part in changes which give them a stable arrangement of electrons. They may do this by either:

- sharing electrons, which is called **covalent bonding**, or
- transferring electrons, which is called **ionic bonding**.

## Losing electrons to form positive ions

In ionic bonding, the atoms involved lose or gain electrons to form charged particles called ions. The ions have the electronic structure of a noble gas. So, for example, if a sodium atom (2,8,1), from Group 1 in the Periodic Table, loses one electron, it is left with the stable electronic structure of neon (2,8).

However, the sodium atom is also left with one more proton in its nucleus than there are electrons around its nucleus. The proton has a positive charge, so the sodium atom has now become a positively charged ion. The sodium ion has a single positive charge. The formula of a sodium ion is written as $Na^+$. The electronic structure of the $Na^+$ ion is 2,8 (Figure 1).

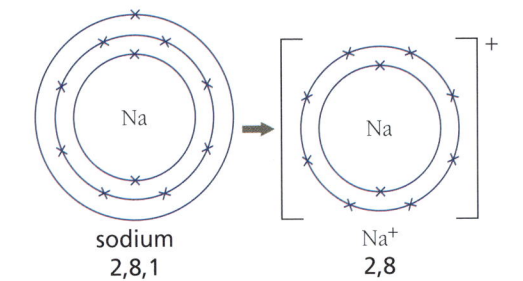

▲ **Figure 1** A positive sodium ion, $Na^+$, is formed when a sodium atom loses an electron during ionic bonding

## Gaining electrons to form negative ions

When non-metals react with metals, the non-metal atoms gain electrons to achieve the stable electronic structure of a noble gas. Chlorine, for example, has the electronic structure 2,8,7. It is in Group 7 of the periodic table. By gaining a single electron, a chlorine atom gets the stable electronic structure of argon (2,8,8). In this case, there is now one more negative electron than there are positive protons in its nucleus. So, the chlorine atom becomes a negatively charged ion. The chloride ion carries a single negative charge. The formula of the chloride ion is written as $Cl^-$. Its electronic structure is 2,8,8 (Figure 2).

▲ **Figure 2** A negative chloride ion, $Cl^-$, is formed when a chlorine atom gains an electron during ionic bonding

## C3 Structure and bonding

## Representing ionic bonding

Metal atoms, which tend to lose electrons, react with non-metal atoms, which tend to gain electrons. So, when sodium reacts with chlorine, each sodium atom loses an electron, and each chlorine atom gains an electron. They both form stable ions. The electrostatic attraction between the oppositely charged $Na^+$ ions and $Cl^-$ ions is called ionic bonding. You can show what happens in a diagram. The electrons of one atom are represented by dots, and the electrons of the other atom are represented by crosses (Figure 3).

2,8,1     2,8,7     2,8     2,8,8
NaCl ($Na^+Cl^-$)

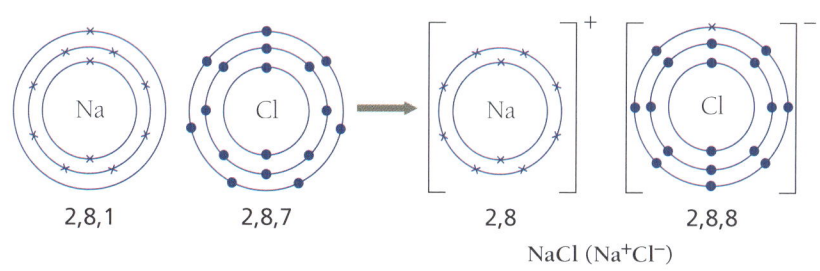

▲ **Figure 3** The formation of sodium chloride, NaCl, an example of ion formation by transferring an electron

This can also be shown more simply by just showing the electrons in the outermost shell of the atoms and ions in a **dot and cross diagram** (Figure 4).

2,8,1     2,8,7     2,8     2,8,8

▲ **Figure 4** The dot and cross diagram to show electron transfer in sodium chloride, NaCl

### Study tip

Remember to use different symbols for electrons from different atoms when drawing ionic bonding. It helps you to see which electrons have been gained or lost by each atom during bonding.

### Synoptic link

You first met the formation of ions in Topic C1.7.

### Study tip

Dot and cross diagrams like Figure 4 just show the electrons in the outermost shell of each atom. This can make it easier to see how the electrons in the outer shell change during ionic bonding.

However, it's helpful to write down the electron structure of the atoms so you can remember the structure of the atoms and see how they change when bonded.

## Summary questions

1  a  What type of bond is formed when atoms *share* electrons?  **1 MARK**
   b  What type of bond is formed when ions bond together by *gaining* or *losing* electrons?  **1 MARK**
2  Write electronic structures to show the ions that would be formed when the following atoms are involved in ionic bonding. For each one, explain how many electrons have been lost or gained and show the charge on the ions formed.
   a  aluminium, Al  **2 MARKS**
   b  fluorine, F  **2 MARKS**
   c  potassium, K  **2 MARKS**
   d  oxygen, O.  **2 MARKS**
3  Explain how and why atoms of Group 1 and Group 7 elements react with each other, in terms of their electronic structures.  **4 MARKS**

### Key points

- Elements react together to form compounds by gaining or losing electrons or by sharing electrons.
- The elements in Group 1 react with the elements in Group 7. As they react, atoms of Group 1 elements can each lose one electron to gain the stable electronic structure of a noble gas. This electron can be given to an atom from Group 7, which then also achieves the stable electronic structure of a noble gas.

37

# C3.3 Ionic bonding

## Learning objectives

*After this topic, you should know:*
- how ionic compounds are held together
- which elements, as well as those in Group 1 and Group 7, form ions
- how the charges on ions are related to group numbers in the Periodic Table.

## Study tip

For an ionic compound, the formula used doesn't tell you exactly how many ions are in the compound because there will be millions! Instead, it shows us the ratio of the types of ions. This is known as the empirical formula.

For example we use the formula $CaCl_2$ for calcium chloride because there is one calcium ion for every two chlorine ions within the giant structure.

When you eat salty food, you probably do not think about the charged particles, called sodium ions and chloride ions, that enter your body. You have seen how positive ions and negative ions form during some reactions. Ionic compounds are usually formed when metals react with non-metals. It is the metals that form positive ions and the non-metals that form negative ions.

The oppositely charged ions formed are held next to each other by very strong forces of attraction between them. These electrostatic forces of attraction, which act in all directions, are called ionic bonds.

## Ions and the Periodic Table

You have seen how atoms in Group 1 of the Periodic Table have one electron in their outermost shell (or highest energy level) and form 1+ ions. Group 7 atoms have seven electrons in their outermost shell and form 1– ions. The group number gives the number of electrons in the outermost shell. So how does the group number relate to the charges on the ions formed from atoms?

Sometimes the atoms reacting need to gain or lose two electrons to achieve the stable electronic structure of a noble gas. An example is when magnesium (2,8,2) from Group 2 reacts with oxygen (2,6) from Group 6. When these two elements react, they form magnesium oxide, MgO. This is made up of magnesium ions with a double positive charge, $Mg^{2+}$, and oxide ions with a double negative charge, $O^{2-}$.

Table 1 shows what type of ionic bonds the atoms from different groups of the Periodic Table form.

**Table 1** The atoms from different groups form different ions depending on the number of electrons in their outermost shell

| Group | Ion formed |
| --- | --- |
| Group 1 | form 1+ ions |
| Group 2 | form 2+ ions |
| Group 3 | form 3+ ions, when they form ions as opposed to sharing electrons |
| Group 4 | do not form ions, apart from tin (Sn) and lead (Pb) at the bottom of the group |
| Group 5 | form 3– ions, when they form ions as opposed to sharing electrons |
| Group 6 | form 2– ions, when they form ions as opposed to sharing electrons |
| Group 7 | form 1– ions, when they form ions as opposed to sharing electrons |
| Group 0 | never form ions in compounds |

Figure 1 shows how the electrons are transferred between a magnesium atom and an oxygen atom during ionic bonding.

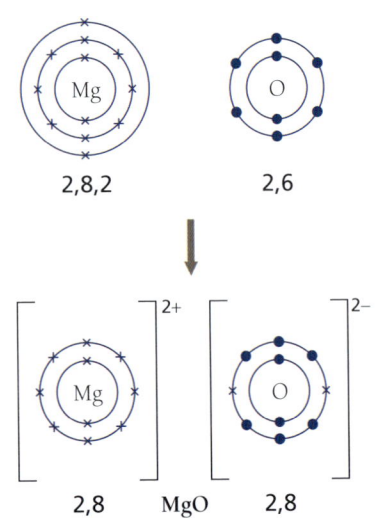

▲ **Figure 1** When magnesium oxide, MgO, is formed, the reacting magnesium atoms lose two electrons, and the oxygen atoms gain two electrons

Another example of an ionic compound is calcium chloride. Each calcium atom (2,8,8,2) needs to lose two electrons, but each chlorine atom (2,8,7) needs to gain only one electron (Figure 2).

This means that two chlorine atoms react with every one calcium atom to form calcium chloride. So, the formula of calcium chloride is $CaCl_2$.

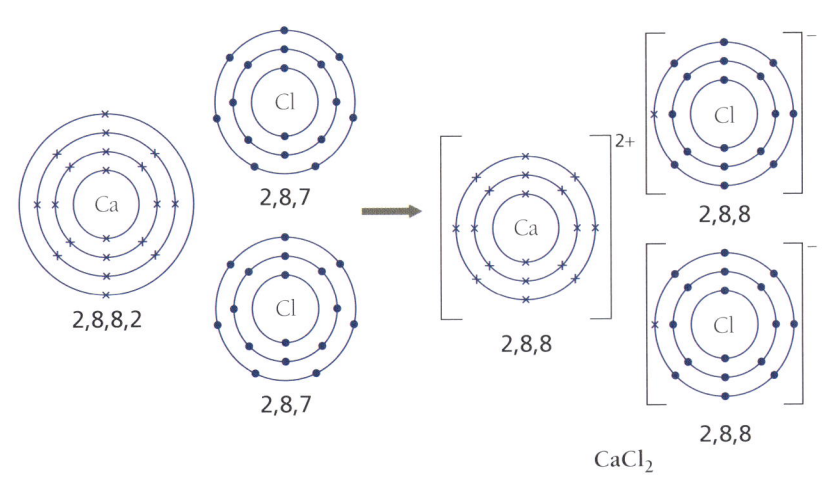

**Figure 2** The formation of calcium chloride, $CaCl_2$

## Study tip

Look carefully at how calcium has shared its electrons in Figure 2.

It had two electrons in its outermost shell at first, and has shared one electron with each chlorine ion. This is why it can bond with two chlorine atoms to make calcium chloride, $CaCl_2$.

## Maths

Notice that the charges in the formula of an ionic compound cancel each other out, as the overall charge on the compound is zero. So aluminium oxide (made up of aluminium ions, $Al^{3+}$, and oxide ions, $O^{2-}$) has the formula $Al_2O_3$. The total charge of 6+ on the two aluminium ions is cancelled out by the total charge of 6− on the three oxide ions.

## Summary questions

1. Copy and complete the table:

| Atomic number | Atom | Electronic structure of atom | Ion | Electronic structure of ion |
|---|---|---|---|---|
| 9 | F | | | 2,8 |
| 3 | | 2,1 | Li⁺ | |
| 16 | S | | S²⁻ | |
| 20 | | 2,8,8,2 | | |

4 MARKS

2. Write down the general rules used to remember the charge on any ions formed by elements in:
   a Group 1, Group 2, and Group 3. 1 MARK
   b Group 5, Group 6, and Group 7. 1 MARK
3. Draw dot and cross diagrams to show how you would expect the following elements to form ions together:
   a potassium and oxygen 3 MARKS
   b aluminium and chlorine. 4 MARKS
4. a Explain why the formula of potassium bromide is KBr but the formula of potassium oxide is $K_2O$. 3 MARKS
   b Explain why the formula of magnesium oxide is MgO but the formula of magnesium chloride is $MgCl_2$. 3 MARKS
5. Explain why metal atoms form positively charged ions, whereas non-metal atoms form negatively charged ions. 6 MARKS

## Key points

- Ionic compounds are held together by strong forces of attraction between their oppositely charged ions. This is called ionic bonding.
- Besides the elements in Group 1 and Group 7, other elements that can form ionic compounds include those from Group 2 (forming 2+ ions) and Group 6 (forming 2− ions).

# C3.4 Giant ionic structures

## Learning objectives

After this topic, you should know:
- why ionic compounds have high melting points
- why ionic compounds conduct electricity when molten or dissolved in water.

An ionic compound consists of a giant structure of ions arranged in a lattice. The attractive electrostatic forces between the oppositely charged ions act in all directions and are very strong. This holds the ions in the lattice together very tightly. Look at the two models showing small parts of a **giant ionic lattice** in Figure 1.

It takes a large amount of energy to break up a giant ionic lattice. There are lots of strong ionic bonds to break. To separate the ions, you have to overcome all those electrostatic forces of attraction acting in all directions. This means that ionic compounds have high melting points and boiling points.

Once you have supplied enough energy to separate the ions from the lattice, they become mobile so can start to move around. This is when the ionic solid melts and becomes a liquid. The ions are free to move anywhere in this liquid. They are attracted to oppositely charged electrodes held in the molten compound. Therefore, they can carry their electrical charge through the liquid (Figure 2).

*3D model of a giant ionic lattice* — strong electrostatic forces of attraction called ionic bonds

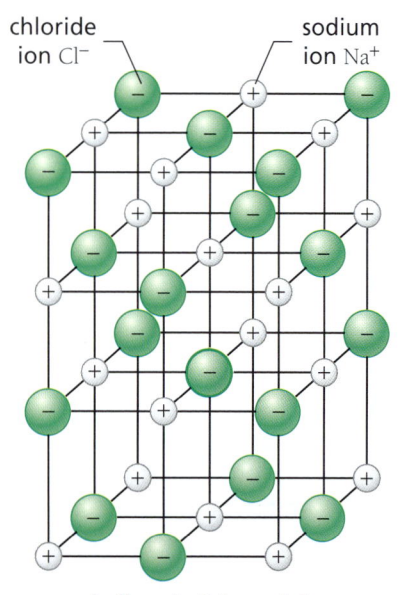

*ball and stick model* — chloride ion $Cl^-$, sodium ion $Na^+$

▲ **Figure 1** The regular arrangement of ions in the giant lattice results in ionic compounds forming crystals. The ball and stick model shows the 1:1 ratio of $Na^+$ and $Cl^-$ ions in NaCl

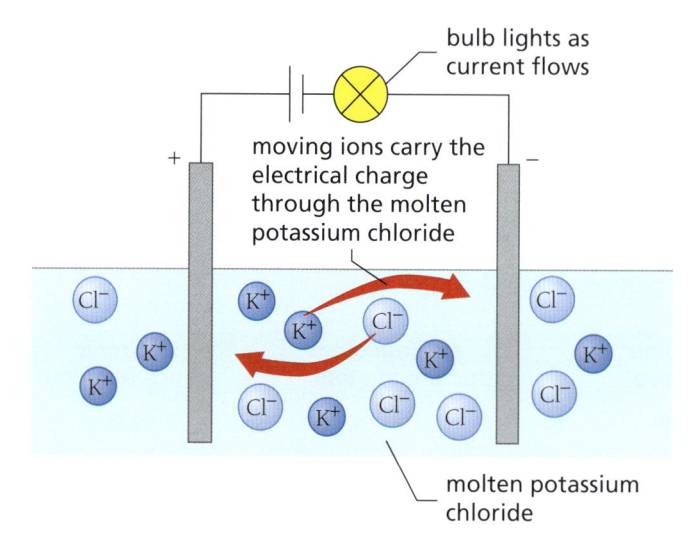

▲ **Figure 2** Because the ions are mobile, a molten ionic compound can conduct electricity

A solid ionic compound cannot conduct electricity because its ions are held in fixed positions in the lattice. The ions in a solid ionic compound cannot move around. They can only vibrate 'on the spot'.

Many, but not all, ionic compounds will dissolve in water. When an ionic compound is dissolved in water, the lattice is split up by the water molecules. The ions are then free to move around within the solution formed. They can carry their charge to oppositely charged electrodes in the solution. Just as molten ionic compounds will conduct electricity, solutions of ionic compounds will also conduct electricity. The ions can move to an oppositely charged electrode dipped in the solution.

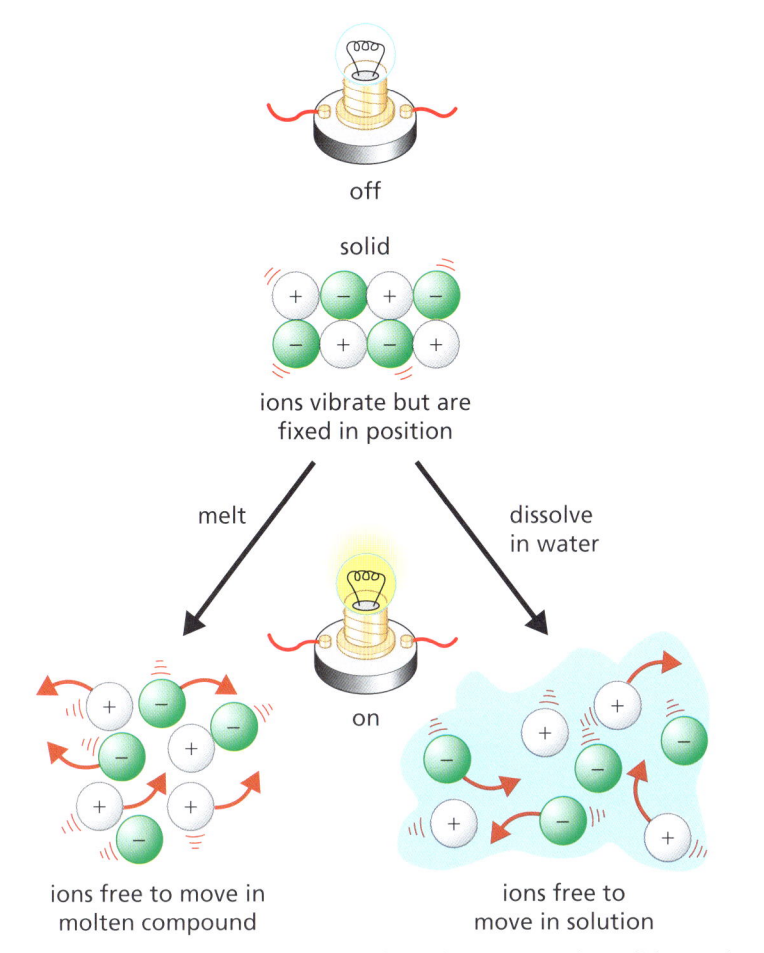

# C3 Structure and bonding

▲ **Figure 3** Ionic compounds do not conduct electricity in the solid state but do when molten or when dissolved in water

| Ionic solid | Molten ionic compound | Ionic compound in solution |
|---|---|---|
| Ions are fixed in position in a giant lattice. They vibrate but cannot move around. It **does not** conduct electricity. | High temperature provides enough energy to overcome the many strong attractive forces between ions. Ions are free to move around within the molten compound. It **does** conduct electricity. | Water molecules separate ions from the lattice. Ions are free to move around within the solution. It **does** conduct electricity. |

## Summary questions

1. Describe a rigid ionic lattice. **2 MARKS**
2. Explain why ionic compounds have high melting points. **4 MARKS**
3. Explain why ionic compounds conduct electricity only when they are molten or dissolved in water. **2 MARKS**
4. Predict which of these two ionic compounds has the higher melting point – sodium oxide or aluminium oxide. Explain your answer. **5 MARKS**

### Study tip

Remember that every ionic compound has a giant structure. The oppositely charged ions in these structures are held together by strong electrostatic forces of attraction. These act in all directions in the giant lattice, resulting in relatively high melting points.

### Synoptic link

You will look at the limitations of using models like those in Figure 1 in Topic C3.6.

### Practical

#### Testing conductivity

Using a simple d.c. circuit (Figure 2) dip a pair of electrodes into a 1 cm depth of sodium chloride crystals. What happens?

Now slowly add water.

- What happens to the bulb?

Repeat the experiment using potassium chloride.

- Explain your observations.

Follow safety advice and take care if you are asthmatic.

### Key points

- It takes a large amount of energy to break the many strong ionic bonds, operating in all directions, which hold a giant ionic lattice together. So ionic compounds have high melting points. They are all solids at room temperature.
- Ionic compounds will conduct electricity when molten or dissolved in water. This is because their ions can then become mobile and can carry electric charge through the liquid.

# C3.5 Covalent bonding

## Learning objectives

After this topic, you should know:
- how covalent bonds are formed
- how covalent bonds can be represented
- what types of substances contain covalent bonds.

Reactions between metals and non-metals usually result in compounds with ionic bonding. However, many more compounds, including the vast majority of those making up your body, are formed in a very different way. When non-metals react together, their atoms share pairs of electrons to form molecules. This is called covalent bonding.

## Simple molecules

The atoms of non-metals generally tend to gain electrons to achieve stable electronic structures. When they react together, neither atom can give away electrons. So, they share pairs of electrons to get the electronic structure of a noble gas. The atoms in the molecules are then held together by shared pairs of electrons creating strong bonds between the atoms called **covalent bonds**.

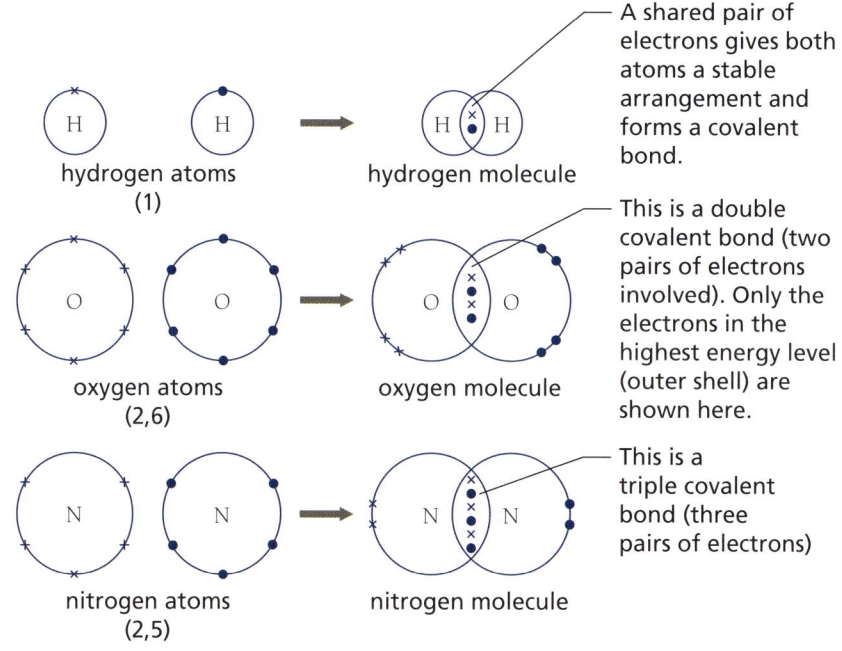

▲ Figure 1 Most of the molecules in substances that make up living things are held together by covalent bonds between non-metal atoms

A shared pair of electrons gives both atoms a stable arrangement and forms a covalent bond.

hydrogen atoms (1) → hydrogen molecule

This is a double covalent bond (two pairs of electrons involved). Only the electrons in the highest energy level (outer shell) are shown here.

oxygen atoms (2,6) → oxygen molecule

This is a triple covalent bond (three pairs of electrons)

nitrogen atoms (2,5) → nitrogen molecule

▲ Figure 2 Atoms of hydrogen, oxygen, and nitrogen join together to form stable molecules. The atoms in $H_2$, $O_2$, and $N_2$ molecules are held together by strong covalent bonds

Sometimes in covalent bonding each atom has the same number of electrons to share (Figure 2) but this is not always the case. Sometimes the atoms of one element will need several electrons, whilst those of the other element only need one more electron, for each atom to get a stable electronic structure. In this case, more atoms become involved in forming the molecule, such as in water, $H_2O$, and methane, $CH_4$ (Figure 3).

You can represent the covalent bonds in substances such as water, ammonia, and methane in several ways. Each way represents the same thing. The method chosen depends on what you want to show (Figure 4).

hydrogen chloride, HCl

water, $H_2O$

methane, $CH_4$

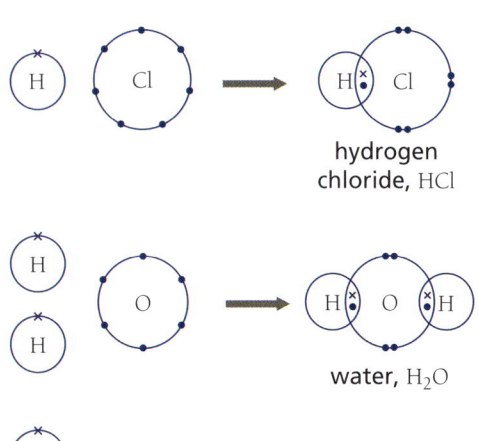

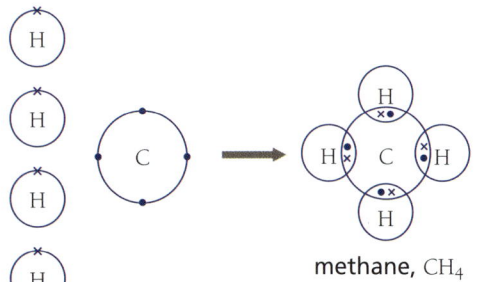

▲ Figure 3 The principles of covalent bonding remain the same however many atoms are involved – the atoms share one or more pairs of electrons to form the electronic structure of a noble gas, for example, He (2), Ne (2,8), and Ar (2,8,8)

42

C3 Structure and bonding

water, H₂O:
a) [dot-and-cross shell diagram of H–O–H]
b) H :Ö: H (dot and cross)
c) H — O — H

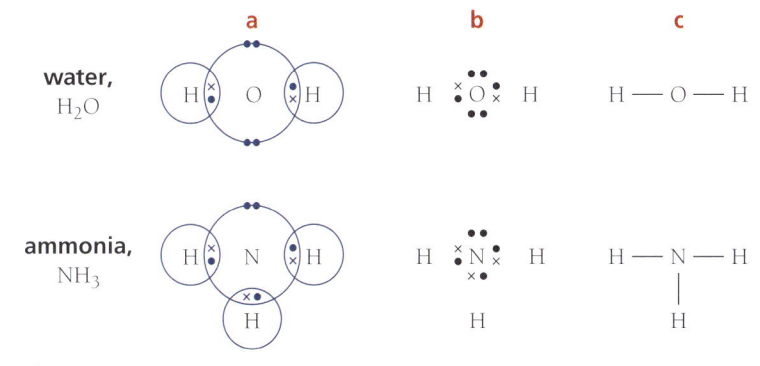

ammonia, NH₃:
a) [dot-and-cross shell diagram with N and three H]
b) H :N: H with H below (dot and cross)
c) H — N — H with H below

▲ **Figure 4** You can represent the bonding in a covalent molecule by showing:
  a the highest energy levels (or outer shells)
  b the outer electrons in a dot and cross diagram
  c the number of covalent bonds.

Double bonds, as in the $O_2$ molecule in Figure 2, can be shown by two lines: O=O in an oxygen molecule. The dot and cross diagram of an oxygen molecule is shown in Figure 5.

[dot and cross diagram of O₂]

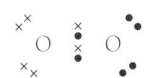

▲ **Figure 5** Notice the two pairs of electrons (four electrons in all) between the two oxygen atoms.

## Giant covalent structures

Many substances containing covalent bonds consist of small molecules, for example, $H_2O$. However, some covalently bonded substances are very different. They have giant structures where huge numbers of atoms are held together by a network of covalent bonds. These giant covalent structures are sometimes referred to as macromolecules.

Diamond has a giant covalent structure (Figure 6). In diamond, each carbon atom forms four covalent bonds with its neighbours. This results in a rigid giant covalent lattice.

### Metacognition

Draw a flow chart of the steps you need to take to draw a dot and cross diagram of covalent bonding for small molecules. This should help you to break this down into manageable chunks. You can then apply this method when asked to draw bonding diagrams involving unfamiliar molecules.

▲ **Figure 6** Diamonds owe their hardness to the way the carbon atoms are arranged in a giant covalent structure

### Synoptic link

You will look at the structure of diamond in more detail in Topic C3.7.

### Summary questions

1 Which of these compounds will contain covalent bonds? Give a reason for your answer.
  hydrogen iodide    iron(II) chloride    lithium oxide
  sulfur dioxide    nitrogen(III) chloride    magnesium nitride    **2 MARKS**

2 Draw diagrams, showing all the electrons, to represent the covalent bonding between the following atoms:
  a two hydrogen atoms    **2 MARKS**
  b two chlorine atoms.    **2 MARKS**

3 Draw dot and cross diagrams to show the covalent bonds when:
  a a phosphorus atom bonds with three hydrogen atoms    **3 MARKS**
  b a carbon atom bonds with two oxygen atoms.    **3 MARKS**

### Key points

- Covalent bonds are formed when atoms of non-metals share pairs of electrons with each other.
- Each shared pair of electrons is a covalent bond.
- Many substances containing covalent bonds consist of simple molecules, but some have giant covalent structures.

# C3.6 Structure of simple molecules

## Learning objectives

*After this topic, you should know:*

- the limitations of using models such as dot and cross, ball and stick, 2D diagrams, and 3D diagrams to represent molecules or giant structures
- why substances made of small molecules have low melting points and boiling points
- why these substances do not conduct electricity.

## Using models

Models are used in everyday life to help us understand things. For example, the map of the London Underground is a simplified model of the maze of tunnels carrying trains beneath the streets. Figure 1 summarises the different models used by chemists to show covalent bonding – a methane molecule, $CH_4$, is used here as an example.

3D ball and stick model

2D ball and stick model

dot and cross diagram (showing outer shells as circles)

dot and cross diagram showing outer shell electrons

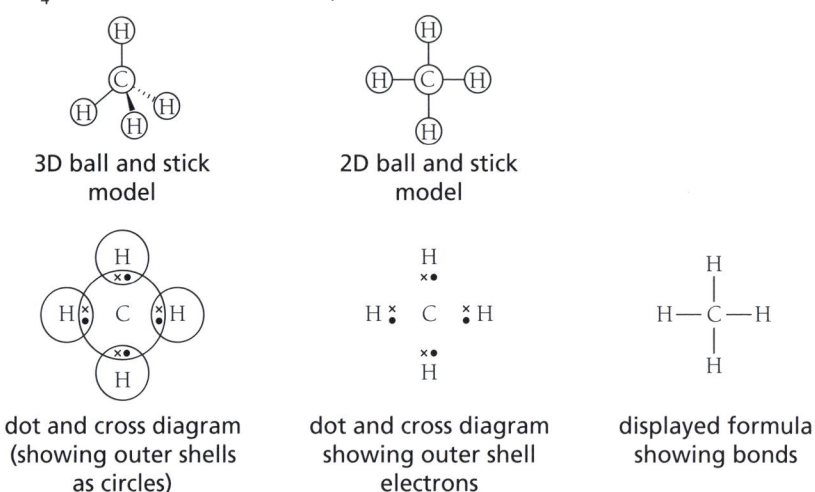

displayed formula showing bonds

▲ **Figure 1** The models used to help us understand covalent bonding

Like all models, each one is useful but has some limitations. In Figure 1, both the 2D and 3D ball and stick models try to show the shape of the molecule, but a molecular model kit is the best way to see its tetrahedral shape (Figure 2).

Dot and cross diagrams show which atom the electrons in the bonds came from originally but, in reality, all electrons are identical. Like all models drawn on paper, the electrons are shown in fixed positions between two atoms. However, scientists believe that the electrons in covalent bonds are constantly moving, but on average are found between the nuclei of the atoms they are bonding together.

In giant structures, the models can never accurately reflect the many millions of atoms (or ions) bonded together. However, they can represent a tiny fraction of a structure. They can indicate the chemical formula of a compound by the simplest **ratio** of the atoms or ions in models of their giant structures. For example, in a ball and stick model of sodium chloride (Figure 1 in Topic C3.4), there will be an equal number of Na⁺ and Cl⁻ ions (ratio 1 : 1), so its formula is NaCl.

▲ **Figure 2** A molecular model of a methane molecule using a molecular model kit. Molecular model kits use plastic rods to join spheres together to construct molecules. These models have rigid bonds and solid atoms, but actual bonds can vibrate, and molecules can bend and twist

## Intermolecular forces

Covalent bonds are very strong. So, the atoms within each molecule are held very tightly together. However, the bonds between molecules within a substance are often quite weak because the molecules are further away from each other. These weak **intermolecular forces** can be broken without much energy.

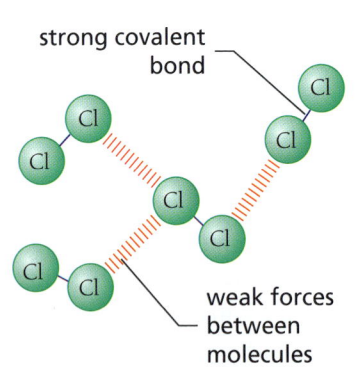

▲ **Figure 3** Covalent bonds and the weak forces between molecules in chlorine gas. It is the weak intermolecular forces that are overcome when substances made of simple molecules melt or boil. The covalent bonds are not broken

44

# C3 Structure and bonding

Intermolecular forces **increase** with the **size** of the molecules.

So substances with larger molecules have higher melting points and boiling points than substances with smaller molecules. For example, molecules in long chains (such as polymers) have stronger intermolecular forces. This is why polymers are solid at room temperature.

**Polymers** are made up of many small reactive molecules that bond to each other to form long chains. The simplest example is poly(ethene), made up from thousands of small ethene molecules, $C_2H_4$, reacting together. We can represent the long polymer chains in poly(ethene) as in Figure 4.

Instead of showing large numbers of covalent bonds, an abbreviated version showing the repeating unit of the polymer chain can be used, as in Figure 5.

▲ **Figure 4** Poly(ethene)

▲ **Figure 5** Long chain of poly(ethene)

## Conductivity

You have seen that ionic compounds will conduct electricity when they are molten or dissolved in water. Although a substance that is made up of relatively small covalently bonded molecules may be a liquid at room temperature, it will not conduct electricity (see Practical box).

Compounds made of small molecules do not conduct electricity, even when they are molten or dissolved in water. This is because there is **no overall charge** on the relatively small molecules in a compound like sucrose, so they cannot carry electrical charge. Molten or aqueous ionic compounds, such as acid molecules, release ions as they melt or dissolve due to the bonds within the molecules breaking. The presence of these ions means they can conduct electricity.

### Practical

**Conductivity of a simple molecular compound**

Sucrose is a sugar used to sweeten food and drinks. It is a compound made up of individual molecules.

▲ **Figure 6** A molecule of sucrose

Watch your teacher test the conductivity of solid sucrose, molten sucrose, and sucrose dissolved in water.

- What happens?
- Compare these results with what would happen in a similar experiment using sodium chloride instead of sucrose.

### Summary questions

1. Describe what is meant by the term intermolecular forces. **1 MARK**
2. Describe the boiling points of small molecules. **1 MARK**
3. **a** Diamond has a very high melting point. Explain why. **2 MARKS**
   **b** Nitrogen gas has a very strong triple covalent bond holding the nitrogen atoms together in a diatomic molecule with the formula $N_2$. Explain why nitrogen has a boiling point of –196 °C. **2 MARKS**
4. A compound called sulfur hexafluoride, $SF_6$, is used to stop sparks forming inside electrical switches designed to control large currents. Explain why the properties of this compound make it particularly useful in electrical switches. **2 MARKS**
5. Explain in detail why substances made of small molecules do not conduct electricity. **2 MARKS**
6. Explain why the melting point of hydrogen chloride is –115 °C, whereas sodium chloride's melting point is 801 °C. **4 MARKS**

### Key points

- The forces between small molecules are weak. These weak intermolecular forces explain why substances made of small molecules have low melting points and boiling points.
- Small molecules have no overall charge, so they cannot carry electrical charge. Therefore, substances made of small molecules do not conduct electricity.
- Models are used to help us understand bonding, but each model has its limitations in representing reality.

# C3.7 Giant covalent structures

### Learning objectives

After this topic, you should know:
- the general properties of substances with giant covalent structures
- why diamond is hard, and graphite is slippery
- why graphite can conduct electricity and thermal energy.

Did you know that diamond is a form of the element carbon, the same element contained in your pencil leads? Diamond is the hardest known natural substance. Artificial diamonds can be made by heating pure carbon to very high temperatures under enormous pressures. 'Industrial diamonds' made like this are embedded in the drills used by oil companies. They must drill through layers of rock to get to the crude oil deep underground.

Many covalently bonded substances are made up of individual molecules. However, some substances, such as diamond, form very different structures. These do not have relatively small numbers of atoms arranged in simple molecules. They form huge networks of atoms held together by strong covalent bonds in **giant covalent structures**.

▲ Figure 1 Hard, shiny and transparent – diamonds make beautiful jewellery

### Study tip

Giant covalent structures are held together by covalent bonds throughout the lattice.

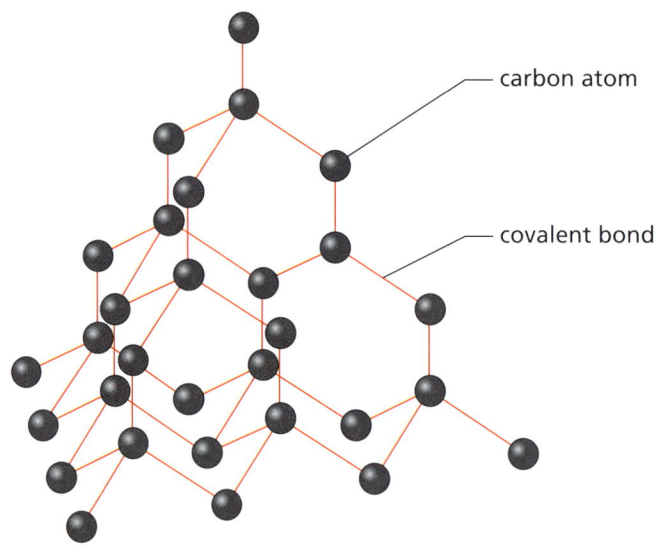

▲ Figure 2 A very small part of the structure of diamond. The giant covalent structure continues on and on in all directions

As well as diamond, graphite and silicon dioxide (silica) also have giant covalent structures.

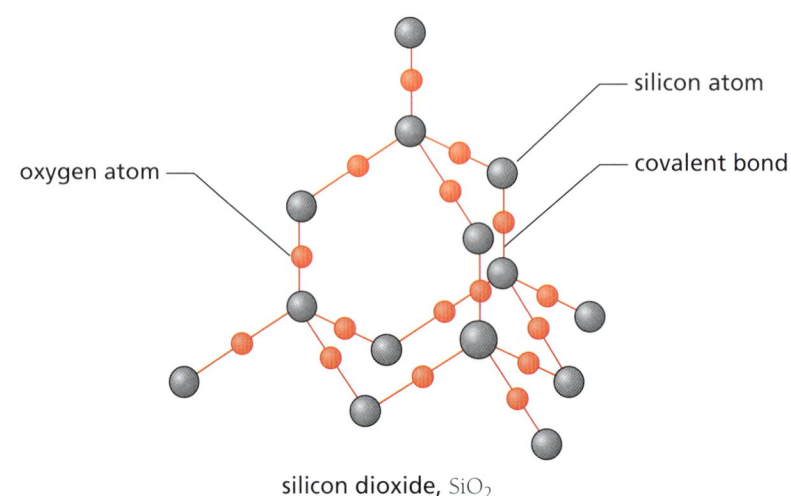

▲ Figure 3 Silicon dioxide has a giant covalent structure similar to that of diamond

**C3 Structure and bonding**

Having a giant covalent structure gives substances some very special properties:
- they have very high melting points and boiling points
- they are insoluble in water
- apart from graphite, they are hard and do not conduct electricity.

For example, as mentioned earlier, diamond is exceptionally hard and it has a boiling point of 4827 °C. Each carbon atom forms four strong covalent bonds, arranged in a perfectly symmetrical giant lattice.

## Bonding in graphite

Carbon is not always found in the form of diamond. Another form of carbon, which we use in pencils, is graphite. In graphite, carbon atoms are only bonded to three other carbon atoms. They form hexagons, which are arranged in giant layers. There are no covalent bonds between the layers, only weak intermolecular forces, so the layers can slide over each other quite easily. It is a bit like the effect of cards sliding off a pack of playing cards. This makes graphite a soft material that feels slippery to the touch.

As the carbon atoms in graphite's layers are arranged in hexagons, each carbon atom forms three strong covalent bonds (Figure 4). Carbon atoms have four electrons in their outer shell available for bonding. This leaves one spare outer electron on each carbon atom in graphite.

These mobile electrons can move freely along the layers of carbon atoms. The mobile electrons found in graphite are called **delocalised electrons**. They no longer belong to any one particular carbon atom. They behave rather like electrons in a metallic structure (which you will look at in detail in Topic C3.9).

These delocalised electrons allow graphite to conduct electricity. The electrons will drift away from the negative terminal of a battery and towards its positive terminal when put into an electrical circuit. Diamond – and most other covalently-bonded substances – cannot conduct electricity. This is because their atoms have no free electrons, as all their outer shell electrons are involved in covalent bonding.

Graphite is also an excellent conductor of thermal energy. As more energy is transferred to the delocalised electrons, they move around faster and rapidly transfer the energy along the layers in the graphite.

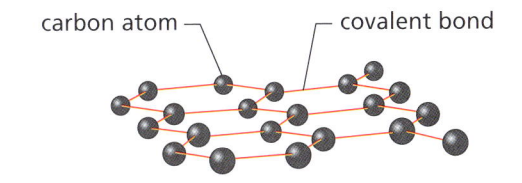

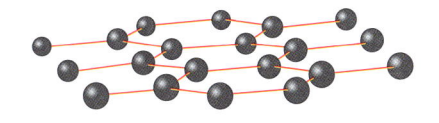

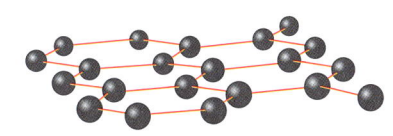

▲ **Figure 4** The giant structure of graphite. When you write with a pencil, some layers of carbon atoms slide off the 'lead' and are left on the paper

### Summary questions

1. Name the general properties of a substance with a typical giant covalent structure. **2 MARKS**
2. Draw a rough sketch of the structure of graphite. Insert a plus sign and a minus sign to represent the terminals of a battery attached to the ends of the graphite.
   On your sketch use arrows to indicate the movement of the electrons when an electric current flows through the graphite. **2 MARKS**
3. Graphite is sometimes used to reduce the friction between two surfaces that are rubbing together.
   Explain how it does this. **2 MARKS**
4. Explain why graphite can conduct electricity but diamond cannot. **6 MARKS**

### Key points

- Some covalently bonded substances have giant structures. These substances have very high melting points and boiling points.
- Graphite contains giant layers of covalently bonded carbon atoms. However, there are no covalent bonds between the layers. This means they can slide over each other, making graphite soft and slippery. The carbon atoms in diamond have a rigid giant covalent structure, making it a very hard substance.
- Graphite can conduct electricity and thermal energy because of the delocalised electrons that can move along its layers.

# C3.8 Fullerenes and graphene

### Learning objectives

After this topic, you should know:
- about the structure of the fullerenes and graphene
- how to recognise fullerenes and graphene from diagrams
- some uses of fullerenes, including carbon nanotubes.

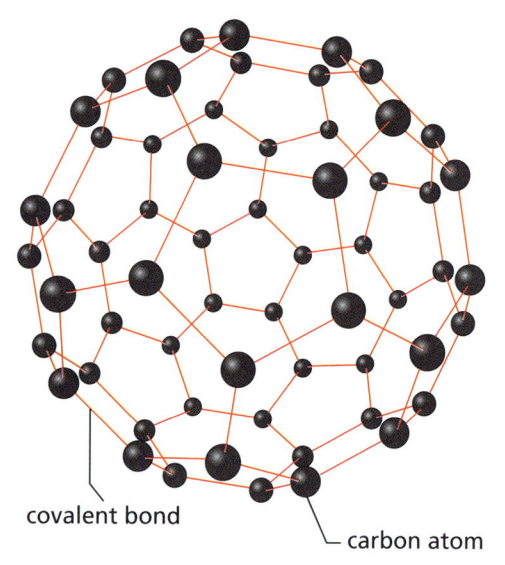

## Fullerenes

Apart from diamond and graphite, there are other structures that carbon atoms can form. In these structures the carbon atoms join together to make large hollow cages, which can have all sorts of shapes.

The ability of carbon to behave in this way was not discovered until 1985. Astronomers had found that long chains of carbon atoms existed in outer space. When scientists tried to recreate the conditions that might account for these carbon chains, they created a new molecule by chance. The molecule was made of 60 carbon atoms, but they did not know how the atoms were arranged within each molecule. Analysis showed that all the carbon atoms in the new molecule were equivalent. There were no carbon atoms stuck at the ends of the molecule.

Other scientists found that it was made of a structure of hexagons and pentagons arranged in a sphere – just like the panels stitched together to make a football (Figure 1). The name buckminsterfullerene was chosen for this $C_{60}$ molecule after the Canadian architect Buckminster Fuller. He designed a similar shaped building in Montreal in 1967. The name is often abbreviated to 'bucky-ball'.

Since then, scientists have made many other new molecules. They can be shaped like rugby balls, doughnuts, onions (spheres within spheres), and cones or tubes (open or closed at the ends). The general name for all these hollow-shaped molecules of carbon are the **fullerenes**. The structure of fullerenes is based mainly on hexagonal rings of carbon atoms, as in graphite (Topic C3.7). However, they may also have rings of five (pentagonal) or seven (heptagonal) carbon atoms.

Cylindrical fullerenes called carbon nanotubes can also be produced. These fullerenes form incredibly thin cylinders, whose length is much greater than their diameter. They have very useful properties, such as:

- high tensile strength (leading to their use in reinforcing composite materials, such as those used in making tennis rackets)
- high electrical conductivity and high thermal conductivity (because their bonding is like the bonding in graphite, giving them delocalised electrons, resulting in their use in the electronics industry).

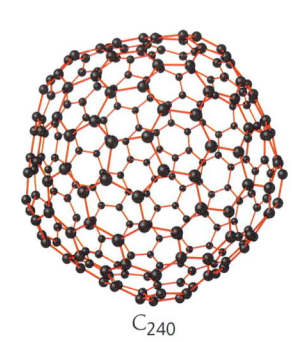

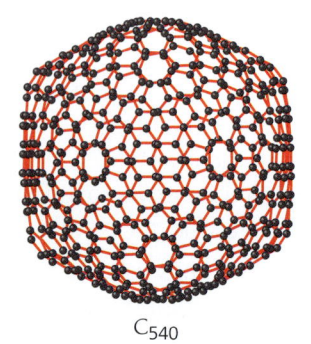

▲ **Figure 1** Buckminsterfullerene, $C_{60}$, was the first fullerene to be discovered

$C_{240}$    $C_{540}$

▲ **Figure 2** Other fullerenes. Some are bigger spheres than buckminsterfullerene

**C3 Structure and bonding**

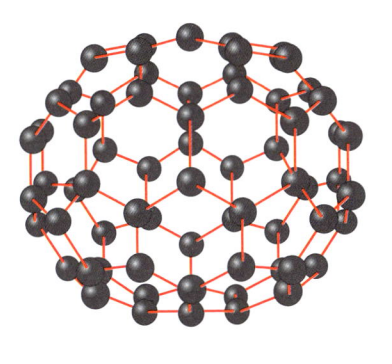

▲ **Figure 3** Some fullerenes are more elliptical in shape than $C_{60}$. The molecule with a ball inside a ball is nicknamed a 'bucky-onion'

Fullerenes could be used for drug delivery into the body. For example, the cage-like structures can be used as 'bucky-mules' to deliver drugs or radioactive atoms to treat cancer at very specific sites within the body. They can also be used as lubricants (as can graphite) and as catalysts because of the large surface area to volume ratio of their nanoparticles.

## Graphene

If you could separate a single sheet of carbon atoms from graphite, you would get a layer of interlocking hexagonal rings of carbon atoms (Figure 4 in Topic C3.7). It would be just one atom thick. Scientists at Manchester University managed to do this in 2004, basically by using a piece of sticky tape. They stuck the tape across a piece of graphite, pulled it off, and looked at the tape under a powerful electron microscope. They had managed to isolate a 2D material – the thinnest ever made.

The new material is called graphene. It is an excellent conductor of thermal energy and electricity (even better than graphite), has a very low density, is the most reactive form of carbon, and pieces of it are incredibly strong for their mass. Graphene can be laid on a solid support so that it can be used to make quicker and more powerful computer chips.

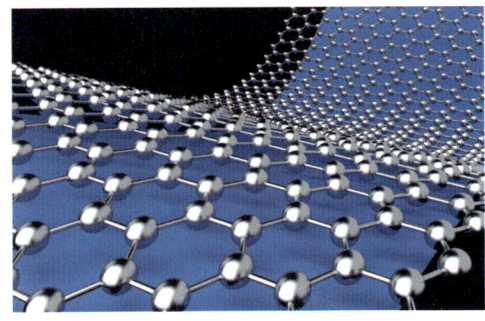

▲ **Figure 4** A computer-generated image of the structure of graphene

### Key points

- As well as diamond and graphite, carbon also exists as fullerenes, which can form large cage-like structures and tubes, based on hexagonal rings of carbon atoms. The first fullerene discovered was buckminsterfullerene, $C_{60}$.
- The fullerenes are finding uses as a transport mechanism for drugs to specific sites in the body, as catalysts, and as reinforcement for composite materials.
- Graphene is a single layer of graphite and so is just one atom thick. Its properties, such as its excellent electrical conductivity, are helping to create new developments in the electronics industry.

### Summary questions

1. Give one difference between graphene and graphite. **1 MARK**
2. List the main physical properties of fullerenes. **3 MARKS**
3. Write the chemical formula of the first fullerene discovered. **1 MARK**
4. Suggest which properties of graphene would make it useful in the manufacture of bullet-proof vests. **2 MARKS**
5. a Explain why graphene is such a good conductor of electricity. **5 MARKS**
   b Suggest why graphene could have many more applications in mobile electronics than graphite. **6 MARKS**
6. Justify in detail a use for nanotubes and fullerenes, based on their features or properties. **4 MARKS**

# C3.9 Bonding in metals

## Learning objectives

*After this topic, you should know:*
- how the atoms in metals are arranged
- how the atoms in metals are bonded to each other.

## Metal crystals

The atoms in metals are built up layer upon layer in a regular pattern (Figure 1).

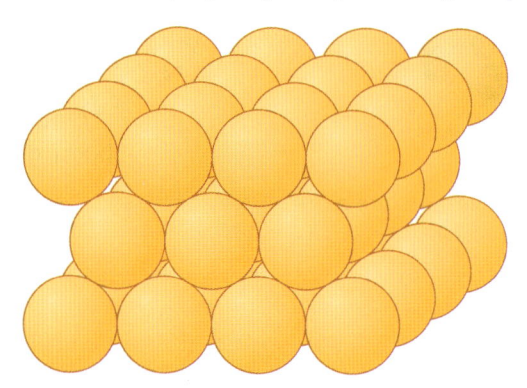

▲ **Figure 1** A model showing the close-packed arrangement of copper atoms in copper metal

This means that metals form crystals, although these are not always obvious to the naked eye. However, sometimes you can see them. You can see zinc crystals on the surface of some steel that has been dipped into molten zinc to prevent it from **rusting**. This is called galvanised steel. For example, look at the surface of a galvanised lamp post (Figure 2).

▲ **Figure 2** Metal crystals, such as the zinc ones shown on this galvanised post, give us evidence that metals are made up of atoms arranged in regular patterns

### Practical

#### Growing silver crystals

You can grow crystals of silver metal by suspending a coiled length of copper wire in silver nitrate solution. Crystals of silver will appear on the wire quite quickly. However, for the best results they need to be left for several hours.

- Describe and explain your observations.

**Safety:** Wear eye protection.

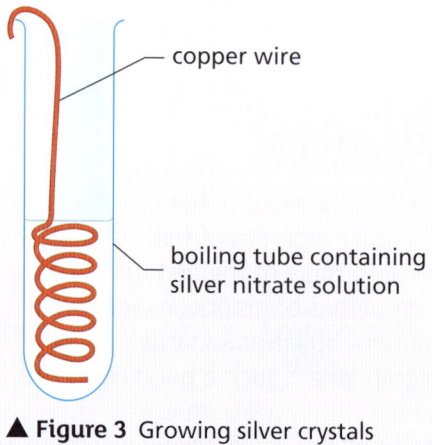

▲ **Figure 3** Growing silver crystals

## C3 Structure and bonding

### Practical

**Survey of metallic crystals**

Look around your school or college to see if you can find any galvanised steel. See if you can spot the metal crystals. You can also look for crystals on brass fittings that have been left outside and not polished.

## Metallic bonding

Metals are another example of giant structures. You can think of a metal as a lattice of positively charged ions. The metal ions are arranged in regular layers, one on top of another.

The outer electrons from each metal atom can easily move throughout the giant structure. The outer electrons (in the highest occupied energy level) form a 'sea' of free-moving electrons surrounding the positively charged metal ions. Strong electrostatic attractions between the negatively charged electrons and the positively charged ions bond the metal ions to each other. These attractions are called metallic bonds.

The electrons in the 'sea' of free-moving electrons are called **delocalised electrons**. They are no longer linked with any particular metal ion in the giant metallic structure. These delocalised electrons help to explain the properties of metals (Topic C3.10).

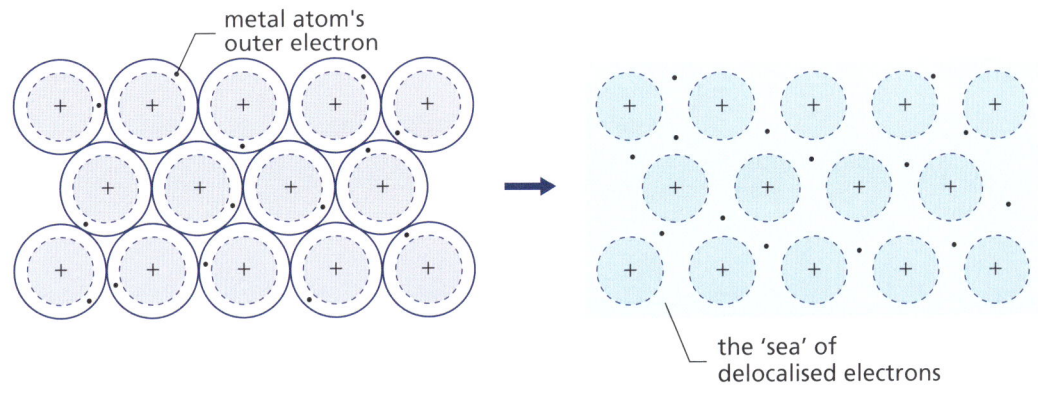

▲ **Figure 4** A metal consists of positively charged metal ions surrounded by a 'sea' of delocalised electrons. This diagram shows a model of metallic bonding

### Summary questions

1. Describe the structure of metals in terms of their arrangement of atoms. **2 MARKS**
2. a Explain why the particles that make up a metal are described as positively charged ions. **3 MARKS**
   b Describe what delocalised electrons are. **2 MARKS**
3. Use the theory of metallic bonding to explain the bonding in magnesium metal. Make sure you mention delocalised electrons. (The atomic number of magnesium is 12.) **4 MARKS**
4. Using a model to explain metallic bonding, delocalised electrons could be thought of as a glue.
   Explain why thinking of delocalised electrons in a metal as a glue is a useful model but one which has a major drawback. **3 MARKS**

### Key points

- Metals form a giant structure.
- The atoms in metals are closely packed together and arranged in regular layers.
- Metallic bonding involves positively charged metal ions, which are held together by electrons from the outermost shell of each metal atom. These delocalised electrons are free to move throughout the giant metallic lattice.

# C3.10 Giant metallic structures

## Learning objectives

After this topic, you should know:
- why metals can be bent and shaped without breaking
- why alloys are harder than pure metals
- why metals conduct electricity and thermal energy.

Metals can be hammered and bent into different shapes and drawn out into wires. This is because the layers of atoms in a pure metal can slide over each other easily.

The atoms in a pure metal, such as iron, are held together in a giant metallic structure. The atoms are arranged in closely packed layers. This regular arrangement allows the atoms to slide over one another quite easily. This is why pure iron is relatively soft and easily bent and shaped.

**Alloys** are usually mixtures of metals. However, most steels contain iron with controlled amounts of carbon, a non-metal, mixed into its structure. The carbon atoms are a different size to the iron atoms. This makes it more difficult for the layers in the metal's giant structure to slide over each other. So, alloys are harder than the pure metals used to make them (Figure 1).

**An alloy is a mixture of two or more elements, at least one of which is a metal.**

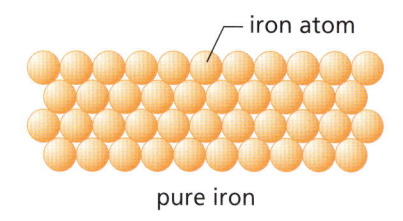

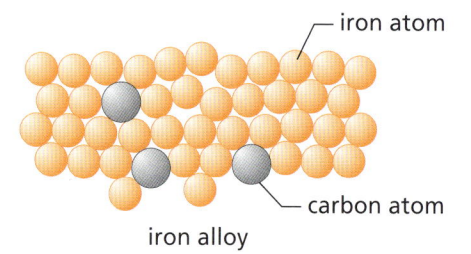

▲ **Figure 1** The atoms in pure iron are arranged in layers, which can easily slide over each other. In alloys, the layers cannot slide so easily, because atoms of other elements distort the layers

▲ **Figure 3** Drawing copper out into wires depends on being able to make the layers of metal atoms slide easily over each other, without breaking the metal

## Practical

### Making models of metals

We can make a model of the structure of a metal by blowing small bubbles onto the surface of a soap solution to represent atoms.

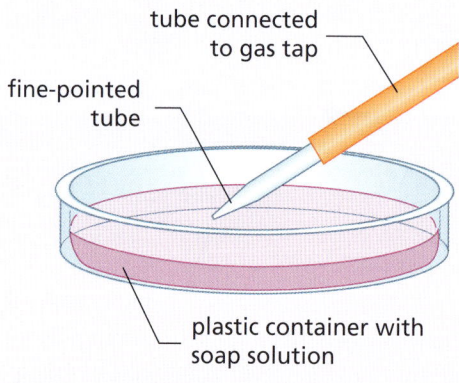

▲ **Figure 2** Making a bubble raft to model the structure of a metal

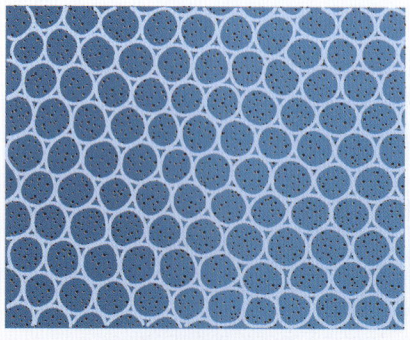

A regular arrangement of bubble 'atoms'

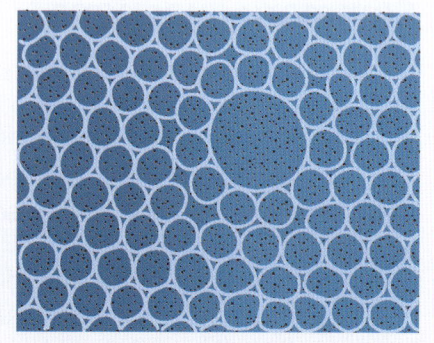

A larger bubble 'atom' disrupts the regular arrangement around it

- Why are models useful in science?

## C3 Structure and bonding

Metal cooking utensils are used all over the world because metals are good conductors of thermal energy and most have high melting points. Pans are usually made of steel (alloys of iron), but aluminium or copper are also used (Figure 4).

Wherever electricity is generated, it passes through metal wires (usually made of copper) to get to where it is needed. All metals are good conductors of electricity (Figure 4).

## Explaining the properties of metals

The positive ions in a metal's giant structure are bonded to each other by a sea of delocalised electrons (Topic C3.9). These electrons are a bit like 'glue'. Their negative charge between the positively charged ions holds the metal ions in position by electrostatic forces of attraction. (Remember that opposite charges attract.)

However, unlike glue, the electrons are able to move throughout the whole giant lattice. Because they can move around and hold the metal ions together at the same time, the delocalised electrons enable the lattice to distort. When struck, the metal atoms can slip past one another without breaking up the metal's structure.

This means that metals are:

- malleable – they can be hammered into different shapes without cracking
- ductile – they can be drawn out into wires (as shown in Figure 3).

The high melting points of metals are explained by their giant structures. The electrostatic forces of attraction extend in all directions, as the electrons move freely between the positive metal ions in the giant lattices. It therefore takes a large amount of energy to separate the metal ions from their fixed positions and break down the lattice, melting the metal.

Metals are also good conductors of thermal energy and electricity. This is because their delocalised electrons can readily flow through the giant metallic lattice. The electrical charge and thermal energy are transferred quickly through the metal by the free-moving delocalised electrons.

▲ **Figure 4** Metals are essential in our lives – the delocalised electrons mean that they are good conductors of both thermal energy and electricity

### Metacognition

At this point, you should review your understanding of chemical bonding.

Draw a concept map with 'Bonding' at its centre. Draw lines from the centre to the three main types of bonding covered in this chapter. Label the lines with a sentence to summarise how electrons are involved in each type of bond.

### Summary questions

1  **a** Describe why metals can be bent, shaped, and pulled out into wires when forces are applied. **1 MARK**
   **b** Name the word used to describe a material, such as a metal, which can be:
      **i** hammered into shapes **1 MARK**
      **ii** drawn out into wire. **1 MARK**
2  Using your knowledge of metal structures, explain why alloying a metal can make the metal harder. **3 MARKS**
3  Explain why metals are good conductors of thermal energy and electricity, in terms of their structure and bonding. **5 MARKS**
4  Explain why aluminium (from Group 3 in the Periodic Table) has a higher melting point than sodium (a Group 1 metal). **6 MARKS**

### Key points

- Metals can be bent and shaped because the layers of atoms (or positively charged ions) in a giant metallic structure can slide over each other.
- Alloys are harder than pure metals because the regular layers are distorted by atoms of different sizes in an alloy.
- Delocalised electrons in metals enable electricity and thermal energy to be transferred through a metal easily.

# C3 Structure and bonding

## Practice questions

1. Name the following changes:
   a. liquid → solid  **1 MARK**
   b. gas → liquid  **1 MARK**
   c. solid → liquid  **1 MARK**
   d. liquid → gas  **1 MARK**
   e. solid → gas (in a single step).  **1 MARK**

2. Write a number to fill in the blanks for parts **a** to **e**:
   a. The elements in Group .... in the Periodic Table all form ions with a charge of 1+.  **1 MARK**
   b. The elements in Group .... in the Periodic Table all form ions with a charge of 2+.  **1 MARK**
   c. The elements in Group .... in the Periodic Table all form ions with a charge of 1−.  **1 MARK**
   d. The elements in Group .... in the Periodic Table all form ions with a charge of 2−.  **1 MARK**
   e. The elements in Group .... in the Periodic Table have atoms that can form four covalent bonds.  **1 MARK**

3. This table contains data about some different substances:

| Substance | Melting point in °C | Boiling point in °C | Electrical conductor |
|---|---|---|---|
| ammonia | −78 | −33 | solid – poor<br>liquid – poor |
| magnesium oxide | 2852 | 3600 | solid – poor<br>liquid – good |
| lithium chloride | 605 | 1340 | solid – poor<br>liquid – good |
| silicon dioxide | 1610 | 2230 | solid – poor<br>liquid – poor |
| hydrogen bromide | −88 | −67 | solid – poor<br>liquid – poor |
| graphite | 3652 | 4827 | solid – good<br>liquid – good |

   a. Make a table with the following headings: *Giant covalent, Giant ionic, Simple molecules*. Now write the name of each substance above in the correct column.  **3 MARKS**
   b. Which substances are gases at 25 °C?  **2 MARKS**
   c. One of these substances behaves in a surprising way. Choose which one and explain why.  **1 MARK**
   d. Draw a diagram to show the electron structures of a lithium atom and a chlorine atom and their ions in lithium chloride. (The atomic number of Li = 3, Cl = 17.)  **4 MARKS**

4. a. Which of the following substances will have covalent bonding?
      hydrogen iodide    chlorine(VII) oxide
      silver chloride    phosphorus(V) fluoride
      calcium bromide    silver nitrate  **3 MARKS**
   b. Explain how you decided on your answers in part **a**.  **1 MARK**
   c. Name the type of bonding that the remaining substances in the list in part **a** have.  **1 MARK**
   d. Give the chemical formula of:
      i. hydrogen iodide  **1 MARK**
      ii. calcium bromide.

5. Copy and complete the following table with the formula of each ionic compound formed. (The first one has been done for you.)

| Element | chloride, $Cl^-$ | oxide, $O^{2-}$ | sulfate, $SO_4^{2-}$ | phosphate(V), $PO_4^{3-}$ |
|---|---|---|---|---|
| potassium, $K^+$ | KCl | | | |
| magnesium, $Mg^{2+}$ | | | | |
| iron(III), $Fe^{3+}$ | | | | |

   **4 MARKS**

6. Draw a diagram which shows the bonding in:
   a. hydrogen, $H_2$  **3 MARKS**
   b. carbon dioxide, $CO_2$.  **3 MARKS**

7. Aluminium is in Group 3 of the Periodic Table. It is a metal with very useful properties, and is often used as one of its many alloys.
   a. Aluminium alloys are used in the manufacture of aeroplanes. Explain, in terms of structure, why aluminium alloys are used instead of pure aluminium.  **3 MARKS**
   b. What is the charge on an aluminium ion? Explain your reasoning.  **3 MARKS**
   c. Predict the chemical formula of aluminium oxide.  **1 MARK**

8. Look back at the ball and stick model of sodium chloride and its caption in Topic C3.4. Explain how you can use it to work out its chemical formula.  **2 MARKS**

# C3 Structure and bonding

## Exam-style questions

**01** Diamond and graphite are the main structures of carbon. However, carbon can form many different structures besides diamond and graphite.

**01.1** Name the type of bond that carbon atoms form. **1 MARK**

**01.2** How many bonds does each carbon atom form in diamond? **1 MARK**

**01.3** Which **two** of the following properties are shown by graphite?

    A low melting point
    B high boiling point
    C electrical insulator
    D electrical conductor
    E hardness
    F soluble in water **2 MARKS**

**01.4** Name the form of carbon that exists as a single layer of carbon atoms. **1 MARK**

**0.1.5** What is the shape of the first fullerene discovered that has a formula of $C_{60}$? **1 MARK**

**02** Properties of five different substances **A**, **B**, **C**, **D**, and **E** are shown in **Table 1**.

Table 1

| Substance | Melting point in °C | Boiling point in °C | Conduction of electricity when solid | Conduction of electricity when liquid |
|---|---|---|---|---|
| substance **A** | 0 | 100 | does not conduct | does not conduct |
| substance **B** | 1538 | 2862 | conducts | conducts |
| substance **C** | 801 | 1413 | does not conduct | conducts |
| substance **D** | 1610 | 2230 | does not conduct | does not conduct |
| substance **E** | −7 | 59 | does not conduct | does not conduct |

Which substance **A**, **B**, **C**, **D**, or **E**:

**02.1** is a liquid at 20 °C? **1 MARK**

**02.2** has a giant covalent structure? **1 MARK**

**02.3** has a giant ionic structure? **1 MARK**

**02.4** The properties of another three substances **X**, **Y**, and **Z** are shown in **Table 2**.

Table 2

| Substance | Melting point in °C | Boiling point in °C | Conduction of electricity when solid | Conduction of electricity when liquid |
|---|---|---|---|---|
| substance **X** | 1064 | 1947 | conducts | conducts |
| substance **Y** | −220 | −188 | does not conduct | does not conduct |
| substance **Z** | 302 | 337 | does not conduct | does not conduct |

Substance **X** is a metal. Describe the structure of a metal and explain why a metal can conduct electricity when it is solid. **3 MARKS**

**02.5** Substances **Y** and **Z** are elements in Group 7 of the Periodic Table. They are both simple molecules with the formula $Y_2$ and $Z_2$. Explain why substance **Z** has a higher boiling point than substance **Y**. **2 MARKS**

**03** The electronic structures of an atom of magnesium and an atom of fluorine are shown in **Figure 1**.

Figure 1

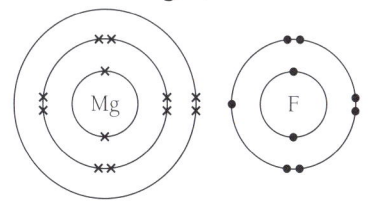

**03.1** Describe in terms of electrons what happens when magnesium reacts with fluorine to form the ionic compound magnesium fluoride $MgF_2$. **3 MARKS**

**03.2** The structure of magnesium fluoride can be represented by the ball and stick model shown in **Figure 2**.

Figure 2

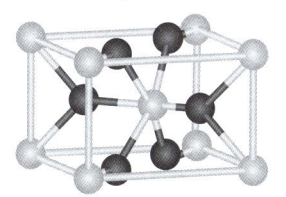

Explain why an ionic substance such as magnesium fluoride will conduct electricity when it is molten. **2 MARKS**

**03.3** The ball and stick model is **not** a good representation of the structure of an ionic compound.

Give **one** reason why. **1 MARK**

55

# C4 Chemical calculations

## C4.1 Relative masses and moles

### Learning objectives

*After this topic, you should know:*
- what we mean by the relative atomic mass of an element
- how to calculate the relative atomic mass of an element and the relative formula mass of a compound
- how to calculate the percentage by mass of each element in a compound
- **H** how to calculate the number of moles, given the mass (or the mass, given the number of moles) of substance.

### Relative atomic masses

The mass of a single atom is so tiny that it would not be practical to use it in experiments or calculations. So instead of working with the actual masses of atoms, the *relative* masses of atoms of different elements are used. These are called **relative atomic masses**, $A_r$.

On any relative scale you need a standard reference point to compare against. In quoting relative atomic masses, the atom of carbon-12, $^{12}_{6}C$, is used as a standard atom. Carbon-12 is given a 'mass' of exactly 12 units because it has six protons and six neutrons. You can then compare the masses of atoms of all the other elements with this standard carbon atom. For example, hydrogen has a relative atomic mass of 1, as most of its atoms have a mass that is $\frac{1}{12}$ of the mass of a $^{12}_{6}C$ atom.

The $A_r$ accounts for the abundance of any isotopes of the element found naturally. So, it is the mean (average) relative mass of the isotopes of an element. That is why chlorine has a relative atomic mass of 35.5, although you could never have half a proton or neutron (see the Maths box on the left). You can find the $A_r$ of each element in the Periodic Table – it is the larger number, usually found above the chemical symbol.

### Maths

You can calculate the relative atomic mass, $A_r$, of an element given the percentage abundance of its isotopes. For example, chlorine has two isotopes, $^{35}Cl$ (abundance = 75%) and $^{37}Cl$ (abundance = 25%). This means that in a sample of 100 chlorine atoms, 75 chlorine atoms would have a relative mass of 35, and the other 25 chlorine atoms would have a mass of 37.
To calculate the mean relative mass of these 100 atoms you use the equation:

$A_r$ of Cl = $\frac{(75 \times 35) + (25 \times 37)}{100}$ = **35.5**

### Relative formula masses

You can use the $A_r$ of the various elements to work out the **relative formula mass**, $M_r$, of compounds. This is true whether the compounds are made up of molecules or ions.

A simple example is a substance such as sulfuric acid, $H_2SO_4$. Hydrogen has an $A_r$ of 1, the $A_r$ of sulfur is 32, and the $A_r$ of oxygen is 16. This means that the $M_r$ of sulfuric acid is:

$(1 \times 2) + 32 + (16 \times 4) = 2 + 32 + 64 =$ **98**

In the case of molecular substances, such as $H_2SO_4$, the relative formula mass can also be referred to as the relative molecular mass.

### Study tip

Sometimes you might need to work out the relative formula mass, $M_r$, of complex compounds like $Al_2(SO_4)_3$. Remember to multiply everything inside the brackets with the subscript number outside the brackets.

### Maths

You can also use relative atomic and formula masses to calculate the percentage by mass of each element in a compound.
For example, $CO_2$ ($A_r$ values: C = 12, O = 16)
The relative formula mass of $CO_2$ is: $12 + (2 \times 16) = 44$

So, the percentage mass of C in $CO_2$ is:
= $\frac{12}{44} \times 100 =$ **27.3%**

The percentage mass of O in $CO_2$ is:
= $\frac{32}{44} \times 100 =$ **72.7%** to three significant figures.

# C4 Chemical calculations

## The mole (mol)

The word **mole** is used to describe the measurement of the relative atomic mass, or relative formula mass, in grams. The symbol for the unit mole is mol. The relative atomic mass in grams of carbon (i.e., 12 g) is a mole of carbon atoms. **One mole is simply the relative atomic mass, or relative formula mass, of any substance in grams.**

A mole of any substance always contains the same number of atoms, molecules, or ions. This is a huge number, and its value is called the **Avogadro constant**. In standard form, it is written as $6.02 \times 10^{23}$ per mole. In fact, if you had as many soft drink cans as there are atoms, molecules, or ions in a mole, they would cover the surface of the Earth to a depth of 200 miles.

## Moles from masses

Chemists prefer to use the mole when describing numbers of particles (atoms, molecules, or ions) in a certain mass of substance.

They use the equation:

$$\text{number of moles} = \frac{\text{mass (g)}}{A_r} \text{ or } \frac{\text{mass (g)}}{M_r}$$

## Masses from moles

Sometimes you will have to work out the mass of a substance from a given number of moles.

By rearranging the equation above, you can calculate the mass of a certain number of moles of substance using the equation:

$$\text{mass (g)} = \text{number of moles} \times A_r \text{ or number of moles} \times M_r$$

### Maths

#### Worked example 1
How many moles of sulfuric acid molecules are there in 19.6 g of sulfuric acid?

**Solution**

number of moles of $H_2SO_4$ molecules
$= \frac{19.6}{98} = \textbf{0.200 mol}$

The answer is given as 0.200 mol, as opposed to 0.2 mol.
The data in the question was provided to 3 significant figures (19.6), so the answer should also be given to 3 significant figures.

### Maths

#### Worked example 2
What is the mass of $7.5 \times 10^{-3}$ moles of aluminium sulfate?

**Solution**

mass of $Al_2(SO_4)_3 = (7.5 \times 10^{-3}) \times 342$
$= \textbf{2.6 g}$

Your calculator will give the number 2.565, which has 4 significant figures. In the question, $7.5 \times 10^{-3}$ moles, is given to 2 significant figures, so the answer should reflect this. Hence 2.565 is rounded up to 2.6.

### Summary questions

1. What is meant by the relative atomic mass of an element? **2 MARKS**
2. Determine the relative formula mass of:
   a. $MgF_2$ ($A_r$ values: Mg = 24, F = 19) **1 MARK**
   b. $C_6H_{12}O_6$ ($A_r$ values: C = 12, H = 1, O = 16). **1 MARK**
3. Calculate the percentage by mass of oxygen in calcium carbonate, $CaCO_3$. ($A_r$ values: Ca = 40, C = 12, O = 16) **2 MARKS**
4. Bromine has two isotopes, $^{79}Br$ (abundance = 51%) and $^{81}Br$ (49%). Calculate the relative atomic mass of bromine. Give your answer to 2 decimal places. **2 MARKS**
5. Ⓗ Calculate:
   a. how many moles of helium atoms there are in 0.02 g of helium. **1 MARK**
   b. how many moles of sulfur atoms there are in 16 tonnes of sulfur (where 1 tonne = 1000 kg). **1 MARK**
6. Ⓗ Determine the mass of:
   a. 50 moles of calcium carbonate, $CaCO_3$ **1 MARK**
   b. 0.05 moles of hydrogen, $H_2$. **1 MARK**

### Key points

- The masses of atoms are compared by measuring them relative to atoms of carbon-12.
- You can work out the relative formula mass of a compound by adding up the relative atomic masses of the elements in it, in the ratio shown by its formula.
- Ⓗ One mole of any substance is its relative formula mass, in grams.
- Ⓗ number of moles
  $= \frac{\text{mass (g)}}{A_r} \text{ or } \frac{\text{mass (g)}}{M_r}$
- Ⓗ Avogadro constant is $6.02 \times 10^{23}$ per mole.

# C4.2 Equations and calculations

### Learning objectives

After this topic, you should know:
- what balanced symbol equations tell you about chemical reactions
- how to use balanced symbol equations to calculate masses of reactants and products.

We know from the *Conservation of mass* in Topic C1.2 that mass cannot be created or destroyed in a chemical reaction. The total mass of the reactants always equals the total mass of the products. Our balanced chemical equations show this. When you want to know how much of each substance is involved in a chemical reaction, you can use the balanced symbol equation.

Think about what happens when hydrogen molecules, $H_2$, react with chlorine molecules, $Cl_2$. The reaction makes hydrogen chloride molecules, HCl:

$$H_2 + Cl_2 \rightarrow HCl \text{ (not balanced)}$$

This equation shows the reactants and the product – but it is not balanced.

Here is the balanced equation:

$$H_2 + Cl_2 \rightarrow 2HCl$$

This balanced equation tells you that one hydrogen molecule reacts with one chlorine molecule to make two hydrogen chloride molecules. The balanced equation also tells you the number of moles of each substance involved. It tells you that 1 mole of hydrogen molecules reacts with 1 mole of chlorine molecules to make 2 moles of hydrogen chloride molecules.

### Study tip

The '2' inserted in front of HCl to balance the equation is called a multiplier.

| one hydrogen molecule | one chlorine molecule | two hydrogen chloride molecules |
|---|---|---|
| $H_2$ + | $Cl_2$ → | 2HCl |
| 1 mole of hydrogen molecules | 1 mole of chlorine molecules | 2 moles of hydrogen chloride molecules |

## Using balanced equations to work out reacting masses

The previous balanced equation is really useful because you can use it to work out the masses of hydrogen and chlorine that react together. You can also calculate how much hydrogen chloride is made (Worked example 1).

### Maths

Sometimes you will see fractions written in balanced equations. Even though you cannot have half an atom, ion, or molecule, you can read these equations as half a mole of the substance. These fractions are usually used in combustion reactions, such as:

$$C_2H_6 + 3\frac{1}{2}O_2 \rightarrow 2CO_2 + 3H_2O$$

Here you have 2 moles of carbon atoms, 6 moles of hydrogen atoms, and 7 moles of oxygen atoms on both sides of the balanced equation. By multiplying all the large numbers (multipliers) in the equation by two you will get all whole numbers and maintain a balanced equation:

$$2C_2H_6 + 7O_2 \rightarrow 4CO_2 + 6H_2O$$

### Maths

**Worked example 1**

What masses of reactants and products are involved in the balanced symbol equation:

$$H_2 + Cl_2 \rightarrow 2HCl$$

**Solution**

To do this, you need to know that the $A_r$ for hydrogen is 1 and the $A_r$ for chlorine is 35.5.

$A_r$ of hydrogen = 1, so mass of 1 mole of $H_2$ = 2 × 1 = 2 g
$A_r$ of chlorine = 35.5, so mass of 1 mole of $Cl_2$ = 2 × 35.5 = 71 g
$M_r$ of hydrogen chloride = 1 + 35.5, so mass of 1 mole of HCl = 36.5 g

58

The balanced equation tells you that 1 mole of hydrogen reacts with 1 mole of chlorine to give 2 moles of hydrogen chloride molecules. So, turning this into masses you get:

1 mole of hydrogen molecules, $H_2 = 1 \times 2 = 2\,g$

1 mole of chlorine molecules, $Cl_2 = 1 \times 71 = 71\,g$

2 moles of hydrogen chloride molecules, $HCl = 2 \times 36.5 =$ **73 g**

… and the conservation of mass law is verified as we have 73 g of reactants and 73 g of products.

## More reacting mass calculations

These calculations are important when you want to know the mass of chemicals that react together.

### Maths

#### Worked example 2

Sodium hydroxide reacts with chlorine gas to make bleach. This reaction happens when chlorine gas is bubbled through a solution of sodium hydroxide. The balanced symbol equation for the reaction is:

$2NaOH + Cl_2 \rightarrow NaOCl + NaCl + H_2O$
sodium hydroxide    chlorine    bleach    salt    water

If you have a solution containing 100.0 g of sodium hydroxide, what is the minimum mass of chlorine gas needed to convert it to bleach?

#### Solution

$A_r$ values: sodium = 23, oxygen = 16, hydrogen = 1

Mass of 1 mole of $NaOH = 23 + 16 + 1 = 40\,g$

$A_r$ value: chlorine = 35.5

Mass of 1 mole of $Cl_2 = 35.5 \times 2 = 71\,g$

The mass of 1 mole of sodium hydroxide is 40 g. So, 100.0 g of sodium hydroxide is $\frac{100}{40} = 2.5$ moles.

The balanced symbol equation tells you that for every 2 moles of sodium hydroxide you need 1 mole of chlorine to react with it.

So, you need $\frac{2.5}{2} = 1.25$ moles of chlorine.

Worked example 1 shows that 1 mole of chlorine has a mass of 71 g.

So, you will need $1.25 \times 71 =$ **88.75 g** of chlorine to react with 100.0 g of sodium hydroxide.

## C4 Chemical calculations

### Key points

- Balanced symbol equations tell you the number of moles of substances involved in a chemical reaction.
- You can use balanced symbol equations to calculate the masses of reactants and products in a chemical reaction.

### Summary questions

1 Give the two meanings of '2HCl'. **1 MARK**

2 Hydrogen and chlorine react to form hydrogen chloride. The equation for this reaction is:
$H_2 + Cl_2 \rightarrow 2HCl$
Use the conservation of mass to calculate the mass of $Cl_2$ that reacts with 1.0 g of $H_2$ to produce 36.5 g of HCl. **1 MARK**

3 Look at this reaction:
$NaOH + HCl \rightarrow NaCl + H_2O$
The relative formula mass of NaOH is 40, of HCl is 36.5 and of $H_2O$ is 18.
Use the conservation of mass to work out the relative formula mass of NaCl. **1 MARK**

4 Magnesium burns in oxygen with a bright white flame:
$2Mg(s) + O_2(g) \rightarrow 2MgO(s)$
Calculate the mass of oxygen that will react exactly with 6.0 g of magnesium.
($A_r$ values: O = 16, Mg = 24) **2 MARKS**

5 a An aqueous solution of hydrogen peroxide, $H_2O_2$, decomposes to form water and oxygen gas. Write a balanced symbol equation, including state symbols, for this reaction. **3 MARKS**

   b Calculate the mass of hydrogen peroxide needed in solution to produce 1.6 g of oxygen gas. **2 MARKS**

59

# C4.3 From masses to balanced equations

## Learning objectives

After this topic, you should know:
- how to balance an equation, given the masses of reactants and products
- why a limiting quantity of a reactant affects the amount of product it is possible to obtain (in terms of amounts in moles or masses in grams).

## Synoptic link

You first met the law of conservation of mass in Topic C1.2.

In Topic C4.2 you saw how to use a balanced chemical equation to calculate the mass of reactants and products in a reaction. Alternatively, if you have the masses of the substances involved in a reaction, you can work out the ratio of the number of moles of each reactant and product (called the stoichiometry of the reaction). The simplest whole-number ratio gives you the balanced equation.

### Maths

**Worked example 1**

Sodium nitrate, $NaNO_3$, decomposes on heating to give sodium nitrite, $NaNO_2$, and oxygen gas, $O_2$.

When 8.5 g of sodium nitrate is heated in a test tube until its mass is constant, 6.9 g of sodium nitrite is produced.

a What mass of oxygen gas must have been given off in the reaction?

b Find the ratio of reactants and products involved in the reaction, and use these to produce the balanced symbol equation for the decomposition of sodium nitrate:
($A_r$ values: Na = 23, N = 14, O = 16)

**Solution**

a You know that the total mass of reactants = total mass of products (from the law of conservation of mass). So, if the mass of oxygen is $x$ g:

sodium nitrate → sodium nitrite + oxygen
8.5 g = 6.9 g + $x$ g
(8.5 − 6.9) g = $x$ g
**1.6 g** = mass of oxygen

b From the masses given in the question and our answer to part **a**, you can work out the numbers of moles of each reactant and product:

First, you will need to calculate the relative formula masses ($M_r$) of the reactants and products using the $A_r$ values provided:

$M_r$ of $NaNO_3$ = [23 + 14 + (16 × 3)] = 85
$M_r$ of $NaNO_2$ = [23 + 14 + (16 × 2)] = 69
$M_r$ of $O_2$ = 32

Then use the equation from Topic C4.1 to convert masses to moles: number of moles = $\dfrac{\text{Mass}}{M_r}$

moles of $NaNO_3$ = $\dfrac{8.5}{85}$ = 0.1 mol

moles of $NaNO_2$ = $\dfrac{6.9}{69}$ = 0.1 mol

moles of $O_2$ = $\dfrac{1.6}{32}$ = 0.05 mol

Then find the simplest whole-number ratio of the numbers of moles:

$NaNO_3$ : $NaNO_2$ : $O_2$
= 0.1 : 0.1 : 0.05

Dividing the ratio by the smallest number (0.05) gives the whole-number ratio:

2 : 2 : 1

So, the balanced equation is:

**$2NaNO_3 \rightarrow 2NaNO_2 + O_2$**

## C4 Chemical calculations

## Limiting reactants

Often, when you carry out a reaction in experiments, you do not use the exact amounts of reactants as predicted in the balanced equation. One of the reactants will be in excess.

For example, if you add dilute hydrochloric acid to magnesium ribbon, hydrogen gas is given off and you see bubbles rising from the magnesium. If the reaction stops (no more bubbles of gas appear) but there is still magnesium ribbon present, then the magnesium is in excess.

The reason the reaction stops is that all the acid has been used up. In this case the hydrochloric acid is called the **limiting reactant**. What would you expect to see at the end of the reaction if the magnesium was the limiting reactant?

*The reactant that gets used up first in a reaction is called the limiting reactant (or limiting reagent).*

You can work out which is the limiting reactant from the balanced equation, if you know the number of moles of reactants you start with. Look at Worked example 2.

### Maths

#### Worked example 2

If you have 4.8 g of magnesium ribbon reacting in a solution of dilute hydrochloric acid containing 7.3 g of HCl, which reactant is the limiting reactant?
($A_r$ values: Mg = 24, H = 1, Cl = 35.5)

#### Solution

The balanced equation for the reaction is:

$Mg(s) + 2HCl(aq) \rightarrow MgCl_2(aq) + H_2(g)$

You are only interested in the reactants in this question.

number of moles
$$= \frac{mass\ (g)}{A_r} \text{ or } \frac{mass\ (g)}{M_r}$$

You start with 4.8 g of Mg, which is $\frac{4.8}{24}$ moles = 0.2 mol
and 7.3 g of HCl, which is $\frac{7.3}{1 + 35.5}$ moles = $\frac{7.3}{36.5}$ = 0.2 mol.
From the balanced equation, you see that 1 mole of Mg will react with 2 moles of HCl.
Therefore 0.2 mol of Mg will need 0.4 mol of HCl to react completely.

In this case, we do not have 0.4 mol of HCl – we only have 0.2 mol – so the dilute **hydrochloric acid is the limiting reactant** (and the magnesium is in excess).

## Summary questions

1. Explain what we mean by a limiting reactant in a chemical reaction. **1 MARK**
2. When copper metal reacts with oxygen gas, black copper oxide, CuO, is formed. In an experiment it was found that when copper reacted completely with oxygen, 6.35 g of copper reacted with 1.60 g of oxygen gas, $O_2$, to form 7.95 g of copper oxide.
   a. Calculate the number of moles of each reactant and product. **3 MARKS**
   b. Show how this relates to the balanced symbol equation for the reaction. **2 MARKS**
3. Aluminium reacts with iron(III) oxide, $Fe_2O_3$, to give iron metal and aluminium oxide, $Al_2O_3$.
   a. Write a balanced symbol equation for this reaction. **3 MARKS**
   b. In an experiment, 32.0 g of iron(III) oxide was reacted with 16.2 g of aluminium.
      Determine which of the two reactants is the limiting reactant. Show your working. **2 MARKS**
   c. Calculate the maximum mass of iron that could be collected at the end of this experiment. **2 MARKS**

### Key points

- You can deduce balanced symbol equations from the masses of substances involved in a chemical reaction.
- The reactant that gets used up first in a reaction is called the limiting reactant.
- The amounts of product formed in a chemical reaction are determined by the limiting reactant.

# C4.4 Expressing concentrations

## Learning objectives

After this topic, you should know:
- that the concentration of solutions can be expressed in grams per dm³ (g/dm³)
- **H** how the mass of a solute and the volume of a solution is related to the concentration of the solution.

## What is the concentration of a solution?

When you make a drink of orange squash, sometimes you put too much squash in the glass – sometimes you add too much water. Then you can add more water or add more squash until the colour looks right for you. A chemist would say that you are adjusting the **concentration** of the solution.

Chemists often carry out their reactions in solution. The solvent is usually water but can be other liquids, such as ethanol.

To record, interpret, and communicate their results, they need to express the concentration of the solutions they use. Other chemists should be able to repeat published experiments to verify data. So, chemists quote the amount of substance (solute) dissolved in a certain volume of the solution. The units they use to express the concentration of a solution is often grams per decimetre cubed (g/dm³). A decimetre cubed (1 dm³) is equal to 1000 cm³.

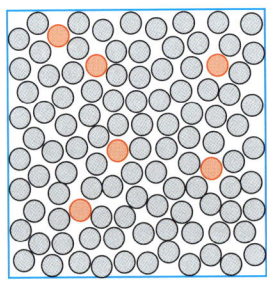

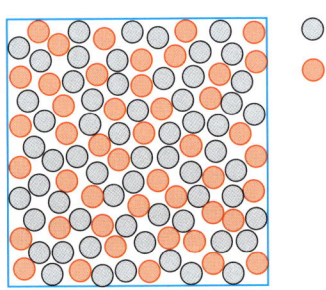

▲ **Figure 1** The orange squash is getting less concentrated going left to right (the darker colour indicates more squash is in the same volume of its solution)

▲ **Figure 2** Adding more solute (like orange squash) to a solvent (like water) makes the solution more concentrated.

## Calculating concentrations

If you know the mass of solute dissolved in a certain volume of solution, you can work out its concentration.

The equation used to calculate concentration is:

$$\text{concentration (g/dm}^3\text{)} = \frac{\text{amount of solute (g)}}{\text{volume of solution (dm}^3\text{)}}$$

If you are working in centimetres cubed (cm³), convert the volume to dm³ by dividing it by 1000, and use the previous equation. Alternatively, substitute your data in cm³ into the equation:

$$\text{concentration (g/dm}^3\text{)} = \frac{\text{amount of solute (g)}}{\text{volume of solution (cm}^3\text{)}} \times 1000$$

As an example, imagine that you make a solution of sodium hydroxide in water. You dissolve exactly 40.0 g of sodium hydroxide in enough water to make exactly 3.00 dm³ of solution. You can calculate the concentration of the solution in g/dm³:

$$\frac{40.0 \text{ g}}{3.00 \text{ dm}^3} = 13.3 \text{ g/dm}^3$$

▲ **Figure 3** Volumetric flasks are used to make up solutions. They have a graduation mark around their narrow necks. Water is added to the solute until the bottom of its meniscus (the curve at the surface of the solution when viewed from the side) is level with the mark

### Study tip

Make sure you are using the correct equation for concentration, depending on the units used for volume.

## C4 Chemical calculations

### Maths

**Worked example 1**

50 g of sodium hydroxide is dissolved in water to make up 200 cm³ of solution. What is its concentration, given in g/dm³? (Remember that 1 dm³ = 1000 cm³.)

**Solution**

To find the concentration of the solution, you should use the equation:

$$\text{concentration (g/dm}^3) = \frac{\text{amount of solute (g)}}{\text{volume of solution (cm}^3)} \times 1000$$

$$\frac{50\,g}{200\,cm^3} = 0.25\,g/dm^3$$

So, 0.25 g/cm³ × 1000 = **250 g/dm³**

### Maths

**Worked example 2**

If you know the concentration of a given volume of solution, you can calculate the amount of solute in the solution.

A solution of sodium chloride has a concentration of 200 g/dm³. What is the mass of sodium chloride in 700 cm³ of the solution?

**Solution**

First, you need to convert 700 cm³ into dm³:

$$\frac{700}{1000} = 0.7\,dm^3$$

Then rearrange the concentration equation to make 'amount of solute (g)' the subject.

$$\text{amount of solute (g)} = \text{concentration (g/dm}^3) \times \text{volume of solution (dm}^3)$$

So, 200 g/dm³ × 0.7 dm³ = **140 g**

There is 140 g of sodium chloride in the solution.

**H**

You can increase the concentration of an aqueous solution by:

- adding more solute and dissolving it in the same volume of its solution

- evaporating off some of the water from the solution so you have the same mass of solute in a smaller volume of solution.

### Summary questions

1. Calculate the concentration, in g/dm³, of a solution made by dissolving 50 g of sodium chloride in 2.5 dm³ of water. **1 MARK**

2. Calculate the concentration, in g/dm³, of a solution made by dissolving 1.8 g of sodium carbonate in 862 cm³ of water. **1 MARK**

3. A technician made up a solution of potassium hydroxide, KOH, by placing 7.00 g of solid potassium hydroxide into a volumetric flask and added water up to the 100 cm³ mark. She then stoppered the flask and shook the solution until the potassium hydroxide had dissolved completely. Calculate the concentration of the solution in g/dm³. **1 MARK**

4. A student had a solution of sodium chloride with a concentration of 93.6 g/dm³.
   Calculate the mass of sodium chloride dissolved in 25.0 cm³ of the solution. **2 MARKS**

5. **H** Explain how the mass of a solute and the volume of water affect the concentration of a solution. **2 MARKS**

### Key points

- concentration (g/dm³) = 
  $$\frac{\text{amount of solute (g)}}{\text{volume of solution (dm}^3)}$$

- amount of solute (g) = concentration (g/dm³) × volume of solution (dm³)

- **H** A more concentrated solution has a greater amount of solute in the same volume of solution than a less concentrated solution does.

63

# C4 Chemical calculations

## Practice questions

1. Calculate the relative formula mass, $M_r$, of each of the following compounds:
   a. $H_2S$ **1 MARK**
   b. $SO_2$ **1 MARK**
   c. $C_2H_4$ **1 MARK**
   d. $NaOH$ **1 MARK**
   e. $Na_2CO_3$ **1 MARK**
   f. $Al_2(SO_4)_3$ **1 MARK**
   g. $NaAl(OH)_4$ **1 MARK**

2. **(H)** Determine the number of moles of:
   a. Ag atoms in 27 g of silver **1 MARK**
   b. Fe atoms in 0.056 g of iron **1 MARK**
   c. $P_4$ molecules in 6.2 g of phosphorus. **1 MARK**

3. In a lime kiln, calcium carbonate is decomposed to calcium oxide:
   $$CaCO_3 \rightarrow CaO + CO_2$$
   Calculate the maximum mass of calcium oxide that 1500 tonnes of calcium carbonate can produce. **2 MARKS**

4. a. Ethene gas, $C_2H_4$, reacting with steam, $H_2O$, to form ethanol gas, $C_2H_5OH$, is a reversible reaction. Write the balanced symbol equation, including state symbols, for this reaction. **1 MARK**
   b. **(H)** 14.00 g of ethene is reacted with excess steam. Calculate the maximum mass of ethanol that can be produced, assuming 100% conversion of reactants to products. **2 MARKS**

5. Knowing the formula of a compound and its relative formula mass, it is possible to work out the percentage by mass of each element in the compound.
   
   Calculate the percentage by mass of each of each element in the following compounds:
   a. water, $H_2O$ **2 MARKS**
   b. aluminium oxide, $Al_2O_3$ **2 MARKS**
   c. iron(II) sulfate, $FeSO_4$ **2 MARKS**
   d. magnesium nitrate, $Mg(NO_3)_2$. **2 MARKS**
   ($A_r$ values: H = 1, O = 16, Al = 27, Fe = 56, S = 32, Mg = 24, N = 14)

6. This question is about calculating masses.
   a. **(H)** There are $6.02 \times 10^{23}$ atoms of carbon in 12.0 g of carbon.
      How many individual carbon atoms are there in 96.0 g of carbon, C? **2 MARKS**
   b. Which has more atoms: 96.0 g of carbon, C or 36.0 g of helium, He? Show your working out. **2 MARKS**
   c. What is the name and unit of the constant that tells us the number of atoms of carbon in 12.0 g of carbon? **2 MARKS**
   d. Calculate the mass of the following amounts of substance, giving your answers to an appropriate number of significant figures.
      i. 0.650 mol silicon, Si **1 MARK**
      ii. 4.87 mol iron, Fe **1 MARK**
      iii. 0.077 mol potassium nitrate, $KNO_3$ **2 MARKS**
   e. Calculate the concentration of 2.525 g of magnesium nitrate, $Mg(NO_3)_2$, dissolved in 50 cm³ of solution. Give your answer in g/dm³. **2 MARKS**

7. Magnesium carbonate, $MgCO_3$, decomposes when heated in a similar reaction to calcium carbonate.
   a. Write a balanced symbol equation for the decomposition of magnesium carbonate. **1 MARK**
   b. **(H)** When a sample of magnesium carbonate was decomposed, 1.10 g of carbon dioxide gas was given off. Calculate the number of moles of carbon dioxide gas that was given off. **2 MARKS**
   c. **(H)** Determine what mass of magnesium carbonate was decomposed in the reaction. **1 MARK**
   d. **(H)** Magnesium carbonate also reacts with dilute hydrochloric acid:
      $$MgCO_3(s) + 2HCl(aq) \rightarrow MgCl_2(aq) + H_2O(l) + CO_2(g)$$
      i. What is the easiest way to tell when this reaction has finished? **1 MARK**
      ii. 8.4 g of magnesium carbonate was added to 25 cm³ dilute hydrochloric acid with a concentration of 7.3 g/dm³. Show which reactant is the limiting reactant. **4 MARKS**
      iii. Calculate the mass of carbon dioxide gas that was given off in the reaction described in part ii. **1 MARK**
   
   $A_r$ values: Mg = 24, C = 12, O = 16

8. Calculate the relative atomic mass of:
   a. bromine (made up of 50% $^{79}Br$ and 50% $^{81}Br$) **1 MARK**
   b. iron (with 5.8% $^{54}Fe$, 91.8% $^{56}Fe$, 2.1% $^{57}Fe$, and 0.3% $^{58}Fe$). **2 MARKS**

# Exam-style questions

**01** This question is about the change in mass when chemical reactions take place in a crucible. A crucible has a loose lid so that gases can get in or get out. A diagram of a crucible is shown in **Figure 1**.

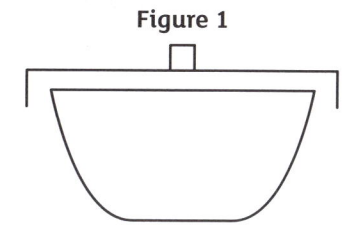

**Figure 1**

**01.1** A student heated a piece of magnesium in a crucible. The magnesium reacts as shown in the equation:

....... Mg(s) + O$_2$(g) → ......... MgO(s)

Balance the equation. **2 MARKS**

**01.2** The student recorded the masses shown in **Table 1**.

**Table 1**

| Mass of crucible | Mass in g |
|---|---|
| at the start of the reaction | 0.24 |
| at the end of the reaction | 0.40 |

Explain why the mass increased. **2 MARKS**

**01.3** The student heated the crucible again at the end of the reaction. Describe what the student could do to make sure the reaction was complete. **2 MARKS**

**01.4** Another student heated lithium carbonate in a crucible. The lithium carbonate reacts as shown in the equation:

Li$_2$CO$_3$(s) → Li$_2$O(s) + CO$_2$(g)

Use the equation to predict whether the mass would increase or decrease. Explain your answer. **3 MARKS**

**02** **H** This question is about the combustion of hydrocarbons.

**02.1** 0.010 moles of hydrocarbon **Z** are burnt completely in an excess of oxygen. The equation for the reaction is:

C$_x$H$_y$ + O$_2$(g) → ........ CO$_2$(g) + ...... H$_2$O

1.76 g of carbon dioxide and 0.90 g of water are produced.

Use this information to determine the balancing numbers for CO$_2$ and H$_2$O.

Relative atomic masses: C = 12; H = 1; O = 16 **4 MARKS**

**02.2** Use your answer from **02.1** to determine the identity of hydrocarbon **Z**. Select the correct answer.

**A** C$_2$H$_4$  **B** C$_3$H$_8$  **C** C$_4$H$_{10}$  **D** C$_8$H$_{18}$  **1 MARK**

**03** **H** This question is about the manufacture of ammonia. Ammonia is made from nitrogen and hydrogen, as shown in the equation:

N$_2$(g) + 3H$_2$(g) ⇌ 2NH$_3$(g)

Two molecules of ammonia are shown in **Figure 2**.

**Figure 2**

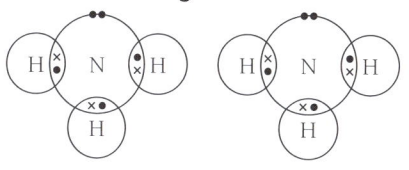

Ammonia is a gas at room temperature because it has a low boiling point.

**03.1** Explain why ammonia has a low boiling point. You should refer to **Figure 2** in your answer. **2 MARKS**

**03.2** 84 tonnes of nitrogen were mixed with 30 tonnes of hydrogen.

Relative atomic masses: N = 14; H = 1.

1 tonne = 1 000 000 g.

Calculate the number of moles of nitrogen and the number of moles of hydrogen and show that nitrogen is the limiting reactant. **3 MARKS**

**03.3** Calculate the maximum mass of ammonia that can be produced from 84 tonnes of nitrogen. **3 MARKS**

**04** Calcium reacts with water forming calcium hydroxide and hydrogen.

**04.1** Balance the equation **1 MARK**

Ca + ........H$_2$O → Ca(OH)$_2$ + H$_2$

The student reacted 5 g of calcium with excess water.

**04.2** Calculate the maximum number of moles of hydrogen the student could produce. **2 MARKS**

In a different experiment a student made 400 cm$^3$ of a solution of calcium hydroxide of concentration 2.00 g/dm$^3$.

**04.3** Calculate the mass of calcium hydroxide dissolved in this solution. **2 MARKS**

**04.4** Give the name of a group 2 metal that would react more violently with water than calcium. **1 MARK**

C4 Chemical calculations

65

# 2 Chemical reactions and energy changes

In the early 19th century, people began experimenting with chemical reactions in a systematic way, organising their results logically. Gradually they began to predict exactly what new substances would be formed and used this knowledge to develop a wide range of different materials and processes. They could extract important resources from the Earth, for example, by using electricity to decompose ionic substances. This is how reactive metals such as aluminium and sodium were first discovered.

Energy changes are an important part of chemical reactions. Transfers of energy take place due to the breaking and formation of bonds. The heating or cooling effects of reactions are used in a range of everyday applications.

| | | |
|---|---|---|
| **1** | Which metal reacts most vigorously with water – lithium, sodium, or potassium? | potassium |
| **2** | What is an ore? | a rock from which a metal can be extracted, and has enough of the metal (or one of its compounds) to make it worthwhile extracting |
| **3** | Complete this general equation: acid + .......... → .......... + water | base (or alkali), a salt |
| **4** | Name the type of reaction in question **3**. | neutralisation |
| **5** | What is the name of the indicator used with the pH scale? | universal indicator |
| **6** | Name a metal that is extracted from its ore by electrolysis. | any metal above carbon in the reactivity series, e.g., lithium, sodium, potassium, magnesium, calcium, aluminium |
| **7** | What is an exothermic reaction? | a reaction in which energy is transferred to the surroundings from the substances that are reacting |
| **8** | Name the type of reaction below: $Mg + FeSO_4 \rightarrow MgSO_4 + Fe$ | displacement |
| **9** | In an experiment, the initial temperature of the reactants was 18 °C and the final temperature after the reaction was 16 °C. Was the reaction exothermic or endothermic? | endothermic |
| **10** | Complete the equation below: $2H_2 + O_2 \rightarrow$ .............. | $2H_2O$ |

# Journey through GCSE Chemistry

**YOU ARE HERE**

### Atoms, bonding, and calculations

- C1  Atomic structure
- C2  The Periodic Table
- C3  Structure and bonding
- C4  Chemical calculations

### Chemical reactions and energy changes

- C5  Chemical changes
- C6  Electrolysis
- C7  Energy changes

### Rates, equilibrium, and organic chemistry

- C8  Rates and equilibrium
- C9  Crude oil and fuels

### Analysis and the Earth's resources

- C10  Chemical analysis
- C11  The Earth's atmosphere
- C12  The Earth's resources

67

# C5 Chemical changes

## C5.1 The reactivity series

### Learning objectives

After this topic, you should know:
- how some common metals react with water and with dilute acid
- how to deduce an order of reactivity of metals based on experimental results
- how to explain reduction and oxidation in terms of loss or gain of oxygen
- how to predict reactions of unfamiliar metals given information about their relative reactivity.

Metals are important in all our lives. For example, in transport metals are used to make bicycles, cars, ships, trains, and aeroplanes. In this chapter you will study the chemistry involved in getting some of these metals from their raw materials, called **ores**. Ores are rocks from which it is economical to extract the metals that they contain. With new techniques, metals can now be extracted from rock that was once thought of as waste.

Most metals in ores are chemically bonded to other elements in compounds. Many of these metals have reacted with oxygen in the air to form their oxides. We say the metals have been **oxidised** (i.e., have had oxygen added). For example:

$$\text{iron} + \text{oxygen} \rightarrow \text{iron(III) oxide}$$
$$4Fe(s) + 3O_2(g) \rightarrow 2Fe_2O_3(s)$$

So, to extract the metals from their oxides, the metal oxides must be **reduced** (i.e., have oxygen removed). To understand how this is done, you will need to know about the **reactivity series** of metals.

**The reactivity series is a list of metals in order of their reactivity, with the most reactive metals at the top and the least reactive ones at the bottom.**

When metal atoms react with other substances, such as water or acids, they form positive ions. It is the strength of the tendency to lose electrons that determines a metal's reactivity. Look back to Topic C2.5 to see a full explanation.

### Metals plus water

You can start putting the metals in order of reactivity by looking at their reactions with water. Most metals do not react vigorously with water. Metals such as copper, which does not react at all with water, can be used to make water pipes. However, there is a great range in reactivity between different metals. For example, in Topic C2.3 you have seen how the alkali metals in Group 1 react with water. They react vigorously, giving off hydrogen gas and producing alkaline solutions.

The reactivity of the metals increases going down Group 1, so of the metals you have observed, the order of reactivity is:

1  potassium (most reactive)
2  sodium
3  lithium (least reactive).

Magnesium lies somewhere between lithium and copper in the reactivity series. If magnesium is left in a beaker of water, it takes several days to collect enough gas to test with a lighted splint. The resulting 'pop' shows that the gas is hydrogen.

▲ **Figure 1** Metals are important materials in transportation

## Metals plus dilute acid

You have now seen how a range of metals react with water, and that you can use your observations of these reactions to arrange the metals into an order of reactivity. However, where the reactions with water are very slow, the task of ordering the metals is difficult. With these metals you can look at their reactions with dilute acid to arrive at an order of reactivity.

Table 1 summarises the reactions of some important metals with water and dilute acid.

**Table 1** The reactivity series. Note: Aluminium is protected by a layer of aluminium oxide, so will not undergo the reactions shown in the table unless the oxide layer is removed. That is why this fairly reactive metal can be used outside, for example, in lighter-weight cars, without corroding.

| Order of reactivity | Reaction with water | Reaction with dilute acid |
|---|---|---|
| potassium | fizz, giving off hydrogen gas, leaving an alkaline solution of metal hydroxide | explode |
| sodium | | |
| lithium | | |
| calcium | | |
| magnesium | | fizz, giving off hydrogen gas and forming a salt |
| aluminium | very slow reaction | |
| zinc | | |
| iron | | |
| tin | slight reaction with steam | react slowly with warm acid |
| lead | | |
| copper | | |
| silver | no reaction, even with steam | no reaction |
| gold | | |

### Summary questions

1. What happens, in terms of oxygen, when:
   a. a metal is oxidised  **1 MARK**
   b. a metal oxide is reduced.  **1 MARK**
2. Explain the following facts in terms of chemical reactivity.
   a. Gold, silver, and platinum are used to make jewellery.  **2 MARKS**
   b. Potassium, lithium, and sodium are stored in jars of oil.  **2 MARKS**
   c. Food cans are plated with tin, but not with zinc.  **2 MARKS**
3. Explain why aluminium can be used outdoors, for example, for window frames, even though it is quite high in the reactivity series.  **1 MARK**
4. Write the word equation and balanced symbol equation for:
   a. lithium reacting with water  **3 MARKS**
   b. zinc reacting with dilute hydrochloric acid  **3 MARKS**
   HINT: metal + acid → a salt + hydrogen
5. A student added a piece of magnesium ribbon to dilute sulfuric acid.
   a. Give three ways she could tell that a chemical reaction was taking place.  **2 MARKS**
   b. Write the word equation and balanced symbol equation, including state symbols, for the reaction between magnesium and dilute sulfuric acid.  **3 MARKS**

### C5 Chemical changes

> **Synoptic link**
>
> For more about the reaction of metals with dilute acid, see Topic C5.4.

> **Practical**
>
> **Metals and acid**
>
> You are given coarse-grained filings of the metals copper, zinc, iron, and magnesium to put into an order of reactivity according to their reactions with dilute hydrochloric acid.
>
> Plan a test to put the metals in order of reactivity based on your observations. Your plan should include the quantities of reactants you intend to use. (You will have access to a balance and measuring cylinders.)
>
> Let your teacher check your plan before you start your tests.
>
> - Give a brief outline of your method, including how you will make it as fair a test as possible. Identify any hazards.
> - Record your results in a suitable table.
> - Put the metals in order of reactivity according to your observations.
> - Evaluate your investigation.
>
> **Safety:** Wear eye protection.

> **Key point**
>
> - The metals can be placed in order of reactivity by their reactions with water and dilute acid.

# C5.2 Displacement reactions

## Learning objectives

*After this topic, you should know:*
- how the reactivity of metals is related to the tendency of the metal to form its positive ion
- the position of carbon and hydrogen in the reactivity series and how to predict displacement reactions
- ⒽHow to write ionic equations for displacement reactions
- ⒽHow to identify in a given reaction, symbol equation, or half equation which species are oxidised and which are reduced, in terms of electron transfer.

You have now seen how to use the reactions of metals with water and dilute acid to get an order of reactivity. You can also judge reactivity by putting the metals 'into competition' with each other. One metal starts off as atoms of the element and the other metal as positive ions in a solution of one of its salts. For example, you might have magnesium metal, Mg(s), and copper(II) ions, $Cu^{2+}$(aq), in a solution of copper(II) sulfate.

**A more reactive metal will displace a less reactive metal from an aqueous solution of one of its salts.**

In this case, magnesium is more reactive than copper. Therefore, the copper ions will be displaced from solution to form copper metal, Cu(s). In this reaction, the magnesium metal forms aqueous magnesium ions, $Mg^{2+}$(aq), and dissolves into the solution. This is a **displacement reaction**.

magnesium + copper(II) sulfate → magnesium sulfate + copper

The balanced symbol equation, including state symbols, is:

$$Mg(s) + CuSO_4(aq) \rightarrow MgSO_4(aq) + Cu(s)$$

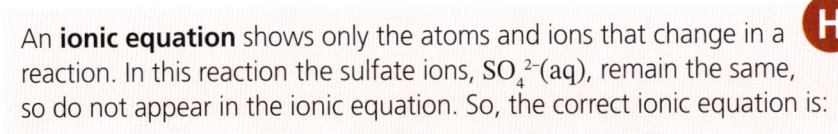

Ⓗ An **ionic equation** shows only the atoms and ions that change in a reaction. In this reaction the sulfate ions, $SO_4^{2-}$(aq), remain the same, so do not appear in the ionic equation. So, the correct ionic equation is:

$$Mg(s) + Cu^{2+}(aq) \rightarrow Mg^{2+}(aq) + Cu(s)$$

This shows that magnesium atoms have a greater tendency to form positive ions than copper atoms.

Zinc is more reactive than silver – it is higher up the reactivity series. Therefore, zinc (metal) displaces silver (ions) from silver nitrate solution:

zinc + silver nitrate → zinc nitrate + silver
$$Zn(s) + 2AgNO_3(aq) \rightarrow Zn(NO_3)_2(aq) + 2Ag(s)$$

In an experiment you would see the silver metal slowly forming on the surface of the zinc.

## Hydrogen and carbon in the reactivity series

We can include the non-metals hydrogen and carbon in the reactivity series using displacement reactions. You can think of the 'metal plus acid' reactions as displacement of hydrogen ions, $H^+$(aq), from solution.

Copper cannot displace the hydrogen from an acid, whereas lead can. So, using the reactivity series in Table 1 in Topic C5.1, hydrogen must be positioned between copper and lead. Carbon can be used in the extraction of metals from their oxides (another type of displacement reaction). However, it can only do this for metals below aluminium in the reactivity series. Carbon is not reactive enough to displace aluminium from aluminium oxide, but it can displace zinc from zinc oxide. So, carbon is placed between aluminium and zinc in the series (Figure 3 in Topic C5.3).

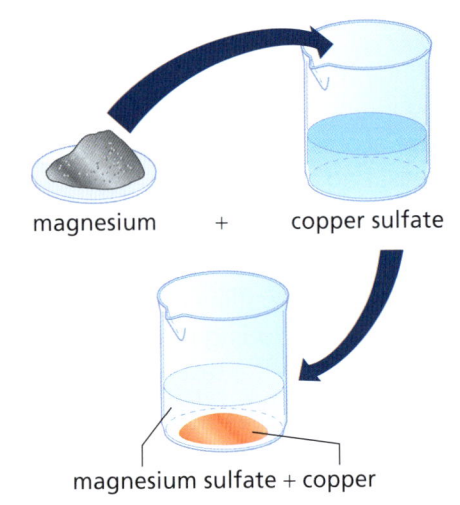

▲ **Figure 1** *Magnesium displaces copper from copper(II) sulfate solution*

## Practical

### Displacing a metal from solution

Set up the test tube as shown:

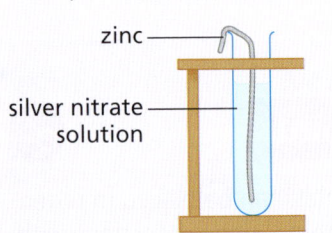

- zinc
- silver nitrate solution

- Explain what happens.

# C5 Chemical changes

## Oxidation and reduction

In Topic C5.1 you saw that oxidation was defined as the chemical addition of oxygen, and reduction defined as the removal of oxygen. A wider definition involves the transfer of electrons rather than oxygen atoms.

**Oxidation is the loss of electrons.**

**Reduction is the gain of electrons.**

You can apply these definitions to displacement reactions in solution. Take, as an example, the displacement of copper(II) ions by iron. This reaction is used in industry to extract copper metal from copper sulfate solution. The iron added to the copper sulfate solution is cheap scrap iron. The ionic equation for the reaction is:

$$Fe(s) + Cu^{2+}(aq) \rightarrow Fe^{2+}(aq) + Cu(s)$$

You can use **half equations** to show what happens to each reactant:

$$Fe(s) \rightarrow Fe^{2+}(aq) + 2e^-$$

The iron atoms lose two electrons to form iron(II) ions. This is oxidation (the loss of electrons). The iron atoms have been oxidised.

The two electrons from iron are gained by the copper(II) ions as they form copper atoms:

$$Cu^{2+}(aq) + 2e^- \rightarrow Cu(s)$$

This is reduction (the gain of electrons). The copper(II) ions have been reduced.

This is why these displacement reactions are also known as redox reactions (reduction-oxidation).

## Practical

### Predicting reactions

You will be provided with small samples of magnesium, copper, zinc, and iron, plus their sulfate solutions. Draw a table to record possible combinations of metal + metal sulfate solution.

Predict which metals and solutions will react (enter a tick in the table), and which will not (enter a cross). Then try out the reactions on a spotting tile.

**Safety:** Wear eye protection. Some solutions are harmful.

## Study tip

You can use the phrase **OILRIG** to remember the definition of oxidation and reduction reactions:

**O**xidation **I**s **L**oss of electrons

**R**eduction **I**s **G**ain of electrons

## Synoptic link

For more about an industrial application of the displacement of copper ions from solution by iron, see Topic C12.4.

## Summary questions

1. Predict whether the following pairs of metals and solutions will result in a reaction. If a reaction is predicted, write a word equation.
   a  iron + zinc sulfate  **1 MARK**
   b  zinc + copper sulfate  **2 MARKS**
   c  magnesium + iron(II) chloride  **2 MARKS**
2. Explain why carbon can reduce zinc oxide, but not magnesium oxide.  **2 MARKS**
3. Hydrogen gas is used in the reduction of tungsten oxide, $WO_3$, to extract tungsten metal, W.
   a  What you can deduce about tungsten metal?  **1 MARK**
   b  Write a balanced symbol equation for this reaction.  **1 MARK**
4. a  Write the ionic equation, including state symbols, for the reaction between zinc and iron(II) sulfate.  **3 MARKS**
   b  Explain, in terms of the transfer of electrons, which species is oxidised, and which is reduced in the reaction.  **4 MARKS**

## Key points

- A more reactive metal will displace a less reactive metal from its aqueous solution.
- Hydrogen and carbon can be given positions in the reactivity series based on the results of displacement reactions.
- Oxidation is the loss of electrons. Reduction is the gain of electrons.

71

# C5.3 Extracting metals

## Learning objectives

After this topic, you should know:
- how metals can be extracted
- how to interpret or evaluate the process used to extract different metals, when given appropriate information
- how to identify substances that are oxidised or reduced in terms of gain or loss of oxygen.

Metals have been important to people for thousands of years. You can follow the course of history by the materials people used. After the Stone Age came the Bronze Age (copper/tin) and then on to the Iron Age.

## Where do metals come from?

Metals are found in the Earth's crust. Most metals are combined chemically with other chemical elements, often with oxygen or sulfur. This means that the metal must be chemically separated from its compounds before it can be used.

When there is enough of a metal or metal compound in a rock to make it worth extracting the metal, the rock is called a metal **ore**. Ores are mined from the ground. Some need to be concentrated before the metal is extracted and purified.

Whether it is worth extracting a particular metal depends on:

- how easy it is to extract it from its ore
- how much metal the ore contains
- the changing demands for a particular metal.

These factors can change over time. For example, a new, cheaper method might be discovered for extracting a metal. You might also discover a new way to extract a metal efficiently from rock that contains only small amounts of a metal ore. An ore that was once thought of as 'low grade' could then become an economic source of a metal.

A few metals, such as gold and silver, are so unreactive that they are found in the Earth as the metals (elements) themselves. They exist in their native state.

Sometimes a nugget of gold is so large it can simply be picked up. At other times, tiny flakes must be physically separated from sand and rocks by panning.

## Reduction of oxide by carbon

The way that a metal is extracted depends on its place in the reactivity series. The reactivity series lists the metals in order of their reactivity (Figure 3, which includes the non-metals carbon and hydrogen).

▲ Figure 1 Copper ore being carried from mines on a conveyor belt

▲ Figure 2 A copper mine in Peru. The rocks containing copper have turned blue-green where the copper ore has reacted with carbon dioxide and water in the air to form copper carbonate

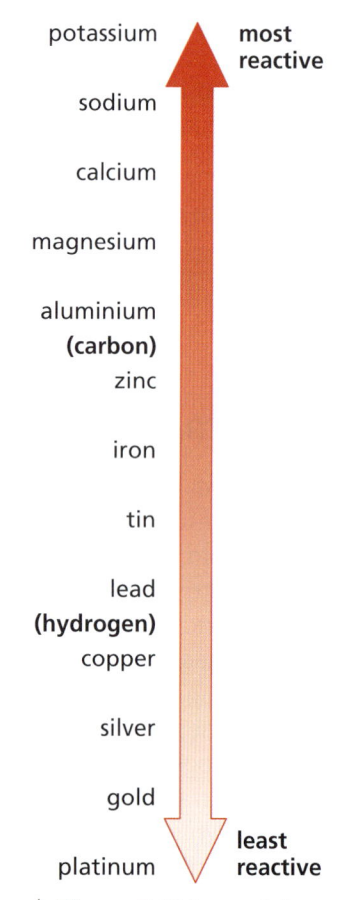

potassium — most reactive
sodium
calcium
magnesium
aluminium
(carbon)
zinc
iron
tin
lead
(hydrogen)
copper
silver
gold
platinum — least reactive

▲ Figure 3 This reactivity series shows the position of the non-metals carbon and hydrogen in the series

As you have seen in Topic C5.2, a more reactive metal will displace a less reactive metal from its compounds. Carbon (a non-metal) will also displace less reactive metals from their oxides. Carbon is used to extract some metals from their ores in industry.

You can find many metals, such as copper, lead, iron, and zinc, combined with oxygen as metal oxides. Because carbon is more reactive than each of these metals, carbon is used to extract the metals from their oxides.

You must heat the metal oxide with carbon. The carbon removes the oxygen from the metal oxide to form carbon dioxide. The metal is also formed, as the element:

$$\text{metal oxide} + \text{carbon} \rightarrow \text{metal} + \text{carbon dioxide}$$

For example:

$$\text{lead oxide} + \text{carbon} \xrightarrow{\text{heat}} \text{lead} + \text{carbon dioxide}$$
$$2PbO(s) + C(s) \rightarrow 2Pb(l) + CO_2(g)$$

The removal of oxygen from a compound is called chemical **reduction**.

## Reduction of oxide by hydrogen

Another metal extracted by reduction of its oxide is tungsten, W. The non-metal used as the reducing agent is hydrogen, not carbon, even though carbon would be cheaper. This is because carbon can form a compound, tungsten carbide, with the tungsten metal formed by reduction. The tungsten obtained from reduction of its oxide by hydrogen is very pure:

$$\text{tungsten oxide} + \text{hydrogen} \xrightarrow{\text{heat}} \text{tungsten} + \text{water (as steam)}$$
$$WO_3(s) + 3H_2(g) \rightarrow W(s) + 3H_2O(g)$$

The metals that are more reactive than carbon are not extracted from their ores by reduction with carbon. Instead, they are extracted by **electrolysis** of the molten metal compound (see Chapter 6).

### Summary questions

1. Define the term metal ore. **2 MARKS**

2. Which substance has been reduced in the reaction below: **1 MARK**
$$2SnO(s) + C(s) \xrightarrow{\text{heat}} 2Sn(l) + CO_2(g)$$

3. Explain why gold is found as a metal rather than combined with other elements in compounds. **1 MARK**

4. Zinc oxide, ZnO, can be reduced to zinc by heating it in a furnace with carbon. Carbon monoxide, CO, gas is given off in the reaction. The zinc formed is molten at the temperature in the furnace.
   a Write a word equation for the reduction of zinc oxide by carbon in the furnace, labelling the species that is reduced and the species that is oxidised. **3 MARKS**
   b Write a balanced symbol equation, including state symbols, for the reaction in part **a**. **3 MARKS**

## C5 Chemical changes

### Practical

**Reduction by carbon**

Heat some copper oxide with carbon powder in a test tube, gently at first, then more strongly.

Empty the contents into an evaporating dish.

You can repeat the experiment with iron oxide and carbon.

- Explain your observations. Include a word equation and a balanced symbol equation with state symbols.

**Safety:** Wear eye protection. Wash hands after experiments. Copper oxide is harmful.

### Synoptic link

To find out more about the use of electrolysis to extract reactive metals, see Topic C6.3.

### Key points

- A metal ore contains enough of the metal to make it economic to extract the metal.
- Gold and some other unreactive metals can be found in their native state.
- The oxides of metals below carbon in the series can be reduced by carbon to give the metal element.

# C5.4 Salts from metals

## Learning objectives

After this topic, you should know:
- the reactions of magnesium, zinc, and iron with hydrochloric acid and sulfuric acid, and how to collect the salts formed
- ⓗ why these reactions are classed as redox reactions
- ⓗ how to identify which species are oxidised and which are reduced in given chemical equations, in terms of electron transfer.

## Acids, metals, and salts

All acids contain hydrogen, which is released as hydrogen ions when the acid is dissolved in water (Topic C5.7). You used the reactions of metals with dilute acid as one of the reactions to deduce the reactivity series in Topic C5.1. Reactions between metals and acids can only occur when the metal is more reactive than the hydrogen in the acid. For example, iron reacts with dilute acids, but silver does not.

Whenever a reaction does take place between a metal and an acid, a **salt** is formed. A salt is the general name for **a compound formed when the hydrogen in an acid is wholly, or partially, replaced by metal (or ammonium) ions**.

So, one way you can make salts is by reacting acids directly with metals that are more reactive than hydrogen.

metal + acid → a salt + hydrogen

iron + hydrochloric acid → iron(II) chloride + hydrogen

$Fe(s) + 2HCl(aq) \rightarrow FeCl_2(aq) + H_2(g)$

If the metal is very reactive, the reaction with acid is too violent to be carried out safely. So, alkali metals are never added to acid.

Pure, dry crystals of a salt (e.g., iron(II) chloride in the previous equation) can be obtained from the solution. Some of the water is evaporated from the solution by heating it until the 'point of crystallisation' is reached. At this point the solution is saturated, and crystals of salt will appear at the edge of the solution in the evaporating dish.

You can also test for the point of crystallisation by dipping a glass rod into the hot salt solution. You then remove the glass rod to see if crystals form in the solution left on the rod as it cools down.

To prepare the best samples of salt crystals, the salt solution should then be left at room temperature. The remaining water will evaporate slowly. You can remove any small amounts of solution left on the crystals by dabbing the crystals with filter papers, then leaving them to dry.

The salt that you make depends on the metal you use, as well as on the acid used. So, magnesium metal will always make salts containing magnesium ions, $Mg^{2+}$. Zinc metal will always make zinc salts, containing $Zn^{2+}$ ions.

The acid used provides the negative ions present in all salts:

- the salts formed when you react a metal with hydrochloric acid, HCl, are always **chlorides** (containing $Cl^-$ ions)
- sulfuric acid, $H_2SO_4$, always makes **sulfates** (containing $SO_4^{2-}$ ions)
- nitric acid, $HNO_3$, always makes **nitrates** (containing $NO_3^-$ ions).

▲ **Figure 1** Heating by using a water bath is a gentler way to evaporate water from the salt solution than heating the solution directly. The slower the water evaporates from the solution, the larger the crystals of the salt collected at the end of the experiment

**C5 Chemical changes**

## Explaining the reaction between a metal and an acid

In the reaction between magnesium, Mg, and dilute sulfuric acid, $H_2SO_4$, hydrogen ions will be displaced from solution by magnesium. This is because magnesium is more reactive than hydrogen. Magnesium has a stronger tendency to form positive ions than hydrogen has, so the following reaction takes place:

$$Mg(s) + H_2SO_4(aq) \rightarrow MgSO_4(aq) + H_2(g)$$

You can summarise this reaction as an ionic equation (see Topic C5.2):

$$Mg(s) + 2H^+(aq) \rightarrow Mg^{2+}(aq) + H_2(g)$$

The sulfate ions in the solution, $SO_4^{2-}(aq)$, do not change in the reaction, so are not included in the ionic equation. They are called spectator ions.

Then you can look more closely at the ionic equation by dividing it into two half equations. You can see what happens to the magnesium atoms when they change into positive magnesium ions:

$$Mg(s) \rightarrow Mg^{2+}(aq) + 2e^-$$

A magnesium atom loses its two electrons from its outer shell. It gives these electrons to two hydrogen ions from the acidic solution, $2H^+(aq)$, forming two H atoms. These bond to each other (sharing a pair of electrons in a covalent bond) to make a molecule of hydrogen gas, $H_2$:

$$2H^+(aq) + 2e^- \rightarrow H_2(g)$$

Remember that oxidation is loss of electrons, and that reduction is gain of electrons (remember OILRIG). So, you can conclude that electrons have been transferred from magnesium atoms to hydrogen ions in the reaction:

- The magnesium atoms have lost electrons, so magnesium atoms have been **oxidised** in the reaction.
- The hydrogen ions have gained electrons, so hydrogen ions have been **reduced** in the reaction.

The reaction of a metal with an acid is always a redox reaction. The metal atoms always donate electrons to the hydrogen ions, displacing hydrogen as a gas and leaving positive metal ions in the solution.

### Practical

**Planning to make a salt**

Given zinc powder and $10\,cm^3$ of dilute hydrochloric acid or dilute sulfuric acid, plan an experiment to make and collect pure, dry crystals of a salt.

- Write a word equation (and balanced symbol equation, with state symbols, if possible) for the reaction chosen.
- Think about how you can make sure that all the dilute acid has reacted. How will you tell when the reaction is finished?
- Then write a step-by-step method that another student could follow to collect a sample of the salt crystals formed when zinc is added to the dilute acid.

**Safety:** Do not try out your plan before your teacher has checked it.

## Summary questions

1. Write the general equation for the reaction between an acid and a metal. **1 MARK**
2. a State why copper sulfate cannot be prepared by adding copper metal to dilute sulfuric acid. **1 MARK**
   b State why potassium chloride is never prepared by reacting potassium metal and dilute hydrochloric acid together. **1 MARK**
3. Write a balanced symbol equation, including state symbols, for:
   a iron + sulfuric acid **3 MARKS**
   b zinc + hydrochloric acid. **3 MARKS**
4. Using the reaction of zinc with dilute hydrochloric acid:
   a Write an ionic equation, including state symbols, for the reaction. **2 MARKS**
   b From your answer to part **a**, construct two half equations to show the electron transfers taking place. **2 MARKS**
   c Explain why this is a redox reaction. **5 MARKS**

### Key points

- Salts can be made by reacting a suitable metal with an acid. Hydrogen gas is also produced.
- Salts can be crystallised out of solution by evaporating off the water.
- The reaction between a metal and an acid is an example of a redox reaction.
- The metal atoms lose electrons and are oxidised. Hydrogen ions from the acid gain electrons and are reduced.

# C5.5 Salts from insoluble bases

## Learning objectives

*After this topic, you should know:*
- the reaction between an acid and a base
- how to prepare pure, dry crystals of the salts formed in neutralisation reactions between acids and insoluble bases
- how to predict products from given reactants
- how to use the formulae of common ions to deduce the formulae of salts.

Acids and bases are an essential part of your understanding of chemistry. They play an important part inside you and all other living things.

When you neutralised acids previously in scientific experiments you will have used an **alkali**, such as sodium hydroxide solution, NaOH(aq). Alkalis are part of a larger class of compounds called **bases**. Bases are compounds that can neutralise acids. Many bases are metal oxides, such as sodium oxide or copper oxide. Alkalis are those bases that are soluble in water. Examples of alkalis are the hydroxides of Group 1 metals.

When you react an acid with a base, a salt and water are formed.

The general equation which describes this **neutralisation** reaction is:

**acid + base → a salt + water**

The oxide of a metal, such as iron(III) oxide, is an example of a base you can use to make a salt in this way:

hydrochloric acid + iron(III) oxide → iron(III) chloride solution + water

$6HCl(aq) + Fe_2O_3(s) \rightarrow 2FeCl_3(aq) + 3H_2O(l)$

## Maths

### Worked example
What is the formula of the salt, iron(III) sulfate?

### Solution
The formulae of the ions in the salt are $Fe^{3+}$ and $SO_4^{2-}$.

All ionic compounds are neutral. They carry no overall charge.

So, the question becomes 'What ratio of $Fe^{3+}$ and $SO_4^{2-}$ will combine to make the overall charge zero (0)?'

Take the magnitude of each charge, which is 3 for $Fe^{3+}$ and 2 for $SO_4^{2-}$.

Then work out the lowest common multiple between 3 and 2. In this case, the smallest whole number that both 3 and 2 will divide evenly into is 6.

So, you will need 6+ charges, from two $Fe^{3+}$ ions, to cancel out 6– charges, from three $SO_4^{2-}$ ions.

Therefore, the $Fe^{3+}$ and $SO_4^{2-}$ must combine in the ratio 2 : 3, making the formula of the salt neutral.

So, the formula of iron(III) sulfate is $\mathbf{Fe_2(SO_4)_3}$.

## Formulae of salts

Salts are made up of positive metal ions (or ammonium ions, $NH_4^+$) and negative ions from an acid. The positive ions can come from a metal, a base, or a metal carbonate. A carbonate reacts with an acid to form a salt, water, and carbon dioxide gas.

Like all ionic compounds, salts have no overall charge, as the sum of the charges on their ions equals zero. So, once you know the charges on the ions that make up a salt, you can work out its formula.

**Table 1** The charge an element has depends on which Group it is in within the Periodic Table

| The charges on common positive ions | The charges on common negative ions |
|---|---|
| ions of Group 1 metals = 1+ (e.g., $Li^+$, $Na^+$, $K^+$) | ions of Group 7 non-metals = 1– (e.g., $F^-$, $Cl^-$, $Br^-$, $I^-$) |
| ions of Group 2 metals = 2+ (e.g., $Mg^{2+}$, $Ca^{2+}$) | nitrate ions = 1–, $NO_3^-$ |
| aluminium ion = 3+, $Al^{3+}$ | sulfate ions = 2–, $SO_4^{2-}$ |
| ammonium ion = 1+, $NH_4^+$ | |

## C5 Chemical changes

### Practical

**Making a copper salt**

You can make copper sulfate crystals from copper(II) oxide (an insoluble base) and sulfuric acid. The equation for the reaction is:

sulfuric acid + copper(II) oxide → copper(II) sulfate + water

$H_2SO_4(aq) + CuO(s) \rightarrow CuSO_4(aq) + H_2O(l)$

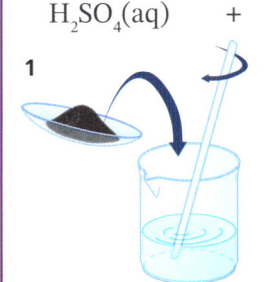

**1** Add insoluble copper oxide to sulfuric acid and stir. Warm gently on a tripod and gauze (do not boil).

**2** warm gently → The solution turns blue as the reaction occurs, showing that copper sulfate is being formed. Excess black copper oxide can be seen.

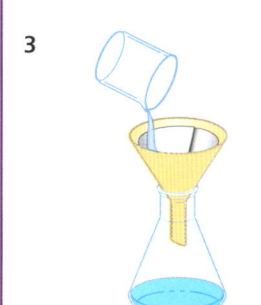

**3** When the reaction is complete, filter the solution to remove excess copper oxide.

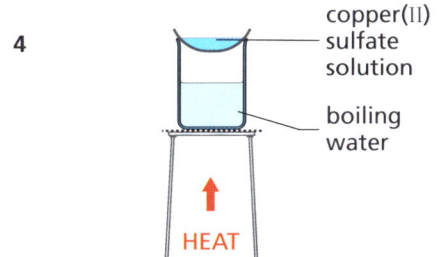

**4** copper(II) sulfate solution / boiling water / HEAT

You can evaporate the water so that crystals of copper sulfate start to form. Stop heating when you see the first crystals appear at the edge of the solution. Then leave for the rest of the water to evaporate off slowly. This will give you larger crystals. Any small excess of solution on the crystals can be removed by dabbing between filter papers (do not touch the solution), then leaving to dry.

- What does the copper(II) sulfate look like? Draw a diagram if necessary.

**Safety:** Wear eye protection. Chemicals in this practical are harmful. Make sure you only warm the acid gently – **do not boil it!**

### Metacognition

Classify the following substances as 'Salt', 'Alkali', 'Base', or 'Product of a neutralisation reaction'. Organise your results in a table. Some substances can be added to more than one column. Explain why.

**hydrogen   calcium sulfate
copper oxide
potassium hydroxide
carbon dioxide   iron oxide
water   lithium oxide
zinc chloride   aluminium nitrate
sodium hydroxide**

Did you find any substances difficult to classify? If so, why?

Discuss your table with a partner.

### Key points

- When an acid reacts with a base, a neutralisation reaction occurs. This produces a salt and water.
- The sum of the charges on the ions in a salt add up to zero. This enables you to work out the formula of salts, knowing the charges on the ions present.
- A pure, dry sample of the salt made in an acid–base reaction can be crystallised out of solution by evaporating off most of the water.

### Summary questions

1. Write the general word equation for an acid–base reaction. **1 MARK**
2. Write the word equation for the reaction between zinc oxide and dilute hydrochloric acid. **1 MARK**
3. Describe in detail how you could prepare a sample of copper(II) sulfate crystals from its solution. **4 MARKS**
4. Give the formula of each of the following salts:
   a. sodium bromide **1 MARK**
   b. magnesium fluoride **1 MARK**
   c. potassium nitrate **1 MARK**
   d. aluminium sulfate. **1 MARK**
5. a. Write a balanced symbol equation, including state symbols, for the reaction of lithium oxide (in excess) and dilute sulfuric acid. **3 MARKS**
   b. **H** Write an ionic equation for the reaction in **5a** and explain what happens in the reaction. **3 MARKS**

# C5.6 Making more salts

## Learning objectives

After this topic, you should know:
- the reactions of acids with alkalis
- the reactions of acids with carbonates
- how to make pure, dry samples of a named soluble salt from information provided.

There are two other important reactions you can use to make salts:
- reacting solutions of an acid and an alkali together
- reacting an acid with a carbonate (usually added as the solid).

## Acid + alkali

When an acid reacts with an alkali, a neutralisation reaction takes place.

Hydrochloric acid reacting with sodium hydroxide solution is an example:

| acid | + | alkali | → | a salt | + | water |
|---|---|---|---|---|---|---|
| HCl(aq) | + | NaOH(aq) | → | NaCl(aq) | + | H$_2$O(l) |
| hydrochloric acid | + | sodium hydroxide solution | → | sodium chloride | + | water |

**H** You can think about neutralisation in terms of H$^+$(aq) ions from the acid reacting with OH$^-$(aq) ions from the alkali. The ions react to form water molecules. You can show this in an ionic equation. Remember that the ionic equation for a reaction just shows the ions, atoms, and molecules that change when the new products are formed:

$$H^+(aq) + OH^-(aq) \rightarrow H_2O(l)$$

You can make ammonium salts, as well as metal salts, by reacting an acid with an alkali. Ammonia reacts with water to form a weakly alkaline solution.

**H**
$$NH_3(aq) + H_2O(l) \rightleftharpoons NH_4^+(aq) + OH^-(aq)$$

Ammonia solution reacts with an acid (e.g., dilute nitric acid):

acid + ammonia solution → an ammonium salt + water

**H**
$$HNO_3(aq) + NH_4^+(aq) + OH^-(aq) \rightarrow NH_4NO_3(aq) + H_2O(l)$$

nitric acid + ammonia solution → ammonium nitrate + water

When you react an acid with an alkali, you need to be able to tell when the acid and alkali have completely reacted. It is not obvious by just observing the reaction. There is no gas given off during the reaction (that would stop when the acid has been neutralised). Also, there is no excess insoluble base visible in the reaction mixture when excess has been added. So, you need to use an acid/base indicator to help decide when the reaction is complete.

To collect a pure, dry sample of crystals of the salt you would:
- carry out the experiment with the indicator added to see how much acid reacts completely with the alkali
- run that volume of acid into the solution of alkali again, but this time without the indicator
- then crystallise and dry the crystals of salt from the reaction mixture, as described previously in Topics C5.4 and C5.5.

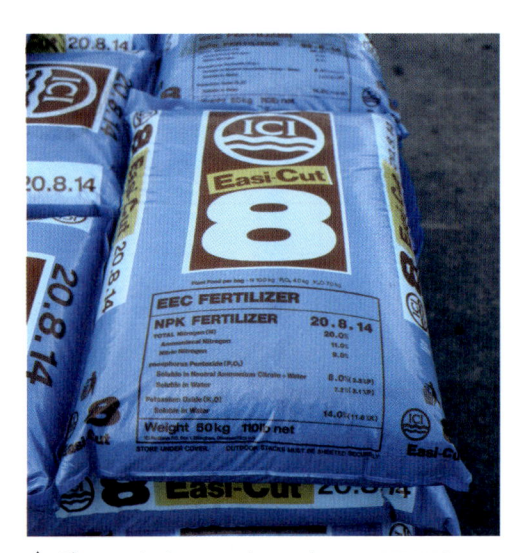

▲ **Figure 1** Ammonium nitrate, NH$_4$NO$_3$, made from ammonia and nitric acid, is used as a fertiliser

## C5 Chemical changes

### Acids + carbonates

Buildings and statues made of limestone suffer badly from damage by acid rain. You might have seen statues where the fine features have been lost. Limestone, which is quarried from the ground, is mostly calcium carbonate. This reacts with acid, giving off carbon dioxide gas in the reaction.

Metal carbonates react with acids to give a salt, water, and carbon dioxide. The general equation is:

**metal carbonate + acid → a salt + water + carbon dioxide**

For calcium carbonate, the reaction with hydrochloric acid is:

calcium carbonate + hydrochloric acid → calcium chloride + water + carbon dioxide

The balanced symbol equation, including state symbols, is:

$$CaCO_3(s) + 2HCl(aq) \rightarrow CaCl_2(aq) + H_2O(l) + CO_2(g)$$

> **Practical**
>
> **Making a salt from a metal carbonate**
>
> Metal carbonates are generally insoluble in water (except the carbonates of the Group 1 metals, such as sodium carbonate).
> - Think of two ways in which you could decide when an acid has been completely neutralised by an insoluble carbonate.
> - You will be given a choice of magnesium carbonate or copper carbonate, plus dilute hydrochloric acid or sulfuric acid. Choose which combination you will react together to make a salt.
> - Name the salt, write an equation, and describe a method for preparing a pure, dry sample of crystals of your salt.
>
> **Safety:** Do not start any practical work before your teacher has checked your planned method.

▲ **Figure 2** Powdered limestone is used to raise the pH of acidic soils or lakes affected by acid rain, making use of the reaction between calcium carbonate and acid

### Summary questions

1. **a** Write the general equation for the neutralisation reaction between an acid and an alkali. *1 MARK*
   **b** Write the general equation for the reaction between an acid and a carbonate. *1 MARK*
2. **a** Write a detailed method to show how to make lithium chloride (a soluble salt) from an acid and an alkali. *6 MARKS*
   **b** Write a balanced symbol equation, including state symbols, for the reaction in part **a**. *3 MARKS*
3. **a** Barium is a Group 2 metal. Give the balanced symbol equation, with state symbols, for the reaction between barium carbonate and dilute nitric acid. *3 MARKS*
   **b** 🄗 Suggest an ionic equation, including state symbols, which can summarise the reaction of any insoluble carbonate with dilute acid. *2 MARKS*

### Key points

- Acids react with alkalis to form a salt and water.
- Metal carbonates react with acids to give a salt, water, and carbon dioxide.

79

# C5.7 Neutralisation and the pH scale

## Learning objectives

After this topic, you should know:
- why solutions are acidic or alkaline
- how to use universal indicator or a wide-range indicator to measure the approximate pH of a solution
- how to use the pH scale to identify acidic or alkaline solutions
- how to investigate pH changes when a strong acid neutralises a strong alkali.

When you dissolve a substance in water, you make an aqueous solution, as happens with the washing powder in a washing machine. Whether the solution formed is acidic, alkaline, or neutral depends on which substance you have dissolved. A solution of washing powder is slightly alkaline.

- Soluble hydroxides are called **alkalis**. Their solutions are alkaline. An example is sodium hydroxide solution.
- **Bases**, which include alkalis, are substances that can neutralise acids. Metal oxides and metal hydroxides are bases. Examples include iron oxide and copper hydroxide, which are both insoluble in water.
- **Acids** include citric acid, sulfuric acid, and ethanoic acid. All acids taste very sour, although many acids are far too dangerous to put in your mouth. Ethanoic acid (in vinegar) and citric acid (in citrus fruit and fizzy drinks) are acids that are weak enough to be edible.
- Pure water is **neutral** – it is neither acidic nor alkaline.

One acid that you use in science labs is hydrochloric acid. This is formed when the gas hydrogen chloride, HCl, dissolves in water:

$$HCl(g) \xrightarrow{water} H^+(aq) + Cl^-(aq)$$

All acids release $H^+(aq)$ ions into solution when added to water. It is these excess $H^+(aq)$ ions that make a solution acidic.

Because alkalis are bases that dissolve in water and form solutions, they are the bases often used in experiments. Sodium hydroxide solution is often found in school labs. You get sodium hydroxide solution when you dissolve solid sodium hydroxide in water:

$$NaOH(s) \xrightarrow{water} Na^+(aq) + OH^-(aq)$$

All alkalis form aqueous hydroxide ions, $OH^-(aq)$, when added to water. It is these excess aqueous hydroxide ions, $OH^-(aq)$, that make a solution alkaline.

▲ **Figure 1** Acids and bases are all around you, in many of the things used in everyday life – and in our bodies too

## Measuring acidity or alkalinity

Indicators are substances which change colour when you add them to acids and alkalis. Litmus is a well-known indicator (red in acid and blue in alkali), but there are many more.

You use the **pH scale** to show how acidic or alkaline a solution is. The scale runs from 0 (most acidic) to 14 (most alkaline). You can use universal indicator to find the pH of a solution. It is a special indicator made from several dyes. It turns a range of colours as the pH changes. Anything in the middle of the pH scale (pH 7) is neutral – neither acidic nor alkaline (Figure 3).

Alternatively, you can use a pH meter (Figure 2). This has a glass probe attached to dip in the solution being tested. Some electronic pH sensors give a digital display of the pH directly, and others can be attached to data-loggers and computers to monitor and record pH changes over time.

▲ **Figure 2** pH probes or sensors can measure pH values accurately

# C5 Chemical changes

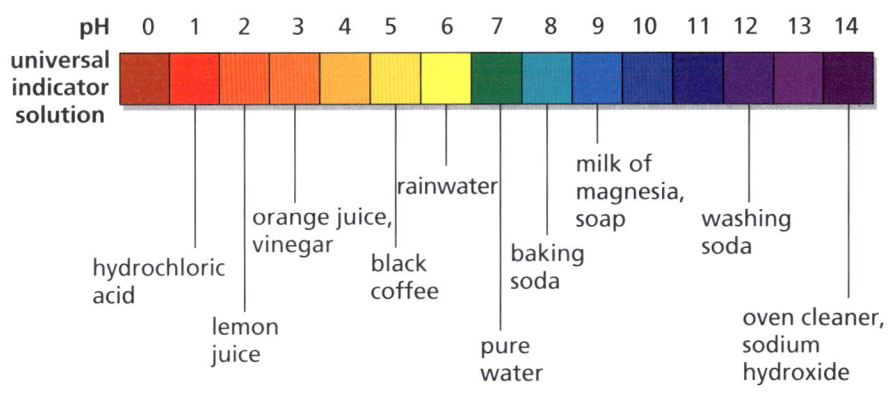

▲ **Figure 3** The pH scale tells you how acidic or alkaline a solution is. The scale starts at red, progressing through orange and yellow (decreasing in acidity) until we get a neutral solution at green. The scale continues through turquoise, and blue until it finishes at a deep purple colour (increasing in alkalinity)

## Maths

You can use the mathematical symbols > (read as 'is greater than') and < (read as 'is less than') when interpreting pH values. You can say:
pH < 7 indicates an acidic solution, that is, pH values less than 7 are acidic.
pH > 7 indicates an alkaline solution, that is, pH values greater than 7 are alkaline.

## Practical

### Obtaining a pH curve

Collect 20 cm³ of sodium hydroxide solution in a small beaker. Measure and record its pH using a pH sensor. Then add dilute hydrochloric acid to a **burette**.

Predict the change of pH you will get in the experiment as you add the hydrochloric acid to the sodium hydroxide solution. You can sketch a predicted line on a graph of 'pH value' against 'volume of dilute hydrochloric acid added'.

Now add the dilute hydrochloric acid from the burette, 1 cm³ at a time, to the alkali. Stir after each addition of acid and take the pH of the solution in the beaker.

Record your data in a table and show it on a graph or use the computer to display the data collected.

- Evaluate your prediction.

**Safety:** Wear eye protection.

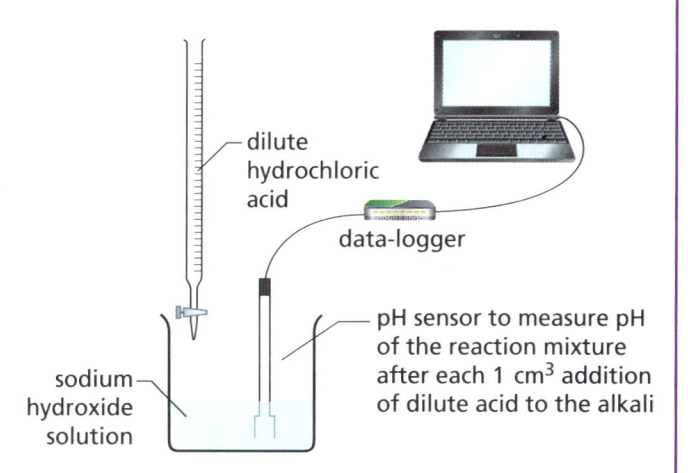

## Summary questions

1. **a** What distinguishes alkalis from other bases? **1 MARK**
   **b** What do all alkalis have in common? **1 MARK**
2. Which ions do all acids produce in aqueous solution? **1 MARK**
3. Describe how you could use universal indicator as a way of distinguishing between distilled water, sodium hydroxide solution, and ethanoic acid solution. **6 MARKS**
4. Describe how the pH changes when a strong acid is added slowly to a strong alkali. **3 MARKS**
5. Using an equation, including state symbols, show the change that happens when:
   **a** potassium hydroxide, KOH, dissolves in water **2 MARKS**
   **b** hydrobromic acid, HBr, dissolves in water. **2 MARKS**
6. Compare the advantages and disadvantages of using universal indicator paper or a pH sensor and data-logger to find the pH of a solution. **3 MARKS**

## Key points

- Acids are substances that produce $H^+(aq)$ ions when you add them to water. Bases are substances that will neutralise acids.
- An alkali is a soluble base. Alkalis produce $OH^-(aq)$ ions when you add them to water.
- On the pH scale, solutions with pH values less than 7 are acidic, pH values greater than 7 are alkaline, and a pH value of 7 indicates a neutral solution.

# C5.8 Strong and weak acids

## Learning objectives

After this topic, you should know:
- how to use and explain the terms 'dilute and concentrated', and 'weak and strong' in relation to acids
- how the concentration of hydrogen ions in a solution affects the numerical value of pH (whole number values of pH only).

## Why are some acids called dilute solutions, and others concentrated solutions?

Some acids are safer to use than others, and you can make acids safer to use by adding water to dilute them. For example, a solution of 219 g/dm³ hydrochloric acid would have to be labelled as corrosive, but when diluted to a concentration of 3.65 g/dm³ hydrochloric acid, it only requires labelling as irritant. Dilute the strong acid enough and it will eventually be harmless.

## Why are some acids called strong acids, and others weak acids?

Although acids such as hydochloric acid are **strong acids**, other acids, such as citric acid, are **weak acids**. Weak acids are not harmful, even when in concentrated solutions.

| Examples of strong acids | Examples of weak acids |
|---|---|
| hydrochloric acid | ethanoic acid (found in vinegar) |
| nitric acid | citric acid (found in citrus fruits) |
| sulfuric acid | carbonic acid (found in rainwater, fizzy drinks) |

Acids must dissolve in water to show their acidic properties. That is because all acids ionise (split up) in water to form H⁺(aq) ions and negative ions. It is the H⁺(aq) ions that all acidic solutions have in common. For example, in hydrochloric acid, all the HCl molecules ionise completely in water:

$$HCl(aq) \rightarrow H^+(aq) + Cl^-(aq)$$

However, in weak acids, most of the molecules stay as they are and do not release their H⁺ ions into the solution. This reaction is reversible for weak acids, unlike the ionisation of a strong acid. This means some molecules will split to form H⁺ ions and negative ions, but others will re-join to form the whole molecule again. A position of **equilibrium** is reached in which both whole molecules (the majority) and their ions (the minority) are present. So, in ethanoic acid you get:

$$\underset{\text{ethanoic acid}}{CH_3COOH(aq)} \rightleftharpoons \underset{\text{ethanoate ions}}{CH_3COO^-(aq)} + \underset{\text{hydrogen ions}}{H^+(aq)}$$

Therefore, given two aqueous solutions of equal concentration, the strong acid will have a higher concentration of H⁺(aq) ions than the solution of the weak acid. So, a weak acid has a higher pH value (and hence reacts more slowly with a metal carbonate).

## Practical

### Comparing ethanoic acid and hydrochloric acid

Ethanoic acid is a weak acid and hydrochloric acid is a strong acid. Write down your observations from these two tests to compare solutions of ethanoic acid with hydrochloric acid, both with the same concentration.

a Take the pH of solutions of both acids.

b Add a little sodium carbonate to solutions of both acids.

- Why did you use the same concentrations of each acid in the experiment?

**Safety:** Wear eye protection.

## Synoptic link

For more information about reversible reactions at equilibrium, see Topic C8.8.

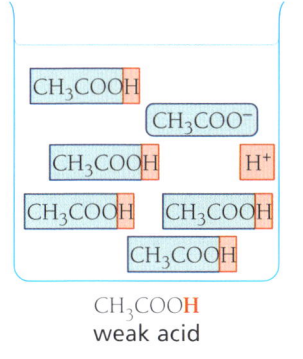

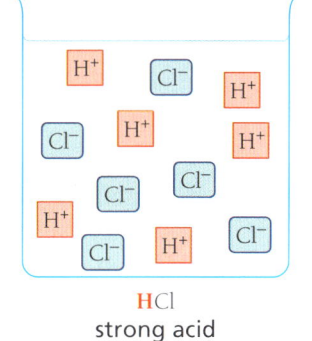

**Figure 1** Weak acids do not ionise completely so they only release a few $H^+$ ions. Strong acids ionise completely

## How are pH values related to the concentration of $H^+(aq)$ ions?

The pH of a 0.10 mol/dm³ solution of dilute hydrochloric acid is 1.0. Remember that all acidic solutions contain $H^+(aq)$ ions. In this solution of hydrochloric acid, the concentration of hydrogen ions, $H^+(aq)$, is also 0.10 mol/dm³, because HCl(aq) ionises completely in solution.

If you make the solution ten times more dilute, the concentration of HCl(aq) would be 0.010 mol/dm³. This has a pH of 2, which is less acidic. If you diluted the solution again to a concentration of 0.0010 mol/dm³, the pH would be 3. Putting these data in a table helps you see the pattern:

| Concentration of $H^+(aq)$ ions in mol/dm³ | pH value |
|---|---|
| 0.10 | 1.0 |
| 0.010 | 2.0 |
| 0.0010 | 3.0 |
| 0.00010 | 4.0 |

As the concentration of hydrogen ions, $H^+(aq)$, decreases by a factor of 10 (i.e., an order of magnitude), the pH value increases by one unit. Therefore, *increasing* the concentration of $H^+$ ions by a factor of 10 (i.e., an order of magnitude) *decreases* the pH by one unit.

## Maths

The pH value can be related to the concentration of $H^+(aq)$ ions expressed in standard form.

Using the values in the table, with concentrations in standard form, you get:

| Concentration of $H^+(aq)$ ions in mol/dm³ | pH value |
|---|---|
| $1.0 \times 10^{-1}$ | 1.0 |
| $1.0 \times 10^{-2}$ | 2.0 |
| $1.0 \times 10^{-3}$ | 3.0 |
| $1.0 \times 10^{-4}$ | 4.0 |

So, looking at the concentration of $H^+(aq)$ ions, if you take minus the value of the power to which 10 is raised, it gives you the pH value of the solution.

## Metacognition

Carrying on the trend, construct a table like the one above for substances with pH values of 8–14. Comment on the concentrations in your table. Are you confident working with negative numbers in standard form and orders of magnitude? (See Maths Skills MS1b and MS2d for support.)

## Summary questions

1. **a** Describe the trend in pH number up to 7 and then after 7. *1 MARK*
   **b** As the pH value increases by one unit, what happens to the concentration of hydrogen ions in a solution? *1 MARK*
2. **a** Determine the pH of a $1.0 \times 10^{-5}$ mol/dm³ solution of dilute hydrochloric acid. *1 MARK*
   **b** A solution of sodium chloride is neutral. Calculate the concentration of hydrogen ions in the solution. Give your answer in mol/dm³ as a decimal and in standard form. *2 MARKS*
3. Explain why it is possible to have a very dilute solution of a strong acid with a lower pH value than a concentrated solution of a weak acid. *4 MARKS*

## Key points

- Aqueous solutions of weak acids have a higher pH value than solutions of strong acids with the same concentration.
- As the pH decreases by one unit, the hydrogen ion concentration of the solution increases by a factor of 10 (i.e., one order of magnitude).

# C5 Chemical changes

## Practice questions

1   a   Identify which of the following pairs of substances will react.
        i    carbon + copper(II) oxide                1 MARK
        ii   iron + zinc nitrate                      1 MARK
        iii  iron + magnesium oxide                   1 MARK
        iv   magnesium + copper(II) sulfate           1 MARK
    b   Write balanced symbol equations, including state symbols, for the pairs that will react.    6 MARKS

2   The reaction between aluminium powder and iron(III) oxide is used in the rail industry.
    a   i   Write a word equation and a balanced symbol equation for the reaction that takes place.    3 MARKS
        ii  What is this type of reaction called?    1 MARK
    b   Compare the reaction described above with the reaction you would expect to see between powdered aluminium and copper(II) oxide.    1 MARK
    c   Predict what would happen if you heated a mixture of aluminium oxide and iron.    1 MARK
    d   Explain why the uses of aluminium metal are surprising, given its position in the reactivity series.    2 MARKS

3   Lead is often found in the ore called galena, which contains lead sulfide, PbS. Before reduction with carbon, the lead sulfide must be converted into lead oxide, PbO, by roasting the ore. This reaction with oxygen from the air also produces sulfur dioxide gas.
    a   Write a word equation for the roasting of lead sulfide.    1 MARK
    b   Write a balanced symbol equation, including state symbols, for the reaction in part a.    3 MARKS
    c   Lead oxide is reduced by heating with carbon. Write a balanced symbol equation for this reaction, assuming $CO_2$ is produced.    3 MARKS

4   Nickel(II) sulfate crystals can be made from an insoluble oxide base and sulfuric acid.
    a   i    Name the insoluble base that can be used to make nickel(II) sulfate.    1 MARK
        ii   Write a balanced symbol equation, including state symbols, to show the reaction.    3 MARKS
        iii  State what type of reaction is shown in part ii.    1 MARK
    b   Describe how you could obtain crystals of nickel(II) sulfate from the reaction in part a ii.    6 MARKS

5   Write balanced symbol equations, including state symbols, to describe the reactions below.
    a   lithium hydroxide solution (in excess) and dilute sulfuric acid    3 MARKS
    b   iron(III) oxide (an insoluble base) and dilute nitric acid    3 MARKS
    c   zinc metal and dilute hydrochloric acid    3 MARKS

6   Imagine that a new metal, given the symbol **X**, has been discovered. It lies between calcium and magnesium in the reactivity series.
    a   Describe the reaction of excess metal **X** with dilute sulfuric acid and give the word and balanced symbol equations (metal **X** forms 2+ ions).    5 MARKS
    b   Explain why you cannot be sure how metal **X** will react with cold water.    2 MARKS
    c   Metal **X** is added to a solution of copper(II) nitrate.
        i    Explain what you would expect to see happen, including a balanced symbol equation with state symbols.    3 MARKS
        ii   **H** Write an ionic equation, including state symbols, showing what happens in the change.    3 MARKS
        iii  **H** Explain which species is oxidised and which is reduced, using ionic half equations.    4 MARKS
    d   Another new metal, **Y**, does not react with water but there is a slight reaction with warm dilute acid.
        i    Where would you place metal **Y** in the reactivity series?    1 MARK
        ii   Explain what you would expect to happen if metal **Y** was added to magnesium sulfate solution.    3 MARKS

# C5 Chemical changes

# Exam-style questions

**01** This question is about the reactivity of metals.
A student dropped five different metals **V**, **W**, **X**, **Y**, and **Z** in water.
Four of the metals reacted to produce a metal hydroxide and hydrogen gas.
The reactions of the five metals are shown in **Figure 1**.

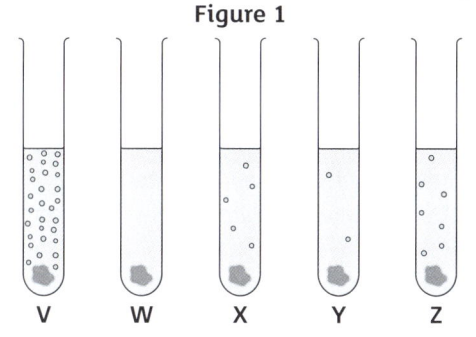

Figure 1

V    W    X    Y    Z

**01.1** Use the information in **Figure 1** to put metals **V**, **W**, **X**, **Y**, and **Z** in order of reactivity. **2 MARKS**

**01.2** Describe the test for hydrogen gas. **2 MARKS**

**01.3** Give two variables that should be controlled. **2 MARKS**

**01.4** Element **V** is a Group 2 metal.
What is the formula for the hydroxide of **V**? **1 MARK**
**A** VOH  **B** V$_2$OH  **C** V(OH)$_2$  **D** V(OH)$_3$

**02** This question is about the preparation of copper sulfate crystals.

Copper metal does not react with dilute sulfuric acid. Copper sulfate can be prepared by reacting copper oxide, CuO, with dilute sulfuric acid, H$_2$SO$_4$.

**02.1** Suggest why copper metal does not react with dilute sulfuric acid. **2 MARKS**

A student used this method to make crystals of copper sulfate.

**Step 1:** Place dilute sulfuric acid into a beaker. Heat for one minute.
**Step 2:** Add one spatula of copper oxide powder.
**Step 3:** Pour the copper sulfate solution into an evaporating basin and heat until all the water has evaporated.

**02.2** Give a reason the student heated the sulfuric acid in **Step 1**. **1 MARK**

**02.3** At the end of the method the student tested the solution with universal indicator paper. The solution was still acidic. Give a colour for universal indicator in acid. **1 MARK**

**02.4** Give an improvement to **Step 2** to ensure all the acid is used up. **2 MARKS**

**02.5** Describe how **Step 3** can be improved to produce large crystals of copper sulfate. **2 MARKS**

**03** The colours of three metals and three metal sulfates are shown in **Table 1**.

Table 1

| Metal | Colour of metal | Formula of the sulfate | Colour of metal sulfate |
|---|---|---|---|
| iron, Fe | grey | FeSO$_4$ | pale green solution |
| copper, Cu | brown | CuSO$_4$ | blue solution |
| magnesium, Mg | silver | MgSO$_4$ | colourless solution |

Use your knowledge of the reactivity series and the information in **Table 1** to give the observations when the following are mixed together.

**03.1** Iron nail with copper sulfate solution. **2 MARKS**

**03.2** Magnesium ribbon with iron sulfate solution. **2 MARKS**

**03.3** Explain why no observable change was seen when a piece of copper was dropped into magnesium sulfate solution. **2 MARKS**

**03.4** 🇭 Write an ionic equation for the reaction between iron and copper sulfate solution in **03.1**. **2 MARKS**

**03.5** 🇭 Write a half equation to show the reduction of Fe$^{2+}$ ions in **03.2**. Use the half equation to explain why Fe$^{2+}$ ions are reduced. **2 MARKS**

**04** Magnesium carbonate reacts with dilute nitric acid to form the soluble salt magnesium nitrate. The equation for the reaction is:
MgCO$_3$(s) + 2HNO$_3$(aq) →
$\qquad$ Mg(NO$_3$)$_2$(aq) + H$_2$O(l) + CO$_2$(g)

**04.1** Plan a method to produce pure, dry crystals of magnesium nitrate. **6 MARKS**

**04.2** 🇭 Magnesium also reacts with dilute ethanoic acid. Nitric acid is a strong acid and ethanoic acid is a weak acid.
What difference would you expect to see if magnesium carbonate were reacted with ethanoic acid of the same concentration as the nitric acid? **2 MARKS**

**04.3** 🇭 The formula of ethanoic acid is CH$_3$COOH. Write an equation to show the ionisation of ethanoic acid. **2 MARKS**

**04.4** 🇭 A solution of ethanoic acid has a pH of 4 and a solution of nitric acid has a pH of 1. Determine how many times greater the concentration of H$^+$ ions is in the nitric acid compared to the concentration of hydrogen ions in the ethanoic acid. **1 MARK**

85

# C6 Electrolysis

## C6.1 Introduction to electrolysis

### Learning objectives

*After this topic, you should know:*
- what happens in electrolysis
- the type of substances that can be electrolysed
- the products of electrolysis.

### Practical

**Electrolysis of zinc chloride**
- When does the bulb light up?
- What is observed at each electrode?

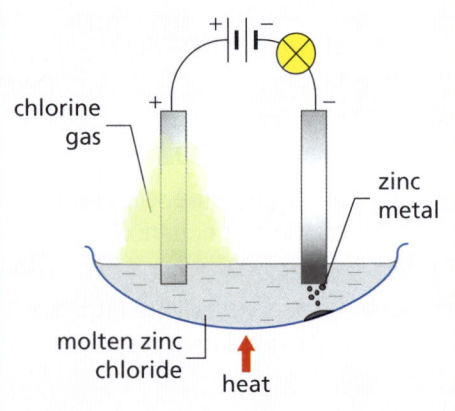

▲ **Figure 1** Passing electricity through molten zinc chloride. Zinc metal forms on one electrode and pale green chlorine gas is given off at the other as the electrolyte (zinc chloride) is broken down by electrolysis

**Safety:** Warn asthmatics. Wear chemical splash-proof eye protection. Chlorine is toxic. Carry out in a fume cupboard. Zinc chloride is corrosive.

### Synoptic links

Look back at Topic C3.3 and Topic C3.4 to remind yourself about ionic bonding and the properties of ionic compounds.

The word electrolysis means 'breaking down using electricity'. In electrolysis you use an electric current to break down an ionic compound. The compound that is broken down by electrolysis is called the **electrolyte**.

To set up an electrical circuit for electrolysis, you have two electrodes that dip into the electrolyte, with a gap between them. The electrodes are conducting rods. One of these is connected to the positive terminal of a power supply. This positive electrode is called the **anode**. The other electrode is connected to the negative terminal and is called the **cathode** (Figure 1).

The electrodes are often made of an unreactive (or **inert**) substance, such as graphite or sometimes expensive platinum metal. This is so that the electrodes do not react with the electrolyte or with the products made in electrolysis.

**During electrolysis, positively charged ions move to the cathode (negative electrode). At the same time, the negative ions move to the anode (positive electrode), as opposite charges attract.**

When the ions reach the electrodes, they lose their charge and become elements. At the electrodes, gases may be given off or metals may be deposited. This depends on the compound used and whether it is molten or dissolved in water (see Topic C6.2).

The equation shows how electricity breaks down zinc chloride into zinc and chlorine:

$$\text{zinc chloride} \rightarrow \text{zinc} + \text{chlorine}$$
$$ZnCl_2(l) \rightarrow Zn(s/l) + Cl_2(g)$$

- Zinc chloride is an ionic compound. Ionic compounds do not conduct electricity when they are solid, as their ions are in fixed positions in their giant lattice.

- However, once an ionic compound is melted, the ions are free to move around within the hot liquid and carry their charge towards the electrodes. Zinc chloride melts at 290 °C.

- The positive zinc ions, $Zn^{2+}$, move towards the cathode (negative electrode).

- At the same time, the negatively charged chloride ions, $Cl^-$, move towards the anode (positive electrode).

Notice the state symbols in the equation. They tell you that the zinc chloride is molten, so it is a *liquid* at the temperature in the evaporating dish, *solid* zinc coats the tip of one electrode (and melts if the temperature of the electrolyte reaches 420 °C), and chlorine *gas* is given off at the other.

# C6 Electrolysis

## Electrolysis of solutions

A lot of ionic substances have very high melting points, so it takes a lot of energy to melt them and free the ions to move to electrodes in electrolysis. However, some ionic substances dissolve in water and when this happens, the ions also become free to move around.

When electrolysing ionic compounds in solution, and not as molten compounds, it is more difficult to predict what will be formed. This is because water also forms ions, so the products at each electrode are not always exactly what you expect (see Topic C6.2). In electrolysis only metals of very low reactivity, below hydrogen in the reactivity series, are deposited from their aqueous solutions.

When you electrolyse an aqueous solution of copper(II) bromide, copper ions, $Cu^{2+}$, move to the cathode (negative electrode). The bromide ions, $Br^-$, move to the anode (positive electrode). Copper(II) bromide is split into its elements at the electrodes (Figure 2).

The equation for this electrolysis is:

copper(II) bromide → copper + bromine
$CuBr_2(aq)$ → $Cu(s)$ + $Br_2(aq)$

The state symbols in the equation tell you that the copper bromide is dissolved in water, the copper is formed as a solid, and the bromine formed dissolves in the water.

Covalent compounds cannot usually be electrolysed unless they react (ionise) in water to form ions. For example, acids in water always contain $H^+(aq)$ ions plus negatively charged aqueous ions.

▲ **Figure 2** If copper(II) bromide is dissolved in water, it can be decomposed by electrolysis. Copper metal, $Cu(s)$, is formed at the cathode (negative electrode). Brown bromine, $Br_2(aq)$, appears in solution around the anode (positive electrode)

## Summary questions

1. **a** Define electrolysis. *1 MARK*
   **b** Give the general name used for the substance broken down by electrolysis. *1 MARK*
   **c** Name the type of bonding present in compounds that can be electrolysed. *1 MARK*
2. Predict the products formed at the cathode and anode when the following compounds are melted and then electrolysed:
   **a** zinc iodide *1 MARK*
   **b** lithium bromide *1 MARK*
   **c** iron(III) fluoride *1 MARK*
   **d** sodium oxide *1 MARK*
   **e** potassium chloride. *1 MARK*
3. **a** Which of the following solutions would deposit a metal at the cathode during electrolysis?
   $KBr(aq)$     $CaCl_2(aq)$     $FeBr_2(aq)$
   $CuCl_2(aq)$     $Na_2SO_4(aq)$     $AgNO_3(aq)$ *2 MARKS*
   **b** Give a reason for your answer to part **a**. *1 MARK*
4. Write a balanced symbol equation, including state symbols, for the electrolytic decomposition of molten sodium chloride. *3 MARKS*
5. Solid ionic substances do not conduct electricity. Using words and diagrams, explain why they conduct electricity when molten or in aqueous solution, but not when solid. *3 MARKS*

### Synoptic links

Remind yourself of the relative reactivity of metals and hydrogen in Topic C5.1 and Topic C5.2.

### Key points

- Electrolysis breaks down a substance using electricity.
- Ionic compounds can only be electrolysed when they are molten or dissolved in water. This is because their ions are then free to move and carry their charge to the electrodes.
- In electrolysis, positive ions move to the cathode (negative electrode), while negative ions move to the anode (positive electrode).

87

# C6.2 Changes at the electrodes

### Learning objectives

*After this topic, you should know:*
- what happens to the ions during electrolysis
- how water affects the products of electrolysis
- (H) how you can represent the reactions at each electrode using half equations.

During electrolysis, mobile ions move towards the electrodes. The direction they move in depends on their charge. As you saw in Topic C6.1, positive ions move towards the cathode (negative electrode) and negative ions move towards the anode (positive electrode).

When ions reach an electrode, they either lose or gain electrons, depending on their charge (Figure 1).

Negatively charged ions *lose* electrons to become neutral atoms.
Positively charged ions *gain* electrons to become neutral atoms.

The easiest way to think about this is to look at an example.

Think about the electrolysis of molten lead bromide, $PbBr_2$ (Figure 2). The lead ions, $Pb^{2+}$, move towards the negative electrode (cathode). When they get there, each ion gains two electrons from the power supply to become a neutral lead atom.

> Gaining electrons is called **reduction**. The lead ions are **reduced**. (H)
> Reduction is simply another way of saying 'gaining electrons'.

The negatively charged bromide ions, $Br^-$, move towards the positive electrode (anode). Once there, each ion loses its one extra electron to become a neutral bromine atom. Two bromine atoms then form a covalent bond to make a bromine molecule, $Br_2$.

> Losing electrons is called **oxidation**. The bromide ions are **oxidised**. (H)
> Oxidation is another way of saying 'losing electrons'.

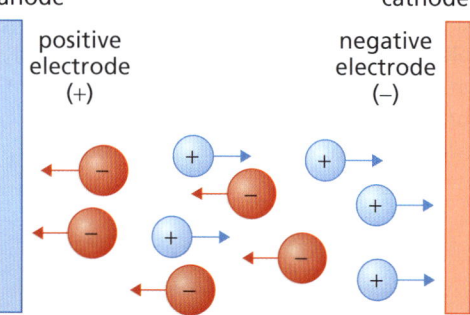

▲ **Figure 1** An ion always moves towards the oppositely charged electrode

## Half equations (H)

You represent what is happening at each electrode using **half equations**. At the cathode (negative electrode) you get reduction of the positive ions:

$$Pb^{2+} + 2e^- \rightarrow Pb$$

At the anode (positive electrode) you get oxidation of the negative ions:

$$2Br^- \rightarrow Br_2 + 2e^-$$

Sometimes half equations at the anode are written to show the electrons being removed from negative ions, like this:

$$2Br^- - 2e^- \rightarrow Br_2$$

You can write the half equation for negative ions either way. They both show the same oxidation of the negatively charged ions.

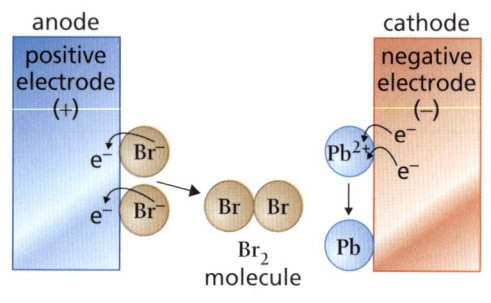

▲ **Figure 2** Changes at the anode and the cathode in the electrolysis of molten lead bromide

### Study tip

(H) Oxidation and reduction reactions don't have to involve oxygen. More generally they involve the transfer of electrons.

Remember **OILRIG** –
**O**xidation **I**s **L**oss (of electrons),
**R**eduction **I**s **G**ain (of electrons).

## The effect of water

In aqueous solutions, electrolysis is more complex, because of the ions formed by water as it ionises:

$$H_2O(l) \rightleftharpoons H^+(aq) + OH^-(aq)$$
water — hydrogen ions — hydroxide ions

88

# C6 Electrolysis

There is a rule for working out what will happen. Remember that if two elements can be produced at an electrode, the less reactive element will usually be formed. In aqueous solutions, there will usually be positively charged metal ions, as well as H⁺(aq) ions (from water), that are attracted to the cathode (negative electrode).

Figure 3 shows what happens in the electrolysis of a solution of a potassium compound. Hydrogen is less reactive than potassium, so hydrogen gas is produced at the cathode rather than potassium metal.

At the cathode (−):

$$2H^+(aq) + 2e^- \rightarrow H_2(g)$$

So, what happens at the anode in the electrolysis of aqueous solutions?

Hydroxide ions, OH⁻(aq), from water are often discharged. When hydroxide ions are discharged, you see oxygen gas given off at the anode (positive electrode).

At the anode (+):

$$4OH^-(aq) \rightarrow 2H_2O(l) + O_2(g) + 4e^-$$

This happens unless the solution contains a reasonably high concentration of a halide (Group 7) ion, such as Cl⁻(aq). In this case, the halide ion is discharged, and the halogen is formed:

At the anode (+):

$$2Cl^-(aq) \rightarrow Cl_2(g) + 2e^-$$

So, the order of discharge at the anode (starting with the 'easiest') is:

**halide ion > hydroxide > all other negatively charged ions**

▲ **Figure 3** Here is the cathode in the electrolysis of a solution of a potassium compound. Hydrogen is less reactive than potassium, so hydrogen gas is given off at the electrode. If there were copper ions in solution instead of potassium ions, hydrogen gas would not be formed at the cathode. This is because copper is less reactive than hydrogen, so copper metal would form on the cathode and hydrogen ions would remain in solution

## Synoptic link

For more information on reduction and oxidation in terms of electron transfer, look back to Topic C5.2.

## Summary questions

1. On which electrodes would oxygen and hydrogen be produced during electrolysis? **2 MARKS**
2. Predict what is formed at each electrode in the electrolysis of:
   a. molten lithium oxide **1 MARK**
   b. copper chloride solution **1 MARK**
   c. sodium sulfate solution. **1 MARK**
3. a i Describe how negatively charged ions become neutral atoms in electrolysis. **1 MARK**
   ii Ⓗ Identify the process described in part **a i**. **1 MARK**
   b i Describe how positively charged ions become neutral atoms in electrolysis. **1 MARK**
   ii Ⓗ Identify the process described in part **b i**. **1 MARK**
4. Ⓗ Copy and, where necessary, balance the following half equations:
   a $Cl^- \rightarrow Cl_2 + e^-$ **1 MARK**
   b $Mg^{2+} + e^- \rightarrow Mg$ **1 MARK**
   c $Al^{3+} + e^- \rightarrow Al$ **1 MARK**
   d $K^+ + e^- \rightarrow K$ **1 MARK**
   e $H^+ + e^- \rightarrow H_2$ **1 MARK**
   f $OH^- \rightarrow O_2 + H_2O + e^-$. **1 MARK**

## Key points

- In electrolysis, the ions move towards the oppositely charged electrodes.
- When electrolysis happens in aqueous solution, at the cathode the less reactive element, either hydrogen or the metal, is usually produced. At the anode, you get either:
  - oxygen gas given off, from discharged hydroxide ions produced from water, or
  - a halogen produced if the electrolyte is a solution of a halide.
- Ⓗ At the negative electrode (cathode), positive ions gain electrons, so are reduced.
- Ⓗ At the positive electrode (anode), negative ions lose their extra electrons, so are oxidised.

89

# C6.3 The extraction of aluminium

### Learning objectives

*After this topic, you should know:*
- why some metals are extracted with carbon and others by electrolysis
- the process of extracting aluminium from its ore
- 🄗 the half equation at each electrode during the electrolysis of aluminium oxide.

You already know that aluminium is a very important metal. The uses of the metal or its alloys include:
- pans
- overhead power cables
- aeroplanes
- cooking foil
- drink cans
- window and patio door frames
- bicycle frames and car bodies.

Aluminium is quite a reactive metal (look back at the reactions of metals and the reactivity series in Topic C5.1 and Topic C5.3). It is less reactive than magnesium, but more reactive than zinc or iron. Carbon is not reactive enough to use in its extraction, as it cannot displace aluminium from its compounds. So, you must use electrolysis. The compound electrolysed is molten aluminium oxide, $Al_2O_3$.

You get aluminium oxide from the ore called bauxite. The ore is mined by open cast mining, digging it directly from the surface. Bauxite contains mainly aluminium oxide. However, it is mixed with other rocky impurities, so the first step is to separate aluminium oxide from the ore. The impurities contain a lot of iron(III) oxide. This makes the waste solution from the separation process a rusty brown colour. The brown wastewater must be stored in large lagoons.

## Electrolysis of aluminium oxide

The electrolysis of aluminium oxide to extract the aluminium metal requires a lot of energy. Once purified, the aluminium oxide must be melted. This enables the ions to move to the electrodes.

Unfortunately, aluminium oxide has a very high melting point of 2050 °C. However, chemists have found a way of saving at least some energy. They mix the aluminium oxide with molten cryolite. Cryolite is another ionic compound. The molten mixture can be electrolysed at about 850 °C. The large amount of electrical energy that is transferred to the mixture keeps it molten (Figure 3).

The overall reaction is:

$$\text{aluminium oxide} \xrightarrow{\text{electrolysis}} \text{aluminium} + \text{oxygen}$$
$$2Al_2O_3(l) \longrightarrow 4Al(l) + 3O_2(g)$$

- Aluminium forms at the negative electrode (cathode).
- Oxygen is produced at the positive electrode (anode).

▲ **Figure 1** Aluminium alloys in this bike have a low density, but are very strong

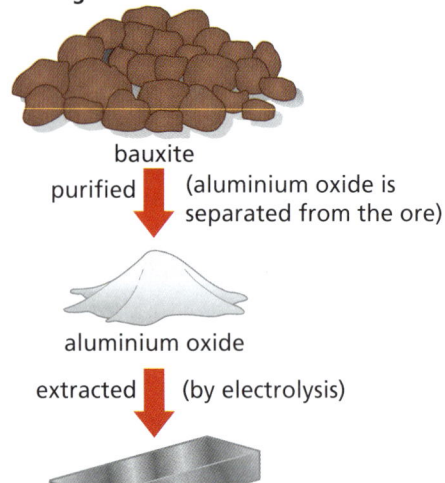

**extracting aluminium from its ore**

bauxite
purified ⬇ (aluminium oxide is separated from the ore)

aluminium oxide
extracted ⬇ (by electrolysis)

aluminium metal

▲ **Figure 2** Extracting aluminium from its ore. This process requires a lot of energy. The purification of aluminium oxide from the ore makes aluminium hydroxide. This is separated from the impurities, but then must be heated to turn it back to pure aluminium oxide. Then even more energy is needed to melt and electrolyse the aluminium oxide

## C6 Electrolysis

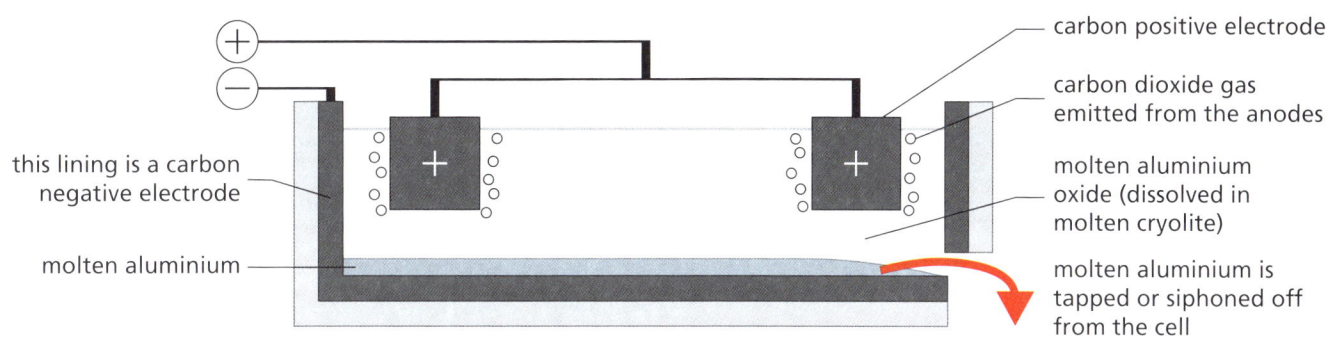

▲ **Figure 3** The setup used in the extraction of aluminium by electrolysis

### At the cathode (negative electrode):

Each aluminium ion, $Al^{3+}$, gains three electrons. The ions turn into aluminium atoms. The $Al^{3+}$ ions are reduced (as they gain electrons) to form Al atoms:

$$Al^{3+}(l) + 3e^- \rightarrow Al(l)$$

The aluminium metal formed is molten at the temperature of the cell and collects at the bottom. It is siphoned or tapped off.

### At the anode (positive electrode):

Each oxide ion, $O^{2-}$, loses two electrons. The ions turn into oxygen atoms. The $O^{2-}$ ions are oxidised (as they lose electrons) to form oxygen atoms. These bond in pairs to form molecules of oxygen gas, $O_2$:

$$2O^{2-}(l) \rightarrow O_2(g) + 4e^-$$

The oxygen reacts with the hot carbon anodes, making carbon dioxide gas:

$$C(s) + O_2(g) \rightarrow CO_2(g)$$

So, the carbon anodes gradually burn away and need to be replaced regularly.

> **Synoptic link**
>
> Revisit Figure 3 in Topic C5.3 to see aluminium's position in the reactivity series.

### Summary questions

1. **a** Explain why aluminium oxide must be molten for electrolysis to take place. **2 MARKS**
   **b** Why is aluminium oxide dissolved in molten cryolite in the extraction of aluminium? **2 MARKS**
2. Why are the carbon anodes replaced regularly in the industrial electrolysis of aluminium oxide? **2 MARKS**
3. **a** Write half equations for the changes at each electrode in the electrolysis of molten aluminium oxide. **2 MARKS**
   **b** Explain which ions are oxidised and which ions are reduced in the electrolysis of molten aluminium oxide. **2 MARKS**
4. **a** Explain why the extraction of aluminium requires so much energy. **3 MARKS**
   **b** Suggest why aluminium metal was only discovered in the early 1800s, despite it being the most common metallic element in the Earth's crust. **3 MARKS**
   **c** Calculate the maximum mass of aluminium metal that can be extracted from 25.5 tonnes of aluminium oxide. ($A_r$ values: Al = 27, O = 16) **3 MARKS**

> **Key points**
>
> - Aluminium oxide is electrolysed in the extraction of aluminium metal.
> - The aluminium oxide is mixed with molten cryolite to lower its melting point, reducing the energy needed.
> - Aluminium forms at the cathode (negative electrode) and oxygen forms at the anode (positive electrode).
> - The carbon anodes are replaced regularly as they gradually burn away as the oxygen reacts with them, forming carbon dioxide gas.

# C6.4 Electrolysis of aqueous solutions

### Learning objectives

After this topic, you should know:
- how to predict the products of the electrolysis of an aqueous solution
- how to investigate the electrolysis of a solution using inert electrodes
- **H** the half equation at each electrode during the electrolysis of an aqueous solution.

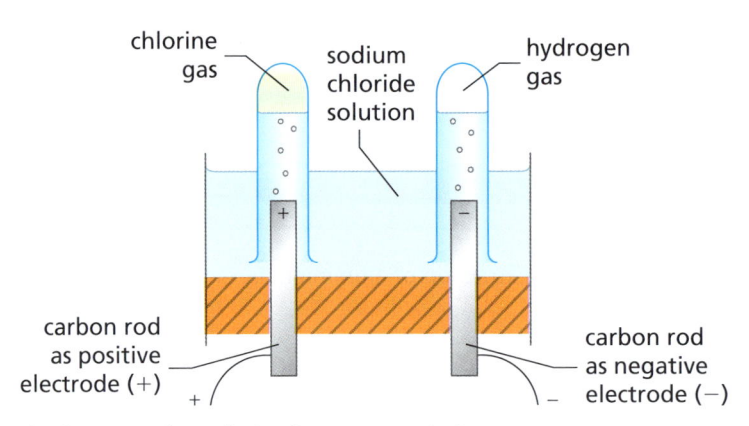

▲ **Figure 1** Electrolysis of aqueous solutions

The electrolysis of brine (concentrated sodium chloride solution) is a very important industrial process. When brine is electrolysed, you get three useful products that are used to make other chemicals:

- chlorine gas is produced at the anode (positive electrode)
- hydrogen gas is produced at the cathode (negative electrode)
- sodium hydroxide solution is also formed.

You can summarise the electrolysis of brine as:

sodium chloride solution →(electrolysis) hydrogen gas + chlorine gas + sodium hydroxide solution

## At the positive electrode (anode)

The negative chloride ions, $Cl^-$, are attracted to the positive electrode. When they get there, they each lose one electron. The chlorine atoms bond together in pairs and are given off as chlorine gas, $Cl_2$.

**H**

The half equation at the anode is:
$$2Cl^-(aq) \rightarrow Cl_2(g) + 2e^-$$
This can also be written as: $2Cl^-(aq) - 2e^- \rightarrow Cl_2(g)$
The chloride ions are oxidised, as they lose electrons.

## At the negative electrode (cathode)

There are $H^+$ ions in brine, formed when water breaks down:
$$H_2O(l) \rightleftharpoons H^+(aq) + OH^-(aq)$$

These positive hydrogen ions are attracted to the negative electrode. The sodium ions, $Na^+(aq)$, are also attracted to the same electrode. But remember in Topic C6.2, you saw what happens when two ions are attracted to an electrode. It is the less reactive element that gets discharged. In this case, hydrogen ions are discharged, and sodium ions stay in solution as aqueous ions.

When the $H^+$ ions reach the negative electrode, they each gain one electron. The hydrogen atoms formed bond together in pairs and are given off as hydrogen gas, $H_2$.

### Metacognition

Electrolysis is a difficult concept to master. Go back and read all four of the 'Key points' boxes in this chapter. Then go through the statements in each box again, making lists of points you are 'confident you understand', points that you are 'not sure' about, and points you 'need to get help' to understand.

You can make a grid with the first two columns as shown in the table to share with your teacher:

| Topic | Key point |
|-------|-----------|
| 6.1   | 1st       |
|       | 2nd       |
|       | 3rd       |
| 6.2   | 1st       |

## C6 Electrolysis

The half equation at the cathode is:
$$2H^+(aq) + 2e^- \rightarrow H_2(g)$$
The hydrogen ions are reduced, as they each gain an electron.

### The remaining solution

You can test the solution around the cathode (negative electrode) with an acid/base indicator. It shows that the solution is alkaline. This is because you can think of brine as containing aqueous ions of $Na^+$ and $Cl^-$ (from salt) and $H^+$ and $OH^-$ (from water). The $Cl^-(aq)$ and $H^+(aq)$ ions are removed during electrolysis. So, this leaves a solution containing $Na^+(aq)$ and $OH^-(aq)$ ions, which is a solution of alkaline sodium hydroxide, $NaOH(aq)$.

### Practical

**Investigating the electrolysis of a solution**

You can now use your knowledge and understanding of electrolysis to investigate the electrolysis of different aqueous solutions using inert electrodes.

Plan your investigation. Think about:
- Which solutions will you test?
- Are there any safety issues with your plan? Are the solutions hazardous? What about the gases that might be given off? How can you reduce any risks?

Predict what products will be formed at each electrode, and explain your choices.
- How will you test and identify any gases formed at the electrodes (Topic C10.3)?

After collecting and recording the data, evaluate your investigation.

If you have time, you can investigate whether changing the concentration of some solutions affects the products formed.

**Safety:** Do not start any practical work until your teacher has checked your plan.

### Summary questions

1. Name the *three* products made when you electrolyse sodium chloride solution (brine). **3 MARKS**
2. Describe how to electrolyse concentrated sodium chloride solution (brine) in terms of ions moving. **6 MARKS**
3. For the electrolysis of sodium chloride solution (brine), write half equations, including state symbols, for the reactions:
   a at the anode **2 MARKS**   b at the cathode. **2 MARKS**
4. You can also electrolyse **molten** sodium chloride.
   a Compare the products formed with those from the electrolysis of sodium chloride solution. **2 MARKS**
   b Explain fully any differences. **4 MARKS**
5. A sodium metal manufacturer completely electrolyses 234 tonnes of sodium chloride. Calculate the maximum mass of sodium metal that could be extracted. ($A_r$ values: Na = 23, Cl = 35.5) **1 MARK**

### Study tip

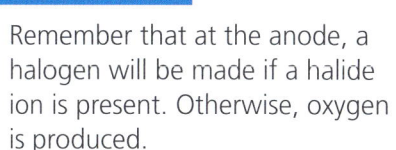

Remember that at the anode, a halogen will be made if a halide ion is present. Otherwise, oxygen is produced.

▲ **Figure 2** Bleach is made from chlorine and sodium hydroxide obtained from the electrolysis of a concentrated solution of sodium chloride (brine)

▲ **Figure 3** The chlorine made when you electrolyse brine in industry is used to kill bacteria in drinking water, and in some swimming pools

### Synoptic link

You will find the tests for gases in Topic C10.3.

### Key points

- When you electrolyse sodium chloride solution (brine), you get chlorine gas and hydrogen gas given off at the electrodes, plus sodium hydroxide solution.
- Hydrogen is produced at the cathode (−), as $H^+(aq)$ ions are discharged from solution in preference to $Na^+(aq)$ ions.
- Chlorine is produced at the anode (+), as $Cl^-(aq)$ ions are discharged from solution in preference to $OH^-(aq)$ ions.

93

# C6 Electrolysis

## Practice questions

1. For each of the following statements, choose whether it is the anode (+) or cathode (−) that is being referred to.
   a. Positive ions move towards this. **1 MARK**
   b. (H) Oxidation happens here. **1 MARK**
   c. This is connected to the negative terminal of the power supply. **1 MARK**
   d. This is connected to the positive terminal of the power supply. **1 MARK**
   e. (H) Reduction happens here. **1 MARK**
   f. Negative ions move towards this. **1 MARK**

2. a. Which of the following ions would move towards the anode (+) and which towards the cathode (−) during electrolysis?

   | potassium ions | oxide ions |
   | iodide ions | magnesium ions |
   | calcium ions | aluminium ions |
   | fluoride ions | bromide ions |

   **2 MARKS**

   b. (H) Write a half equation for the discharge of:
      i. magnesium ions **3 MARKS**
      ii. bromide ions. **3 MARKS**

3. The diagram shows the electrolysis of sodium chloride solution in the laboratory.

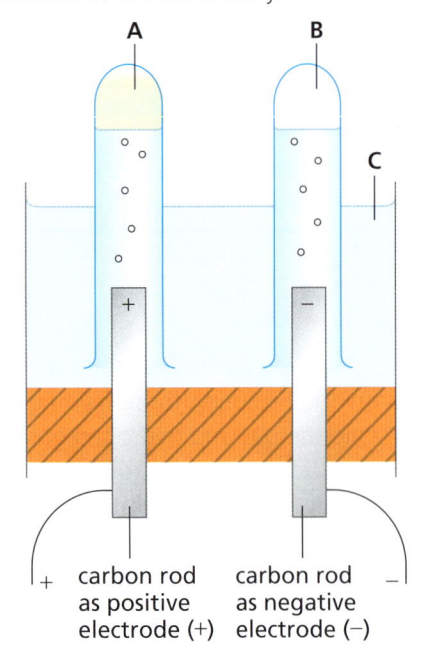

   a. Identify the products **A**, **B**, and **C** on the diagram. **3 MARKS**
   b. Give two uses for substance **A**. **2 MARKS**
   c. What would be the pH of the solution around the cathode? **1 MARK**
   d. Describe how you would carry out a positive test on product **B**. **1 MARK**
   e. (H) Write the half equations, including state symbols, for the changes at the anode and cathode. **6 MARKS**

4. Water can be slightly acidified and broken down into hydrogen and oxygen using electrolysis. The word equation for this reaction is:

   water → hydrogen + oxygen

   a. Write a balanced symbol equation for this reaction, including state symbols. **3 MARKS**
   b. In water, a small percentage of molecules ionise (split up). Write a balanced symbol equation, including state symbols, for the ionisation of water molecules. **3 MARKS**
   c. (H) Write half equations to show what happens at the positive and negative electrodes in the electrolysis of water. **3 MARKS**
   d. (H) When some water is electrolysed, it produces 0.20 moles of hydrogen gas. Calculate the mass of oxygen gas produced. **2 MARKS**
   e. During electrolysis, where does the energy needed to split water into hydrogen and oxygen come from? **1 MARK**

5. (H) Complete the following half equations:
   a. $Li^+ \rightarrow Li$ **1 MARK**
   b. $Sr^{2+} \rightarrow Sr$ **1 MARK**
   c. $F^- \rightarrow F_2$ **1 MARK**
   d. $O^{2-} \rightarrow O_2$ **1 MARK**

6. (H) 'Electrolysis can be thought of as a redox reaction.' Evaluate this statement by explaining the changes that take place at the anode and cathode during electrolysis, using an example of a molten ionic compound. Write half equations for the reactions occurring at each electrode. **6 MARKS**

# Exam-style questions

**01** This question is about the electrolysis of lead bromide, PbBr$_2$.
Lead bromide contains Pb$^{2+}$ and Br$^-$ ions.

The apparatus for the electrolysis of lead bromide is shown in **Figure 1**.

**Figure 1**

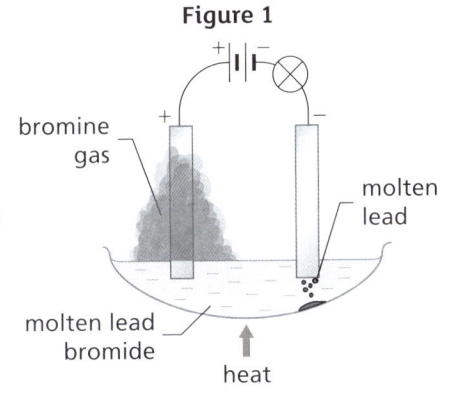

The electrodes were placed in solid lead bromide and the lead bromide was heated. The bulb did not light initially but lit when the lead bromide was completely molten.

**01.1** Explain why molten lead bromide conducts electricity. **2 MARKS**

**01.2** Explain why the metal in the wire conducts electricity. **2 MARKS**

**01.3** (H) Explain the formation of the brown gas at the anode (the positive electrode).
Include a half equation in your answer. **4 MARKS**

**01.4** (H) Explain the formation of the grey droplets at the cathode (the negative electrode).
Include a half equation in your answer. **4 MARKS**

**02** This question is about extracting metals.

**02.1** Iron can be extracted by reacting iron(III) oxide with carbon.
Aluminium cannot be extracted by reacting aluminium oxide with carbon.
Explain why. **2 MARKS**

Aluminium is extracted from aluminium oxide by electrolysis. The electrolysis of aluminium oxide Al$_2$O$_3$ is shown in **Figure 2**.
Aluminium oxide contains Al$^{3+}$ and O$^{2-}$ ions.

**Figure 2**

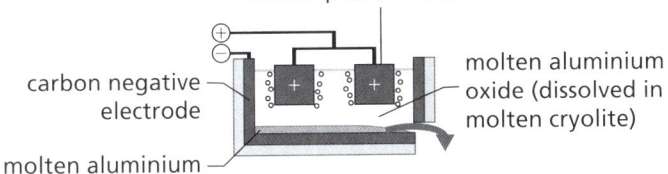

**02.2** Explain why molten aluminium oxide is dissolved in molten cryolite. **2 MARKS**

**02.3** (H) The positive electrodes need frequent replacement. Explain why. **4 MARKS**

**02.4** (H) Write a half equation to show how aluminium is formed at the negative electrode. **1 MARK**

**02.5** (H) Why are aluminium ions reduced? **1 MARK**

**03** This question is about the electrolysis of potassium bromide solution. The electrolysis of potassium bromide solution is shown in **Figure 3**.

**Figure 3**

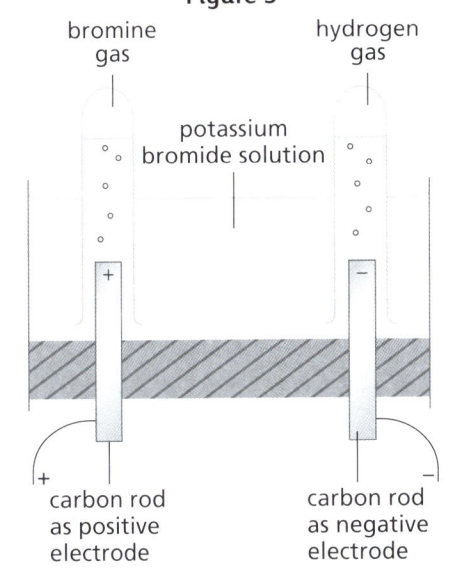

**03.1** Give the test and the result for hydrogen gas. **2 MARKS**

Potassium bromide solution can conduct electricity because the ions can move. Some electrodes are made of carbon in the form of graphite.

**03.2** Explain why electrodes that are made of graphite can conduct electricity. **2 MARKS**

**03.3** The solution contains K$^+$ ions and H$^+$ ions, which are both attracted to the negative electrode. Explain why hydrogen gas forms instead of potassium metal. **2 MARKS**

**03.4** A few drops of universal indicator were added to the solution. The universal indicator turned blue. Explain why. **2 MARKS**

**03.5** (H) Complete the half equation for the formation of bromine gas at the positive electrode. **2 MARKS**
Br$^-$ → Br$_2$

**03.6** (H) Complete the half equation for the formation of hydrogen gas at the negative electrode. **2 MARKS**
H$^+$ → H$_2$

# C7 Energy changes

## C7.1 Exothermic and endothermic reactions

### Learning objectives

After this topic, you should know:
- energy cannot be created or destroyed in a chemical reaction
- that energy is transferred to or from the surroundings in chemical reactions, and some examples of these exothermic and endothermic reactions
- how to distinguish between exothermic and endothermic reactions based on the temperature change
- how to carry out an investigation into energy changes in chemical reactions.

### Synoptic link

Remind yourself about neutralisation reactions in Topic C5.7.

▲ **Figure 1** When a fuel burns in oxygen, energy is transferred to the surroundings. You usually don't need a thermometer to know that there is a temperature change!

### Study tip

Make sure that you do not say energy is 'lost'. It is not lost in reactions but is transferred to the environment.

Have you ever warmed up by a fire? If so, you will have felt the effects of energy being transferred during a chemical reaction. In fact, whenever chemical reactions take place, energy is always transferred, as chemical bonds in the reactants are broken and new bonds are made in the products. However, the total energy remains the same before and after a reaction. Energy cannot be created or destroyed in any chemical reaction.

Many reactions transfer energy from the reacting substances to their surroundings. These are called **exothermic** reactions. The energy transferred from the reacting substances often heats up the surroundings. As a result of this, you can measure an increase in temperature as the reaction happens.

Other reactions transfer energy from the surroundings to the reacting substances. These are called **endothermic** reactions. Because they take in energy from their surroundings, these reactions cause a decrease in temperature as they happen.

### Exothermic reactions

The burning of fuels, such as the combustion of methane gas, is an obvious example of exothermic reactions. When methane, $CH_4$ (the main gas present in natural gas), burns, it gets oxidised and releases energy to its surroundings.

Neutralisation reactions between acids and alkalis are also exothermic. You can easily measure the rise in temperature using simple apparatus (see the practical 'Investigating temperature changes' on the next page).

▲ **Figure 2** All warm-blooded animals rely on exothermic reactions in respiration to keep their body temperatures steady

The products of exothermic reactions have a lower energy content than the reactants. The actual differences in energy are usually expressed in kilojoules per mole (kJ/mol).

For example, for the reaction:

$$CH_4(g) + 2O_2(g) \rightarrow CO_2(g) + 2H_2O(l)$$

the energy transferred to the surroundings is 890 kJ/mol.

### Endothermic reactions

Endothermic reactions are much less common than exothermic ones. The reaction between citric acid and sodium hydrogencarbonate ($NaHCO_3$) is a good example to try in the lab, as it is easy to measure the fall in temperature.

Thermal decomposition reactions are also endothermic. An example is the decomposition of calcium carbonate ($CaCO_3$). When heated, it forms calcium oxide ($CaO$) and carbon dioxide ($CO_2$). This reaction only takes place if you keep heating the calcium carbonate strongly. In order to be broken down, calcium carbonate needs to absorb energy from the surroundings, such as the energy from a roaring Bunsen flame.

In endothermic reactions the products have a higher energy content than the reactants, so energy is transferred to the products from the surroundings.

For example, for the reaction:

$$CaCO_3(s) \rightarrow CaO(s) + CO_2(g)$$

the energy transferred from the surroundings is 178 kJ/mol.

▲ **Figure 3** When you eat sherbet you can feel an endothermic reaction. Sherbet dissolving in the water in your mouth takes in energy. It provides a slight cooling effect

### Practical

#### Investigating temperature changes

You can use very simple apparatus to investigate the energy changes in reactions involving at least one solution. You could use a poly(styrene) cup and a thermometer.

For example, you can investigate the temperature changes when you mix different combinations of reactants.

- Record the initial temperatures of any solutions and the maximum or minimum temperature reached during the reaction.

To extend yourself, you could consider how the quantities of reactants used might affect the temperature change.

- Make a quantitative prediction and explain your reasoning. This hypothesis could include a sketch graph.
- Test your hypothesis, recording and displaying your data using a suitable table and graph.
- Draw your conclusions.

thermometer used to measure temperature change

reactants are mixed in the cup

poly(styrene) cup provides insulation – reducing the rate energy is transferred to or from the mixture

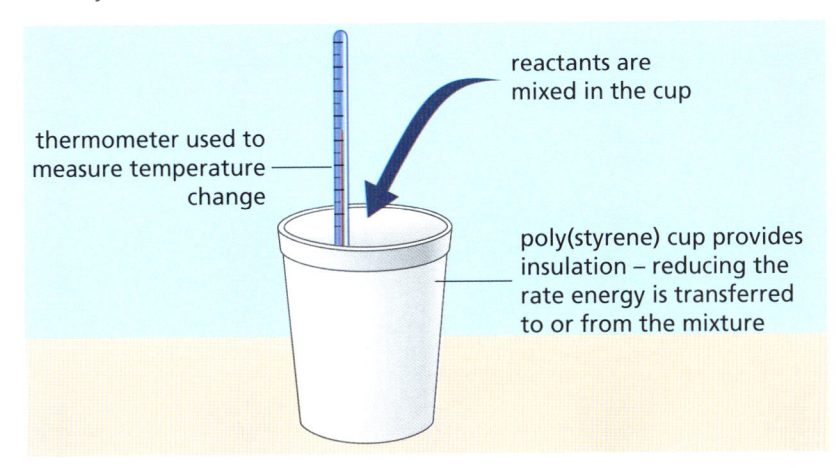

- Evaluate your investigation, including at least two ways in which you could make the data you collect more accurate.

**Safety:** Wear eye protection.

## C7 Energy changes

### Summary questions

1. **a** What do you call a reaction that transfers energy to its surroundings? **1 MARK**
   **b** What do you call a reaction that takes in energy transferred from its surroundings? **1 MARK**
   **c** Give **two** examples of:
      **i** an exothermic reaction **2 MARKS**
      **ii** an endothermic reaction. **2 MARKS**

2. Potassium nitrate dissolving in water is an endothermic process. Explain what you would feel if you held a beaker of water in your hand as you stirred in potassium nitrate. **3 MARKS**

3. Two solutions are added together and the temperature changes from 19 °C to 27 °C. Explain what you can deduce about the energy transferred between the reaction mixture and its surroundings. **3 MARKS**

4. The energy required for the thermal decomposition of 16.8 g of magnesium carbonate is 23.4 kJ.
   **a** Write a balanced symbol equation, including state symbols, for the reaction. **3 MARKS**
   **b** ⓗ Calculate the number of moles of magnesium carbonate that decompose. **2 MARKS**

### Key points

- Energy is conserved in chemical reactions. It is neither created nor destroyed.
- A reaction in which energy is transferred from the reacting substances to their surroundings is called an exothermic reaction.
- A reaction in which energy is transferred to the reacting substances from their surroundings is called an endothermic reaction.

# C7.2 Using energy transfers from reactions

## Learning objectives

*After this topic, you should know:*

- how you can make use of the energy from exothermic reactions
- how you can use the cooling effect of endothermic reactions
- how to evaluate uses and applications of exothermic and endothermic reactions given appropriate information.

## Warming up

Chemical hand warmers and body warmers can be very useful. These products use exothermic reactions. People can take hand warmers to places they know will get very cold. For example, spectators at outdoor sporting events in winter can use chemical hand warmers to warm their hands. Chemical body warmers are often used to help ease aches and pains.

Some hand warmers can only be used once. An example of this type makes use of the energy transferred to the surroundings in the oxidation of iron:

– Iron turns into hydrated iron(III) oxide in an exothermic reaction. The reaction is like rusting. Sodium chloride (common salt) is used as a catalyst.

This type of hand warmer is disposable. It can only be used once, but it lasts for hours.

Other hand warmers can be reused many times (Figure 1). These are based on the formation of crystals from solutions of a salt. The salt used is often sodium ethanoate.

1. A supersaturated solution is prepared by dissolving as much of the salt as possible in hot water.
2. The solution is then allowed to cool.
3. A small metal disc in the plastic pack is used to start the exothermic change.
4. When you press this metal disc a few times, small particles of metal are scraped off from its surface. These particles 'seed' (or start off) the crystallisation process.
5. The crystals formed spread throughout the solution, transferring energy to the surroundings in an exothermic change. They work for about 30 minutes.
6. To reuse the warmer, you simply put the solid pack into boiling water to re-dissolve the crystals. Once it has cooled down, the pack is ready to activate again.

▲ **Figure 1** During the recrystallisation of sodium ethanoate in a hand warmer, energy is transferred from the reaction system to the surroundings, increasing the temperature of the surroundings – that is, your hand

## C7 Energy changes

Exothermic reactions are also used in self-heating cans (Figure 2) that make drinks such as hot coffee without any external heating device (e.g., a kettle). The reaction used to transfer energy to the food or drink is usually:

calcium oxide + water → calcium hydroxide

You press a button in the base of the can. This breaks a seal and lets the water and calcium oxide mix. Then the exothermic reaction can begin.

Development of the self-heating can has taken several years and cost millions of pounds. Even now, the design could be further improved as over a third of the can is taken up with the reactants needed to transfer enough energy to the drink (Figure 2).

Some early versions of the design did not produce sufficient heat to increase the temperature of the drink enough in cold conditions.

## Cooling down

Endothermic processes can be used to cool things down. For example, chemical cold packs usually contain ammonium nitrate and water. When ammonium nitrate dissolves, it absorbs energy from its surroundings, making them colder.

These cold packs are used as emergency treatment for sports injuries (Figure 3). The decrease in temperature reduces swelling and numbs pain.

The ammonium nitrate and water (sometimes present in a gel) are kept separate in the pack. When squeezed or struck, the bag inside the water pack breaks, releasing ammonium nitrate. The instant cold packs work for about 20 minutes.

Instant cold packs can only be used once but are ideal where there is no ice available to treat a knock or strain. This type of cold pack is often included in the first aid kit at venues used for amateur sports or outdoor pursuits.

The same endothermic change can also be used to chill cans of drinks.

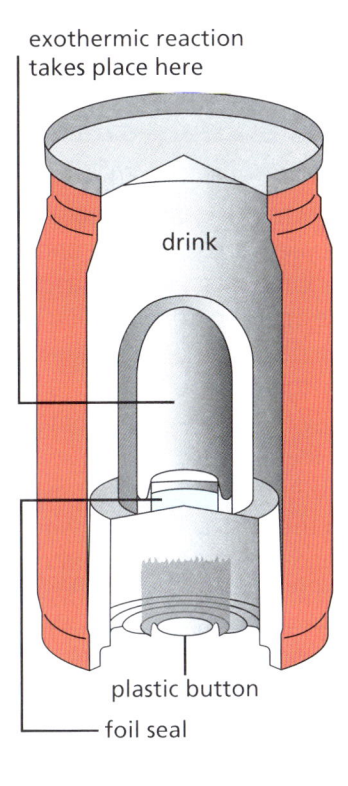

▲ **Figure 2** Development of the self-heating can in the USA took about 10 years

▲ **Figure 3** Instant cold packs can be applied as soon as an injury occurs to minimise damage

### Summary questions

1. **a** Give **two** uses of endothermic changes. *2 MARKS*
   **b** Which endothermic change is often used in cold packs? *1 MARK*
2. **a** Which solid is usually used in the base of self-heating coffee cans? *1 MARK*
   **b** Write a balanced symbol equation, including state symbols, for the reaction of water with the solid in part **a**. *3 MARKS*
   **c** Why is it essential that the coffee stays out of contact with the solid in part **a**? *1 MARK*
3. **a** Describe the chemical reaction which takes place in a disposable hand warmer. *4 MARKS*
   **b** Describe how a reusable hand warmer works. *4 MARKS*
   **c** Give an advantage and a disadvantage of each type of hand warmer. *2 MARKS*
   **d** Name **one** use of an exothermic reaction in the food industry. *1 MARK*

### Key points

- Exothermic changes can be used in hand warmers and self-heating cans.
- Endothermic changes can be used in instant cold packs for sports injuries, and to chill drinks.

# C7.3 Reaction profiles

## Learning objectives

*After this topic, you should know:*

- how to draw simple reaction profiles for exothermic and endothermic reactions, including the activation energy
- the definition of activation energy
- how to use reaction profiles to identify reactions as exothermic or endothermic
- **H** the energy changes when bonds are broken and when bonds are made.

You can find out more about what is happening in a particular reaction by looking at its **reaction profile**. These diagrams show the relative amounts of energy contained in the reactants and the products, measured in kilojoules per mole (kJ/mol). A curved line, drawn from reactants to products, shows the course of the reaction. The difference in energy between the reactants and the peak of the curve indicates the energy input needed for the reaction to take place.

## Exothermic reactions

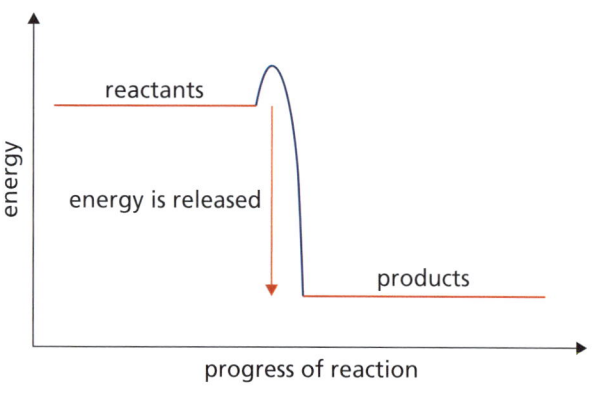

Figure 1 shows the reaction profile for an exothermic reaction. The products are at a lower energy level than the reactants. This means that when the reactants form the products, energy is transferred to the surroundings.

The difference between the energy levels of the reactants and the products is the energy change during the reaction, measured in kJ/mol.

An amount of energy equal to the difference in energy between the products and the reactants is transferred to the surroundings. Therefore, in an exothermic reaction, the surroundings get hotter, and their temperature rises.

▲ **Figure 1** The reaction profile for an exothermic reaction

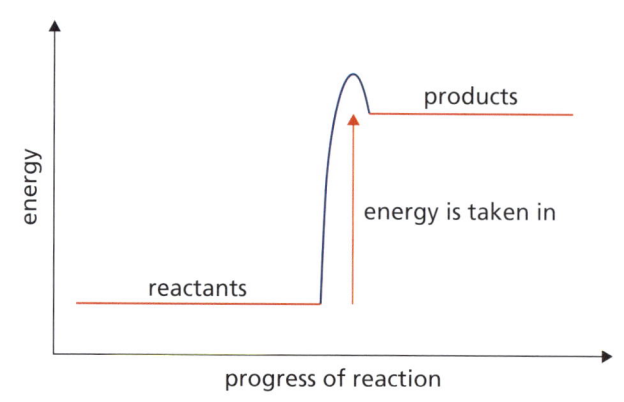

▲ **Figure 2** The reaction profile for an endothermic reaction

## Endothermic reactions

Figure 2 shows the reaction profile for an endothermic reaction.

Here the products are at a higher energy level than the reactants. As the reactants react to form products, energy is transferred from the surroundings to the reaction mixture. The temperature of the surroundings decreases because energy is taken in during the reaction. The surroundings get colder.

## Metacognition

To learn about different types of the same thing, it is helpful to make comparisons. To compare exothermic and endothermic reactions, draw two overlapping circles. Label one exothermic and the other endothermic. In the overlap, list things that are true for both. In the other parts of the circles, list things that are true for exothermic or endothermic reactions only.

## Activation energy

There is a minimum amount of energy needed before colliding particles of reactants have sufficient energy to cause a reaction. This is called the **activation energy**. This activation energy is shown on reaction profiles. Figure 3 shows the activation energy of an exothermic reaction, and Figure 4 shows that of an endothermic reaction.

## Bond breaking and bond making (H)

When a chemical reaction takes place, first the chemical bonds between the atoms or ions in the reactants are broken. Then new chemical bonds are formed to make the products.

- Energy must be supplied to break chemical bonds. This means that **breaking bonds is an endothermic** process. Energy is taken in from the surroundings.
- However, when new bonds are formed, energy is transferred to the surroundings. **Making bonds is an exothermic** process.

H–H + O=O → H₂O + H₂O (with bonds shown breaking)

▲ **Figure 5** Hydrogen and oxygen react to make water. The bonds in the hydrogen and oxygen molecules must be broken so that bonds between oxygen and hydrogen atoms in water can be formed

In reality, the two processes do not happen in sequence – it is not the case that all the bonds break and then all the new bonds form. The bond breaking and bond making processes happen at the same time. However, comparing the energy required to break the bonds with the energy released when the new bonds form gives a good guide to the overall energy change.

### Summary questions

1. Define the term activation energy. **1 MARK**
2. Draw reaction profiles for the following reactions:
   a. $H_2(g) + Cl_2(g) \rightarrow 2HCl(g)$
   For this reaction, the energy transferred to the surroundings is 184 kJ/mol. **3 MARKS**
   b. $H_2(g) + I_2(g) \rightarrow 2HI(g)$
   For this reaction, the energy taken in from the surroundings is 26.5 kJ/mol. **3 MARKS**
3. (H) Explain why some reactions are exothermic and some are endothermic, in terms of the processes of bond making and bond breaking. **3 MARKS**
4. (H) a. Explain why bond breaking is an endothermic process. **3 MARKS**
   b. Using a diagram like **Figure 5**, show the bonds being broken and new bonds being made in the reaction between methane, $CH_4$, and oxygen, which produces carbon dioxide and water. **2 MARKS**
   c. Give the number and type of each bond broken and formed in your answer to part **b**. **4 MARKS**

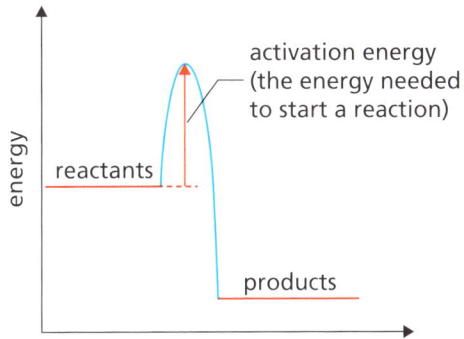

▲ **Figure 3** This reaction profile shows the activation energy for an **exothermic** reaction

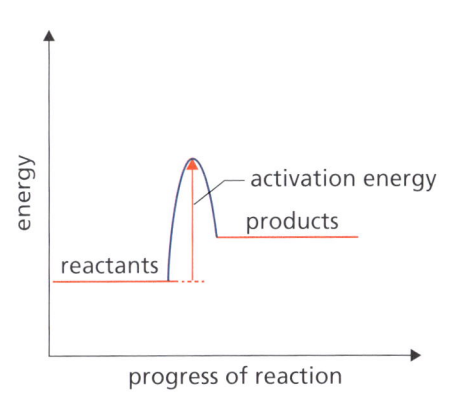

▲ **Figure 4** This reaction profile shows the activation energy for an **endothermic** reaction

### Synoptic link

For information about how catalysts can increase the rate of a reaction by providing an alternative reaction pathway that has a lower activation energy, see Topic C8.5.

### Study tip

Remember that **B**reaking bonds a**b**sorbs energy; fo**R**ming bonds **R**eleases energy.

### Key points

- You can show the relative difference in the energy of reactants and products on reaction profiles.
- (H) Bond breaking is endothermic, whereas bond making is exothermic.

# C7.4 Bond energy calculations

## Learning objectives

After this topic, you should know:
- how the balance between 'bond breaking' in the reactants and 'bond making' in the products affects the overall energy change of a reaction
- how to calculate the energy transferred in chemical reactions when supplied with bond energies.

## Making and breaking bonds

There is always a balance between the energy needed to break bonds and the energy released when new bonds are made in a chemical reaction. This is what decides whether the reaction is endothermic or exothermic.

- In some reactions, the energy released when new bonds are formed (as the products are made) is more than the energy needed to break the bonds in the reactants. These reactions transfer energy to the surroundings. They are **exothermic**.

- In other reactions, the energy needed to break the bonds in the reactants is more than the energy released when new bonds are formed in the products. These reactions transfer energy from the surroundings to the reacting chemicals. They are **endothermic**.

## Bond energy

The energy needed to break the bond between two atoms is called the **bond energy** for that bond.

Bond energies are measured in kJ/mol. You can use bond energies to work out the energy change for many chemical reactions. Before you can do this, you need to have a list of the most common bond energies (Table 1).

**Table 1** Common bond energies

| Bond | Bond energy in kJ/mol |
|---|---|
| C—C | 347 |
| C—O | 358 |
| C—H | 413 |
| C—N | 286 |
| C—Cl | 346 |
| Cl—Cl | 243 |
| H—Cl | 432 |
| H—O | 464 |
| H—N | 391 |
| H—H | 436 |
| O=O | 498 |
| N≡N | 945 |

To calculate the energy change for a chemical reaction, you need to work out:

1. how much energy is needed to break the chemical bonds in the reactants
2. how much energy is released when the new bonds are formed in the products.

The data in Table 1 is the energy required for *breaking* bonds. When you want to know the energy released as these bonds are formed, the amount of energy involved is the same (see Figure 1).

For example, the bond energy needed to break a C—C bond is 347 kJ/mol, which is taken in from the surroundings (an endothermic change). This means that the energy released when *forming* a C—C bond is 347 kJ/mol, which is transferred to the surroundings (an exothermic change).

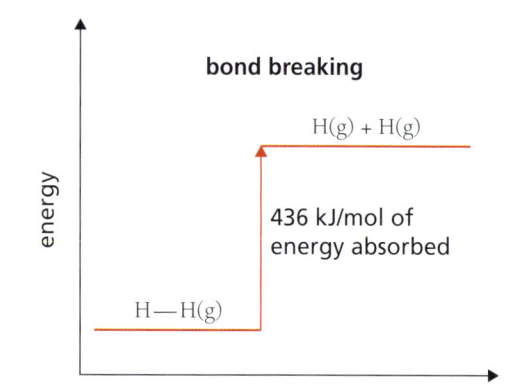

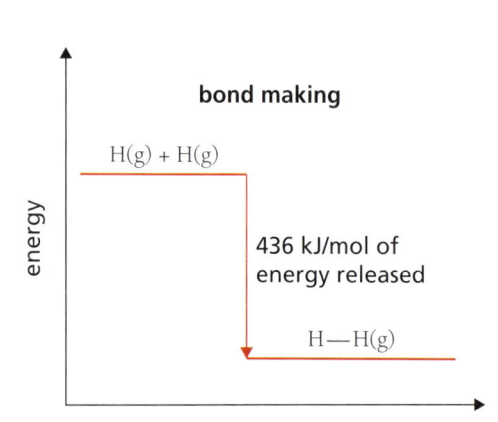

▲ **Figure 1** Breaking or making a particular bond, such as an H—H bond, always involves the same amount of energy

# C7 Energy changes

## Maths

### Worked example
In industry ammonia is made from nitrogen and hydrogen in the Haber process. The balanced symbol equation for this reaction is:

$$N_2(g) + 3H_2(g) \rightleftharpoons 2NH_3(g)$$

Calculate the overall energy change for the forward reaction using bond energies.

### Solution
This equation tells you that the bonds in 1 mole of nitrogen molecules and 3 moles of hydrogen molecules need to break in this reaction (see Figure 2).

N≡N    H—H
       H—H    ◀ **Figure 2** These bonds are
       H—H    broken in the forward reaction

Nitrogen molecules are held together by a triple bond (written like this: N≡N). This bond is very strong. Using data from Table 1, its bond energy is 945 kJ/mol.

Hydrogen molecules are held together by a single bond (written like this: H—H). From Table 1, the bond energy for this bond is 436 kJ/mol. The energy needed to break 1 mole of N≡N and 3 moles of H—H bonds = 945 + (3 × 436) kJ = 2 253 kJ taken in from the surroundings (an endothermic process).

When these atoms form ammonia ($NH_3$), six new N—H bonds are made since 2 moles of $NH_3$ are formed (see Figure 3). The bond energy of the N—H bond is 391 kJ/mol.

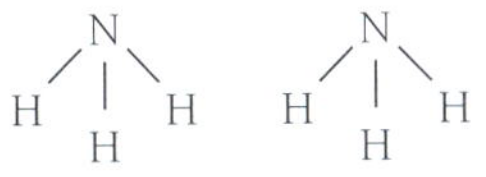

◀ **Figure 3** These bonds are made in the forward reaction

Energy transferred to the surroundings when 6 moles of N—H bonds are made = 6 × 391 kJ = 2 346 kJ

So, the **overall** energy change = (2 253 kJ − 2 346 kJ) = **−93 kJ**

This shows that the energy released by the bonds formed is greater than the energy absorbed by the breaking of the bonds. So, energy is transferred to the surroundings and it is an exothermic process. The reaction profile in Figure 4 shows the overall energy change for the formation of ammonia.

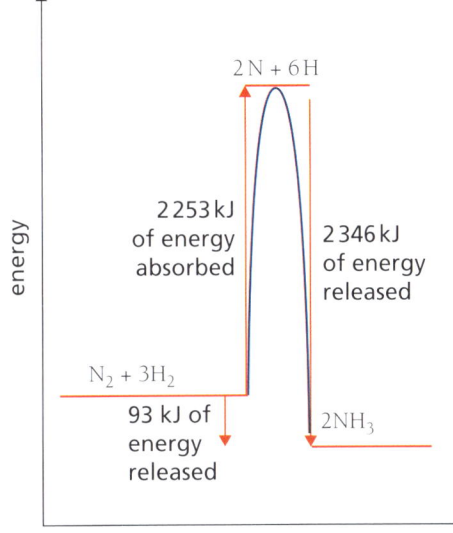

▲ **Figure 4** The formation of ammonia. The energy released, 93 kJ, is from the formation of 2 moles of ammonia, as shown in the balanced equation. So, if you wanted to know the energy change for the reaction per mole of ammonia formed, it would release exactly half this, that is, 46.5 kJ/mol

## Summary questions

1. In an example reaction the energy required to break bonds is greater than the energy transferred to the surroundings when bonds are made. State whether the reaction is exothermic or endothermic. **1 MARK**
2. What is the 'bond energy of a chemical bond'? **1 MARK**
3. Using Table 1, calculate the energy needed to break all the bonds in 0.0960 g of oxygen gas. ($A_r$ of O = 16) **3 MARKS**
4. Using Table 1, write balanced symbol equations and calculate the energy changes for the following chemical reactions:
   a  hydrogen + chlorine → hydrogen chloride **6 MARKS**
   b  hydrogen + oxygen → water. **6 MARKS**

## Key points

- In an exothermic reaction, the energy released when new bonds are formed is greater than the energy absorbed when bonds are broken.
- In an endothermic reaction, the energy released when new bonds are formed is less than the energy absorbed when bonds are broken.
- You can calculate the overall energy change in a chemical reaction using bond energies.

# C7 Energy changes

## Practice questions

1. Two solutions are mixed and react in an endothermic reaction. When the reaction has finished, the reaction mixture is allowed to stand until it has returned to its starting temperature.
   a. Sketch a graph of temperature (*y*-axis) against time (*x*-axis) to show how the temperature of the reaction mixture changes. **1 MARK**
   b. Label the graph clearly and explain what is happening wherever you have shown that the temperature is changing. **6 MARKS**

2. a. Draw a reaction profile to show the exothermic reaction between nitric acid and sodium hydroxide, including the activation energy. **3 MARKS**
   b. Draw a reaction profile to show the endothermic change when ammonium nitrate dissolves in water, including the activation energy. **3 MARKS**

3. When you eat sugar, you break it down to eventually produce water and carbon dioxide.
   a. Complete the balanced symbol equation:
   $C_{12}H_{22}O_{11} + O_2 \rightarrow$ .................................... **2 MARKS**
   b. 🅗 State why your body must **supply** energy to break down a sugar molecule. **1 MARK**
   c. 🅗 When you break down sugar in your body, energy is released. Explain where this energy comes from in terms of the bonds in molecules. **3 MARKS**
   d. You can get about 1700 kJ of energy by breaking down 100 g of sugar. If a heaped teaspoon contains 5 g of sugar, calculate how much energy this releases when broken down by your body. **1 MARK**

4. 🅗 Hydrogen peroxide has the structure H—O—O—H. It decomposes slowly to form water and oxygen:
   $$2H_2O_2(aq) \rightarrow 2H_2O(l) + O_2(g)$$
   The table shows the bond energies for different types of bonds.

   | Bond | Bond energy in kJ/mol |
   | --- | --- |
   | H—O | 464 |
   | H—H | 436 |
   | O—O | 144 |
   | O=O | 498 |

   a. Use the bond energies to calculate the energy change for the decomposition of hydrogen peroxide, as shown in the equation above. **4 MARKS**
   b. Explain exothermic and endothermic reactions in terms of bond breaking and bond making. **4 MARKS**

5. A student carried out an investigation into the temperature changes when different combinations of chemicals were mixed together. The results were recorded in Table 1.

   | Reactants | Initial temperature of each reactant in °C | Maximum or minimum temperature recorded after mixing in °C |
   | --- | --- | --- |
   | A. dilute hydrochloric acid + sodium hydroxide solution | 18.2 | 22.3 |
   | B. magnesium + iron(II) sulfate | 18.3 | 28.8 |
   | C. sodium hydrogencarbonate + citric acid | 18.3 | 16.2 |
   | D. zinc + iron(II) sulfate | 18.4 | 23.0 |

   a. i. What is the scientific name given to the reaction vessel used in experiments investigating the energy transferred during chemical reactions? **1 MARK**
      ii. Name and explain the choice of material for the reaction vessel. **3 MARKS**
      iii. Suggest the interval between the scale division marks on the thermometer. Give a reason for your choice. **2 MARKS**
   b. Classify reactions **A** to **D** as exothermic or endothermic. **2 MARKS**
   c. Which reaction involved the largest transfer of energy? **1 MARK**
   d. i. Write a balanced symbol equation, including state symbols, for reaction **A**. **3 MARKS**
      ii. 🅗 Predict the temperature change when dilute nitric acid reacts with potassium hydroxide solution (using reactants of the same concentration and volume as those used in reaction **A**). Explain your answer. Your explanation should include an ionic equation. **3 MARKS**
   e. i. What type of reaction is taking place in reactions **B** and **D**? **1 MARK**
      ii. Explain what the results of the experiment indicate about the relative reactivity of magnesium, iron, and zinc. **3 MARKS**

# Exam-style questions

**01** 🇭 **Figure 1** shows an incomplete reaction profile for the reaction of ethene and bromine.

**Figure 1**

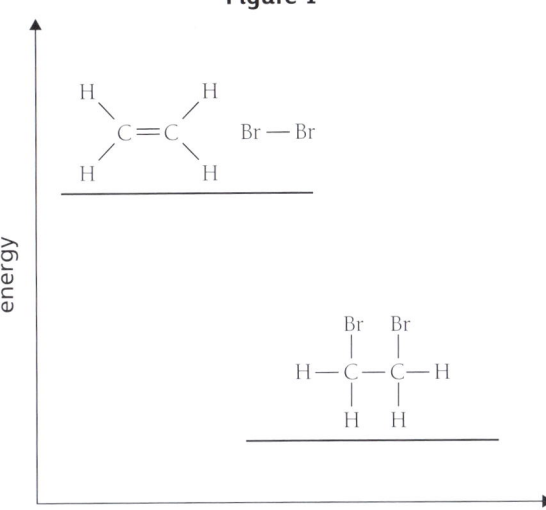

**01.1** Copy and complete the diagram and use arrows to label:
- activation energy, $E_a$
- energy released. **3 MARKS**

**01.2** Explain why, in terms of the energy involved in bond breaking and bond making, this reaction is exothermic. **3 MARKS**

**02** 🇭 A molecule of hydrogen is shown in **Figure 2**.

**Figure 2**

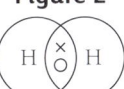

**02.1** Describe the attractions in a covalent bond and explain why bond breaking is endothermic. **5 MARKS**

**02.2** Hydrogen reacts with chlorine as shown in the equation.

$$H—H + Cl—Cl \rightarrow 2H—Cl$$

The bond energies are shown in **Table 1**.

**Table 1**

| Bond | Bond energy in kJ/mol |
|---|---|
| H—H | 436 |
| Cl—Cl | 243 |
| H—Cl | 432 |

Calculate the energy change for the reaction in kJ/mol. **3 MARKS**

**03** A more reactive metal will displace a less reactive metal from a solution of its compound.

A group of students did an experiment to put metals in order of reactivity. The students poured 50 cm³ of copper nitrate solution into a glass beaker and recorded the temperature.

The students added a spatula of metal and stirred the mixture. The students recorded the temperature of the solution at the end of the reaction **(Table 2)**.

**Table 2**

| Metal | Temperature at the start/°C | Temperature at the end/°C |
|---|---|---|
| gold | 20 | 20 |
| iron | 20 | 28 |
| tin | 20 | 25 |
| zinc | 20 | 41 |
| silver | 20 | 20 |
| magnesium | 20 | 52 |

**03.1** What name is given to a reaction that transfers energy to the surroundings? **1 MARK**

**03.2** Give two variables that would need to be controlled to make this a fair test. **2 MARKS**

**03.3** Another group repeated the experiment using a polystyrene cup rather than a glass beaker. Suggest why a polystyrene cup would give better results than a glass beaker. **1 MARK**

The students looked at the results from the experiment and concluded that the order of reactivity was:

magnesium
zinc
iron
tin
copper
silver
gold

**03.4** Why can the results not be used to place silver and gold in the correct position in the reactivity series? **1 MARK**

A teacher said that the order of reactivity was correct.

**03.5** Suggest a modification to the experiment to confirm that gold is the least reactive metal. Explain your answer. **3 MARKS**

C7 Energy changes

105

# 3 Rates, equilibrium, and organic chemistry

Chemical reactions can occur at vastly different rates, and many variables can be manipulated to change their speed. Chemical reactions may also be reversible, so changing conditions will affect the yield of a desired product. In industry, chemists and chemical engineers determine the effect of different variables on rate of reaction and yield of product.

The great variety of organic compounds is possible because carbon atoms can form chains and rings linked by C—C bonds. Chemists can modify these organic molecules in many ways to make new and useful materials such as polymers, pharmaceuticals, perfumes, flavourings, dyes, and detergents.

| | | |
|---|---|---|
| **1** | A gas is cooled down in a sealed container. What happens to the gas pressure inside the container? | the pressure decreases |
| **2** | Why do many industrial processes use catalysts in their reaction vessels when making new substances? | to speed up the reaction |
| **3** | Name the process used to collect a solvent from a solution. | distillation |
| **4** | Name the product formed when carbon burns in plenty of oxygen. | carbon dioxide |
| **5** | Name the type of reaction taking place in question 4. | combustion / oxidation |
| **6** | Complete the word equation for this reaction which takes place at a high temperature:<br>calcium carbonate $\xrightarrow{heat}$ ............ ............ + carbon dioxide | calcium oxide |
| **7** | Name the type of reaction that takes place in question 6. | thermal decomposition |
| **8** | Write a balanced symbol equation for the reaction in question 6. | $CaCO_3 \rightarrow CaO + CO_2$ |

# Journey through GCSE Chemistry

**YOU ARE HERE**

### Atoms, bonding, and calculations

- C1 Atomic structure
- C2 The Periodic Table
- C3 Structure and bonding
- C4 Chemical calculations

### Chemical reactions and energy changes

- C5 Chemical changes
- C6 Electrolysis
- C7 Energy changes

### Rates, equilibrium, and organic chemistry

- C8 Rates and equilibrium
- C9 Crude oil and fuels

### Analysis and the Earth's resources

- C10 Chemical analysis
- C11 The Earth's atmosphere
- C12 The Earth's resources

# C8 Rates and equilibrium

## C8.1 Rate of reaction

### Learning objectives

*After this topic, you should know:*
- what we mean by the rate of a chemical reaction
- how to collect data on the rate of a chemical reaction
- how to calculate the mean rate of a reaction
- Ⓗ how to calculate the rate of reaction at a specific time.

The rate of a chemical reaction tells you how fast reactants turn into products. In your body, there are lots of reactions taking place all the time. They happen at the correct rate to supply your cells with what they need, whenever it is required.

Reaction rate is also very important in the chemical industry. Any industrial process has to make money by producing useful products. This means the amount of product needed must be made as cheaply as possible. If it takes too long to produce, it will be hard to make a profit when it is sold. The rate of the reaction must be high enough to make the product quickly but safely.

### How can you find out the rate of reactions?

Reactions happen at all sorts of different rates. Some are really fast, such as the combustion of chemicals inside a firework exploding. Others are very slow, such as an old piece of iron rusting.

There are two ways you can work out the rate of a chemical reaction. You can find out how quickly:
- the reactants are used up as they make products, or
- the products of the reaction are made.

Here are three techniques you can use to collect this type of data in experiments.

### Maths

You can use a reaction graph to find the rate of the reaction at a given time:
- Draw a tangent to the curve at that time (a straight line that just touches the curve at that point).
- Then construct a right-angled triangle, using the tangent as its longest side (the hypotenuse).
- Ⓗ Finally, calculate the gradient of the tangent, as shown on the graph.
- Make sure you include the units of rate, usually g/s, cm$^3$/s or mol/s.

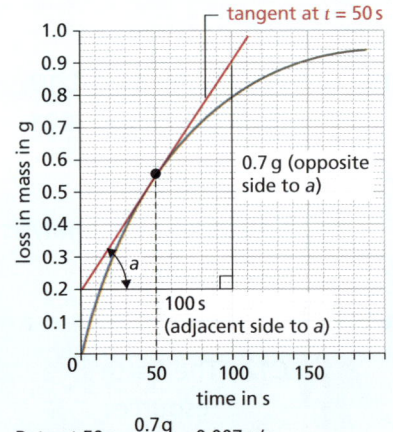

Rate at 50 s = $\frac{0.7\,g}{100\,s}$ = 0.007 g/s

(The gradient is the tangent of angle *a* in the right-angled triangle, i.e. opposite side divided by adjacent side.)

### Practical

**Measuring the decreasing mass of a reaction mixture**

You can measure the rate at which the **mass** of a reaction mixture changes if the reaction gives off a gas. As the reaction takes place, the mass of the reaction mixture decreases. You can measure and record the mass at regular time intervals.

Some balances can be attached to a data-logger to monitor the loss in mass continuously.

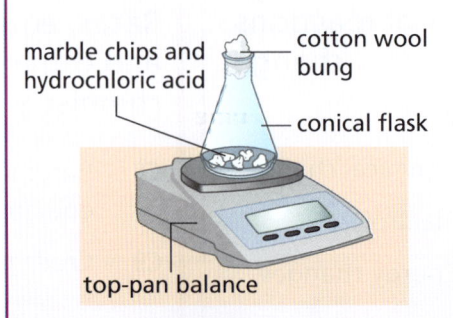

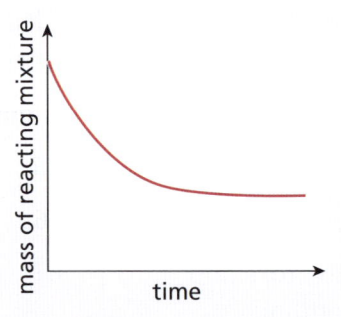

- Why is the cotton wool placed in the neck of the conical flask?
- How would the line on the graph differ if you plotted 'loss of mass' on the vertical axis?

**Safety:** Wear eye protection.

108

## C8 Rates and equilibrium

### Practical

**Measuring the increasing volume of gas given off**

If a reaction produces a gas, you can use the gas to find out the rate of the reaction. You do this by collecting the gas and measuring the volume given off at time intervals.

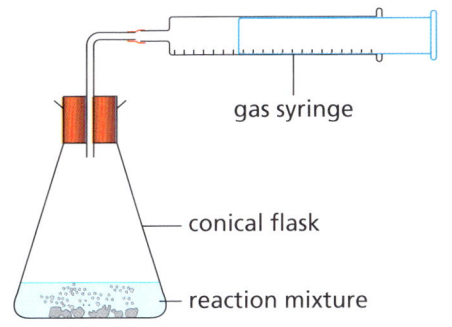

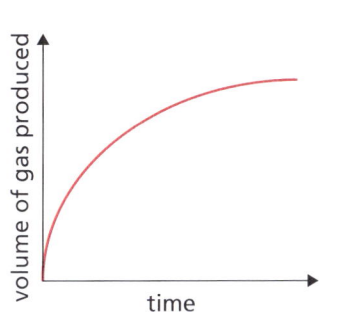

- What are the sources of error when measuring the volume of gas?

**Safety:** Wear eye protection.

### Practical

**Measuring the decreasing light passing through a solution**

Some reactions in solution make a suspension of an insoluble solid (**precipitate**). This makes the solution go cloudy. You can use this to measure the rate at which the precipitate appears (Topic C8.4).

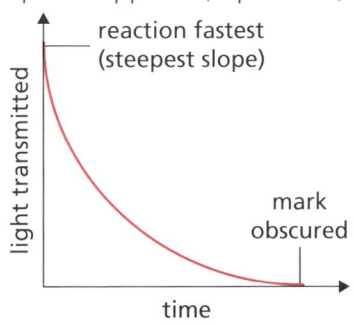

- What are the advantages of using a light sensor rather than the 'disappearing cross' method to monitor precipitation?

You can calculate the mean rate of reaction after a given time using the equation:

$$\text{mean rate of reaction} = \frac{\text{quantity of reactant used}}{\text{time}} \text{ or } \frac{\text{quantity of product formed}}{\text{time}}$$

See Worked example 1 in Topic C8.2.

### Summary questions

1. Write an equation you could use to calculate rate of reaction. **1 MARK**
2. Sketch a graph to show the results of measuring the mass of a product formed in a reaction over time. **2 MARKS**
3. ⓗ Describe how to use a graph to calculate the rate of reaction at a specific time. **5 MARKS**

### Study tip

The steeper the line on the graph, the faster the rate of reaction.

### Study tip

The units of quantity that you measure will usually be grams (g) with solids, or centimetres cubed ($cm^3$) with liquids or gases. The units of time will be seconds (s) or minutes (min). So, the units of a typical rate of reaction could be $cm^3$/min or g/s.

### Key points

- Rate of reaction can be found by measuring the amount of reactants used up or products made, over time.
- The gradient on a reaction graph tells you the rate of reaction at a specific time. The steeper the gradient, the faster the reaction.
- ⓗ To calculate the rate of reaction at a specific time, draw the tangent to the curve at that time, then calculate its gradient.

109

# C8.2 Collision theory and surface area

## Learning objectives

After this topic, you should know:
- the factors that can affect the rate of a chemical reaction
- collision theory
- how to use collision theory to explain the effect of surface area on reaction rate.

## Synoptic link

For more information about the activation energy of a reaction, look back to Topic C7.3.

In everyday life you often control the rates of chemical reactions without thinking about it. For example, when cooking cakes in an oven or by adding more detergent to a washing machine. In chemistry you need to know what factors affect the rate of reactions. You also need to be able to explain why each factor affects the rate of a reaction.

There are four main factors that affect the rate of chemical reactions:
- temperature
- surface area of solids
- concentration of solutions or pressure of gases
- the presence of a catalyst.

Reactions can only take place when the particles (atoms, ions, or molecules) of reactants come together. The reacting particles do not only have to bump into each other, but also need to collide with enough energy to cause a reaction to take place. This is known as **collision theory**.

The minimum amount of energy that particles must have before they can react is called the **activation energy**.

So, reactions are more likely to happen between reactant particles if you:
- increase the frequency of reacting particles colliding with each other
- increase the energy they have when they do collide.

If you increase the chances of particles reacting, you will also increase the rate of the reaction.

## Surface area and reaction rate

Imagine lighting a campfire. It is not a good idea to pile large logs together and try to set them alight. You use small pieces of wood to begin with. Doing this increases the surface area of the wood. This results in more wood being exposed to react with oxygen in the air.

When a solid reacts in a solution, the size of the pieces of solid affects the rate of the reaction. The particles inside a large lump of solid are not in contact with the reactant particles in the solution, so they cannot react.

When smaller lumps or a powder are used, each tiny piece of solid is surrounded by solution. Many more particles of the solid are exposed and able to react at a given time. This means that reactions can take place much more quickly.

You can compare solids with different surface areas quantitatively by looking at their surface area to volume ratio (SA : V). The smaller the size of the pieces of a solid material, the larger its SA : V. As the side of a cube decreases in size by a factor of 10, its SA : V increases times 10. The larger the SA : V ratio, the faster the reaction.

▲ **Figure 1** The collision theory is used to explain how reactant particles (atoms, molecules, or ions) react together and why their rate of reaction can vary

## Study tip

Particles collide all the time, but only some collisions lead to reactions.

Increasing the number of collisions in a certain time and the energy of collisions produce faster rates of reaction.

A larger surface area does not result in collisions with more energy but does increase the frequency of collisions.

C8 Rates and equilibrium

## Maths

### Worked example 1

A group of students timed how long it took before no more gas was given off when calcium carbonate was added to excess dilute hydrochloric acid. They performed three experiments using the same volume and concentration of acid, and 2.50 g of large, medium, and then small marble chips. Here are their results:

| Size of marble chips | Time until no more bubbles of gas appeared in s |
|---|---|
| small | 102 |
| medium | 188 |
| large | 294 |

Calculate the mean rate of reaction of each size of marble chips used.

### Solution

Using the equation in Topic C8.1:

$$\text{mean rate in g/s} = \frac{\text{mass of reactant used up in g}}{\text{time in s}}$$

**small chips**
$\frac{2.50\,g}{102\,s}$
= 0.0245 g/s
(fastest mean rate)

**medium chips**
$\frac{2.50\,g}{188\,s}$
= 0.0133 g/s

**large chips**
$\frac{2.50\,g}{294\,s}$
= 0.008 50 g/s
(slowest mean rate)

Notice that the data is given to three significant figures, so the answers are consistent with the data provided.

## Maths

### Worked example 2

On a nanoscale, an individual nanoparticle could have a size of 10 nm. Remember that a nanometre is just $1 \times 10^{-9}$ m. So what would the SA:V ratio be for a cube of side 10 nm?

### Solution

$SA = (10 \times 10^{-9}) \times (10 \times 10^{-9}) \times 6\,m^2$
$\phantom{SA}= 600 \times 10^{-18}\,m^2$
$V = (10 \times 10^{-9})^3\,m^3$
$\phantom{V}= 1000 \times 10^{-27}\,m^3$

So the SA:V ratio is:
$600 \times 10^{-18}\,m^2 : 1000 \times 10^{-27}\,m^3$
$= 0.6 \times 10^9\,/m$
$= \mathbf{6 \times 10^8\,/m}$ (in standard form)

So with a surface area to volume ratio of 600 million per metre, it is no wonder nanoparticles are reactive.

## Summary questions

1. Name the factors that can affect the rate of a chemical reaction. **4 MARKS**

2. Explain why the acid in your stomach can help you digest your food more quickly if you chew it well before you swallow. **2 MARKS**

3. In an investigation of the reaction between zinc and dilute sulfuric acid, a student compared the rates of reaction by measuring the time taken for a set volume of hydrogen gas to be given off. The student tested zinc granules, and then zinc pellets of an equal mass. It was found that the granules gave off 25.0 cm³ of hydrogen in 225 s, whereas with the pellets it took 114 s to collect the same volume of gas.
   a Calculate the mean rate of reaction with:
      i zinc granules **1 MARK**
      ii zinc pellets. **1 MARK**
   b Draw a conclusion from this data using the collision theory. **6 MARKS**
   c ⒽCalculate the mass of zinc that reacted with the sulfuric acid to give off $2.08 \times 10^{-3}$ g of hydrogen gas. Show the steps in your calculation. **3 MARKS**

## Key points

- Particles must collide, and must have a certain minimum amount of energy, before they can react.
- The minimum amount of energy that particles must have in order to react is called the **activation energy** of a reaction.
- The rate of a chemical reaction increases if the surface area to volume ratio of any solid reactants is increased. This increases the frequency of collisions between reacting particles.

111

# C8.3 The effect of temperature

### Learning objectives

*After this topic, you should know:*
- how increasing the temperature affects the rate of reactions
- how to use collision theory to explain this effect.

When you increase the temperature, it increases the rate of reaction. You can use fridges and freezers to reduce the temperature and slow down the rate of reaction. Food goes bad because of chemical reactions, so reducing the temperature slows down these unwanted reactions (Figure 1).

Collision theory tells you why raising the temperature increases the rate of a reaction. There are two reasons:

- particles collide more often
- particles collide with more energy.

## Particles collide more frequently

When you heat up a substance, energy is transferred to its particles. In solutions, and in gases, this means that the particles move around faster. When particles move around faster, they also collide more often. Imagine many people walking around in the school playground blindfolded. They may bump into each other occasionally. However, if they start running around, they will bump into each other much more often.

When particles collide more frequently, there are more chances for them to react. This increases the rate of the reaction.

## Particles collide with more energy

Particles that are moving around more quickly have more energy. This means that any collisions they have are much more energetic. It is like two people colliding when they are running rather than when they are walking.

When you increase the temperature of a reacting mixture, a higher proportion of the collisions will result in the reaction taking place in any given time. This is because a higher proportion of particles have energy greater than the activation energy (Figure 3).

▲ **Figure 1** Lowering the temperature will slow down the reactions that make foods go off

▲ **Figure 2** Moving faster means it is more likely that you will bump into someone else – and the collision will be harder (more energetic) too

cold – slow movement, less frequent collisions, little energy

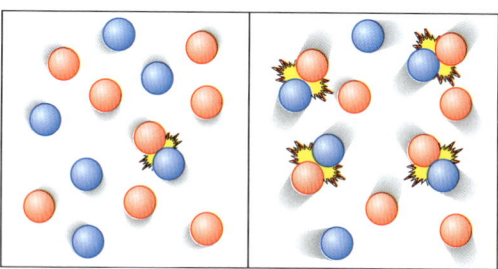

hot – fast movement, more frequent collisions, more energy

▲ **Figure 3** More frequent collisions, with more energy – both factors lead to the increase in the rate of a chemical reaction that is caused by increasing the temperature

**An increased proportion of particles exceeding the activation energy has a greater effect on rate than the increased frequency of collisions.**

Around room temperature, if you increase the temperature of a reaction by 10 °C, the rate of the reaction will roughly double.

### Study tip

When explaining rates of reaction, make sure you refer to the *rate* at which the particles collide. You can describe the collisions as 'more frequent' or that they 'occur more often' or 'more in a given time'. However, **do not** just say that there are 'more collisions'.

C8 Rates and equilibrium

## Practical

### The effect of temperature on rate of reaction

Alka-Seltzer tablets are a well-known indigestion remedy. They fizz when added to water (Figure 4). The fizzing is caused by carbon dioxide gas, produced by the reaction of sodium hydrogencarbonate and citric acid, both contained in the tablets. These compounds can come into contact once the tablet is added to water. By varying the temperature of the water, you can measure its effect on the rate of reaction.

▲ **Figure 4** When indigestion tablets dissolve in water, sodium hydrogencarbonate and citric acid mix and react to produce carbon dioxide

- How could you vary the temperature in the investigation?
- How could you measure the mean rate at different temperatures?

Check your ideas with your teacher before you start your investigation.

- Which variables do you have to control to make this a fair test?
- Why is it difficult to get accurate timings in this investigation?
- How can you improve the **precision**, and hence the accuracy in this case, of any data that has random measurement errors?

**Safety:** Wear eye protection. Do not raise the temperature above 50 °C.

The results of an investigation like this can be plotted on a graph.

The graph in Figure 5 shows how the time taken for the reaction to finish changes with temperature. The negative slope shows that as the *temperature increases*, the *time* it takes for the reaction to finish *decreases*. As the *temperature increases*, the *rate* of the reaction (or 'mean rate of reaction' in this case) also *increases*.

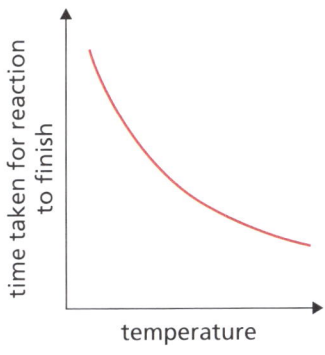

▲ **Figure 5** Example results for an investigation into the effect of temperature on the rate of a reaction

## Summary questions

1. **a** Why does increasing the temperature increase the rate of a reaction? *2 MARKS*
   **b** Estimate by how much a 10 °C rise in temperature increases the reaction rate at room temperature. *1 MARK*
2. Look at the experiment in the previous Practical box.
   **a** Why does the tablet fizz in the water? *2 MARKS*
   **b** Predict what happens to the time it takes for the reaction to finish as the temperature increases. *1 MARK*
   **c** Explain your answer to part **b** by using collision theory. *3 MARKS*
3. Water in a pressure cooker boils at a much higher temperature than water in a saucepan because it is under pressure. Explain why food takes longer to cook in a pan than it does in a pressure cooker. *2 MARKS*

## Key points

- Reactions happen more quickly as the temperature increases.
- Increasing the temperature increases the rate of reaction because particles collide more frequently and more energetically.
- More of the collisions occurring in a given time result in a reaction because a higher proportion of particles have energy greater than the activation energy.

# C8.4 The effects of concentration and pressure

## Learning objectives

After this topic, you should know:
- how, and why, increasing the concentration of reactants in solutions affects the rate of reaction
- how, and why, increasing the pressure of reacting gases affects the rate of reaction.

Some of the most beautiful buildings and statues are made of limestone or marble. These have stood for centuries. However, they are now crumbling away at a greater rate than before. This is because both limestone and marble are mainly calcium carbonate. This compound reacts with acids, leaving the stone soft and crumbly. The rate of this reaction has speeded up because the concentration of acids in rainwater has increased.

Increasing the concentration of reactants in a solution increases the rate of reaction because there are more particles of the reactants moving around in the same volume of solution. The more 'crowded together' the reactant particles are, the more likely it is that they will collide. So the increased frequency of collisions results in a faster reaction.

Increasing the pressure of reacting gases has the same effect. Increased pressure squashes the gas particles more closely together. There are more particles of gas in a given space. This increases the chance that they will collide and react. So, increasing the pressure produces more frequent collisions, which will increase the rate of the reaction (Figures 1 and 2).

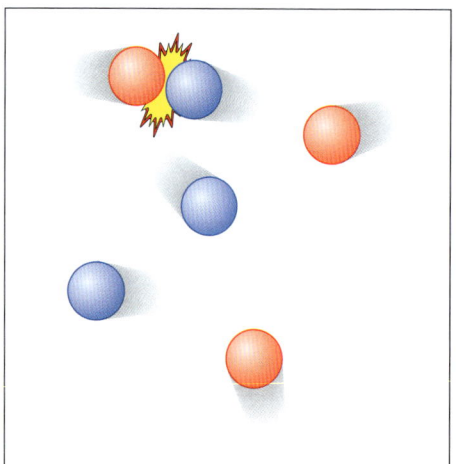

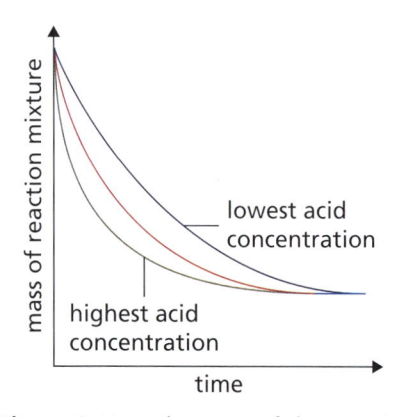

▲ Figure 2 How the mass of the reaction mixture of marble chips and dilute hydrochloric acid decreases over time at three different concentrations of acid

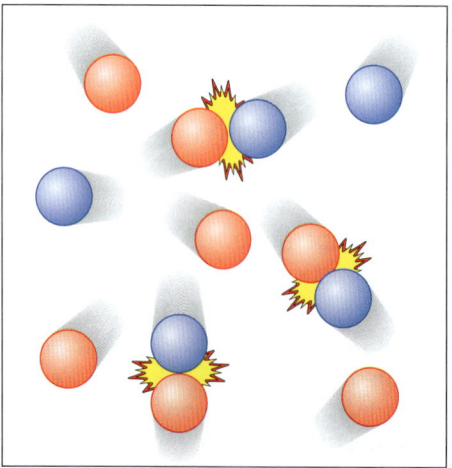

▲ Figure 1 Increasing the concentration of solutions or the pressure of gases both mean that particles are closer together. This increases the frequency of collisions between reactant particles, so the reaction rate increases

# C8 Rates and equilibrium

## Practical

### Concentration and rate of reaction

**A** You can investigate the effect of changing concentration by reacting marble chips with different concentrations of hydrochloric acid:

$$CaCO_3(s) + 2HCl(aq) \rightarrow CaCl_2(aq) + CO_2(g) + H_2O(l)$$

You can find the rate of a reaction by plotting the volume of carbon dioxide gas given off as the reaction progresses over time. You can measure the volume of gas at regular time intervals using the method shown in the Practical box in Topic C8.5. Alternatively, you might choose to time how long it takes to collect a fixed volume of gas using the same apparatus.

- Write a hypothesis explaining your prediction of what will happen. (You might include a sketch graph of your expected results.)
- How do you make this a fair test?
- What conclusion can you draw from your results?

**B** Consider the reaction between sodium thiosulfate and dilute hydrochloric acid:

$$Na_2S_2O_3(aq) + 2HCl(aq) \rightarrow 2NaCl(aq) + SO_2(aq) + S(s) + H_2O(l)$$

Plan an investigation to see how varying the concentration of sodium thiosulfate affects the rate of this reaction. Your timing method should use the increasing cloudiness (turbidity) of the reaction mixture as the reaction proceeds (final Practical box in Topic C8.1).

Make sure your teacher checks your plan before any practical work is attempted.

**Safety:** Wear eye protection.

## Study tip

The balanced equation for a reaction tells us nothing about its rate of reaction.

## Summary questions

1. A metal carbonate reacts with an acid to produce a gas. Sketch a graph of volume of gas against time for three different concentrations of the acid. Label the lines as high, medium, and low concentration. **2 MARKS**

2. **a** Explain how you know which line on the graph in **Figure 2** shows the fastest reaction. **2 MARKS**
   **b** The electric balance used in the experiment needs a high resolution. Explain what 'high resolution' means. **1 MARK**

3. Acidic cleaners are designed to remove limescale (calcium carbonate) when they are used neat (undiluted). They do not work as well when they are diluted. Explain this using your knowledge of collision theory. **4 MARKS**

## Key points

- Increasing the concentration of reactants in solutions increases the frequency of collisions between particles, and so increases the rate of reaction.
- Increasing the pressure of reacting gases also increases the frequency of collisions, and so increases the rate of reaction.

115

# C8.5 The effect of catalysts

### Learning objectives

*After this topic, you should know:*
- what a catalyst is
- how catalysts work
- why catalysts are important in industry.

### Synoptic link

To remind yourself about reaction profiles and exothermic reactions look back to Topic C7.3.

Sometimes a reaction might only take place if you use very high temperatures or pressures. This can cost industry a lot of money. However, you can speed up some reactions and reduce energy costs by using **catalysts**.

A catalyst is a substance that changes the rate of a reaction. However, it is not changed chemically itself at the end of the reaction. A catalyst is not used up in the reaction, so it can be used over and over again.

Different catalysts are needed for different reactions. Many of the catalysts used in industry involve metals. Examples include iron, used to make ammonia, and platinum, used to make nitric acid. Catalysts are normally used in the form of powders, pellets, or fine gauzes. This gives them the biggest possible surface area to volume ratio, making them as effective as possible, as the reactions they catalyse often involve gases reacting on their surfaces (Figure 2).

## How catalysts work

Catalysts do not increase the frequency of collisions between reactant particles, nor do they make collisions any more energetic. They increase rates of reaction by providing an alternative reaction pathway to the products, with a lower activation energy than the reaction without the catalyst present (Figure 3). So, with a catalyst, a higher proportion of the reactant particles have sufficient energy to react. This means that the frequency of *effective* collisions (i.e., collisions that result in a reaction) increases and the rate of reaction speeds up.

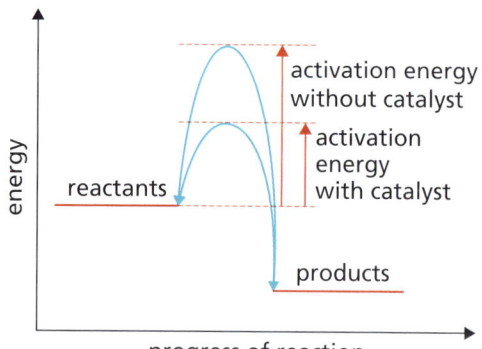

▲ **Figure 1** Biological catalysts in living things are called **enzymes**. These are large protein molecules that are folded into intricate shapes to accommodate the reactant molecules (called substrates). Enzymes work at relatively low temperatures, conserving energy in industry

▲ **Figure 3** The reaction profile of an uncatalysed and a catalysed exothermic reaction. The catalyst lowers the activation energy of the reaction

## Advantages of catalysts in industry

Catalysts are often very expensive precious metals. Gold, platinum, and palladium are all costly, but are the most effective catalysts for certain reactions. It is usually cheaper to use a catalyst than to pay for the extra energy needed without one. To get the same rate of reaction without a catalyst would require higher temperatures and/or pressures.

So, catalysts save money and help the environment. That is because using high temperatures and pressures often involves burning fossil fuels. Operating at lower temperatures and pressures conserves these **non-renewable** resources. It also stops more carbon dioxide entering the atmosphere when fossil fuels are burnt, helping to combat **climate change**.

▲ **Figure 2** The metals platinum and palladium are used in catalytic converters in cars. They are coated onto a honeycombed support to maximise their surface area to volume ratio

C8 Rates and equilibrium

Not only does a catalyst speed up a reaction, but it also does not get used up in the reaction, so a tiny amount of catalyst can be used to speed up a reaction repeatedly.

However, the catalysts used in chemical plants eventually become 'poisoned', so that they do not work anymore. This happens because impurities in the reaction mixture combine with the catalyst and stop it working properly.

> **Metacognition**
>
> Write a quiz with five questions, which have one-word answers, to test a partner on 'rates of reaction'. Mark each other's answers and discuss your results.

## Practical

### Investigating catalysis

You can investigate the effect of different catalysts on the rate of a reaction, for example hydrogen peroxide solution decomposing:

$$2H_2O_2(aq) \rightarrow 2H_2O(l) + O_2(g)$$

The reaction produces oxygen gas, which can be collected in a gas syringe. Alternatively, you can use an inverted measuring cylinder, or burette, filled with water.

You can investigate the effect of many different substances on the rate of this reaction. Examples include manganese(IV) oxide, **MnO₂**, and potassium iodide, **KI**.

- Name the independent variable in this investigation.

A table of the time taken to produce a certain volume of oxygen gas can then tell you which catalyst makes the reaction go fastest.

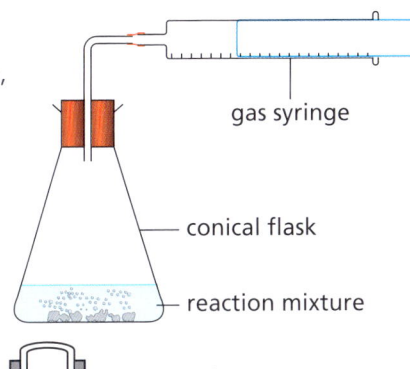

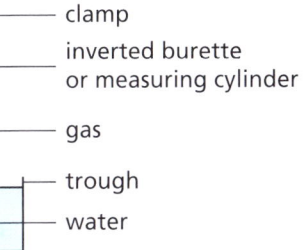

- What type of graph would you use to show the results of your investigation? Why?

**Safety:** Wear eye protection. If the syringe is glass, ensure that the piston does not fall out and break. Manganese(IV) oxide is harmful.

## Summary questions

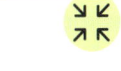

1. How is a catalyst affected by a chemical reaction that it speeds up? **1 MARK**
2. In the reaction shown in the previous Practical box, with one of the catalysts tested it took 3 minutes and 12 seconds to collect 50 cm³ of oxygen gas. Calculate the mean rate of the reaction, giving your answer in cm³/s. **2 MARKS**
3. Solid catalysts used in chemical processes are often shaped as tiny beads or cylinders with holes through them. Why are they made in these shapes? **1 MARK**
4. Suggest why the volume of catalyst needed to speed up a chemical reaction is very small compared with the volume of reactants. **2 MARKS**
5. Research four industrial processes that make products using catalysts. Write a word equation for each reaction and name the catalyst used. **4 MARKS**
6. Evaluate the use of catalysts in the chemical industry. **6 MARKS**

> **Study tip**
>
> Catalysts change only the **rate** of reactions. The products do not change. So, catalysts do not appear in the balanced equation for a reaction but can be written above reaction arrows.

> **Key points**
>
> - A catalyst speeds up the rate of a chemical reaction but is not used up itself during the reaction.
> - Different catalysts are needed for different reactions.
> - Catalysts are used whenever possible in industry to increase rates of reaction and reduce energy costs.

117

# C8.6 Reversible reactions

### Learning objectives

*After this topic, you should know:*
- what a reversible reaction is
- how you can represent reversible reactions.

In most chemical reactions, the reactants react completely to form the products. You show this by using an arrow pointing *from* the reactants *to* the products:

$$\underset{\text{reactants}}{A + B} \rightarrow \underset{\text{products}}{C + D}$$

However, in some reactions the products can react together to make the original reactants again. This is called a **reversible reaction**.

A reversible reaction can go in both directions, so two 'half-arrows' are used in the equation. One arrow points in the forwards direction and one in the backwards direction:

$$A + B \rightleftharpoons C + D$$

You still call the substances on the left-hand side of the equation the 'reactants' and those on the right-hand side the 'products'. So, it is important that you write down the equation of the reversible reaction you are referring to when you use the words 'reactants' and 'products'. If the equation is written as:

$$C + D \rightleftharpoons A + B$$

the reactants are **C** and **D**, and the products are **A** and **B**!

## Examples of reversible reactions

Have you ever tried to neutralise an alkaline solution with an acid? It is very difficult to get a solution that is exactly neutral. You can use an indicator to tell when just the right amount of acid has been added. An indicator forms compounds that are different colours in acidic solutions and in alkaline solutions.

Litmus is a complex molecule. This can be represented as HLit (where H is hydrogen). HLit is red. If you add alkali, HLit turns into the Lit$^-$ ion by losing an H$^+$ ion. Lit$^-$ is blue. If you then add more acid, blue Lit$^-$ changes back to red HLit, and so on (Figure 1).

$$\underset{\text{red litmus}}{HLit(aq)} \rightleftharpoons \underset{\text{blue litmus}}{H^+(aq) + Lit^-(aq)}$$

Other reversible reactions involve salts and their water of crystallisation.

For example:

hydrated copper(II) sulfate $\rightleftharpoons$ anhydrous copper(II) sulfate + water
(blue)  (white)

$$CuSO_4 \cdot 5H_2O \rightleftharpoons CuSO_4 + 5H_2O$$

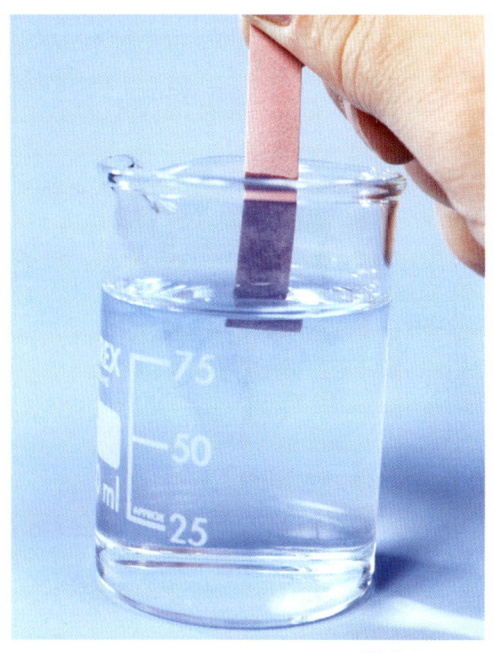

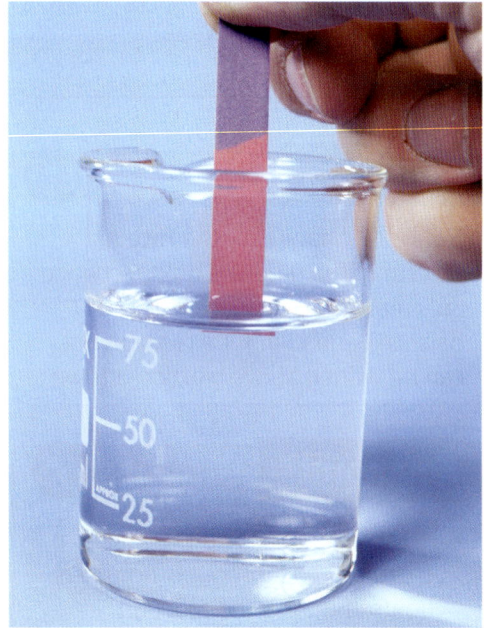

▲ **Figure 1** Indicators undergo reversible reactions, changing colour to show you whether solutions are acidic or alkaline. Blue litmus paper turns red in an acidic solution, and red litmus paper turns blue in an alkaline solution and back to red in acid

When you heat ammonium chloride, a reversible reaction takes place.

## Practical

### Heating ammonium chloride

Gently heat a small amount of ammonium chloride (harmful) in a test tube with a loose plug of mineral wool. Use test tube holders or clamp the test tube at an angle. Make sure you warm the bottom of the tube.

- What do you see inside the test tube? Explain the changes.

**Safety:** Wear eye protection. Take care if you are asthmatic.

Ammonium chloride breaks down on heating. It forms ammonia gas and hydrogen chloride gas. This is an example of thermal decomposition:

$$\text{ammonium chloride} \xrightarrow{\text{heat}} \text{ammonia} + \text{hydrogen chloride}$$
$$NH_4Cl(s) \longrightarrow NH_3(g) + HCl(g)$$

The two hot gases rise up the test tube. When they cool down near the mouth of the tube, they react with each other (Figure 2). The gases re-form ammonium chloride again. The white ammonium chloride solid forms on the inside of the glass test tube:

$$\text{ammonia} + \text{hydrogen chloride} \xrightarrow{\text{cool}} \text{ammonium chloride}$$
$$NH_3(g) + HCl(g) \longrightarrow NH_4Cl(s)$$

You can show the reversible reaction as:

$$\text{ammonium chloride} \rightleftharpoons \text{ammonia} + \text{hydrogen chloride}$$
$$NH_4Cl(s) \rightleftharpoons NH_3(g) + HCl(g)$$

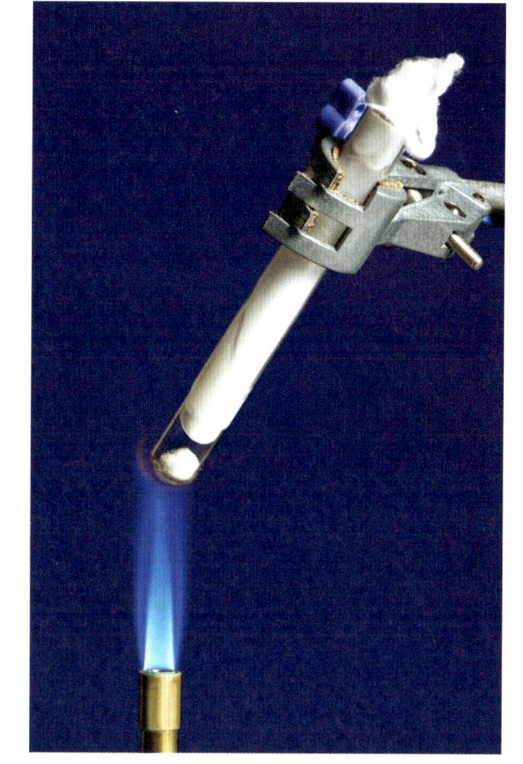

▲ **Figure 2** An example of a reversible reaction – heating ammonium chloride to break it down into ammonia gas and hydrogen chloride gas. When the gases cool down, they recombine to form the white solid ammonium chloride again

## Summary questions

1. What do chemists mean by a reversible reaction? **1 MARK**

2. Phenolphthalein is an indicator. It is colourless in acid and pure water but is pink-purple in alkali. In a demonstration, a teacher started with a beaker containing a mixture of water and phenolphthalein. In two other beakers she had different volumes of acid and alkali. The acid and alkali had the same concentration. She poured the mixture into the beaker containing 2 cm³ of sodium hydroxide solution. She then poured the mixture into a third beaker containing 5 cm³ of hydrochloric acid.
Describe what you would observe happening in the demonstration. **1 MARK**

3. You can represent the phenolphthalein indicator in question **2** as HPhe. Assuming it behaves like litmus, write a balanced symbol equation to show the reversible reaction of phenolphthalein in acid and in alkali. **1 MARK**

4. Thermochromic materials change colours at different temperatures. The change is reversible. Give a use or potential use for thermochromic materials in the home. **1 MARK**

### Key points

- In a reversible reaction, the products of the reaction can react to make the original reactants.
- You can show a reversible reaction using the $\rightleftharpoons$ sign.

# C8.7 Energy and reversible reactions

## Learning objectives

After this topic, you should know:
- what happens in the energy transfers in reversible reactions.

## Synoptic link

To remind yourself about energy transferred in chemical reactions, look back to Topic C7.1.

In Topic C7.1, you saw examples of reactants forming products in exothermic reactions and endothermic reactions. These energy changes are involved in reversible reactions too. An example is given here.

Figure 1 shows a reversible reaction where **A** and **B** react to form **C** and **D**. The products of this reaction (**C** and **D**) can also react to form **A** and **B** again.

If the reaction **transfers** energy to the surroundings when it goes in this direction …

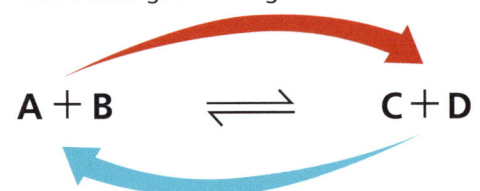

$$A + B \rightleftharpoons C + D$$

… it will **take in** exactly the same amount of energy from the surroundings when it goes in this direction.

▲ **Figure 1** A reversible reaction

If the reaction between **A** and **B** is exothermic, energy will be transferred to the surroundings when the reaction forms **C** and **D**.

If **C** and **D** then react to make **A** and **B** again, the reverse reaction must be endothermic. It will take in the same amount of energy as was transferred when **C** and **D** were formed from **A** and **B**.

Energy cannot be created or destroyed in a chemical reaction. The amount of energy transferred to the surroundings when the reaction goes in one direction in a reversible reaction must be exactly the same as the energy transferred back in when the reaction goes in the opposite direction.

You can see how this works if you look at what happens when blue copper(II) sulfate crystals are heated. The crystals contain water as part of the lattice formed when the copper(II) sulfate crystallised. The copper sulfate is **hydrated**. Heating the copper(II) sulfate drives off the water from the crystals, producing white **anhydrous** ('without water') copper(II) sulfate (Figure 2). This is an endothermic reaction.

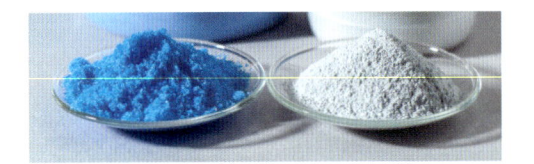

▲ **Figure 2** Blue hydrated copper(II) sulfate and white anhydrous copper(II) sulfate

$\xrightarrow{\text{endothermic (in forward reaction)}}$

hydrated copper(II) sulfate ⇌ anhydrous copper(II) sulfate + water
(blue)                                        (white)

$CuSO_4 \cdot 5H_2O$ ⇌ $CuSO_4$ + $5H_2O$

$\xleftarrow{\text{exothermic (in reverse reaction)}}$

When you add water to anhydrous copper(II) sulfate, hydrated copper(II) sulfate is formed. The colour change in the reaction, from white to blue, is a useful test for the presence of water. The reaction in this direction is exothermic (Figure 3). In fact, you may see steam rising if you add water drop by drop to anhydrous copper(II) sulfate powder.

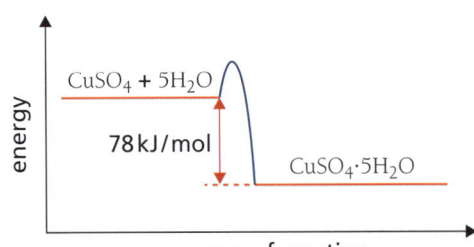

▲ **Figure 3** The reaction profile of the reversible reaction involving anhydrous and hydrated copper(II) sulfate

(Graph shows: energy axis vs progress of reaction; $CuSO_4 + 5H_2O$ at higher level, 78 kJ/mol drop to $CuSO_4 \cdot 5H_2O$)

120

# C8 Rates and equilibrium

## Practical

### Energy changes in a reversible reaction

Gently heat a few copper(II) sulfate crystals in a test tube (Figure 4). Observe the changes.

When the crystals are completely white, allow the tube to cool to room temperature (this takes several minutes).

Add two or three drops of water from a dropper and observe the changes. Carefully feel the bottom of the test tube.

- Explain the changes you have observed.

You can try this same thing with other hydrated crystals, such as cobalt(II) chloride. Some are not so colourful, but the changes are similar.

**Safety:** Wear eye protection. Avoid skin contact with cobalt(II) chloride, which is toxic. Copper salts are harmful.

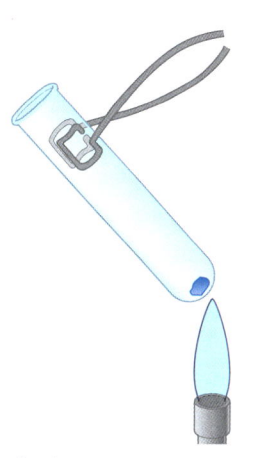

▲ **Figure 4** Heating hydrated copper(II) sulfate

You can soak filter paper in cobalt(II) chloride solution and allow it to dry in an oven. The blue paper that is produced is called cobalt(II) chloride paper. The paper turns pale pink when water is added to it, and so can be used as an indicator for the presence of water (Figure 5).

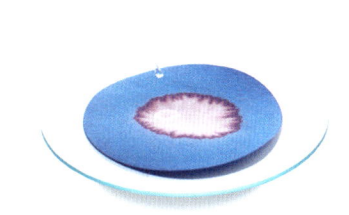

▲ **Figure 5** Blue cobalt(II) chloride paper turns pink when water is added

## Summary questions

1. **a** How does the energy change for a reversible reaction in one direction compare with the energy change for the reaction in the opposite direction? *1 MARK*
   **b** What can anhydrous copper(II) sulfate be used to test for? *1 MARK*

2. A reversible reaction transfers 50 kilojoules (kJ) of energy to the surroundings in the forward reaction. In this reaction **W** and **X** react to give **Y** and **Z**.
   **a** Write an equation to show the reversible reaction. *1 MARK*
   **b** Give the energy transfer in the reverse reaction. *1 MARK*

3. Blue cobalt(II) chloride crystals turn pink when they become damp. The formula for the two forms can be written as $CoCl_2 \cdot 2H_2O$ and $CoCl_2 \cdot 6H_2O$.
   **a** ❶ Determine the number of moles of water that will combine with 1 mole of $CoCl_2 \cdot 2H_2O$. *1 MARK*
   **b** Write a balanced chemical equation for the reaction, which is reversible. *1 MARK*
   **c** How can pink cobalt(II) chloride crystals be changed back to blue cobalt(II) chloride crystals? *1 MARK*
   **d** ❶ Calculate the mass of water lost when 0.50 moles of pink cobalt(II) chloride are turned completely into blue cobalt(II) chloride. *2 MARKS*

### Key points

- In reversible reactions, one reaction is exothermic and the other is endothermic.
- In any reversible reaction, the amount of energy transferred to the surroundings when the reaction goes in one direction is exactly equal to the energy transferred back when the reaction goes in the opposite direction.

# C8.8 Dynamic equilibrium

## Learning objectives

After this topic, you should know:
- how a reversible reaction in a closed system can be 'at equilibrium'
- **H** that the composition of an equilibrium mixture can be altered by changing conditions, such as concentration.

Some reactions are reversible. The products formed can react together to make the original reactants again:

$$A + B \rightleftharpoons C + D$$

So, what happens when you start with just the reactants in a reversible reaction in a **closed system**, in which no reactants or products can get in or out?

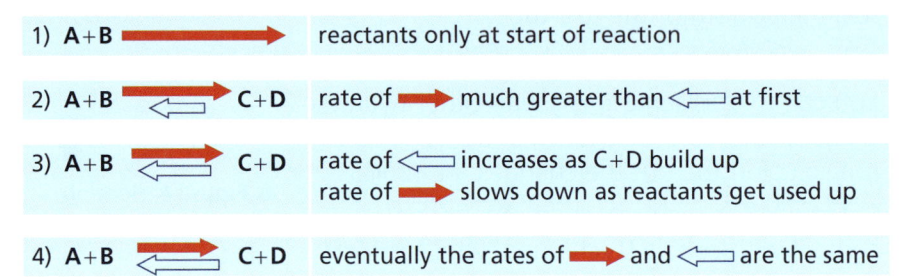

1) A+B ⟶   reactants only at start of reaction
2) A+B ⇌ C+D   rate of ⟶ much greater than ⟵ at first
3) A+B ⇌ C+D   rate of ⟵ increases as C+D build up
   rate of ⟶ slows down as reactants get used up
4) A+B ⇌ C+D   eventually the rates of ⟶ and ⟵ are the same

So, in a reversible reaction, as the concentration of products builds up, the rate at which they react to re-form reactants increases. As this starts to happen, the rate of the forward reaction is decreasing. That is because the concentration of reactants is decreasing from its original maximum value. Eventually both forward and reverse reactions are happening at the same rate, but in opposite directions (Figure 1).

When this happens, the reactants are making products at the same rate as the products are making reactants. Overall, there is *no change* in the amount of products and reactants. The reaction has reached **equilibrium**.

**At equilibrium, the rate of the forward reaction equals the rate of the reverse reaction.**

As the forward and reverse reactions are continuously taking place (unnoticed because they occur at the atomic level), a state of 'dynamic' equilibrium has been reached (Figure 2).

▲ **Figure 1** The situation at equilibrium is just like running up an escalator that is going down – if you run up as fast as the escalator goes down, you will get nowhere!

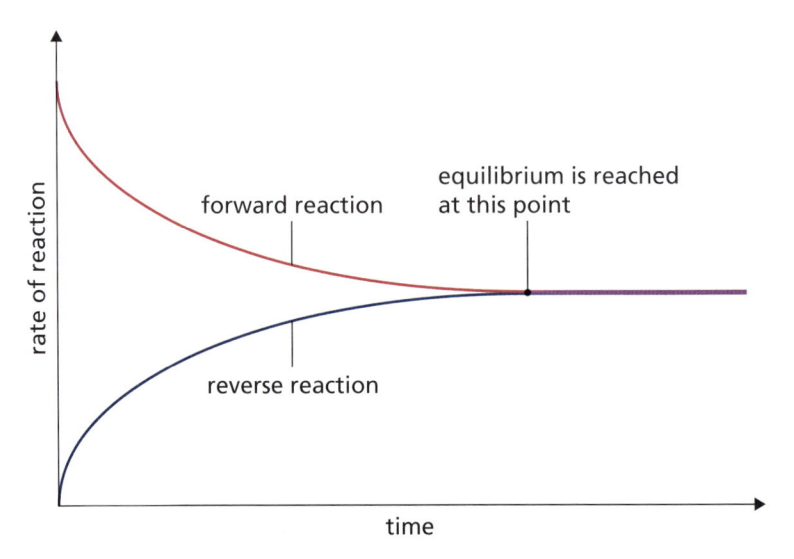

▲ **Figure 2** In a reversible reaction at equilibrium, the rate of the forward reaction is the same as the rate of the reverse reaction

## C8 Rates and equilibrium

### Affecting the composition of an equilibrium mixture

**H**

One example of a reversible reaction is the reaction between iodine monochloride, ICl, and chlorine gas. Iodine monochloride is a brown liquid, whilst chlorine is a yellowish green gas. These substances can be reacted together to make yellow crystals of iodine trichloride, $ICl_3$.

When there is plenty of chlorine gas, the forward reaction makes iodine trichloride crystals, which are quite stable. However, if the concentration of chlorine gas is lowered, the rate of the forward reaction decreases and the rate of the reverse reaction increases. This starts turning more iodine trichloride back to iodine monochloride and chlorine, until equilibrium is established again (Figure 3).

You can change the relative amounts of the reactants and products in a reacting mixture at equilibrium by changing the conditions. This is an application of **Le Châtelier's Principle**. Henry Louis Le Châtelier was a French chemist who observed equilibrium mixtures. He noticed that whenever a change in conditions is introduced to a system at equilibrium, the position of equilibrium shifts to cancel out the change. The change in conditions can be changes in concentration, pressure, or temperature.

This principle is very important in the chemical industry. In a process with a reversible reaction, industrial chemists need to find the conditions that give as much product as possible, in as short a time as possible.

However, there are always other economic and safety factors to consider when chemists manipulate reversible reactions in industry.

with plenty of chlorine gas

iodine monochloride + chlorine ⇌ iodine trichloride
$ICl$ + $Cl_2$ ⇌ $ICl_3$
(brown liquid) (yellow crystals)

remove chlorine gas

▲ **Figure 3** This reacting mixture can be changed by adding or removing chlorine from the mixture

### Summary questions

1. How does the rate of the reverse reaction compare with the rate of the forward reaction in a reaction at equilibrium? **1 MARK**
2. Complete the following sentence: In a reversible reaction at equilibrium, the concentration of ….
   A …reactants is changing constantly.
   B …reactants remain constant.
   C …products increase. **1 MARK**
3. Explain why chemists describe chemical equilibrium as dynamic as opposed to static. **2 MARKS**
4. **H** An equilibrium mixture is set up in a closed system with iodine monochloride, chlorine gas, and iodine trichloride. In order to make more iodine trichloride, would you pump more chlorine gas into the mixture or remove chlorine gas? Explain your answer using Le Châtelier's Principle. **2 MARKS**

### Key points

- In a reversible reaction, the products of the reaction can react to re-form the original reactants.
- In a closed system, the rate of the forward and reverse reactions is equal at equilibrium.
- **H** Changing the reaction conditions can change the amounts of products and reactants in a reaction mixture at equilibrium.

# C8.9 Altering conditions

## Learning objectives

After this topic, you should know:
- how changing the pressure affects reversible reactions involving gases
- how changing the temperature affects reversible reactions.

## Pressure and equilibrium

You saw in Topic C8.8 how changing concentration can affect a reversible reaction at equilibrium. In general, the position of equilibrium shifts as if trying to cancel out any change in conditions. Think about increasing the concentration of a reactant. This will cause the position of equilibrium to shift to the right, in favour of the products, to reduce the concentration of that reactant. It opposes the change that is introduced.

If a reversible reaction involves changing numbers of gas molecules, altering the pressure can also affect the equilibrium mixture. In many reversible reactions, there are more molecules of gas on one side of the equation than on the other. By changing the pressure at which the reaction is carried out, you can change the amount of products that are made.

Look at the table:

| If the forward reaction produces *more* molecules of gas ... | If the forward reaction produces *fewer* molecules of gas ... |
|---|---|
| ... an increase in pressure decreases the amount of products formed. | ... an increase in pressure increases the amount of products formed. |
| ... a decrease in pressure increases the amount of products formed. | ... a decrease in pressure decreases the amount of products formed. |

You can show this with the reversible reaction equation:

$$2NO_2(g) \rightleftharpoons N_2O_4(g)$$
brown gas  pale yellow gas

In this reaction you can see from the balanced symbol equation that there are two moles of gas on the left-hand side of the equilibrium equation and one mole of gas on the right-hand side.

Imagine that you increase the pressure in the reaction vessel. The position of equilibrium will shift to reduce the pressure. It will move in favour of the reaction that produces fewer gas molecules. In this case that is to the right, in favour of the forward reaction. So, more $N_2O_4$ gas will be made. The colour of the gaseous mixture will get lighter (Figure 1).

Note that pressure changes do not affect all gaseous reversible reactions at equilibrium. When there are *equal* numbers of molecules of gas on both sides of the balanced equation, changing the pressure has no effect on the composition of the equilibrium mixture. However, increasing the pressure will speed up both the forward and reverse reactions by the same amount.

▲ **Figure 1** The effect of changing the pressure on $2NO_2(g) \rightleftharpoons N_2O_4(g)$

## Temperature and equilibrium

When you have a closed system, no substances are added or taken away from the reaction mixture. In a closed system, the relative amounts of the reactants and products in a reversible reaction at equilibrium depend on the temperature.

### Study tip

Changing the pressure affects the equilibrium only if there are different numbers of molecules of gases on each side of the balanced equation.

## C8 Rates and equilibrium

By changing the temperature, you can plan to get more of the products and less of the reactants. Look at the table:

| If the forward reaction is exothermic ... | If the forward reaction is endothermic ... |
| --- | --- |
| ... an increase in temperature decreases the amount of products formed. | ... an increase in temperature increases the amount of products formed. |
| ... a decrease in temperature increases the amount of products formed. | ... a decrease in temperature decreases the amount of products formed. |

You can show this by looking at the reaction involving $NO_2(g)$ and $N_2O_4(g)$ again. The forward reaction is exothermic, so the reverse reaction is endothermic.

$$2NO_2(g) \underset{\text{endothermic}}{\overset{\text{exothermic}}{\rightleftharpoons}} N_2O_4(g)$$

If the temperature is increased, the equilibrium shifts as if to try to reduce the temperature. The reaction that is endothermic (taking in energy from the surroundings) will cool it down. So, in this case, the reverse reaction is favoured and more $NO_2(g)$ is formed (Figure 2).

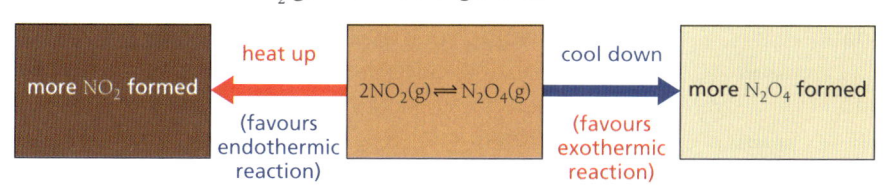

▲ **Figure 2** The effect of changing the temperature on $2NO_2(g) \rightleftharpoons N_2O_4(g)$

### Metacognition

Flashcards are a great way to summarise important facts. Being able to make your own cards will help you to remember the information in this chapter. Make a flashcard for each spread, then test yourself to see how much you can remember from each card. As you go through the course you can mix flashcards with different topics or subjects.

### Summary questions

1. Name the conditions that affect the position of equilibrium. **2 MARKS**
2. The equation for a reversible reaction is:
$$H_2O(g) + C(s) \rightleftharpoons CO(g) + H_2(g)$$
The forward reaction is endothermic.
Describe how the amount of hydrogen gas formed will change if the temperature is increased. **1 MARK**
3. a In **Figure 1**, how will increasing the pressure affect the colour of a mixture of $NO_2$ and $N_2O_4$ gases? Explain your answer. **2 MARKS**
   b In **Figure 2**, what will happen to the colour of a mixture of $NO_2$ and $N_2O_4$ gases if you increase the temperature? Explain your answer. **2 MARKS**
4. Explain what effect increasing the pressure would have on the equilibrium mixture shown in the equation:
$$H_2(g) + I_2(g) \rightleftharpoons 2HI(g)$$
**1 MARK**

### Key points

- Pressure can affect reversible reactions involving gases at equilibrium. Increasing the pressure favours the reaction that forms fewer molecules of gas. Decreasing the pressure favours the reaction that forms the greater number of molecules of gas.
- You can change the relative amount of products formed at equilibrium, by changing the temperature at which you carry out a reversible reaction.
- Increasing the temperature favours the endothermic reaction. Decreasing the temperature favours the exothermic reaction.

# C8 Rates and equilibrium

## Practice questions

1 Two students investigated the reaction of some marble chips with dilute nitric acid.

| Time in minutes | Investigation A: Mass of gas produced in g | Investigation B: Mass of gas produced in g |
|---|---|---|
| 0.0 | 0.00 | 0.00 |
| 0.5 | 0.56 | 0.28 |
| 1.0 | 0.73 | 0.36 |
| 1.5 | 0.80 | 0.39 |
| 2.0 | 0.82 | 0.41 |
| 2.5 | 0.82 | 0.41 |

a Name the gas produced in the reaction. Describe the positive test for this gas. **2 MARKS**

b i Marble chips contain calcium carbonate. Write a word equation for the reaction investigated. **1 MARK**

ii Write a balanced symbol equation, including state symbols, for the reaction. **3 MARKS**

c The students were investigating the effect of concentration on rate of reaction. Describe the method the students used to collect the data for their table. **6 MARKS**

d Plot a graph of these results, with time on the x-axis. **4 MARKS**

**H** e i Use your graph to calculate the rate of reaction at 30 seconds in both investigations, and give your answers in units of g/min and in mol/s. **2 MARKS**

ii Compare the rate of reaction in Investigation **B** with the rate of reaction in Investigation **A**. **1 MARK**

f Compare the final mass of gas produced in Investigation **B** with that produced in Investigation **A**. **1 MARK**

g From the results table, deduce the relative concentrations of the acids in Investigations **A** and **B**. **1 MARK**

h Use the collision theory to explain the data obtained. **4 MARKS**

2 A pair of students are studying the effect of surface area on rate of reaction. They test the reaction of zinc metal with dilute hydrochloric acid.

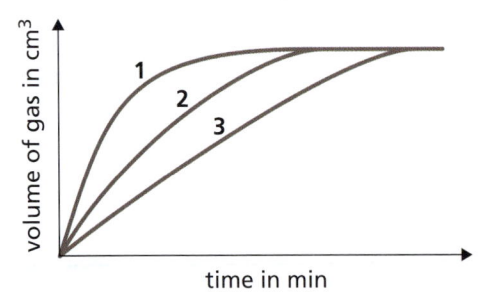

a What would the students investigating the reaction need to do to make it a **fair test**? **3 MARKS**

b Which gas was given off in the reaction? How could you test for this gas? **2 MARKS**

c Write a balanced symbol equation, including state symbols, for the reaction under investigation. **3 MARKS**

d Which line (**1**, **2**, or **3**) shows results for the zinc with the largest surface area to volume ratio? **1 MARK**

e What size of zinc pieces would react most slowly? **1 MARK**

f The students doing the experiments also tried reacting the same mass of **powdered** zinc with the acid. What would their results look like on the graph? **2 MARKS**

g Use the collision theory to explain the results in this investigation. **3 MARKS**

h **H** The students had reacted zinc with excess dilute hydrochloric acid. If they had added 0.13 g of zinc, calculate the total mass of hydrogen gas collected when the reaction had finished. **3 MARKS**

3 a Define the word 'catalyst'. **2 MARKS**

b Hydrogen peroxide, $H_2O_2$, solution decomposes to form water and oxygen gas. Write a balanced symbol equation, including state symbols, for this reaction. **3 MARKS**

c The reaction is catalysed by some metal oxides. You are provided with oxides of copper, lead, manganese, and iron. Describe how you can test which is the best catalyst for the decomposition of hydrogen peroxide, collecting quantitative (measured) data to support your conclusion. **5 MARKS**

d **H** In one test, it was found that 40 cm³ of oxygen gas was collected in 16 s. Calculate the mean rate of reaction in that test, expressing your answer in cm³/s. **3 MARKS**

e Describe how you can get a pure dry sample of the metal oxides from the mixture left at the end of the reaction. **3 MARKS**

# Exam-style questions

**01** This question is about the reactions of sodium thiosulfate.

A student investigated the rate of reaction between sodium thiosulfate and hydrochloric acid. The reaction was set up in a conical flask as shown in **Figure 1**.

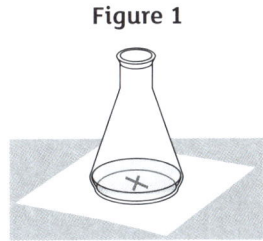

**Figure 1**

The student recorded the time from mixing the sodium thiosulfate and hydrochloric acid until the mixture became so cloudy that the cross below the flask was no longer visible.

The equation for the reaction is:

$Na_2S_2O_3(aq) + 2HCl(aq) \rightarrow 2NaCl(aq) + H_2O(l) + SO_2(g) + S(s)$

**01.1** Name which product caused the mixture to become cloudy. **1 MARK**

**01.2** The student changed the concentration of sodium thiosulfate. The student did each reaction at the same temperature.

Give one other variable the student should control. **1 MARK**

**01.3** The rate of reaction increased as the concentration of sodium thiosulfate increased. Explain why. **2 MARKS**

**01.4** The rate of reaction would also increase as the temperature increased. Explain why. **4 MARKS**

**02** A student investigated the rate of reaction between calcium carbonate chips and dilute hydrochloric acid. The apparatus is shown in **Figure 2**.

**Figure 2**

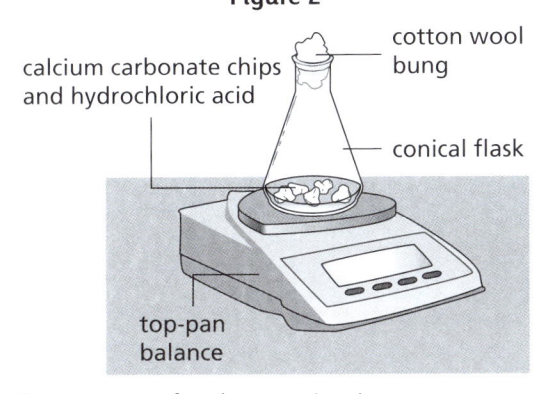

calcium carbonate chips and hydrochloric acid
cotton wool bung
conical flask
top-pan balance

The equation for the reaction is:

$CaCO_3(s) + 2HCl(aq) \rightarrow CaCl_2(aq) + H_2O(l) + CO_2(g)$

The mass decreased during the reaction. The student's results are shown in **Figure 3**.

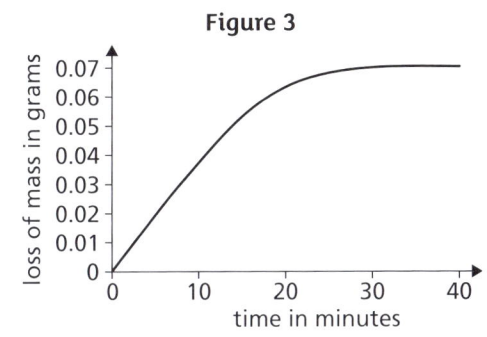

**Figure 3**

**02.1** Use the equation to explain why the mass decreased during the reaction. **2 MARKS**

**02.2** Suggest why the student used a cotton wool plug. **1 MARK**

**02.3** The student used an excess of calcium carbonate chips. Explain why the rate of reaction slows down as the reaction proceeds. **2 MARKS**

**02.4** The same mass of calcium carbonate powder was used in another experiment. Suggest one reason the rate of reaction was higher. Explain your answer. **3 MARKS**

**03** **H** This question is about reversible reactions.

**03.1** Consider the two reversible reactions.

**Reaction 1:** $C_2H_4(g) + H_2O(g) \rightleftharpoons C_2H_5OH(g)$ exothermic

**Reaction 2:** $N_2O_4(g) \rightleftharpoons 2NO_2(g)$ endothermic

Use the equations to fill in the gaps in **Table 1**.

**Table 1**

| Reaction | Effect of increasing pressure on rate | Effect of increasing pressure on yield | Effect of increasing temperature on yield |
|---|---|---|---|
| Reaction 1 | increases | | |
| Reaction 2 | increases | | |

**4 MARKS**

**03.2** Explain why increasing the pressure increases the rate of a reaction involving gases. **2 MARKS**

The equation for the industrial manufacture of ammonia is:

$N_2(g) + 3H_2(g) \rightleftharpoons 2NH_3(g)$

The reaction is exothermic in the forwards direction.

Explain why high pressure is used for the process. **3 MARKS**

# C9 Crude oil and fuels

## C9.1 Hydrocarbons

### Learning objectives

*After this topic, you should know:*
- what crude oil is made up of
- what alkanes are
- how to represent alkanes by their chemical formula or displayed formula
- the names and formulae of the first four alkanes.

So far, some of the 21st century's most important chemicals have come from the organic carbon compounds found in crude oil. The massive variety of natural and synthetic carbon compounds occur due to the ability of carbon atoms to form families of similar compounds. The carbon atoms can bond to each other to form chains and rings that form the 'skeletons' of organic molecules. In the recent past, organic compounds were the main fuels used to warm homes and to generate electricity. However, renewable and alternative sources of energy (wind, solar, hydroelectric, and nuclear) are taking over as oil supplies dwindle and concerns about climate change grow.

### Crude oil

Crude oil is a finite resource found in rocks. It was formed over millions of years from the remains of tiny, ancient sea animals and plants, mainly plankton, that were buried in mud. Over time, layer upon layer of rock was laid down on top. This created the conditions (high pressure and temperature, in the absence of oxygen) to make crude oil.

The crude oil formed is a dark, smelly liquid. It is a **mixture** of many different carbon compounds. A mixture contains two or more elements or compounds that are not chemically combined together. Nearly all of the compounds in crude oil are compounds containing *only hydrogen and carbon* atoms. These compounds are called **hydrocarbons**.

▲ **Figure 1** The price of nearly everything you buy is affected by oil prices. The cost of the fuels used to move goods to the shops affects how much you have to pay for them

### Practical

**Distillation of crude oil**

Mixtures of liquids can be separated using distillation. This can be done in the lab on a small scale. Your teacher will heat the crude oil mixture so that it boils. The different fractions vaporise between different ranges of temperature. The vapours can be collected by cooling and condensing them.

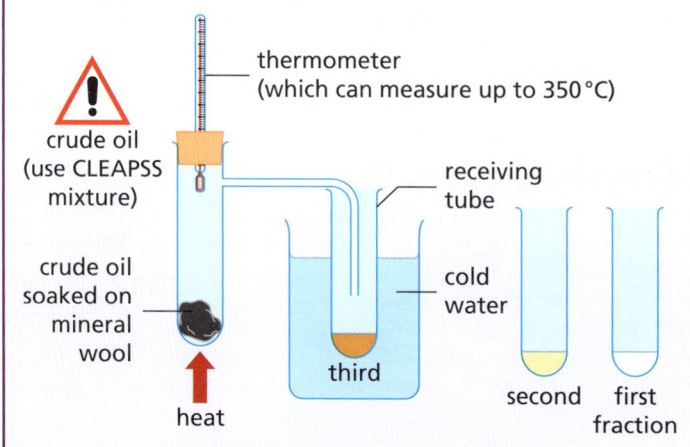

▲ **Figure 2** The distillation of crude oil in the lab

### Synoptic link

For more information about the Earth's finite (non-renewable) resources, see Topic C12.1.

128

C9 Crude oil and fuels

Crude oil straight from the ground is not much use. There are too many substances in it, all with different boiling points. Before crude oil can be used, it must be separated into different substances with similar boiling points. These are known as **fractions**. The mixtures of substances in crude oil can be separated in the lab by **distillation**. Distillation separates liquids with different boiling points.

## Alkanes

Most of the hydrocarbons in crude oil are **alkanes**. You can see some examples of alkane molecules in Figure 3. Notice how all their names end in '-ane'.

The first part of the name of each alkane tells you how many carbon atoms are in its molecules (Table 1).

**Table 1** Prefixes of alkanes

| Prefix (start of name) | meth- | eth- | prop- | but- |
|---|---|---|---|---|
| Number of carbon atoms | 1 | 2 | 3 | 4 |

Alkanes are **saturated hydrocarbons**. All the carbon–carbon bonds are single covalent bonds. This means that alkanes contain as many hydrogen atoms as possible in each molecule. No more hydrogen atoms can be added.

The formulae of the first four alkane molecules are:

$CH_4$ (methane)

$C_2H_6$ (ethane)

$C_3H_8$ (propane)

$C_4H_{10}$ (butane)

Can you see a pattern in the formulae of the alkanes? You can write the **general formula** for alkane molecules like this:

$$C_nH_{(2n+2)}$$

This means that in alkane molecules 'for every $n$ carbon atoms, there are $(2n + 2)$ hydrogen atoms'. For example, if an alkane molecule contains 12 carbon atoms, its formula will be $C_{12}H_{26}$.

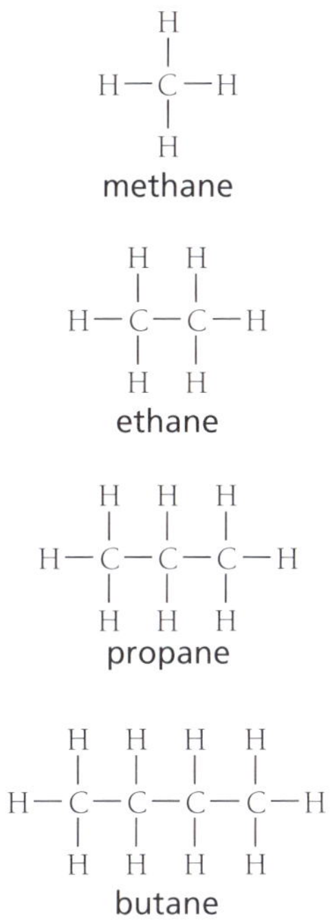

▲ **Figure 3** You can represent alkanes like this, showing all the atoms in the molecule. These are called **displayed formulae**. A single line drawn between two atoms in a molecule represents a single covalent bond

## Synoptic link

To remind yourself about covalent bonding, look back at Topic C3.5.

## Summary questions

1. **a** What is crude oil made up of? *1 MARK*
   **b** Why can you separate crude oil using distillation? *1 MARK*
2. Crude oil is drilled from beneath the land or seabed. Why is this crude oil not very useful as a product itself? *2 MARKS*
3. **a** Write the general formula of the alkanes. *1 MARK*
   **b** Give the names and formulae for the first four alkanes. *4 MARKS*
4. **a** Draw the displayed formula of octane, whose molecules have eight carbon atoms. *2 MARKS*
   **b** Determine the number of hydrogen atoms there are in an alkane molecule that has 22 carbon atoms. *1 MARK*
   **c** Determine the number of carbon atoms there are in an alkane molecule that has 32 hydrogen atoms. *1 MARK*
   **d** Why are alkanes described as saturated hydrocarbons? *2 MARKS*

## Key points

- Crude oil is a mixture of many different compounds. Most of these compounds are hydrocarbons – they contain only hydrogen and carbon atoms.
- The first four alkanes are methane ($CH_4$), ethane ($C_2H_6$), propane ($C_3H_8$), and butane ($C_4H_{10}$).
- The general formula of an alkane is: $C_nH_{(2n+2)}$.

# C9.2 Fractional distillation of oil

## Learning objectives

After this topic, you should know:
- how the boiling point, viscosity, and flammability of hydrocarbons are affected by the size of their molecules
- how to separate crude oil into fractions
- how to explain the separation of crude oil by fractional distillation
- how the fractions from crude oil are used.

## The properties of hydrocarbons

There is a great variety of hydrocarbon molecules. Some are quite small, with relatively few carbon atoms in short chains. These short-chain molecules make up the hydrocarbons that tend to be most useful. These hydrocarbons make good fuels as they ignite easily and burn well, with less smoky flames than hydrocarbons made up of larger molecules. They are described as very **flammable** (Figure 1). Other hydrocarbons have lots of carbon atoms in their long-chain molecules and may have branches (side chains) or form rings.

Figure 1 shows the trends in the properties of hydrocarbons.

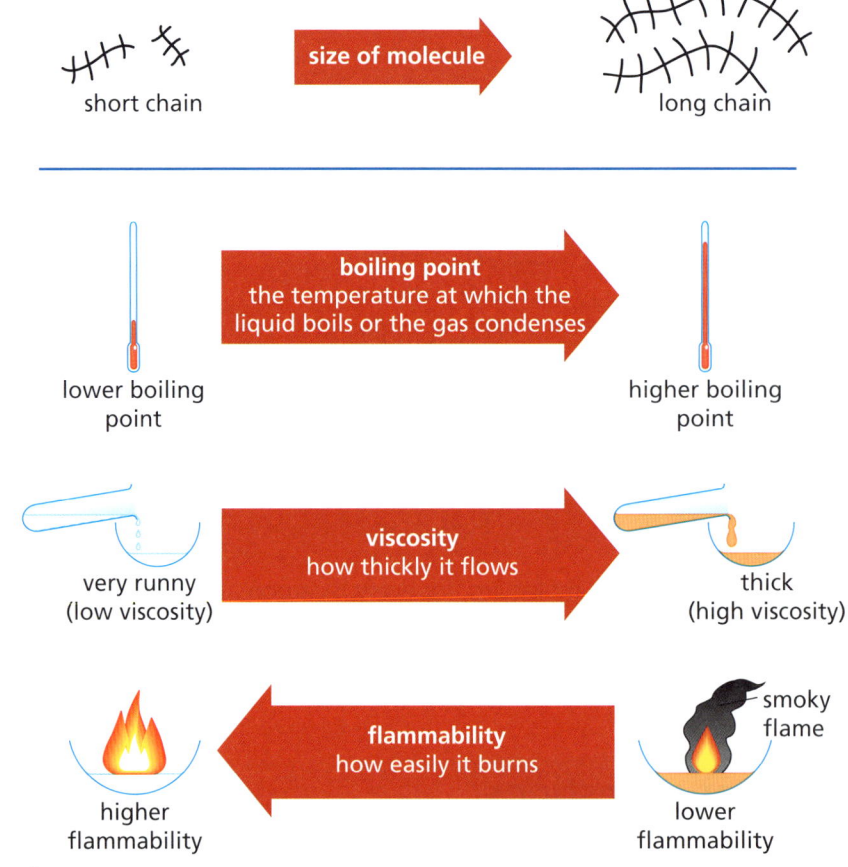

▲ Figure 1 The properties of hydrocarbons depend on the chain length of their molecules

## Fractional distillation of crude oil

Crude oil is separated into hydrocarbons with similar boiling points, called fractions. This process is called **fractional distillation** (Figure 2). Each hydrocarbon fraction contains molecules with similar numbers of carbon atoms. Each of these fractions boils at a different temperature range because of the different sizes of the molecules in it.

## Synoptic links

To remind yourself about the process of fractional distillation, look back to Topic C1.4. To revise intermolecular forces, refer to Topic C3.6.

# C9 Crude oil and fuels

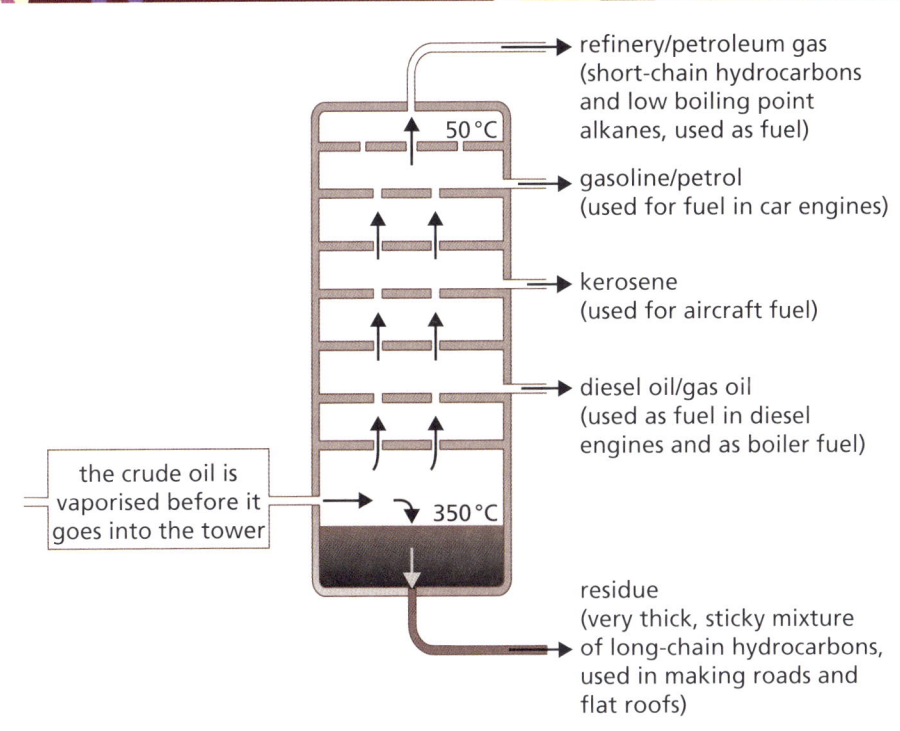

▲ **Figure 2** The boiling point of a hydrocarbon depends on the size of its molecules. Differences in boiling points can be used in fractional distillation to separate the hydrocarbons in crude oil into fractions

Crude oil is heated and fed in near the bottom of a tall tower (called a fractionating column) as hot vapour. The column is kept very hot at the bottom and much cooler at the top, so the temperature decreases going up the column. The gases move up the column and the hydrocarbons condense when they reach the temperature of their boiling points. The different fractions are collected as liquids at different levels in a continuous process.

Hydrocarbons with the smallest molecules have the lowest boiling points. They are piped out of the cooler top of the column as gases. At the bottom of the column, the fractions have high boiling points. They cool to form very thick liquids or solids, such as bitumen, at room temperature.

Once collected, the fractions need more processing before they can be used (Figure 3).

▲ **Figure 3** An oil refinery at night

## Summary questions

1 Name the process used to separate crude oil into its fractions. **1 MARK**

2 a How does the size of a hydrocarbon molecule affect:
   i the boiling point **1 MARK**
   ii the viscosity of a hydrocarbon? **1 MARK**
  b A hydrocarbon catches fire very easily. Write whether it is likely to have molecules with long hydrocarbon chains or short ones and whether it will give off lots of black smoke when it burns. **2 MARKS**

3 Describe how the properties of petrol make it appropriate for its use. **3 MARKS**

4 Explain the steps involved in the fractional distillation of crude oil. **6 MARKS**

## Key points

- Crude oil is separated into fractions using fractional distillation.
- The boiling point, viscosity, and flammability of each fraction depends on the size of the hydrocarbon molecules.
- Lighter fractions make better fuels as they ignite more easily and burn well, with cleaner (less smoky) flames.

# C9.3 Burning hydrocarbon fuels

## Learning objectives

*After this topic, you should know:*
- the products formed when you burn hydrocarbon fuels in a good supply of air
- how to test for the products of complete combustion of a hydrocarbon
- why carbon monoxide gas is given off when incomplete combustion takes place
- how to write balanced equations for the complete combustion of hydrocarbons with a given formula.

## Complete combustion

The lighter fractions from crude oil can be used as fuels. When hydrocarbons burn in plenty of air, they transfer lots of energy to the surroundings.

For example, you might have seen orange gas cylinders used in mobile heaters and for gas cookers in areas without mains gas. These cylinders contain propane, one of the petroleum gases that come from the top of the fractionating column in oil refineries. When propane gas burns:

$$\text{propane} + \text{oxygen} \rightarrow \text{carbon dioxide} + \text{water}$$
$$C_3H_8(g) + 5O_2(g) \rightarrow 3CO_2(g) + 4H_2O(g)$$

The carbon and hydrogen in the fuel are **oxidised** completely when they burn like this. Remember that one definition of oxidation means adding oxygen in a chemical reaction.

**The products of the complete combustion of a hydrocarbon are carbon dioxide and water.**

### Practical

**Products of complete combustion**

You can test the products given off when a hydrocarbon burns.

- What happens to the limewater? Which gas is given off?
- What happens in the U-tube? Which substance is present?

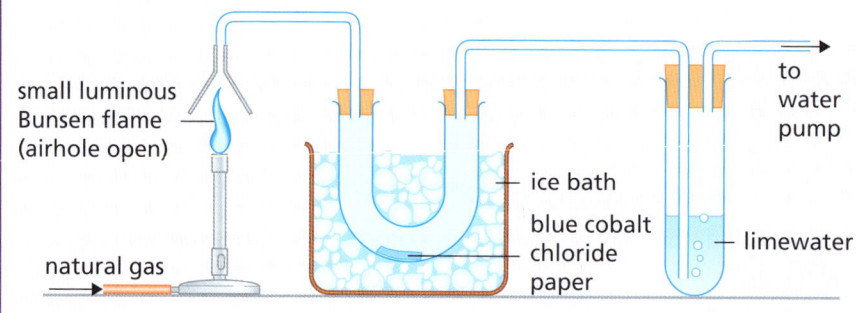

[Diagram: apparatus with small luminous Bunsen flame (airhole open) burning natural gas, connected to a U-tube in an ice bath containing blue cobalt chloride paper, then to limewater, then to water pump]

**Safety:** Wear eye protection. Handle cobalt chloride paper as little as possible.

▲ **Figure 1** On a winter's day you can often see the water produced when the hydrocarbons in petrol or diesel burn, as the steam formed in combustion of the fuel condenses when it cools down

As well as using blue cobalt chloride paper to test for the water formed in the complete combustion of a hydrocarbon, you can also use white anhydrous copper sulfate. On contact with water, the white powder turns blue.

## Incomplete combustion

All fossil fuels – oil, coal, and natural gas – produce carbon dioxide and water when they burn in plenty of air, reacting with oxygen. However, when there is not enough oxygen, for example, inside an engine, there is **incomplete combustion**. Instead of all the carbon in the fuel turning into carbon dioxide, carbon monoxide gas, CO, is also formed. Carbon monoxide is a toxic gas. It is colourless and odourless. Your red blood cells pick up this gas and carry it around in your blood instead of oxygen.

### Synoptic links

To revise the tests for water and the reactions they are based on, look back to Topic C8.7.

You will look at testing for gases in more detail in Topic C10.3.

**C9 Crude oil and fuels**

## Maths

### Worked example

A typical small cylinder of butane, $C_4H_{10}$, used for camping contains 5.000 kg of liquefied butane.

a Write a balanced symbol equation, including state symbols, for the complete combustion of butane.

b If all the gas were burnt in a plentiful supply of air, what would be the maximum mass of carbon dioxide released into the atmosphere?

### Solution

a $2C_4H_{10}(g) + 13O_2(g) \rightarrow 8CO_2(g) + 10H_2O(g)$

b In the cylinder we have 5.000 kg of butane, that is, 5000 g of the gas. Using $A_r$ of C = 12 and H = 1, the $M_r$ of $C_4H_{10}$ = $(4 \times 12) + (10 \times 1) = 58$.

So, knowing that 1 mole of butane = 58 g, in 5000 g we have $\frac{5000}{58}$ moles of butane (from number of moles = $\frac{\text{mass}}{M_r}$).

The balanced equation tells us that 2 moles of butane gives off 8 moles of $CO_2$, so 1 mole of butane gives off 4 moles of $CO_2$ and $\frac{5000}{58}$ moles of butane give off $\left(\frac{5000}{58}\right) \times 4$ moles of $CO_2$.

1 mole of $CO_2$ has a mass of $[12 + (2 \times 16)]$ g = 44 g

So, using mass = number of moles × $M_r$:

$\left(\frac{5000}{58}\right) \times 4$ moles of $CO_2$ will have a mass of:

$[\left(\frac{5000}{58}\right) \times 4] \times 44$ g

= **15 170 g (or 15.17 kg)**

The answer is given to four significant figures in line with the mass of butane provided in the question.

▲ **Figure 2** Compressed butane gas is sold in blue cylinders and is used to fuel camping stoves

## Summary questions

1 Name the products of the complete combustion of a hydrocarbon. **2 MARKS**

2 Describe a positive test for each of the products of combustion. **2 MARKS**

3 a Natural gas is mainly methane, $CH_4$. Write a balanced symbol equation, including state symbols, for its complete combustion. **3 MARKS**

b When natural gas burns in a faulty gas heater, it can produce carbon monoxide (and water). Write a balanced symbol equation, including state symbols, to show just this reaction. **3 MARKS**

c Describe why victims of carbon monoxide poisoning are unaware that carbon monoxide is building up in the air they breathe. **2 MARKS**

4 **H** A cylinder of propane, $C_3H_8$, contains 16.00 kg of liquefied gas. Using the balanced chemical equation, calculate the minimum mass of oxygen gas needed for complete combustion of the gas in the cylinder. **6 MARKS**

## Key points

- When hydrocarbon fuels are burned in plenty of air, the carbon and hydrogen in the fuel are completely oxidised. They produce carbon dioxide and water.

- You can test the gases formed in complete combustion of a hydrocarbon: the carbon dioxide turns limewater cloudy, and the water turns blue cobalt chloride paper pink (or white anhydrous copper sulfate blue).

- Incomplete combustion of a hydrocarbon produces carbon monoxide (a toxic gas) as one of its products.

133

# C9.4 Cracking hydrocarbons

## Learning objectives

*After this topic, you should know:*
- how and why larger, less useful hydrocarbon molecules are cracked to form smaller ones
- examples to illustrate the usefulness of cracking
- what alkenes are and how they differ from alkanes.

## Why crack hydrocarbons?

Some of the heavier fractions from the fractional distillation of crude oil are not in high demand. The hydrocarbons in them are made up of large molecules. They are thick liquids or solids with high boiling points. They are difficult to vaporise and do not burn easily – so they are poor fuels, although they do have their uses (see Topic C9.2). Yet the main demand from crude oil is for fuels and starting materials (feedstock) for the chemical industry. Fortunately, the larger, less useful hydrocarbon molecules can be broken down into smaller, more useful ones in a process called **cracking**.

The process takes place at an oil refinery in steel vessels called crackers (Figure 1). In the cracker, a heavy fraction distilled from crude oil is heated to vaporise the hydrocarbons. The vapour is then either:

- passed over a hot catalyst, or
- mixed with steam and heated to a very high temperature.

The hydrocarbons are cracked as **thermal decomposition** reactions take place. The large molecules split apart to form smaller, more useful ones.

## An example of cracking

Decane, $C_{10}H_{22}$, is a medium-sized alkane molecule. When it is heated to 500 °C with a catalyst, it breaks down. One of the molecules produced is pentane, $C_5H_{12}$, which is used in petrol.

pentane (displayed formula)

Propene and ethene are also made, which the chemical industry can use to produce polymers and other chemicals, such as solvents:

$$C_{10}H_{22} \xrightarrow{500°C + catalyst} C_5H_{12} + C_3H_6 + C_2H_4$$
decane → pentane + propene + ethene

This cracking reaction is an example of thermal decomposition.

Notice how cracking produces different types of molecules. One of the molecules is pentane. The first part of its name tells us that it has five carbon atoms (*pent-*). The last part of its name (*-ane*) shows that it is an alkane. Like all other alkanes, pentane is a saturated hydrocarbon. Its molecules have as much hydrogen as possible in them.

The other molecules in this reaction have names that end slightly differently. They end in -ene. We call this type of molecule an **alkene**. The different ending tells us that these molecules are **unsaturated**. Unsaturated compounds contain at least one **double bond** between their carbon atoms. In Figure 2, you can see that these alkenes have one C=C double covalent bond in their molecules. As carbon atoms form four covalent bonds, it means that the unsaturated alkene molecules have two fewer hydrogen atoms in their molecules than the saturated alkane molecules with the same number of carbon atoms.

▲ **Figure 1** In an oil refinery, huge crackers like this are used to break down large hydrocarbon molecules into smaller, more useful ones. The petrochemical industry provides the chemicals used to make products such as solvents, lubricants, polymers, and detergents, as well as fuels

# C9 Crude oil and fuels

The experiment outlined in Figure 3 shows how cracking can be done in the lab.

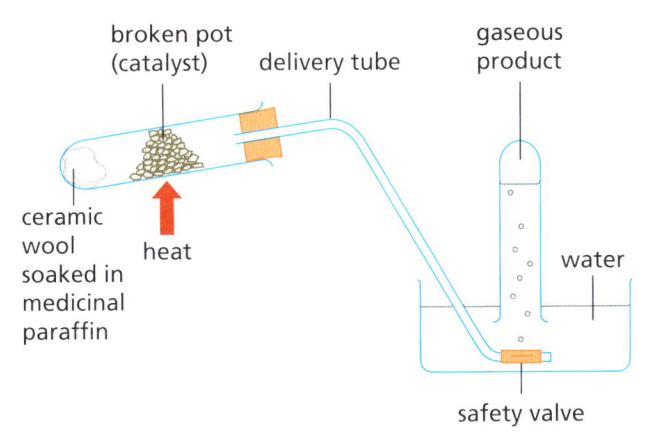

**Figure 3** Apparatus for cracking medicinal paraffin

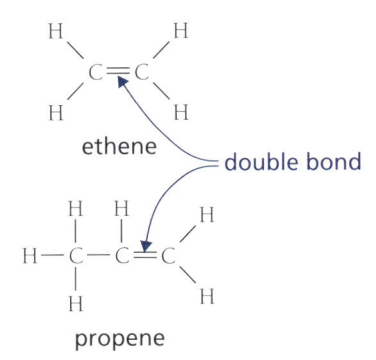

**Figure 2** A molecule of ethene, $C_2H_4$, and a molecule of propene, $C_3H_6$. These are both alkenes – each molecule has a carbon–carbon double bond in it

Tests on the gaseous products from this experiment show that alkenes:

- burn in air (but not as well as equivalent small alkanes that are used as fuels)
- react with bromine water, which is orange in colour, decolourising it.

Alkenes are generally more reactive than alkanes. The reaction with bromine water is used as a test to see if an organic compound is unsaturated (like the alkenes with their C=C double bond).

**A positive test for an unsaturated hydrocarbon is that it turns orange bromine water colourless.**

The alkanes do not react with bromine water, so you can use this test to distinguish between an alkene and an alkane.

## Metacognition

Nonane, $C_9H_{20}$, is an alkane found in crude oil. Describe its journey from entering an oil refinery to leaving it as smaller more useful molecules. You could write a 'story', draw a comic strip, or show a sequence on a flow map.

## Summary questions

1. Define the process of cracking. **1 MARK**
2. Describe the process of cracking a heavy fraction distilled from crude oil. **2 MARKS**
3. Cracking a hydrocarbon makes two new hydrocarbons, **A** and **B**. When bromine water is added to **A**, nothing happens. Bromine water added to **B** turns from an orange solution to a colourless solution.
   - a  i  Which hydrocarbon, **A** or **B**, is unsaturated? **1 MARK**
     - ii Name the type of unsaturated hydrocarbon formed in cracking. **1 MARK**
   - b  i  Which hydrocarbon, **A** or **B**, is used as a fuel? **1 MARK**
     - ii Name the type of saturated hydrocarbon formed in cracking. **1 MARK**
   - c  Name the type of reaction cracking is an example of. **1 MARK**
4. Dodecane (an alkane with 12 carbon atoms) can be cracked into octane (with eight carbon atoms) and ethene. Write a balanced symbol equation for this reaction. **2 MARKS**

## Key points

- Large hydrocarbon molecules can be broken up into smaller molecules by passing the vapours over a hot catalyst, or by mixing them with steam and heating them to a very high temperature.
- Cracking produces saturated hydrocarbons, used as fuels, and unsaturated hydrocarbons (called alkenes).
- Alkenes react with orange bromine water, turning it colourless.

# C9 Crude oil and fuels

## Practice questions

1 One alkane, **A**, has a boiling point of 344 °C and another, **B**, has a boiling point of 126 °C.
   a Which one will be collected nearer the top of a fractionating column in an oil refinery? Explain your choice. *2 MARKS*
   b Which one will be the better fuel? Explain your choice. *2 MARKS*
   c Explain the difference you would expect between **A** and **B** in terms of their viscosity. *1 MARK*

2 a The alkanes are all saturated hydrocarbons.
     i Define a hydrocarbon. *1 MARK*
     ii What does 'saturated' mean when describing an alkane? *1 MARK*
   b i Give the name and formula of this alkane:

   $$H-\overset{\overset{H}{|}}{\underset{\underset{H}{|}}{C}}-\overset{\overset{H}{|}}{\underset{\underset{H}{|}}{C}}-\overset{\overset{H}{|}}{\underset{\underset{H}{|}}{C}}-H$$
   *1 MARK*

     ii What do the letters represent in this displayed formula? *1 MARK*
     iii What do the lines between the letters represent? *1 MARK*
   c The alkane in part **b** is used in portable gas heaters.
     i Write a word equation to show its complete combustion. *1 MARK*
     ii Write a balanced symbol equation, including state symbols, for its complete combustion. *3 MARKS*
   d There must be good ventilation in the room when using a portable gas heater. Name the toxic gas that will be produced if there is a poor supply of air into the heater. *1 MARK*

3 a i Copy and complete this general formula for the alkanes: $C_nH_{\_\_\_}$? *1 MARK*
     ii Give the formula of the alkane with 18 carbon atoms. *1 MARK*
     iii Give the formula of the alkane with 18 hydrogen atoms. *1 MARK*
   b Look at the boiling points in this table:

| Alkane | Number of carbon atoms | Boiling point in °C |
|---|---|---|
| methane | 1 | −161.0 |
| ethane | 2 | −88.0 |
| propane | 3 | −42.0 |
| butane | 4 | −0.5 |
| pentane | 5 | |
| hexane | 6 | 69.0 |

   Draw a graph of the alkanes' boiling points (vertical axis) against the number of carbon atoms (horizontal axis). *3 MARKS*
   c Describe the general pattern you see from your graph. *1 MARK*
   d Use your graph to predict the boiling point of pentane. *1 MARK*

4 Two students are testing the products formed when the hydrocarbons in wax burn. They set up the experiment as shown in the diagram below:

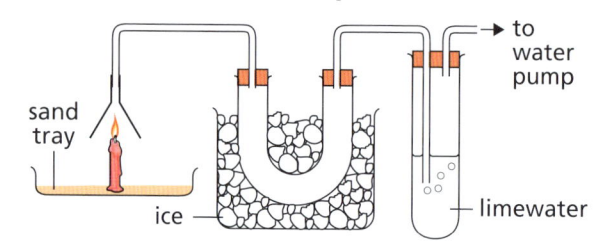

   a Why did they put ice around the U-tube? *1 MARK*
   b How can they test for the substance formed in the U-tube? *1 MARK*
   c Explain what would happen to the limewater. *2 MARKS*
   d There is a small amount of carbon dioxide in the air. How can they show that the carbon dioxide they test for is not just the result of the carbon dioxide in the air? *1 MARK*
   e One of the hydrocarbons found in candle wax is pentacosane, a straight-chain alkane containing 25 carbon atoms.
     i Write the chemical formula of pentacosane. *1 MARK*
     ii Write a word equation for its complete combustion. *1 MARK*
     iii Write a balanced symbol equation, including state symbols, for its complete combustion. *3 MARKS*

5 The equation for a reaction that can take place in an oil refinery is:
   $$C_{15}H_{32} \rightarrow C_8H_{18} + C_3H_6 + 2C_2H_4$$
   a Give the name for this type of thermal decomposition reaction. *1 MARK*
   b Give two ways in which the reaction could be carried out using gaseous $C_{15}H_{32}$. *2 MARKS*
   c Why is this reaction carried out? *2 MARKS*

# C9 Crude oil and fuels

## Exam-style questions

**01** The displayed formulae of five hydrocarbons are shown in **Figure 1**.

**Figure 1**

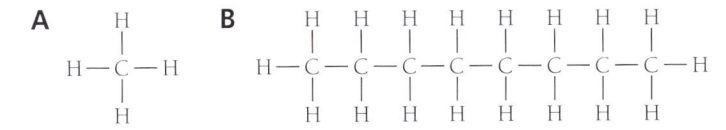

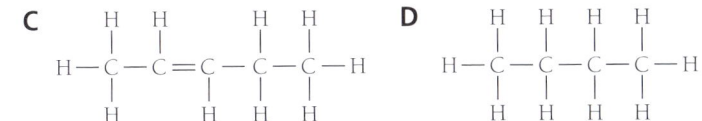

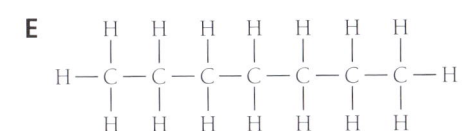

A: CH₄ (methane displayed)

B: C₈H₁₈ (octane, straight chain displayed)

C: H–C(H)(H)–C(H)=C–C(H)(H)–C(H)(H)–H (an alkene)

D: C₄H₁₀ (butane displayed)

E: C₇H₁₆ (heptane displayed)

**01.1** Define the term hydrocarbon. **2 MARKS**

Choose which hydrocarbon **A**, **B**, **C**, **D**, or **E** is the answer to questions **01.2** to **01.6**.

**01.2** Which hydrocarbon has the lowest boiling point? **1 MARK**

**01.3** Which hydrocarbon has the general formula $C_nH_{2n}$? **1 MARK**

**01.4** Which hydrocarbon can be cracked to form **D** and $C_3H_6$ as the only products? **1 MARK**

**01.5** Which hydrocarbon decolourises bromine water? **1 MARK**

**01.6** Which hydrocarbon has a relative formula mass $M_r$ of 58? **1 MARK**

**01.7** The fractional distillation of crude oil produces too much $C_{14}H_{30}$.

Describe how $C_{14}H_{30}$ can be cracked to produce shorter chain hydrocarbons. **2 MARKS**

**02** Crude oil is a mixture of many useful substances. Crude oil is separated into fractions by fractional distillation, as shown in **Figure 2**.

**02.1** Describe and explain how crude oil is separated into fractions by fractional distillation. Use **Figure 2** to help you answer this question. **4 MARKS**

**02.2** The fractional distillation of crude oil produces more kerosene than required. Kerosene can be cracked. Complete the equation for the cracking of $C_{12}H_{26}$ to produce $C_7H_{16}$ and two different alkenes.

$C_{12}H_{26} \rightarrow C_7H_{16} + \ldots\ldots + \ldots\ldots$ **2 MARKS**

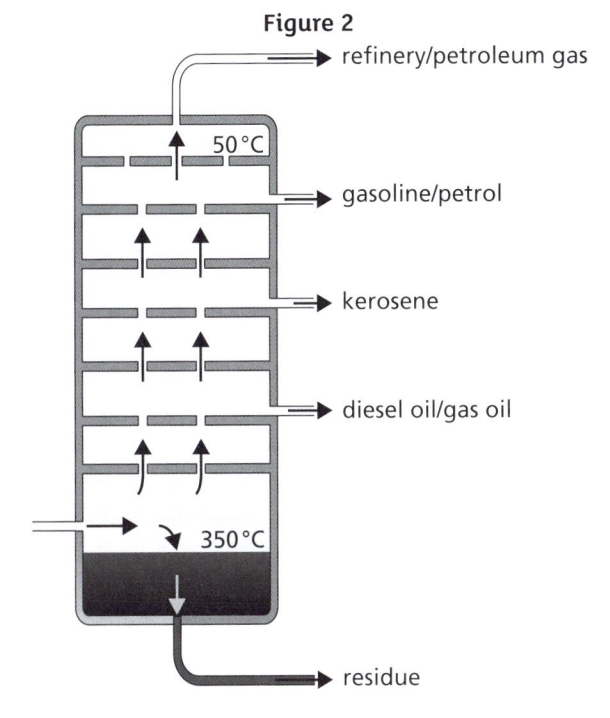

**Figure 2**

(Fractional distillation column showing: refinery/petroleum gas at top (50 °C), gasoline/petrol, kerosene, diesel oil/gas oil, residue at bottom (350 °C))

**02.3** The equation shows the incomplete combustion of $C_{12}H_{26}$.

$C_{12}H_{26} + \ldots\ldots O_2 \rightarrow 9CO + 3CO_2 + 13H_2O$

Complete the balancing of the equation. **1 MARK**

**02.4** Explain why the incomplete combustion of $C_{12}H_{26}$ is dangerous. **3 MARKS**

**03** The equation shows the cracking of $C_{18}H_{38}$ to produce two liquid products.

$C_{18}H_{38} \rightarrow C_{13}H_{28} + C_5H_{10}$

**03.1** Explain why $C_{18}H_{38}$ needs to be heated to produce $C_{13}H_{28}$ and $C_5H_{10}$. **2 MARKS**

**03.2** The two liquid products were poured into separate test tubes.

Describe a chemical test that would show which tube contained $C_5H_{10}$.

Explain your answer. **3 MARKS**

**03.3** Explain why $C_{18}H_{38}$ has a higher boiling point than $C_{13}H_{28}$. **3 MARKS**

# 4 Analysis and the Earth's resources

Analytical chemists have developed many tests to detect specific chemicals. These tests are based on reactions that produce a gas with distinctive properties, or a colour change, or an insoluble solid that appears as a precipitate. Instrumental analysis provides fast, sensitive, and accurate results, as used by forensic scientists and anti-doping scientists.

The Earth's atmosphere is dynamic and is always changing. Some of these changes are man-made and some are part of natural cycles. Scientists and engineers are trying to solve the problems caused by increased levels of air pollutants and global climate change. Industries use the Earth's natural resources to manufacture useful products. In order to operate sustainably, chemists seek to minimise the use of limited resources, the use of energy, waste produced, and environmental impact.

| | | |
|---|---|---|
| **1** | Name the experimental technique that can separate a mixture of dyes. | chromatography |
| **2** | The Earth's atmosphere is mainly made up of two gases. Name the gases. | nitrogen and oxygen |
| **3** | What is a greenhouse gas? | a gas that contributes to global climate change |
| **4** | The increase in which gas is mainly responsible for global climate change? | carbon dioxide (or $CO_2$) |
| **5** | Name the solution used to test for carbon dioxide gas. | Limewater (calcium hydroxide solution) |
| **6** | What colour change happens when litmus indicator is added to an alkali, such as sodium hydroxide solution? | red changes to blue |
| **7** | What is a composite? | a mixture of materials with properties that are a combination of those of the materials in it |
| **8** | What are the missing words? Metals can be drawn out into long, thin wires and can be hammered into shapes without smashing. Scientists say that the metals can be described as ………….. and ………….. when they display these properties. | ductile and malleable |

# Journey through GCSE Chemistry

**YOU ARE HERE**

### Atoms, bonding, and calculations

- C1 Atomic structure
- C2 The Periodic Table
- C3 Structure and bonding
- C4 Chemical calculations

### Chemical reactions and energy changes

- C5 Chemical changes
- C6 Electrolysis
- C7 Energy changes

### Rates, equilibrium, and organic chemistry

- C8 Rates and equilibrium
- C9 Crude oil and fuels

### Analysis and the Earth's resources

- C10 Chemical analysis
- C11 The Earth's atmosphere
- C12 The Earth's resources

# C10 Chemical analysis

## C10.1 Pure substances and mixtures

### Learning objectives

After this topic, you should know:
- how to use melting point data to distinguish pure from impure substances
- how to identify examples of useful mixtures called formulations, given appropriate information.

▲ **Figure 1** This mineral water might be described as pure as a mountain stream, but it would not be called a pure substance by a chemist

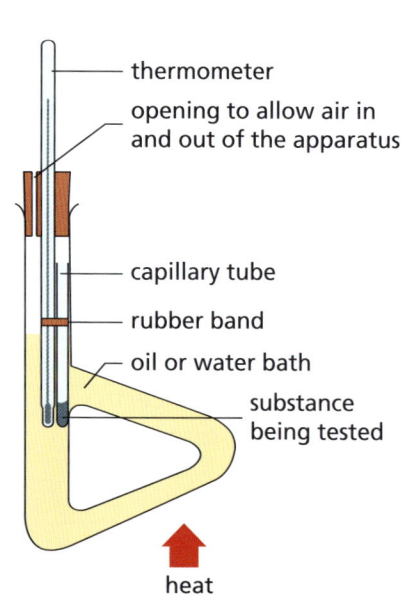

▲ **Figure 2** This apparatus can be used to determine the melting point of a solid in powdered or crystal form

### What is meant by purity?

When you talk about something being *pure* in everyday life, often you are not referring to its chemical purity. For example, you often see orange juice or mineral water being advertised as 'pure' (Figure 1). However, a bottle of mineral water is not chemically pure.

When advertising a product, pure is taken to mean that it is in its natural state and 'has had nothing added to it'. For example, 'pure orange juice' means it comes from freshly squeezed oranges.

However, to a chemist:

**A pure substance is one that is made up of just one substance. That substance can be either an element or a compound.**

### Analysing pure substances and mixtures

You can use boiling points and melting points to identify pure substances.

Do you remember a test for water? For example, it turns white anhydrous copper sulfate blue. But that only tells you that water is present. It does not tell you whether the water is pure or not. The test for pure water is that its melting point is exactly 0 °C, and its boiling point is exactly 100 °C.

**The melting and boiling points of an element or a compound are called 'fixed points'.**

You can use melting points or boiling points to identify substances because pure substances have characteristic, specific temperatures at which they melt and boil. These fixed points can be looked up in databooks or databases stored on computers.

The melting point and boiling point of a mixture will vary, depending on the composition of the mixture. A mixture does not have a sharp melting point or boiling point. It changes state over a range of temperatures. This difference between pure substances and mixtures can be used to distinguish whether an unknown sample is a pure substance or a mixture of substances. So, doing an experiment to find a melting point (or melting range) is a quick and easy test of a compound's purity.

Impurities tend to lower the melting point of a substance and raise its boiling point. The size of the difference from the fixed point of a pure substance depends on the amount of any impurities mixed with it. The purer the compound is, the narrower the melting point range. For example, the melting point range of a purified sample of caffeine is 234–237 °C. However, crude caffeine extracted from tea melts in the range 180–220 °C, showing it is an impure sample.

## Formulations

A **formulation** is a mixture, made up in definite proportions, that has been designed to produce a useful product. Many consumer products are made up of complex mixtures. For example, medicinal drugs are formulations. They will often only contain between 5% and 10% of the active drug. This is the specific compound that affects the body to relieve symptoms or cure an illness. If taken in tablet form, they can also contain colorants, sweeteners, smooth coatings to aid swallowing, and fillers. There may also be other compounds present to aid the dissolving of the tablet at the most effective place in the digestive tract.

Paints are also common formulations. In general, paints will contain:

- a pigment, to provide colour
- a binder, to help the paint attach itself to an object and to form a protective film when dry
- a solvent, to help the pigment and binder spread well during painting by thinning them out.

Other formulations are found in the range of cleaning agents used in the home. For example, washing-up liquids generally contain:

- a surfactant, the actual detergent that removes grease
- water, to thin out the mixture so it can squirt more easily from the bottle
- colouring and fragrance additives, to improve the appeal of the product to potential customers
- rinse agent, to help water drain off crockery.

Fuels, alloys, fertilisers, pesticides, cosmetics, and food products are other examples of formulations.

▲ **Figure 3** Scientists must test the effects that the other compounds in a formulation will have on the active drug in medicines

### Synoptic link

To remind yourself about the differences between mixtures and compounds, look back to Topic C1.3.

### Summary questions

1. What is the difference between the use of the term pure in advertising and its use in chemistry? **2 MARKS**

2. A white powder was placed in the melting point apparatus shown in Figure 2. The oil in the apparatus had a high boiling point. The chemist carrying out the test noted that the white powder started to melt at 158 °C and finished melting at 169 °C.
   a. Determine the melting range of the white powder. **1 MARK**
   b. What does this information tell us about the white powder? **1 MARK**
   c. Explain why oil, and not water, was used in the apparatus. **1 MARK**

3. An insecticide formulation contains a very powerful toxic substance to kill the insects that feed on crops.
   Suggest two reasons why most of this pesticide formulation is made up of a solvent. One reason should benefit the environment and the other should benefit the farmer. **2 MARKS**

### Key points

- Pure substances can be compounds or elements, but they contain only one substance.
- Pure elements and compounds melt and boil at specific temperatures, and these fixed points can be used to distinguish pure substances from mixtures.
- Formulations are useful mixtures, made up in definite proportions.

# C10.2 Analysing chromatograms

## Learning objectives

After this topic, you should know:
- how chromatography can be used to distinguish pure substances from impure substances
- how paper chromatography separates mixtures
- how to interpret chromatograms
- how to determine $R_f$ values from chromatograms.

## Synoptic link

To remind yourself about how to set up a paper chromatogram, look back to Topic C1.4.

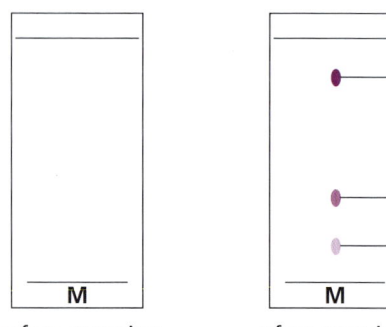

Scientists have many instruments that they can use to identify unknown compounds. Many of these are more sensitive, automated versions of the techniques that you have used. For example, chromatography can be used to separate and identify mixtures of amino acids. The amino acids are colourless, but they appear as purple spots on the paper when sprayed with a locating agent, and then dried (Figure 1).

You will have tried paper chromatography before, and probably used it to separate dyes in inks or food colourings (Figure 2).

Chromatography always involves a mobile phase and a stationary phase. The mobile phase moves through the stationary phase, carrying the components of the mixture under investigation with it. Each component in the mixture will have a different attraction for the mobile phase and the stationary phase. A substance with stronger forces of attraction between itself and the mobile phase than between itself and the stationary phase will be carried a greater distance in a given time. A substance with a stronger force of attraction to the stationary phase will not travel as far over the same time.

In paper chromatography the mobile phase is the solvent chosen, and the stationary phase can be thought of as the paper.

In Figure 1, amino acid **X** from the mixture **M** has the strongest attraction to the solvent, and amino acid **Z** has the strongest attraction to the paper.

Given an unknown organic solution, chromatography can usually tell you if it is a single compound or a mixture. If the unknown sample is a mixture of compounds, there will probably be more than one spot formed on the chromatogram. On the other hand, a single spot indicates the possibility of a pure substance.

▲ **Figure 1** A chromatogram produced by a mixture of amino acids

## Identifying unknown substances using chromatography

Once the compounds in a mixture have been separated using chromatography, they can be identified. You can compare spots on the chromatogram with others obtained from known substances (Figure 2).

The chromatogram in Figure 2 shows that mixture **A** still has one substance left unknown. A scientist making the chromatogram often does not know which pure compounds to include in their experiment to make a positive identification. It is also not practical to store actual chromatograms or their images, even on a computer. To make valid comparisons, every variable that affects a chromatogram would need to be exactly the same in all the chromatograms.

It is far more effective to measure data taken from any chromatogram of the unknown sample, then match it against a database. So, the data is presented as **retention factor** ($R_f$) values. An $R_f$ value is a ratio, calculated by dividing the distance a spot travels up the paper (measured to the centre of the spot) by the distance the solvent front travels:

$$R_f = \frac{\text{distance moved by substance}}{\text{distance moved by solvent}}$$

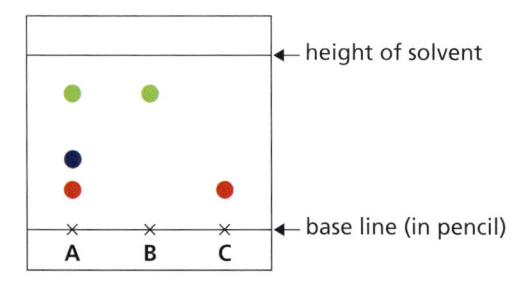

▲ **Figure 2** This chromatogram shows that **A** is a mixture of three substances. These are **B** and **C** plus one other unknown substance

## C10 Chemical analysis

As the number generated in the calculation is a ratio, it does not matter how long you run your chromatography experiment or what quantities you use. For comparisons against an $R_f$ database to be valid, you just have to ensure that the solvent used and the temperature are the same as those quoted in the database or databook. Figure 4 shows how to get the measurements to calculate $R_f$ values.

▲ **Figure 3** Black ink can be separated out into its different colours on a chromatogram

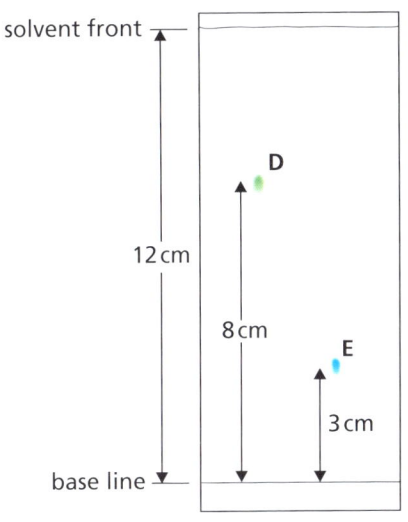

### Practical

#### Finding $R_f$ values

Using a capillary tube, pencil, **pipette**, water, boiling tube, and a narrow strip of chromatography paper, find out the $R_f$ values of the different dyes in the mixture of food colourings provided.

Present your evidence clearly. Include your dried chromatogram, calculations, and an evaluation.

### Maths

#### Worked example

Find the $R_f$ value of compounds **D** and **E** using the chromatogram shown in Figure 4.

#### Solution

The $R_f$ value of **D** = $\frac{8\,cm}{12\,cm}$ = **0.67**

The $R_f$ value of **E** = $\frac{3\,cm}{12\,cm}$ = **0.25**

▲ **Figure 4** The $R_f$ values from this chromatogram are calculated in the Maths box opposite. The $R_f$ value of an unknown substance, in a particular solvent at a given temperature, can be compared with values in a database to identify the substance

### Summary questions

1. Describe how you calculate an $R_f$ value from a chromatogram. **3 MARKS**

2. Use the chromatogram below to determine the $R_f$ value of substance **X**. **1 MARK**

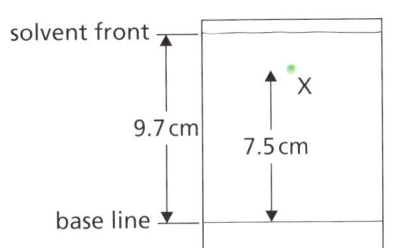

3. The $R_f$ values of two substances, **Y** and **Z**, were taken from a chromatogram run in 50% water and 50% ethanol solvent at 20 °C. The $R_f$ value of **Y** was 0.54 and that of **Z** was 0.79. What can you deduce about the solubility of **Y** and **Z** from these values, and how could you use them to identify **Y** and **Z**? **3 MARKS**

4. To positively identify a compound from a chromatogram, explain why the solvent and temperature must be the same as those used to generate the $R_f$ values in a database. **4 MARKS**

### Key points

- Scientists can analyse unknown substances in solution by using paper chromatography.
- $R_f$ values can be measured and matched against databases to identify specific substances.
- $R_f = \dfrac{\text{distance moved by substance}}{\text{distance moved by solvent}}$

143

# C10.3 Testing for gases

### Learning objectives

After this topic, you should know:
- the tests and the positive results for the gases:
  - hydrogen
  - oxygen
  - carbon dioxide
  - chlorine.

### Synoptic links

To revise how you can use the gases given off in reactions to monitor rates of reaction, look back to Topic C8.1.

To remind yourself about the reaction of metals with dilute acids, look back to Topic C5.1 and Topic C5.4.

### Study tip

When asked how to identify a given gas, always give the test **and** its result.

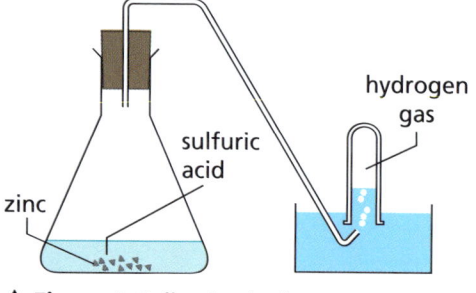

▲ **Figure 1** Collecting hydrogen over water

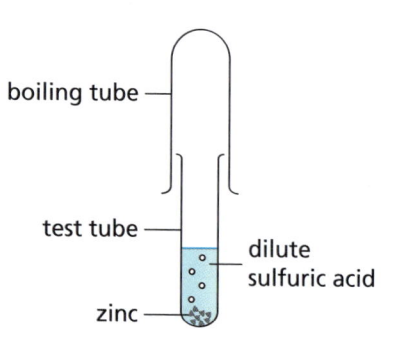

▲ **Figure 2** Collecting hydrogen by upward delivery (downward displacement of air)

Many of the reactions you will study in chemistry give off gases as a product. So, chemists have devised quick and easy tests to identify different gases.

## Test for hydrogen

The reaction between zinc and dilute acid is a convenient way to make some hydrogen gas to test:

$$\text{zinc} + \text{sulfuric acid} \rightarrow \text{zinc sulfate} + \text{hydrogen}$$
$$Zn(s) + H_2SO_4(aq) \rightarrow ZnSO_4(aq) + H_2(g)$$

If you want the gas to be produced more quickly, a few crystals of copper(II) sulfate can be added, or magnesium can be used instead of zinc.

### Practical

**Testing for hydrogen gas**

Collect a test tube of hydrogen gas, using either of the sets of apparatus shown in Figures 1 and 2.
- Record your observations when you hold a lighted splint at the open end of the test tube of hydrogen gas.
- Explain your observations.
- What do the methods of collecting hydrogen gas tell you about its properties?

**Safety:** Wear eye protection. Hydrogen gas is flammable.

**Positive test for hydrogen gas: a lighted splint 'pops', when held at the end of a test tube.**

## Test for oxygen

A convenient way to make some oxygen gas to test is the decomposition of hydrogen peroxide solution, with a little manganese(IV) oxide added as a catalyst.

$$\text{hydrogen peroxide} \xrightarrow{\text{manganese(IV) oxide}} \text{water} + \text{oxygen}$$
$$2H_2O_2(aq) \longrightarrow 2H_2O(l) + O_2(g)$$

### Practical

**Testing for oxygen gas**

Collect 15 cm³ hydrogen peroxide solution in a small conical flask.

Add a small amount of manganese(IV) oxide from the end of a spatula.

Insert a glowing splint (made by blowing out a lighted splint) in the mouth of the flask.
- Record and explain your observations.

**Safety:** Wear eye protection.

Positive test for oxygen gas: a glowing splint relights, when inserted into the gas.

## Test for carbon dioxide

You can make carbon dioxide gas to test by reacting marble chips (calcium carbonate) and dilute hydrochloric acid:

calcium carbonate + hydrochloric acid → calcium chloride + water + carbon dioxide

$CaCO_3(s) + 2HCl(aq) \rightarrow CaCl_2(aq) + H_2O(l) + CO_2(g)$

### Practical

**Testing for carbon dioxide gas**

Bubble carbon dioxide gas through limewater (calcium hydroxide solution), using the apparatus shown below:

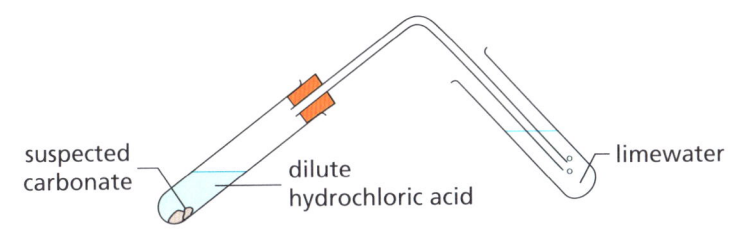

- Record your observations.
- Explain your observations.

**Safety:** Wear eye protection.

**Positive test for carbon dioxide gas:** limewater turns milky (cloudy white) when the gas is bubbled through.

## Test for chlorine

Chlorine is a toxic gas, so care must be taken when working with this gas. Your teacher will show you the test for chlorine gas (see the 'Testing for chlorine gas' box).

**Positive test for chlorine gas:** damp blue litmus paper turns white (as it gets bleached).

### Synoptic link

You might be asked to test the chlorine gas given off during the electrolysis of a chloride solution, as in Topic C6.4.

### Practical

**Testing for chlorine gas**

Your teacher will carefully add concentrated hydrochloric acid (corrosive) to a spatula of moistened potassium manganate(VII) crystals in a boiling tube held in a rack inside a fume cupboard.

A piece of damp blue litmus paper can be held in the mouth of the boiling tube.

Record and explain your observations.

### Summary questions

1. How would you test a gas to see if it was hydrogen? **1 MARK**
2. Describe the test for oxygen gas and its positive result. **2 MARKS**
3. During the electrolysis of a chloride solution, a student predicted that a mixture of chlorine and oxygen gases would be given off from the anode. Suggest how you could test this prediction. **6 MARKS**
4. Explain why limewater (a solution of calcium hydroxide, $Ca(OH)_2$) turns milky when it reacts with carbon dioxide. Use a balanced symbol equation, including state symbols, in your explanation. **3 MARKS**

### Key points

- Hydrogen gas burns rapidly with a 'pop' when you apply a lighted splint.
- Oxygen gas relights a glowing splint.
- Carbon dioxide gas turns limewater milky (cloudy white).
- Chlorine gas bleaches damp blue litmus paper white.

145

# C10 Chemical analysis

## Practice questions

1. As well as pigments (25% by mass), binders (30%), and solvents (40%), the formulation used to make a gloss paint has additives included in the mixture.
   a. Calculate the percentage of additives in the formulation to make gloss paint. **1 MARK**
   b. Explain what a formulation is and why they are manufactured in the chemical industry. **2 MARKS**
   c. **H** Titanium(IV) oxide, $TiO_2$, is used to give a brilliant white colour to paint. Assuming all the pigment is titanium(IV) oxide, how many moles of the oxide would be in a tin containing 6.00 kg of paint. Give your answer to 3 significant figures. **5 MARKS**

2. The diagram below shows the apparatus used to identify an unknown solid.

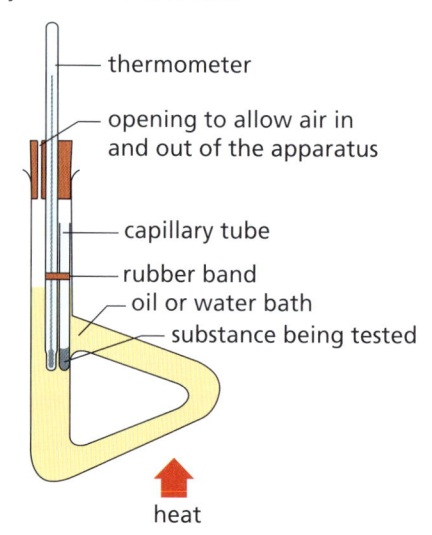

   [Diagram: apparatus with thermometer, opening to allow air in and out of the apparatus, capillary tube, rubber band, oil or water bath, substance being tested, heat applied from below]

   The solid started to melt at 81 °C, and was completely melted at 85 °C.
   a. Explain what information can be deduced about the unknown solid tested. **2 MARKS**
   b. A different solid was tested in the same apparatus. It was found that the whole sample melted at 62 °C.
      i. What can be deduced about this second solid? **1 MARK**
      ii. Both solids tested were found to be made up of covalently bonded molecules. Explain in detail the difference in the melting temperatures of the two samples in terms of their structure and bonding. **3 MARKS**

3. A student carried out a paper chromatography experiment on a mixture of the food colourings used to coat a chocolate-centred sweet.
   a. What would the student use to mark the baseline on the chromatogram? **1 MARK**
   b. Suggest how the student could effectively spot the mixture on the baseline. **3 MARKS**
   c. The student ran the experiment and found that, when the solvent front had almost reached the top of the paper, the food colourings had hardly moved from the baseline, so there was poor separation of the different colours. Suggest a way the student could try to improve the results on the chromatogram. **1 MARK**

4. A sample of solid sodium nitrate, $NaNO_3$, was heated in a test tube. A gas was given off and collected over water in an inverted measuring cylinder. At the end of the experiment, 96 cm³ of gas had been collected.

   $$...NaNO_3 \xrightarrow{heat} ...NaNO_2 + ............$$  **2 MARKS**

   a. Complete and balance the equation.
   b. Draw the apparatus used to carry out the experiment. **3 MARKS**
   c. Describe a positive test for the gas collected. **1 MARK**
   d. Explain what precaution should be taken before the heating is stopped. **3 MARKS**
   e. **H** Calculate the mass of $NaNO_3$ that decomposed in the experiment. **4 MARKS**

5. The chromatogram below is for two unknown substances, **X** and **Y**. Ethanol was used as the solvent.

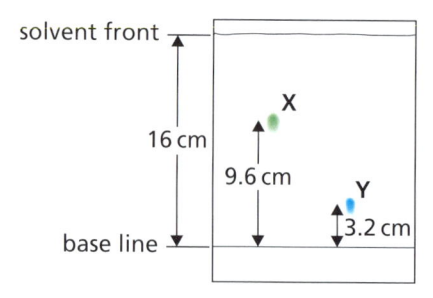

   [Diagram: chromatogram showing solvent front at top, X spot at 9.6 cm from base line, Y spot at 3.2 cm from base line, total 16 cm from base line to solvent front]

   a. Using the chromatogram above, determine the $R_f$ values of the unknown substances **X** and **Y**. **2 MARKS**
   b. Explain the difference in the $R_f$ values of **X** and **Y**. **2 MARKS**
   c. Describe how you could use the $R_f$ values to positively identify **X** and **Y**. **1 MARK**
   d. Before you could be certain of the identification made, identify what other condition, besides the solvent used, should be controlled when obtaining the $R_f$ values for **X** and **Y**. **1 MARK**

146

# C10 Chemical analysis

## Exam-style questions

**01** A group of students were investigating a water filter. They had two samples of water. The students used the filter as shown in **Figure 1** and analysed the filtered water.

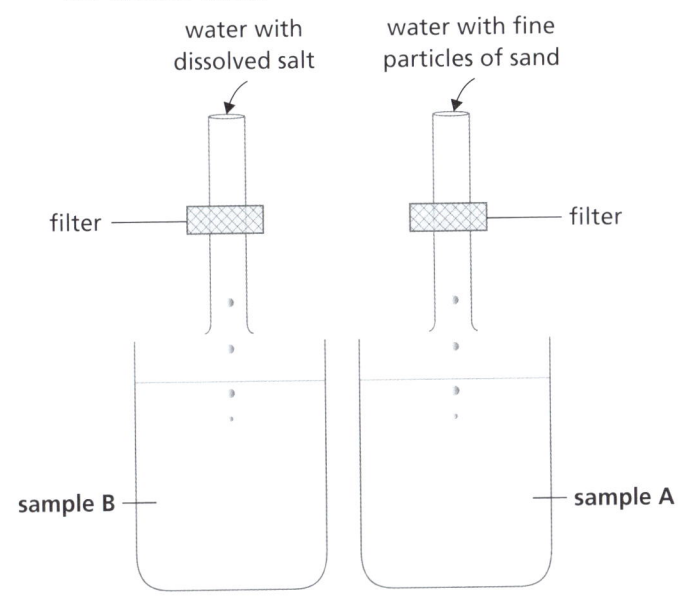

▲ **Figure 1**

Both samples of filtered water were colourless.

The students' teacher said that the filtered water in **sample A** was pure, but the filtered water in **sample B** still contained dissolved salts.

**01.1** Select the correct definition for pure. *1 MARK*

> a single element or compound, not mixed with any other substance
>
> two or more elements or compounds not chemically combined together
>
> two or more elements chemically combined in fixed proportions

**01.2** What physical property can be used to show that the filtered water in **sample A** is pure? *2 MARKS*

**01.3** Suggest how the students could show that the filtered water in **sample B** still contains dissolved salts. You do not need to do a chemical test. *2 MARKS*

**01.4** Explain why filtering the water did not remove the dissolved salts in **sample B**. *3 MARKS*

**02** A class of students were given three colourless solutions:

potassium chloride solution

potassium nitrate solution

potassium carbonate solution.

The solutions were in unlabelled beakers. The teacher told the students that only potassium carbonate solution would effervesce when dilute hydrochloric acid was added to it. The gas produced would be carbon dioxide.

**02.1** Give the test and the result of the test for carbon dioxide. *2 MARKS*

**02.2** Name **one** other product made when potassium carbonate and dilute hydrochloric acid react. *1 MARK*

The students decided to electrolyse potassium chloride solution and potassium nitrate solution separately using the apparatus in **Figure 2**.

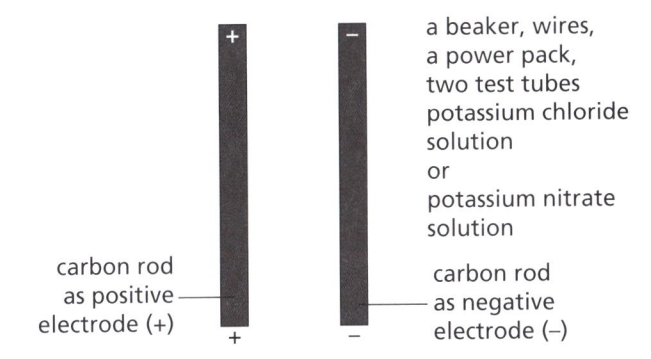

▲ **Figure 2**

Bubbles of gas were produced at each electrode. The students collected the gases.

The gases produced at each electrode are shown in **Table 1**.

Table 1

| Solution | Gas produced at the positive (+) electrode | Gas produced at the negative (−) electrode |
|---|---|---|
| potassium chloride | chlorine | hydrogen |
| potassium nitrate | oxygen | hydrogen |

**02.3** How could the students collect a pure sample of hydrogen gas? *2 MARKS*

**02.4** Describe a test and the result of the test to show which colourless solution was potassium nitrate. You should refer to **Table 1** in your answer. *2 MARKS*

**02.5** Explain how chlorine gas forms at the positive electrode in the electrolysis of potassium chloride solution. *2 MARKS*

147

# C11 The Earth's atmosphere

## C11.1 History of our atmosphere

**Learning objectives**

After this topic, you should know:
- a theory about how our atmosphere developed
- how to interpret evidence and evaluate different theories about the Earth's early atmosphere, given appropriate information.

Scientists think that the Earth was formed about 4.6 billion years ago, and that, to begin with, it was a molten ball of rock and minerals. For the first billion years, the planet was a very hot, turbulent place. The Earth's surface was covered with volcanoes that belched fire and gases into the **atmosphere**.

### The Earth's early atmosphere

There are several theories about the Earth's early atmosphere, although there is little direct evidence to draw on from billions of years ago. However, scientists have reconstructed what they think the atmosphere must have been like, based on evidence from gas bubbles trapped in ancient rocks. They also use data gathered from the atmospheres of other planets and their moons in the Solar System.

One theory suggests that:

- Volcanoes released carbon dioxide, $CO_2$, water vapour, $H_2O$, and nitrogen gas, $N_2$, plus traces of methane, $CH_4$, and ammonia, $NH_3$, and that these gases formed the early atmosphere.

- As the Earth gradually cooled down, the water vapour in the atmosphere condensed and fell as rain.

- The water collected in hollows that had formed in the crust as the rock solidified and the first oceans were formed.

- As the Earth began to stabilise, the atmosphere was probably mainly carbon dioxide. There could also have been some water vapour and nitrogen gas, and traces of methane, $CH_4$, and ammonia, $NH_3$. There would have been very little or no oxygen gas, $O_2$, at that time. This resembles the atmospheres that are known to exist today on the planets Mars and Venus. Our nearest neighbours have atmospheres made up mainly of carbon dioxide with little or no oxygen.

After these initial violent years of the history of the Earth, the atmosphere remained quite stable. That is until life first appeared on Earth.

### Oxygen in the atmosphere

There are many theories as to how life was formed on Earth billions of years ago. Scientists think that life began about 3.4 billion years ago, when the first simple organisms, similar to bacteria, appeared. These organisms could use the breakdown of substances as a source of energy.

Then, about 2.7 billion years ago, bacteria and other simple organisms, such as algae, evolved. Algae used the energy from the Sun to make their own food by photosynthesis. This produced oxygen gas, $O_2$, as a waste product. Over the next billion years or so, the levels of oxygen rose steadily as the algae and bacteria thrived in the seas. More plants evolved – all of them were photosynthesising, removing carbon dioxide, and making oxygen.

▲ **Figure 1** Volcanoes moved substances from inside the Earth to the surface and to the newly forming atmosphere

▲ **Figure 2** The surface of one of Jupiter's moons, Io, with its active volcanoes releasing gases into its sparse atmosphere. This is likely to be what our own Earth was like billions of years ago

## C11 The Earth's atmosphere

$$\text{carbon dioxide} + \text{water} \xrightarrow{\text{(energy from sunlight)}} \text{glucose} + \text{oxygen}$$
$$6CO_2 + 6H_2O \longrightarrow C_6H_{12}O_6 + 6O_2$$

As plants evolved, they successfully colonised most of the surface of the Earth. So, the atmosphere became richer in oxygen. This made it possible for the first animals to evolve. These animals could not make their own food like the algae and plants could. They relied on the algae and plants for their food and on oxygen to respire.

On the other hand, many of the earliest living microorganisms could not tolerate a relatively high oxygen concentration, because they had evolved without it. They largely died out, as there were fewer places where they could survive.

### Study tip

Remember that oxygen was not one of the gases in the Earth's original atmosphere. It was only made after the first simple organisms that could carry out photosynthesis had evolved.

▲ **Figure 3** Some of the first photosynthesising bacteria probably lived in colonies like these stromatolites. They grew in water and released oxygen into the early atmosphere

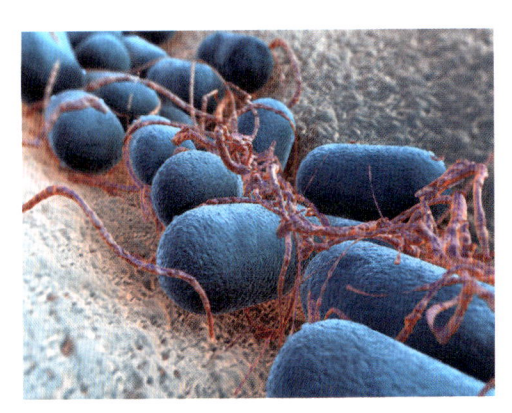

▲ **Figure 4** Not only do bacteria such as these not need oxygen – they die if they are exposed to it. However, they can survive and breed in rotting tissue and other places where there is no oxygen

### Summary questions

1. Name and give the chemical formulae of five gases that scientists speculate were found in the Earth's early atmosphere. Display your answer in a table. **5 MARKS**
2. Where do scientists think the first gases in the Earth's atmosphere came from? **1 MARK**
3. a Suggest why scientists believe there was no life on Earth for its first billion years. **1 MARK**
   b Suggest a possible source of the water that collected and formed our early oceans. **1 MARK**
4. Explain in detail how the levels of oxygen in our atmosphere increased and why this was significant in the history of the Earth. Include any relevant chemical equations in your answer. **6 MARKS**

### Key points

- The Earth's early atmosphere was formed by volcanic activity.
- It probably consisted mainly of carbon dioxide. There may also have been nitrogen and water vapour, together with traces of methane and ammonia.
- As plants spread over the Earth, the levels of oxygen in the atmosphere increased.

149

# C11.2 Our evolving atmosphere

## Learning objectives

After this topic, you should know:
- the main changes in the atmosphere over time and some of the likely causes of these changes
- the relative proportions of gases in our atmosphere now.

Scientists think that the early atmosphere of the Earth contained mainly carbon dioxide. Yet the Earth's atmosphere today only has around 0.04% of $CO_2$. So where has it all gone? The answer is mostly into living organisms and into materials formed from living organisms. As you saw in Topic C11.1, algae and plants decreased the percentage of carbon dioxide in the early atmosphere by photosynthesis.

### Carbon 'locked into' rock

Carbon dioxide, along with water, is taken in by plants and converted to glucose and oxygen during photosynthesis. The carbon in the glucose can then end up in new plant material. When animals eat the plants, some of this carbon can be transferred to the animal tissues, including their skeletons and shells.

Over millions of years, the skeletons and shells of huge numbers of these marine organisms built up at the bottom of vast oceans. There they became covered with layer upon layer of fine sediment. Under the pressure caused by being buried by all these layers of sediment, eventually the deposits formed sedimentary carbonate rocks such as limestone. Limestone is rock containing mainly calcium carbonate, $CaCO_3$.

Some of the remains of ancient living things (animals and plants) were crushed by large-scale movements of the Earth and were heated within the Earth's crust over very long periods of time. They formed the fossil fuels coal, crude oil, and natural gas.

- Coal is classed as a sedimentary rock, and was formed from thick deposits of plant material, such as ancient trees and ferns. When the plants died in swamps, they were buried, in the absence of oxygen, and compressed over millions of years.
- Crude oil and natural gas were formed from the remains of plankton deposited in mud on the seabed. These remains were covered by sediments that became layers of rock when compressed over millions of years. The crude oil and natural gas formed is found trapped beneath these layers of rock.

Carbon dioxide gas was also removed from the early atmosphere by dissolving in the water of the oceans. It reacted, for example, with metal oxides, and made insoluble carbonate compounds. These fell to the seabed as sediments and helped to form more carbonate rocks.

In this way, much of the carbon from the old carbon dioxide-rich atmosphere became locked up within the Earth's crust in rocks and fossil fuels.

Over the past 200 million years, the level of carbon dioxide in the atmosphere has not changed much. This is due to the natural cycle of carbon in which carbon moves between the oceans, rocks, and the atmosphere.

### Ammonia and methane

Volcanoes also produced nitrogen gas, $N_2$, which gradually built up in the early atmosphere, and there may have also been small proportions of methane and ammonia gases.

▲ **Figure 1** There is clear fossil evidence in carbonate rocks of the organisms which lived millions of years ago

### Practical

**Shelly carbonates**

Carry out a test with dilute hydrochloric acid to see if crushed samples of shells contain carbonates. Think of the general reaction that all carbonates undergo with acid.

How will you test any gas given off?

- Record your findings.

Any methane and ammonia found in the Earth's early atmosphere reacted with the oxygen formed by the evolving algae and plants:

$$CH_4 + 2O_2 \rightarrow CO_2 + 2H_2O$$
$$4NH_3 + 3O_2 \rightarrow 2N_2 + 6H_2O$$

This removed the methane and ammonia from the atmosphere. However, the levels of nitrogen gas in the atmosphere could build up over time, as the element nitrogen, $N_2$, exists as a very unreactive gas.

## The atmosphere today

By 200 million years ago, the proportions of gases in the Earth's atmosphere had stabilised. These were much the same as they are today.

Look at the percentage of gases in the atmosphere today shown in the pie chart in Figure 2.

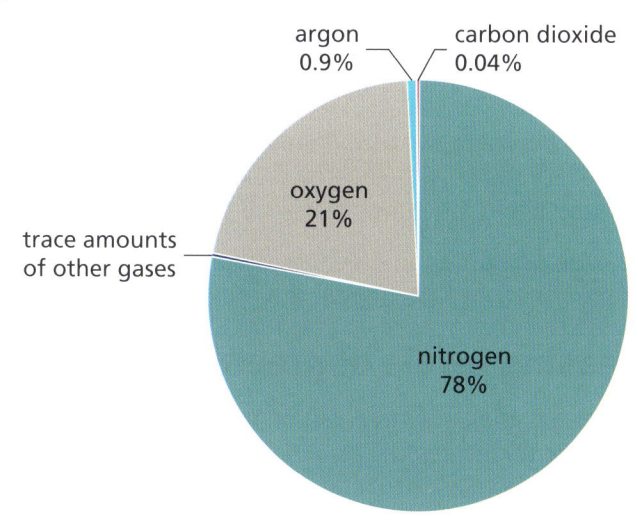

▲ **Figure 2** The relative proportions of nitrogen, oxygen, and other gases in the Earth's atmosphere

The noble gases are all found in air, with argon, Ar, being the most abundant at about 0.9%. Neon, Ne, krypton, Kr, and xenon, Xe, together make up less than 0.1% of clean, dry air.

The Earth's atmosphere also contains water vapour but the percentage in the atmosphere varies.

### Synoptic link

To see where the noble gases are situated in the Periodic Table, look back at Topic C2.2.

### Key points

- Photosynthesis by algae and plants decreased the percentage of carbon dioxide in the early atmosphere. The formation of sedimentary rocks and fossil fuels also contributed.
- The atmosphere today is approximately 80% nitrogen and 20% oxygen, along with small proportions of other gases, including carbon dioxide, water vapour, and noble gases.

### Summary questions

1 Complete the table to show the percentage proportions of gases in the Earth's atmosphere today. **3 MARKS**

| Nitrogen | Oxygen | Argon | Carbon dioxide | Other gases |
|----------|--------|-------|----------------|-------------|
|          |        |       |                |             |

2 Explain how most of the carbon dioxide in the Earth's early atmosphere was removed to arrive at a level of around 0.04% of today's atmosphere. **4 MARKS**

3 Explain why the composition of carbon dioxide in the Earth's atmosphere has not changed much for 200 million years. **1 MARK**

# C11.3 Greenhouse gases

## Learning objectives

After this topic, you should know:
- how the greenhouse effect operates
- how to evaluate the quality of evidence in a report about global climate change, given appropriate information
- how to describe uncertainties in the evidence base
- the importance of peer review of results and of communicating results to a wide range of audiences.

Carbon dioxide along with methane and water vapour are the main 'greenhouse gases' in the Earth's atmosphere. These are the main gases that absorb energy radiated from the surface of the Earth. Without carbon dioxide in the Earth's atmosphere, the average temperature on Earth would be about −19 °C. Life as it is now could never have evolved without liquid water.

So how do greenhouse gases warm up the Earth?

- The Earth is heated by the Sun. Not all the energy reaching the Earth warms up our planet. Almost 30% is reflected back into space from Earth's atmosphere and surface.
- The greenhouse gases let short-wavelength electromagnetic radiation (e.g., ultraviolet light) pass through.
- The surface of the Earth cools down by emitting longer wavelength infrared (thermal) radiation.
- However, greenhouse gases absorb infrared radiation, which raises their temperature. So, some of the energy radiated from the surface of the Earth gets trapped in the atmosphere and the temperature rises.
- The higher the proportion of greenhouse gases in the air, the more energy is absorbed, and the greater the temperature increase becomes.

▲ **Figure 1** The molecules of a 'greenhouse gas' absorb the energy radiated by the Earth as it cools down at night. This increases the store of energy of the gases in the atmosphere and warms the Earth

## The increasing levels of greenhouse gases

Over the past century the amount of carbon dioxide released into the atmosphere has greatly increased. This is due to the use of fossil fuels to make electricity, heat homes, and run cars.

The carbon in fossil fuels has been 'locked up' for hundreds of millions of years. It is released as carbon dioxide into the atmosphere when used as fuel. For example:

propane + oxygen → carbon dioxide + water

$$C_3H_8 + 5O_2 \rightarrow 3CO_2 + 4H_2O$$

Methane is also a greenhouse gas. It is released into the atmosphere from swamps and rice fields, by the growing number of grazing cattle, and from their decomposing waste. It is also produced by waste in landfill sites.

There is no doubt amongst scientists that the levels of greenhouse gases in the atmosphere, especially carbon dioxide, are increasing. So, there is an enhanced greenhouse effect, much greater than the warming effect in pre-industrial times.

Figure 2 shows the data collected by scientists monitoring the proportion of carbon dioxide in the atmosphere at one location. The overall trend over the recent past has been ever increasing.

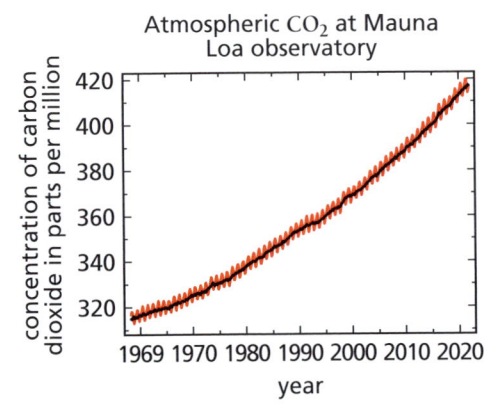

▲ **Figure 2** The change in the levels of carbon dioxide in the atmosphere

The balance between the carbon dioxide produced and the carbon dioxide absorbed by 'CO$_2$ sinks', such as tropical rainforests and the oceans, is affected by human activity. As more trees are cut down for timber and to clear land (deforestation), the carbon dioxide removed from the air as the trees photosynthesise is reduced. Also, as the temperature rises, carbon dioxide gets less and less soluble in water. This makes the oceans less effective as 'CO$_2$ sinks'.

## Weighing up the evidence

The vast majority of scientists agree that a trend in global warming has started. Their views are based on evidence presented in scientific journals. Such evidence must be checked by other scientists working in the same area of expertise. However, a minority of scientists argue that rises observed are due to natural variations that have always happened throughout the long history of the Earth. Sometimes media reports are biased or over-simplified, as they tend to seek out sensational headlines from scientific research without presenting the whole picture. Therefore, they can be misleading.

Now scientists have 'hard' evidence of the link between the levels of carbon dioxide and the climate. One source is ice cores drilled from Greenland's ice sheet, which have gases trapped inside.

Scientists can analyse the trapped air to find how the composition of the gases in the atmosphere has changed over time. Analysis suggests that the current levels of carbon dioxide are higher than at any time in the last 440 000 years. Figure 3 shows changes in temperature and the concentration of CO$_2$ in the atmosphere over the past 150 000 years.

Despite advances in science, predicting with absolute certainty the effects of increasing levels of greenhouse gases is difficult. However, changes in global weather patterns and extreme weather events look like the signs of climate change. Enhanced global warming, causing climate change, is a vital issue that needs to be addressed urgently.

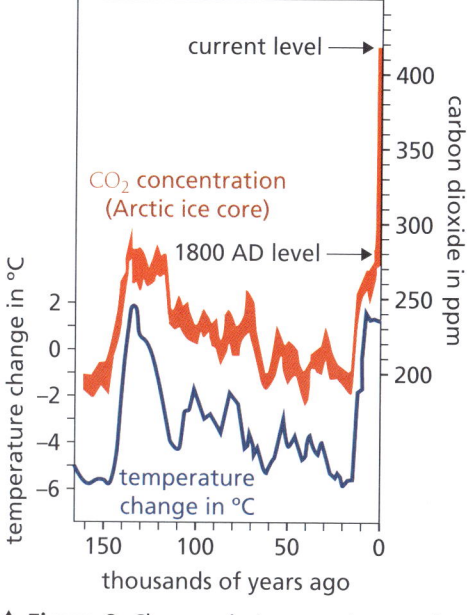

▲ **Figure 3** Changes in temperature and the concentration of CO$_2$ in the atmosphere in the past 150 000 years, using data from gases trapped in ice core samples. The temperature change is relative to the 1850–1900 average

## Summary questions

1. Name three greenhouse gases. **3 MARKS**

2. How does travelling by aeroplane increase the amount of carbon dioxide in the Earth's atmosphere? **1 MARK**

3. Give three reasons why the amount of carbon dioxide in the Earth's atmosphere has increased so much in the recent past. **3 MARKS**

4. Look at the graph in Figure 2:
    a. A closer look at the data would show annual variations of a peak and a trough in each year. Explain these variations. **5 MARKS**
    b. Describe the overall trend shown by the data. **2 MARKS**
    c. Explain how increasing the levels of greenhouse gases in the atmosphere can result in a rise in the temperature of the Earth's atmosphere. **6 MARKS**

5. Explain the difference between the greenhouse effect and global warming. **3 MARKS**

## Key points

- The amount of carbon dioxide in the Earth's atmosphere has risen in the recent past, largely due to the amount of fossil fuels now burnt.
- It is difficult to predict with complete certainty the effects on climate of rising levels of greenhouse gases on a global scale.
- However, the vast majority of peer-reviewed evidence agrees that increased proportions of greenhouse gases from human activities are increasing average global temperatures.

# C11.4 Global climate change

### Learning objectives

After this topic, you should know:
- how emissions of carbon dioxide and methane can be reduced
- why actions to reduce greenhouse gas emissions might be limited
- how to explain the scale, risk, and environmental implications of global climate change.

Some scientists predict that global warming may mean that the Earth's average temperature could rise by as much as 2.1 to 4.3 °C by the year 2100 if we take no action to cut emissions of greenhouse gases. This would have a significant effect on weather patterns all over the world.

## Consequences of rising levels of greenhouse gases

People are worried about changing global climates. For example, in Europe it has been estimated that winters are already almost two weeks shorter than they were 40 years ago. The changing weather patterns all over the world could have the following consequences:

- rising sea levels, as a result of melting ice caps and expansion of the warmer oceans. For example, the Arctic ice cap appears to be shrinking at such a rate that an area of ice the size of the Netherlands melts every year. This can cause the flooding of low-lying land and increased coastal erosion. Some islands are in danger of disappearing

- increasingly common extreme weather events, such as more frequent and severe storms

- changes in temperature and the amount, timing, and distribution of rainfall. This could have impacts on the food-producing capacity of different regions. People have speculated that dry areas will get even drier and that monsoons in Asia will get heavier

- changes to the distribution of wildlife, with some species becoming extinct. Rapid changes in the global climate will put ecosystems around the world under stress

▲ **Figure 1** Hurricanes could become more common in some areas because of global climate change

### Study tip

There have always been greenhouse gases in the Earth's atmosphere, making the planet warmer than it would otherwise have been. However, it is the rapid increase of the levels of greenhouse gases over the recent past that are enhancing this warming effect. This will have consequences for the global climate.

## Thinking of solutions

To tackle the problem of global climate change, it is widely agreed that levels of greenhouse gases must be controlled. You have probably heard that you should be thinking of ways to 'reduce your **carbon footprint'**.

**The carbon footprint of a product, service, or event is the total amount of carbon dioxide and other greenhouse gases emitted over its full life cycle.**

- World leaders meet regularly to negotiate limits on greenhouse emissions. Many governments are taxing fossil fuels and cars that burn large volumes of petrol or diesel, and funding renewable energy sources such as solar, wind, and hydroelectric.

- The methane produced from cattle could be decreased if there was less demand for beef. Plant-based diets offer a more efficient use of land, with farmers using their fields to grow crops and vegetables rather than to feed animals.

- Much of the electricity used in the UK is made by burning fossil fuels, which releases carbon dioxide into the atmosphere. One solution would be to pump the carbon dioxide produced in fossil fuel power stations

C11 The Earth's atmosphere

deep underground to be absorbed into porous rocks. This could be done in old, redundant oil fields. The technique is called carbon capture and storage. However, there is a cost involved in this process that may be passed on to the consumer.

- Governments can also support the use of biofuels. Biofuels are often made from plant material that absorbs carbon dioxide during photosynthesis, and effectively just return it to the atmosphere when they are burnt, so these fuels can be thought of as a 'low-carbon alternative'.

- Incentives can also be given to improve home insulation to conserve energy and plant new trees whenever trees are cut down.

- Every individual can make a positive contribution. If you can use less electricity, less fossil fuel will be used, and less $CO_2$ will be released. If you need to travel by car, it is more efficient to share lifts, or use public transport. However, to have any effect, more people must start to believe that their small contributions will help!

At present there is incomplete international co-operation on setting targets for reducing greenhouse gas emissions. Reductions are likely to have cost implications in all manufacturing and transport industries and could hinder economic growth in some countries.

### Synoptic link

To find out about assessing the life cycle of a product in terms of its environmental impact, see Topic C12.5.

▲ **Figure 2** In some areas, people who car share (reducing their carbon footprint) can use special lanes that are less congested on busy roads

## Summary questions

1. Give three possible consequences of global climate change. **3 MARKS**

2. Describe why the consequences of global climate change are difficult to predict. **2 MARKS**

3. Describe three ways in which emissions of greenhouse gases can be reduced. **3 MARKS**

4. Justify why reducing greenhouse gas emissions can be difficult to achieve. **3 MARKS**

### Key points

- Reducing greenhouse gases in the atmosphere relies on reducing the use of fossil fuels, mainly by using alternative sources of energy and conserving energy.

- The economies of many countries around the world are based on energy obtained from fossil fuels, so changes will cost money to implement.

- Changes are needed because of the potential risks arising from global climate changes, such as rising sea levels, threats to ecosystems, and different patterns of food production around the world.

# C11.5 Atmospheric pollutants

## Learning objectives

After this topic, you should know:
- that sulfur dioxide, carbon monoxide, particulates, and nitrogen dioxide can be produced when burning fuel
- the products of combustion of a fuel, given the composition of the fuel and the conditions in which it is used
- the problems caused by increased amounts of pollutants in the air.

▲ **Figure 1** Pollutants from fossil fuel power stations, especially old coal-fired power stations, can be deposited on land and waterways hundreds of miles away by acid rain and as tiny acidic particles

▲ **Figure 2** Petrol and diesel motor vehicles cause air pollution

## Sulfur in fuels

All fossil fuels – oil, coal, and natural gas – produce carbon dioxide and water when they burn in plenty of air. But as well as hydrocarbons, these fuels also contain other substances, including sulfur impurities.

All fossil fuels contain at least some sulfur. This reacts with oxygen when a fossil fuel is burnt and forms a gas called sulfur dioxide, $SO_2$. This acidic gas is toxic. This is bad for the environment, as it is a cause of acid rain which damages trees, as well as killing animal and plant life in lakes. Acid rain also attacks buildings, especially those made of limestone, and metal structures.

The sulfur impurities can be removed from a fuel before it is burnt. They are removed from petrol and diesel used for vehicles, and from natural gas in gas-fired power stations.

In coal-fired power stations, sulfur dioxide can also be removed from the waste or 'flue' gases by reacting it with the bases calcium oxide or calcium hydroxide. The bases neutralise the acidic sulfur dioxide. However, some sulfur dioxide is still released into the atmosphere.

## Other pollutants from fuels

When fuel burns in a vehicle engine, other pollution can be produced, including:

- **Carbon dioxide** – When any fuel containing carbon is burnt, it makes carbon dioxide. As discussed in Topic C11.3, carbon dioxide is the main greenhouse gas in the air. It absorbs energy released as radiation from the surface of the Earth, which causes warming of the atmosphere, leading to climate change.

- **Carbon monoxide** – When there is not enough oxygen inside an engine, **incomplete combustion** occurs. Instead of all the carbon in the fuel turning into carbon dioxide, carbon monoxide gas, CO, is also formed. Carbon monoxide is a toxic gas. It is colourless and odourless, so you cannot tell that you are breathing it in. Your red blood cells pick up the carbon monoxide instead of oxygen and carry it around your body in your blood stream. The carbon monoxide takes up the sites on haemoglobin in the red blood cells that usually bond to oxygen. So, a victim of carbon monoxide poisoning will become starved of oxygen, get drowsy, lose consciousness, and then die if not removed from the source of the gas.

- **Nitrogen oxides** – The high temperature inside a combustion engine also allows the normally unreactive nitrogen gas in the air to react with oxygen. This reaction makes nitrogen oxides, $NO_x$. These are toxic and can trigger some people's asthma. Like sulfur dioxide, nitrogen oxides also cause acid rain.

- **Particulates** – Diesel engines burn hydrocarbons with bigger molecules than those burnt in petrol engines. When these larger molecules react with oxygen in an engine, they do not always burn completely. Tiny solid particles containing carbon and unburnt hydrocarbons are

C11 The Earth's atmosphere

produced. These particulates get carried into the air. They travel into the upper atmosphere, reflecting sunlight back into space, causing global dimming. These particulates can damage the cells in our lungs and can even cause cancer.

## Metacognition

Figure 4 tells us how pollutant gases are released into our atmosphere. Work out a way to extend the information given to include the problems each of the gases cause. Make it suitable to keep for your revision later in the course. Compare your work with a partner, if possible, and note its strengths and weaknesses as a revision tool.

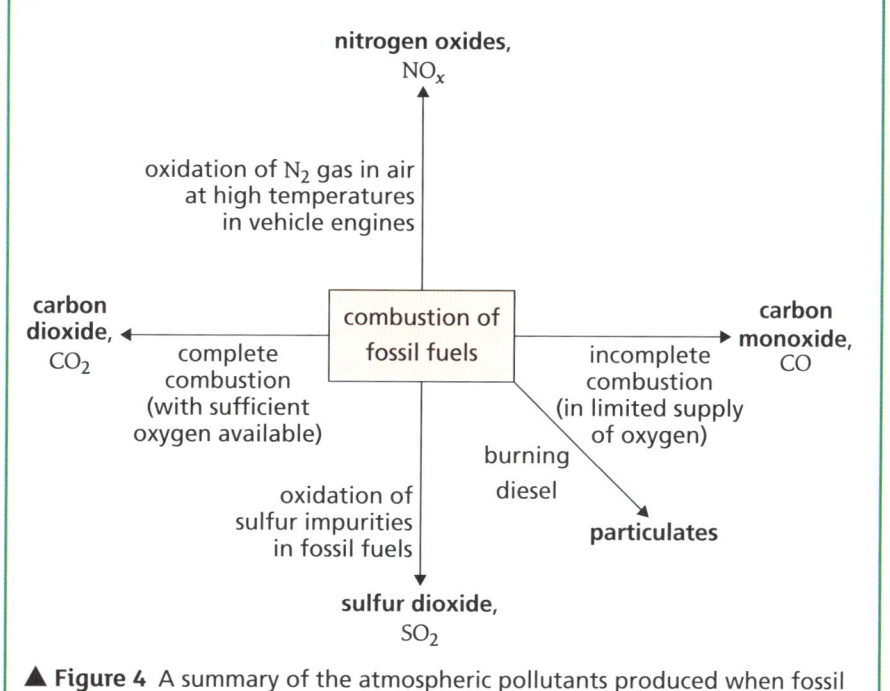

▲ **Figure 3** A combination of many cars in a small area and the right weather conditions can cause smog to be formed. This is a mixture of SMoke and fOG. Some of the yellowish brown colouration is caused by the presence of nitrogen dioxide gas, $NO_2$

▲ **Figure 4** A summary of the atmospheric pollutants produced when fossil fuels are burnt under different conditions

## Summary questions

1   a   Which element present in impurities can produce sulfur dioxide when a fossil fuel is burnt? **1 MARK**
    b   Which pollution problem does sulfur dioxide gas contribute to? **1 MARK**
    c   Which other non-metal oxides released from diesel and petrol cars also cause this pollution problem? **1 MARK**
2   Describe how the following substances are produced when fuels burn in vehicles:
    a   sulfur dioxide **1 MARK**
    b   nitrogen oxides **2 MARKS**
    c   particulates. **1 MARK**
3   a   When natural gas, $CH_4$, burns in an engine that does not have enough oxygen, predict the products of combustion. Write a balanced symbol equation to show this reaction. **3 MARKS**
    b   Explain why one of the products of this reaction is dangerous. **6 MARKS**

## Key points

- When hydrocarbon fuels are burnt **in plenty of air**, the carbon and hydrogen in the fuel are completely oxidised. In **insufficient oxygen**, poisonous carbon monoxide gas is formed, as well as particulates of carbon (soot) and unburnt hydrocarbons.
- Sulfur impurities in fuels burn to form sulfur dioxide, which can cause acid rain.
- At the high temperatures in combustion engines, nitrogen from the air reacts with oxygen to form oxides of nitrogen.

# C11 The Earth's atmosphere

## Practice questions

1 The pie charts show the atmosphere of a planet shortly after it was formed (**A**) and then millions of years later (**B**).

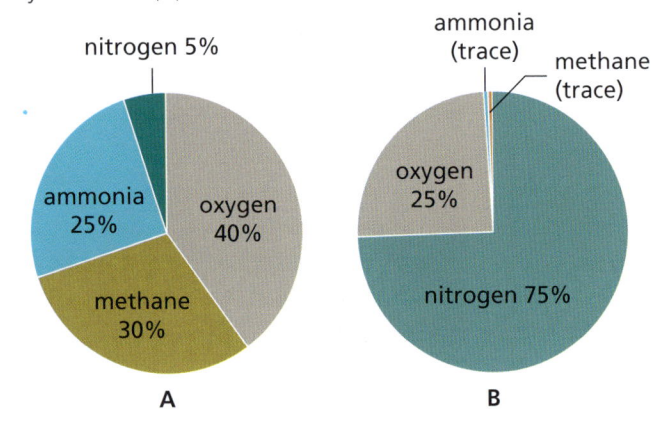

**A**
- nitrogen 5%
- ammonia 25%
- oxygen 40%
- methane 30%

**B**
- ammonia (trace)
- methane (trace)
- oxygen 25%
- nitrogen 75%

  a Using this information, describe the changes in the planet's atmosphere over time. **2 MARKS**
  b Explain what might have caused the changes you described in part **a**. **2 MARKS**
  c Copy and complete the word equations showing the chemical reactions that may have taken place in the atmosphere.
   i methane + _____ → carbon dioxide + _____ **1 MARK**
   ii ammonia + _____ → nitrogen + _____ **1 MARK**
   iii Write both the equations in part **c** as balanced symbol equations. **6 MARKS**

2 a i Name the gas that causes acid rain, formed in fossil fuel power stations. **1 MARK**
   ii Give **two** ways of stopping this acidic gas getting into the atmosphere. **2 MARKS**
   iii Name the other cause of acid rain, which comes from car engines, and explain how it arises. **2 MARKS**
  b Suggest the main reason why levels of carbon dioxide in the Earth's atmosphere have increased so sharply over the past 100 years. **1 MARK**

3 Gases that cause global warming are called 'greenhouse gases'.
  a Write the formulae of three of these greenhouse gases and explain how they cause the temperature of the Earth to rise. **6 MARKS**
  b Explain the effect of planting more trees on the levels of carbon dioxide in the Earth's atmosphere. **4 MARKS**
  c Explain how a change in lifestyle can help to reduce the levels of carbon dioxide in the air. **4 MARKS**

4 Core samples have been taken from the ice in Antarctica. The deeper the sample, the longer the ice has been there. It is possible to date the ice and to take air samples from it. The air was trapped when the ice was formed. It is, therefore, possible to test samples of trapped air in the ice from many thousands of years ago.

**Table 1** shows some of these results. The more recent results are from actual air samples taken from a Pacific island.

Table 1

| Year | $CO_2$ concentration in ppm | Source |
|---|---|---|
| 2020 | 414 | Pacific island |
| 2015 | 401 | Pacific island |
| 2010 | 390 | Pacific island |
| 2005 | 379 | Pacific island |
| 1995 | 360 | Pacific island |
| 1985 | 345 | Pacific island |
| 1975 | 331 | Pacific island |
| 1965 | 320 | Antarctica |
| 1955 | 313 | Antarctica |
| 1945 | 310 | Antarctica |
| 1935 | 309 | Antarctica |
| 1925 | 305 | Antarctica |
| 1915 | 301 | Antarctica |
| 1905 | 297 | Antarctica |
| 1895 | 294 | Antarctica |
| 1890 | 294 | Antarctica |

(ppm = parts per million)

  a If you have access to a spreadsheet program, or similar software, enter the data and produce a line graph. **3 MARKS**
  b Draw a line of best fit on your graph. **1 MARK**
  c Describe the pattern shown in the graph. **3 MARKS**
  d Describe your conclusion from the data. **3 MARKS**
  e Explain how the data coming from two different sources might affect your conclusion. **3 MARKS**

# C11 The Earth's atmosphere

# Exam-style questions

**01** Methane, $CH_4$, and carbon dioxide, $CO_2$, are both greenhouse gases. The percentage of carbon dioxide is increasing in the atmosphere.

**01.1** Give **one** human activity that is causing carbon dioxide to increase in the atmosphere. **1 MARK**

**01.2** Suggest **one** way in which the amount of methane released into the atmosphere could be reduced. **1 MARK**

A large volume of carbon dioxide gas is released into the atmosphere by generating electricity in power stations.

**01.3** Suggest **one** way a government could encourage energy companies to release less carbon dioxide into the atmosphere. **1 MARK**

**01.4** Some cars use hydrogen gas, $H_2$, as an alternative fuel to diesel. Give the only product when hydrogen is burnt. **1 MARK**

**01.5** Suggest **one** problem with using hydrogen as a fuel in a car. **1 MARK**

**01.6** Ⓗ A diesel car produces 88 g of carbon dioxide, $CO_2$, per kilometre. Calculate the number of moles of carbon dioxide formed in a 10 km journey. **3 MARKS**

**02** Most diesel is obtained by the fractional distillation of crude oil.
$C_{18}H_{38}$ is one of the compounds present in diesel. Biodiesel is made from plants. Plants are grown, harvested, and their oil is made into biodiesel. $C_{16}H_{33}COOCH_3$ is one of the compounds present in biodiesel.

**02.1** Give the general formula of $C_{18}H_{38}$. **1 MARK**

**02.2** Explain why $C_{16}H_{33}COOCH_3$ is not a hydrocarbon. **2 MARKS**

**02.3** Both $C_{18}H_{38}$ and $C_{16}H_{33}COOCH_3$ produce carbon dioxide when they are burnt. Carbon dioxide is a greenhouse gas.

Describe how greenhouse gases such as carbon dioxide maintain temperatures on Earth that are high enough to support life.

You should refer to short- and long-wavelength radiation in your answer. **3 MARKS**

**02.4** Complete the balanced equation for the complete combustion of $C_{18}H_{38}$.

$2C_{18}H_{38}$ + ....... $O_2$ → $36CO_2$ + ....... $H_2O$ **2 MARKS**

**02.5** Explain how the equation shows the complete combustion of $C_{18}H_{38}$. **2 MARKS**

**02.6** The vast majority of scientists believe that increasing levels of greenhouse gases such as carbon dioxide are causing global temperatures to rise. Name **one** other greenhouse gas. **1 MARK**

**02.7** Give **two** effects of increasing global temperatures. **2 MARKS**

**02.8** Use the information provided and your own knowledge to explain why many scientists think that the use of biodiesel as a fuel causes less of an increase in carbon dioxide than the use of diesel as a fuel. **3 MARKS**

**02.9** Carbon footprint is defined as the total amount of carbon dioxide and other greenhouse gases emitted into the atmosphere.

Other than using more biofuels, give **two** ways in which a family might reduce their carbon footprint. **2 MARKS**

**03** The formulae of several products formed from the use of fuels are shown in the box.

| NO | CO | C | $CO_2$ | $SO_2$ |
|---|---|---|---|---|

Choose a product from the box to answer questions **03.1** to **03.4**.

**03.1** Which product would be formed from the complete combustion of a hydrocarbon such as $C_8H_{18}$? **1 MARK**

**03.2** Which product is a gas formed from the incomplete combustion of a hydrocarbon such as $C_8H_{18}$? **1 MARK**

**03.3** Which product is a solid that causes global dimming? **1 MARK**

**03.4** Which product is formed in car engines from the reaction of two gases that occur naturally in the air? **1 MARK**

# C12 The Earth's resources

## C12.1 Finite and renewable resources

### Learning objectives

*After this topic, you should know:*

- examples of natural products that are supplemented or replaced by agricultural and synthetic products
- how to distinguish between finite and renewable resources, given appropriate information
- how to extract and interpret information about resources from charts, graphs, and tables
- how to use orders of magnitude to evaluate the significance of data.

We all rely on the Earth's natural resources to live. The Earth's natural resources are used to make homes to live in, provide food, fuel transport, and for the energy needed to cook and stay warm. Humankind has found ever more ways to make use of the natural resources in the Earth's crust, oceans, rivers, lakes, and atmosphere.

People have always used natural products, gathered from their environment. The farming of plants and animals has increased the supply of these products. Not only that but chemists have developed synthetic alternatives to these natural products (Table 1).

**Table 1** Examples of natural products that are supplemented or replaced by agricultural and synthetic products

| Natural resources | Use | Alternative synthetic product |
|---|---|---|
| wool | clothes, carpets | acrylic fibre (polyacrylonitrile), poly(propene) |
| cotton | clothes, textiles | polyester |
| silk | clothes | nylon |
| linseed oil | paint | acrylic resin |
| rubber | tyres, washers | various synthetic polymers, such as poly(butadiene) |
| wood | construction | PVC, composites (e.g., MDF) |

We can classify natural resources as finite or renewable.

Finite resources are those that are being used up at a faster rate than they can be replaced. If we carry on using these resources at current rates, finite resources will eventually run out. Fossil fuels (coal, crude oil, and natural gas) and metal ores are examples of finite resources.

Renewable resources are those that can be replaced at the same rate at which they are used up. The crops used to make biofuels are examples of renewable resources.

▲ **Figure 1** Brown bauxite is the finite resource from which we extract aluminium metal

### Examples of finite resources

The chemical industry uses natural resources as the raw materials to make new products. Consider the following examples:

- metal ores used to extract metals
- crude oil used to make polymers
- limestone to make cement and concrete
- crude oil to make petrol, diesel, and kerosene used for transport.

Depending on the assumptions made, estimates of how long the finite resources will last differ by orders of magnitude. There are many uncertainties: for example, what will the future rate of use be? How accurately do we know the amounts of finite resources on the Earth? Will new sources be discovered?

C12 The Earth's resources

## Examples of renewable resources

Wherever possible, industries are moving towards renewable resources to conserve finite resources and to improve sustainability. We can think of sustainability as developments that meet the needs of society now, without endangering the ability of future generations to meet their needs.

For example, in the plastics industry, many of the polymers produced use ethene made from crude oil as their raw (starting) material. Crude oil is a finite resource. However, ethene can also be made from ethanol, and ethanol can be made by fermenting glucose from sugar cane or sugar beet. Sugar cane and sugar beet are examples of agricultural resources that are renewable.

So, using a renewable crop as the raw material for ethene makes plastics such as poly(ethene) more sustainable than ones made using up finite supplies of crude oil.

Another example of sustainability is the use of wood chips instead of fossil fuels to fuel power stations, linked to a programme of planting new trees (Figure 2).

▲ **Figure 2** Wood chips from sustainable forests can be used to fuel biomass power stations like this one

### Summary questions

1 Give two examples of:
   a finite resources **2 MARKS**
   b renewable resources. **2 MARKS**
2 Explain the difference between 'finite resources' and 'renewable resources'. **2 MARKS**
3 a Explain how the raw materials for the manufacture of a polymer such as poly(ethene) can be sourced renewably. **2 MARKS**
   b Describe why the renewable raw material in your answer to part **a** can also be described as the 'sustainable' option. **1 MARK**
4 a As a rough estimate, there is $1.5 \times 10^{16}$ metric tonnes of 'fossil carbon' on Earth. In a year it is also estimated that $9.2 \times 10^9$ metric tonnes of carbon are burnt worldwide. Assuming that this rate of carbon use was to continue, calculate an order of magnitude estimate of how long 'fossil carbon' will last. **2 MARKS**
   b However, very rough estimates predict there are only $5.5 \times 10^{12}$ metric tonnes of fossil fuels that could actually be used as a useful resource existing on Earth. Assuming an approximate rate of fossil fuel use of $1 \times 10^{10}$ metric tonnes per year, calculate an order of magnitude estimation of the time left before the fossil fuel reserves run out. **2 MARKS**
   c Give two reasons why the estimations calculated in parts **a** and **b** should only be expressed in terms of order of magnitudes. **2 MARKS**

### Synoptic link

For help with question 4, refer to Maths Skills MS2d.

### Key points

- We rely on the Earth's natural resources to make new products and to provide us with energy.
- Some of these natural resources are finite and others are renewable.
- Estimates of the time left before finite resources run out can only be rough estimates, because of the uncertainty involved in the calculations.

# C12.2 Water safe to drink

## Learning objectives

*After this topic, you should know:*

- the difference between potable water and pure water
- the differences in treatment of ground water and salty water
- how to carry out a simple distillation of salt solution and test the distillate to determine its purity.

## Potable water

Water is a vital and useful resource. We use it for agriculture and in industry. It is important as a raw material, as a solvent, and as a coolant. Other uses of water are for washing and cleaning – and, of course, for drinking. Providing people with water that is fit to drink, called potable water, is a major issue all over the world.

Water circulates around our planet in the water cycle. In countries such as the UK, rainwater falls to the ground, replenishing our supplies of fresh water in rivers and lakes. It also seeps down through soil and rocks to underground sources of water.

The rainwater itself dissolves some gases from the air as it falls to the ground. Then, once in contact with solid land, the water will dissolve soluble substances as it passes over them. So, water from natural sources will always contain dissolved minerals (salts), as well as microorganisms from soil and decaying matter. The levels of both these impurities must be reduced to meet strict safety standards for drinking water.

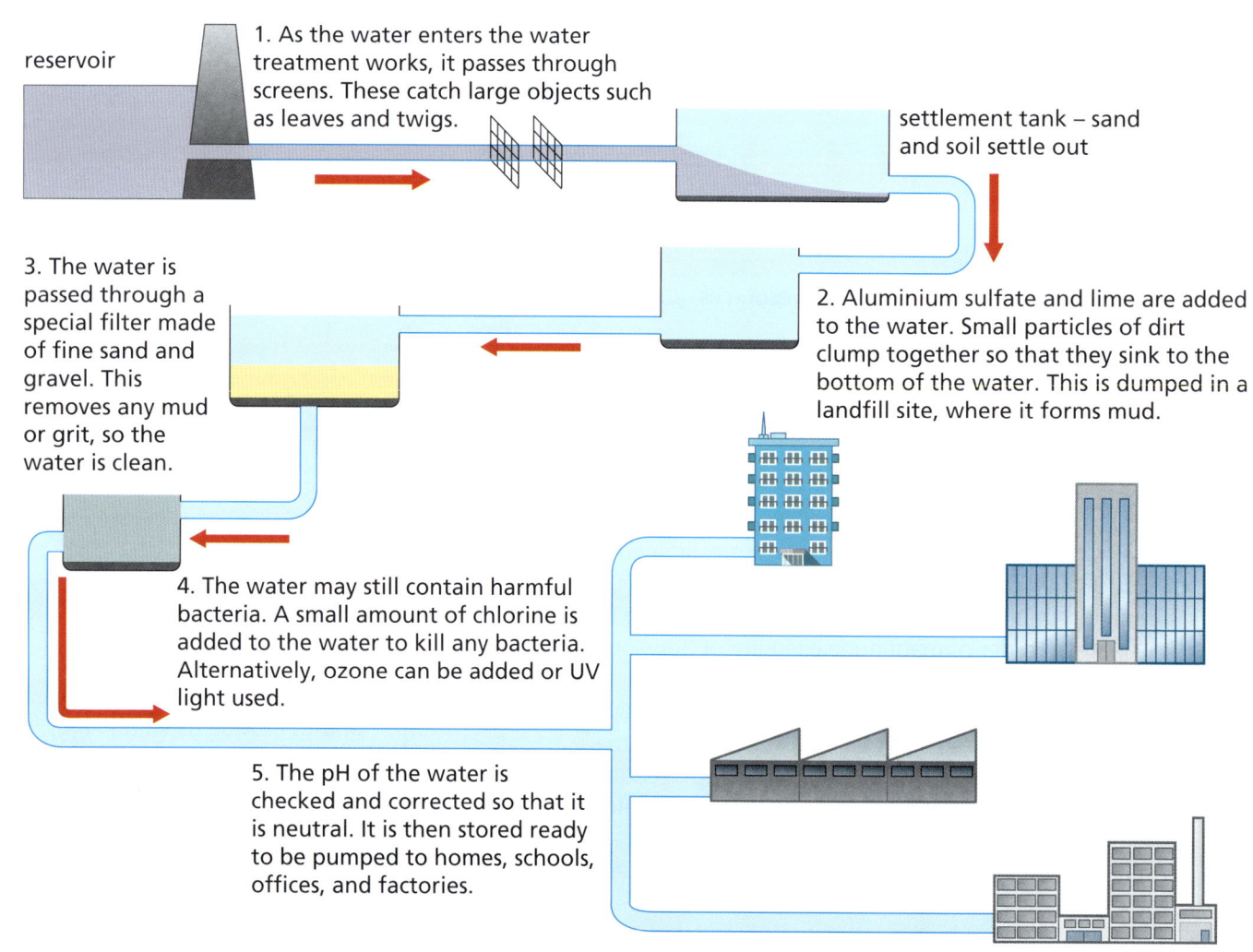

1. As the water enters the water treatment works, it passes through screens. These catch large objects such as leaves and twigs.

2. Aluminium sulfate and lime are added to the water. Small particles of dirt clump together so that they sink to the bottom of the water. This is dumped in a landfill site, where it forms mud.

settlement tank – sand and soil settle out

3. The water is passed through a special filter made of fine sand and gravel. This removes any mud or grit, so the water is clean.

4. The water may still contain harmful bacteria. A small amount of chlorine is added to the water to kill any bacteria. Alternatively, ozone can be added or UV light used.

5. The pH of the water is checked and corrected so that it is neutral. It is then stored ready to be pumped to homes, schools, offices, and factories.

▲ **Figure 1** From freshwater reservoir to end-user – the treatment of water from a reservoir to make potable water

The best sources of fresh water contain low levels of minerals and microorganisms to start with. When water is taken from rivers or reservoirs, made to store fresh water, it must be treated to make it safe to drink. This treatment involves techniques such as:

- passing the untreated water through filter beds made of sand and gravel to remove solid particles
- the addition of chlorine or ozone to sterilise the water by killing microorganisms – passing ultraviolet light through the water is an alternative to adding chemical sterilising agents.

## Purifying salty water

In the UK, there is sufficient rain and natural supplies of fresh water to satisfy the needs of the population and industry. However, in countries with much drier climates and with few sources of natural fresh water, obtaining enough potable water can be difficult.

Salty water can be made into potable water by desalination. There are two types of desalination:

- Distillation – Water can be made pure by distilling it. However, distillation is an expensive process. This is because of the high energy costs involved in boiling large volumes of water. Under reduced pressure, water boils below 100 °C, saving on some of the energy costs of distilling salty water in a desalination plant. Desalination is used in the Middle East in some oil-rich nations, and on some islands with no natural sources of water apart from occasional, insufficient, rainwater.

- Reverse osmosis – A process called reverse osmosis can also be used to desalinate water. This uses membranes to separate the water and the salts dissolved in it. The membranes can remove 98% of dissolved salts from seawater. There is no heating involved, so it uses less energy than distillation. However, energy is still needed to pressurise the water passing through.

### Summary questions

1. Name three possible sterilising agents used to sterilise fresh water, making it potable. **3 MARKS**
2. a How is water from a natural source converted into pure water? **1 MARK**
   b How could you test that the water is pure? **1 MARK**
   c Explain why anhydrous copper(II) sulfate or blue cobalt(II) chloride are not used to test the purity of water. **1 MARK**
3. Explain why bottled water sold in the supermarket should not be described as 'pure' water. **2 MARKS**
4. a Why is a shortage of water a problem for some hot countries, even though they have large coastlines? **1 MARK**
   b Define the term 'desalination'. **1 MARK**
   c i What is the main disadvantage of desalination using distillation? **1 MARK**
      ii Name another process that can be used instead of distillation. **1 MARK**

## C12 The Earth's resources

### Practical

**Analysis and purification of water samples**

a Your teacher will give you a sample of salty water to test its pH, and another sample to desalinate by distillation (Topic C1.3).

Once you have distilled the water, test its purity by measuring its boiling point. Pure water boils at 100 °C.

Note that chemical tests for water (white anhydrous copper(II) sulfate turns blue or blue cobalt(II) chloride paper turns pink) only test for the presence of water. They do not tell you if the water is pure or not.

Using the other half of your distilled water sample, test its pH value. Record the results of your tests on salty water.

b Now, collect more water samples from different sources and find their pH. Also find out whether they contain any dissolved solids.

- Record your results in a table.
- Explain how you would ensure any samples collected are representative of that source.

**Safety:** Wear eye protection.

### Key points

- Water is made potable by filtering and then sterilising with chlorine, ozone, or ultraviolet light.
- Salty water can be desalinated by distillation or reverse osmosis, but both processes require a large amount of energy.

# C12.3 Treating waste water

## Learning objectives

After this topic, you should know:
- how waste water is made safe to release into the environment
- the relative ease of obtaining potable water from waste water, ground water, and salt water.

## Down the drain

Have you ever wondered what happens to all the waste that leaves our homes down the drains? Everything that drains from washing machines, dishwashers, sinks, baths, and toilets, flows down along pipes and enters the larger sewer pipes. All this, along with waste water from businesses and industry, is given the general name 'sewage'. This, together with waste water from farming activities, must be treated at sewage treatment plants to make it safe. Only then can it be returned to the environment, usually into rivers or piped out to sea.

## Sewage treatment

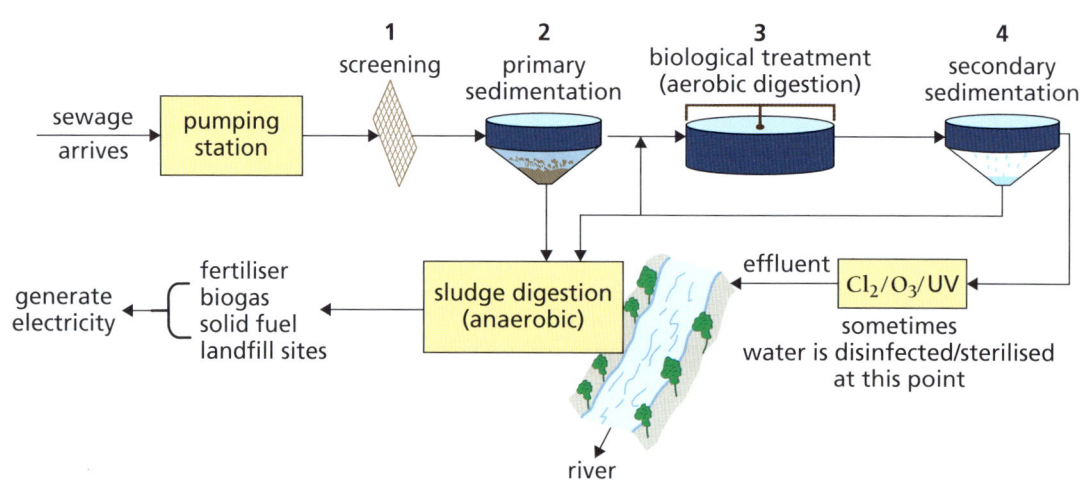

▲ **Figure 1** The steps needed to make our waste water from urban and rural sources safe to return to the environment

Sewage treatment involves a series of steps, which are described here and in Figure 1.

1. **Screening**

   Once the sewage arrives at the sewage treatment plant, the first step is to remove large solid objects and grit from the rest of the waste water. The sewage passes through a metal grid that traps the large objects.

2. **Primary sedimentation**

   In the first circular tank, the solid sediments are allowed to settle out from the mixture. Large paddles rotate, pushing the solids, called sludge, towards the centre of the tank. There the sludge is piped down into a storage tank for further treatment.

   The watery liquid (effluent) above the sludge flows into the next tank. Although no solid matter is visible, this effluent still contains many potentially harmful microorganisms.

3. **Biological treatment**

   In the second tank, useful bacteria feed on any remaining organic matter and harmful microorganisms still present, breaking them down

▲ **Figure 2** A sewage treatment plant

C12 The Earth's resources

aerobically (in the presence of oxygen). The tank is aerated by bubbling air through the waste water. This can take from several hours to several days, depending on the quality of the waste water, size of the tank, rate of aeration, and temperature.

**4 Secondary sedimentation**

In the last tank, the useful bacteria are allowed to settle out to the bottom of the tank as a sediment. The sediment is either recycled back into the secondary treatment tank or passed into the tank where the sludge is treated. At this point, the treated waste water is safe enough to be discharged back into rivers.

However, if the river is a particularly sensitive ecosystem, the water can be filtered one more time through a bed of sand. If necessary, the water can then be sterilised by ultraviolet light, ozone, or chlorine. However, the release of chlorine into rivers does cause concern, as toxic organic compounds of chlorine can be formed in the environment.

## Treating the sewage sludge

The sludge separated off during the primary treatment of the sewage is not wasted. After further treatment, most can be dried and used as fertiliser on farmland to improve the soil or used as a source of renewable energy.

The sludge contains organic matter, including human waste, suspended solids, water, and dissolved compounds. It is digested anaerobically (without oxygen) by microorganisms beneath the surface in the treatment tank.

This biological treatment can be carried out at a relatively high temperature of about 55 °C or a lower temperature of about 35 °C, which can take up to 30 days to complete. The higher temperature has the benefit of speeding up the breakdown of the organic matter, but energy has to be supplied to heat the sludge.

The breakdown products include biogas (a mixture of methane, carbon dioxide, and some hydrogen sulfide). Biogas can be burnt and used to power the sewage treatment plant or provide electricity for the surrounding area. It can also be further cleaned to make methane, the main gas in natural gas, and piped into the gas supply.

Alternatively, the sludge can be dried out and turned into a crusty solid 'cake' that can be burnt to generate electricity (Figure 3).

▲ **Figure 3** Dried sludge can be used as a renewable energy source, along with biogas and biomethane. All of these are made from sewage

### Study tip

When sewage sludge is dried it takes up a lot less space, so it becomes easier to transport it away from the sewage treatment plant.

### Key points

- Waste water requires treatment at a sewage works to remove organic matter as well as harmful microorganisms and chemicals before being released into the environment.
- The stages include screening to remove large solids and grit, sedimentation to produce sewage sludge, and aerobic biological treatment of the safe effluent, which is then released into environment.
- The sewage sludge is separated, broken down by anaerobic digestion, and dried. It can provide us with fertiliser and a source of renewable energy.

### Summary questions

1. Draw a basic flow diagram listing the main steps used in a sewage treatment plant to make waste water safe to discharge into the environment. **4 MARKS**
2. a Describe what takes place in a primary treatment tank. **2 MARKS**
   b Give two uses of sewage sludge. **2 MARKS**
3. Describe how the processes involving microorganisms in a biological treatment tank and a sewage sludge tank differ. **2 MARKS**
4. Using the information here, and in Topic C12.2, evaluate the use of waste water, salt water, and ground water from an aquifer as sources of potable water. **6 MARKS**

165

# C12.4 Extracting metals from ores

## Learning objectives

*After this topic, you should know:*

- how to evaluate alternative biological methods of metal extraction, given appropriate information.

▲ **Figure 1** Mining copper ores can leave huge scars on the landscape. This quarrying of ores is called open-cast mining. About 90% of copper comes from open-cast mines. Our supplies of copper-rich ores are a limited, finite resource

## Metacognition

Look at the method for 'Extracting copper from malachite' in the Practical box. Draw scientific, labelled diagrams in the style of Figure 2 to make a 'visual map' of the method. Write a chemical equation next to each reaction that takes place. Which method is easier to follow – the method in the book or your 'visual map'? Why? Share your method with a partner and discuss the good and bad points of both methods – visual steps and written steps.

## Extracting copper from copper-rich ores

Most copper is extracted from copper-rich ores. These are a finite resource and are in danger of running out.

There are two main methods used to obtain the copper metal from the ore.

- In one method sulfuric acid is used to produce copper(II) sulfate solution, before extracting the copper metal.
- The other process is called smelting (roasting). Copper ore is heated to a high temperature in a furnace with air, to produce impure copper.

Then we use the impure copper as the positive electrode in electrolysis cells to make pure copper (Figure 3). About 80% of copper is still produced by smelting. Smelting and purifying copper ore uses huge amounts of energy and electricity. This costs a large amount of money and causes pollution of the environment.

### Practical

**Extracting copper from malachite**

Malachite is a copper ore containing copper carbonate (harmful). To extract the copper, you first heat the copper carbonate in a boiling tube. **Thermal decomposition** takes place. Copper oxide is left in the tube. Which gas is given off?

After cooling, you then add dilute sulfuric acid to the copper oxide (harmful). Stopper and shake the tube. This makes copper(II) sulfate solution (harmful). Filter off any excess black copper oxide in the solution.

To extract the copper metal, either:

1. Put an iron nail into the copper(II) sulfate solution. What happens to the iron nail?

or

2. Collect some extra copper(II) sulfate solution and place it in a small beaker. Set up the circuit as shown in Figure 2. Turn the power on until you see copper metal collecting. Which electrode does the copper metal form on?

**Safety:** Wear eye protection. Chemicals used here are harmful.

▲ **Figure 2** Extracting copper metal from a solution containing $Cu^{2+}$(aq) ions using electrolysis. In industry, copper electrodes are used to obtain very pure copper metal at the negative electrode

Metal ions are always positively charged. Therefore, in electrolysis they are attracted to and deposited at the negative electrode. In industry, the electrolysis of copper is carried out on a large scale. This method gives the very pure copper needed to make electrical wiring. Electrolysis is also used to purify the impure copper extracted by smelting.

C12 The Earth's resources

Look at Figure 3. We can show what happens with half equations.

**Negative electrode**    $Cu^{2+}(aq) + 2e^- \rightarrow Cu(s)$

$Cu(s) \rightarrow Cu^{2+}(aq) + 2e^-$    **Positive electrode**

The copper can also be extracted from copper(II) sulfate solution in industry by adding scrap iron. Iron can displace copper from its solutions:

iron + copper(II) sulfate → iron(II) sulfate + copper

## Extracting copper from low-grade copper ores

Instead of extracting copper from our limited copper-rich ores, scientists are developing ways to get copper from low-grade ores. This would be uneconomical using traditional methods. New techniques use biological methods to help extract copper:

- **Phytomining** – In this process, plants that can absorb copper ions are grown on soil containing low-grade copper ore. This could be on slag heaps of previously discarded waste from the processing of copper-rich ores. Then the plants are burnt, and copper is extracted from copper compounds in the ash. The copper ions can be 'leached' (dissolved) from the ash by adding sulfuric acid. This makes a solution (called the leachate) of copper(II) sulfate. Displacement by scrap iron and then electrolysis makes pure copper metal.

- **Bioleaching** – In this process bacteria feed on low-grade metal ores. By a combination of biological and chemical processes, a solution of copper ions (the leachate) can be obtained from waste copper ore. Once again, scrap iron and electrolysis are used to extract the copper from the leachate. About 20% of copper comes from bioleaching. This is likely to increase as sources of copper-rich ores run out. Bioleaching is a slow process, so scientists are researching ways to speed it up. At present it can take years to extract 50% of the metal from a low-grade ore.

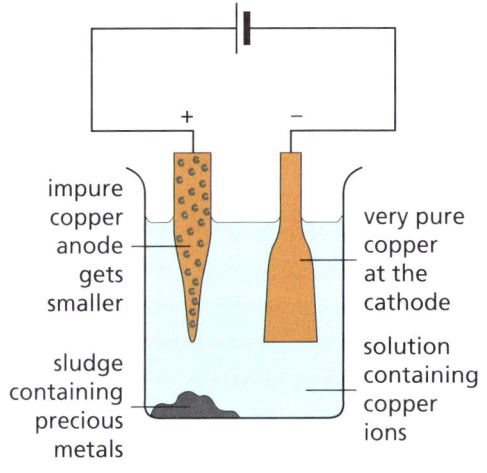

▲ **Figure 3** The cathodes (negative electrodes) are removed about every two weeks

### Synoptic links

For information on the half equations at electrodes in electrolysis, see Topic C6.2.

For information on the displacement (redox) reaction between copper ions in solution and iron metal, look back at Topic C5.2.

### Summary questions

1. Give the two alternative biological methods of metal extraction. **2 MARKS**
2. a Give two traditional ways of extracting copper metal. **2 MARKS**
   b Name one advantage of extracting copper using bacteria over traditional methods. **1 MARK**
   c Why can copper occasionally be found native? **1 MARK**
   d Which electrode does pure copper collect at when copper is purified by electrolysis? Explain your answer. **2 MARKS**
3. Write a balanced chemical equation, including state symbols, for the extraction of copper from copper(II) sulfate solution by displacement. **3 MARKS**
4. a Write half equations for the reactions at each copper electrode in the electrolysis of copper(II) sulfate solution. **4 MARKS**
   b Explain where reduction and oxidation occur in part **a**. **4 MARKS**
5. Explain how copper is extracted by phytomining and why this method will become increasingly important. **6 MARKS**

### Key points

- Most copper is extracted by smelting (roasting) copper-rich ores, although supplies of ores are becoming increasingly scarce.
- Copper can be extracted from solutions of copper compounds by electrolysis or by displacement using scrap iron. Electrolysis is also used to purify impure copper, for example, the copper metal obtained from smelting.
- Scientists are developing ways to extract copper that use low-grade copper ores. Bacteria are used in bioleaching and plants are used in phytomining.

167

# C12.5 Life cycle assessments

**Learning objectives**

*After this topic, you should know:*
- how to carry out simple comparative life cycle assessments for shopping bags made from plastic and paper
- how to interpret life cycle assessments of materials or products, given appropriate information.

You are probably familiar with the life cycles of animals and plants from studying Biology. However, the same principle of mapping the journey from 'cradle to grave' has now been adapted for manufactured products. The technique used by government agencies, businesses, and industry is called a **life cycle assessment** (**LCA**). It is used to assess the impact on the environment caused by:

- getting and processing the raw materials
- making the product (and any packaging)
- using, reusing, and maintaining the product
- disposing of a product at the end of its useful 'life'.

The total energy needed to extract raw materials, make the product, and distribute it, plus any other transport involved, are all considered.

An LCA is carried out by:

- listing all the energy and material inputs and all the outputs into the environment (Figure 2)
- evaluating the potential environmental impacts from these inputs and outputs
- interpreting the results to help make decisions about which material, process, product, or service is the best to use.

An LCA starts with the process of gathering raw materials needed to make the product. It ends when all the materials are returned to the environment. So, an LCA provides an estimate of the total environmental impact resulting from all stages in the product's life cycle.

The outputs back into the environment include atmospheric emissions, waterborne wastes, solid wastes, and energy dissipation to the surroundings (Figure 2).

The four stages in an LCA can be summarised as:

**Raw material extraction → Manufacture → Use/Reuse/Maintenance → Recycle/Waste management**

However, the results of an LCA will always be open to debate. When considering the environmental impact (and health implications), it is common to convert data collected into a single 'impact score'. This requires subjective judgments to be made, usually by the people who paid for the study, an expert panel, or the analyst who devised that particular LCA.

The scale of the impacts is also important. But what weighting should be applied to global impacts (e.g., global warming or the depletion of natural resources), compared with regional impacts (e.g., acid rain or smog), and local impacts (e.g., water loss from ground water or toxic emissions into a stream)? These are not objective scientific judgements.

Such judgements are also made when trying to quantify all the inputs and outputs listed in the LCA. Consider the impact of 5000 tonnes of sulfur

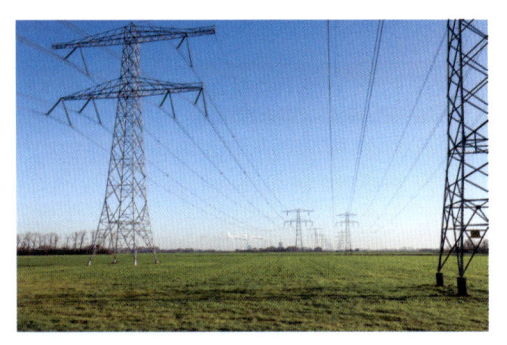

▲ **Figure 1** Think about the raw materials and energy needed to manufacture these electricity cables containing the metals aluminium and copper

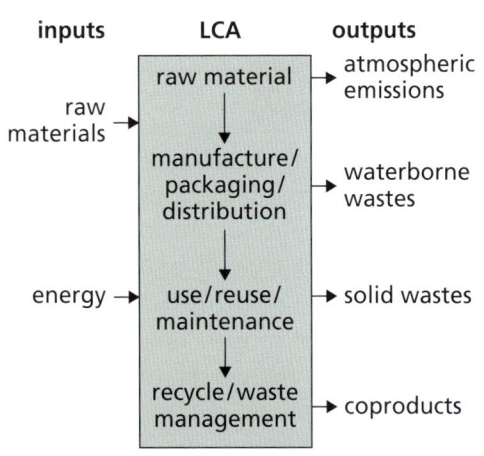

▲ **Figure 2** This shows the inputs and outputs in an LCA

dioxide gas or 2000 tonnes of nitrogen dioxide gas released into the atmosphere. What potential impact does the release of each gas have on smog, and on acid rain? What are the effects on asthma sufferers?

Sometimes there is no hard factual data available, so estimations are made, for example, from articles in journals or from a company's published figures. Calculations of data based on assumptions should include an indication of the uncertainty. Numerical values should only be used in LCAs where widely accepted and accurate data is available for details of energy, water, resources, and wastes.

LCAs will highlight environmental impact and health issues when comparing products or processes, but do not consider differences in the cost or performance. The best practice should incorporate a peer review process into the LCA to check the data and validity of conclusions drawn. This is especially desirable if an LCA is conducted by the company that makes the product that is being assessed, and its results are then used to make claims in advertising.

## Plastic or paper bags?

Your task is to carry out a simplified LCA for a supermarket that is deciding whether to use plastic poly(ethene) bags or paper bags at its checkouts (Figure 3).

- Identify the inputs and outputs in terms of raw materials, energy, and environmental impacts that would have to be considered by the supermarket's management team.
- Try to give the environmental impacts a numerical rating (1 to 10, with 10 having the most serious consequences). What is the problem with this approach?
- Justify the choice you would make from a purely environmental point of view.
- What other considerations might the management team consider before making the final decision?

▲ **Figure 3** Using life cycle assessments, should you use a plastic bag or a paper bag when shopping?

### Synoptic links

For information on crude oil and ethene, see Topics C9.2 and C9.4.

### Key points

- Life cycle assessments (LCAs) are carried out to assess the environmental impact of products, processes, or services.
- LCAs analyse each of the stages of a life cycle, from extracting and processing raw material to disposal at the end of its useful life, including any transport and distribution at each stage.
- LCAs involve some subjective judgements, so they have limitations.

### Summary questions

1 Name the stages in an LCA of a product. **4 MARKS**

2 Explain why an LCA should be carried out on new products. **1 MARK**

3 a Name the input shown on an LCA report that would be the raw material used to make an aluminium alloy for the wings of an aeroplane. **1 MARK**
  b Name the output shown on an LCA that would be:
   i the greenhouse gas given off when a product is distributed from a factory to shops around the country on lorries **1 MARK**
   ii the gas that causes acid rain given off as a result of using electricity generated in a coal-fired power station when making a product. **1 MARK**

4 Explain why parts of some LCAs may not be totally objective. **4 MARKS**

169

# C12.6 Reduce, reuse, and recycle

### Learning objectives

After this topic, you should know:
- how using less, reusing, and recycling materials decreases their environmental impact
- how to evaluate ways of reducing the use of limited supplies of metal ores, given appropriate information.

'Reduce, reuse, and recycle' is a message you might have seen in campaigns asking us to take action to help the environment. The aim is to reduce:

- our use of limited resources
- our use of energy
- the waste we produce.

If we can manage this, then every individual's impact on the environment will also be reduced.

For example, metals, glass, building materials, clay **ceramics**, and most plastics are all produced from limited supplies of raw materials. Converting raw materials into the finished products requires a large amount of energy. Much of the energy used in the processes also comes from limited resources.

However, some products, such as glass bottles or car parts, can be reused. Some other products cannot be reused but can be recycled for a different use. For example, glass bottles can be crushed and melted to make different glass products, and the same applies to parts of cars at the end of their life cycle.

## Recycling aluminium

It is important to **recycle** aluminium to help conserve the Earth's reserves of aluminium ore. Aluminium is extracted from molten aluminium oxide at high temperatures using electrolysis. The process requires huge amounts of electrical energy. Recycling saves energy, and therefore money, since recycling aluminium does not involve electrolysis. When comparing recycled aluminium with aluminium extracted from its ore, there is a 95% energy saving.

▲ **Figure 1** Recycling cans saves energy, as well as our limited supplies of metal ores. It also reduces pollution

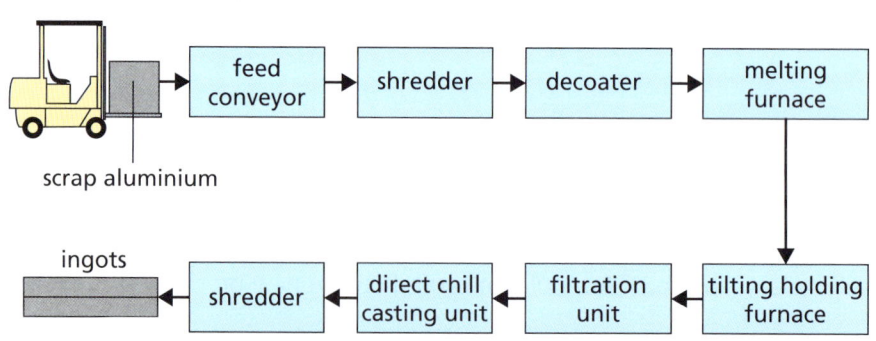

▲ **Figure 2** The recycling of aluminium involves melting the scrap metal, but still uses less energy than extracting aluminium from its ore, bauxite

### Synoptic link

To remind yourself about the production of aluminium, look back at Topic C6.3.

## Recycling iron and steel

We also recycle iron and steel, for example, from the bodywork and engines of scrap cars. 'Tin cans' are another source of scrap iron. These are usually steel cans with a very thin coating of tin to prevent rusting. The cans are easy for waste centres to separate from other domestic rubbish, as they are magnetic.

### C12 The Earth's resources

Using recycled steel saves about 50% of the energy used to extract iron and turn it into steel. This scrap steel can be added to the **blast furnace** to reduce the amount of iron that needs to be mined and extracted from iron ore.

## Recycling copper

Copper is also recycled but the process is more difficult as copper is often alloyed with other metals. An example is the copper in brass where it is mixed with zinc. Impure copper from recycling must be purified for use in electrical wiring, unless it has been reclaimed solely from old electricity wires. High-quality copper from wires can be recycled by melting and/or reusing it.

## Environmental considerations

Recycling metals reduces the need to mine the metal ore and conserves the Earth's limited reserves of metal ores. It also prevents any pollution problems that arise from extracting the metal from its ore. For example, open-cast mining or quarrying is often used to get copper ore from the ground.

The ores of iron and aluminium are also mainly mined like this. Huge pits that scar the landscape are made, creating noise and dust, and destroying the habitats of plants and animals. The mines also leave large heaps of waste rock.

The water in an area subjected to the mining of metal ores can also be affected. As rain drains through exposed ores and slag heaps of waste, the groundwater can become acidic.

Once ores are mined, they must be processed to extract the metals. For example, sulfide ores are heated to high temperatures in smelting. Any sulfur dioxide gas that escapes into the air will cause acid rain.

In the extraction of iron, carbon dioxide is given off, which can contribute to the enhanced greenhouse effect and global warming issues. Reducing these factors is why recycling metals is so important.

> **Synoptic link**
>
> For more information about the pollution caused by fossil fuels, look back at Topic C11.5.

▲ **Figure 3** Scrap copper can be recycled as copper alloy, but for many uses it must be pure. Extraction by electrolysis works if the scrap has a high proportion of copper. If the proportion of copper is low, electrolysis only works if pure copper is added to increase the percentage of copper. This makes the process expensive

▲ **Figure 4** Recycling helps to reduce the pollution problems that result from the energy needed to process metal ores

## Summary questions

1. Describe how glass is recycled. **3 MARKS**

2. It is thought that each person in the UK uses about 8 kg of aluminium each year, on average. Recycling 1 kg of aluminium saves about enough energy to run a small electric fire for 14 hours. If you recycle 50% of the aluminium you use in one year, calculate how long you could run a small electric fire on the energy saved. **1 MARK**

3. Explain why the energy savings are so great when recycling aluminium compared with extracting aluminium from its ore. **3 MARKS**

4. Explain why it is difficult to recycle some metals, such as copper, and how this can be overcome. **4 MARKS**

5. Explain how pollution problems are reduced by recycling metals. **3 MARKS**

> **Key points**
>
> - There are social, economic, and environmental issues associated with exploiting the Earth's limited supplies of raw materials, such as metal ores.
> - Recycling saves energy and finite resources. The pollution caused by the mining and extraction of metals is also reduced by recycling.

171

# C12 The Earth's resources

## Practice questions

1 In some hot countries, getting sufficient fresh water is difficult. However, countries with large coastlines have plenty of seawater available. They can use desalination plants, such as the one in the photo. These use a process called 'flash distillation' to turn the salty water into drinking water. Inside the desalination plant, seawater is boiled under reduced pressure, then the water vapour given off is cooled and condensed.

   a Why is the pressure reduced before boiling the seawater? Explain how this keeps costs down. **2 MARKS**
   
   b An alternative process uses 'reverse osmosis' to remove the salts from seawater. This passes seawater through a membrane. The latest membranes can remove 98% of the salts from seawater. Why is reverse osmosis a better option than flash distillation for obtaining drinking water? **2 MARKS**

2 Scrap car dealers are required to recover 95% of all materials used to make a car. The table shows the metals in an average car:

| Material | Average mass in kg | % mass |
|---|---|---|
| ferrous metal (steels) | 780 | 68.3 |
| light non-ferrous metal (mainly aluminium) | 72 | 6.3 |
| heavy non-ferrous metal (e.g., lead) | 17 | 1.5 |

Other materials used include plastics, rubber, and glass.

   a Determine the average mass of metal in a car. **1 MARK**
   
   b Determine what percentage of a car's mass is made up of **non-metallic** materials. **1 MARK**
   
   c i Name the main metal found in cars. **1 MARK**
   
   ii Which property of this metal allows it to be separated from other scrap materials? **1 MARK**

3 Pure gold is said to be 24 carats. A carat is a twenty-fourth, so $24 \times \frac{1}{24} = 1$ of pure gold. So, a 9-carat gold ring will have $\frac{9}{24}$ gold and $\frac{15}{24}$ of another metal, probably copper or sometimes silver.

How hard the 'gold' is will depend on the amount of gold and on the type of metal used to make the alloy.

| Gold alloy in carats | Maximum hardness in BHN |
|---|---|
| 9 | 170 |
| 14 | 180 |
| 18 | 230 |
| 22 | 90 |
| 24 | 70 |

(BHN = Brinell Hardness Number)

   a i Name the independent variable in this investigation. **1 MARK**
   
   ii Which type of variable is 'the maximum hardness of the alloy' – categoric or continuous? **1 MARK**
   
   iii Plot a graph of the results. **4 MARKS**
   
   iv Describe the pattern in the results. **2 MARKS**
   
   b A Life Cycle Assessment (LCA) was commissioned by a jewellery manufacturer on the 18-carat wedding rings sold.
   
   i If the copper used was obtained from ore containing copper(I) sulfide, $Cu_2S$, name an output of the LCA that would cause concern and explain why. **2 MARKS**
   
   ii Besides the copper ore, name two other inputs into the LCA process that would also cause depletion of natural resources. **2 MARKS**

4 a **H** Name the method of extracting copper from an ore:
   
   i using bacteria **1 MARK**
   
   ii using plants **1 MARK**
   
   iii by roasting **1 MARK**
   
   iv using electricity. **1 MARK**
   
   b Choose which methods in part **a** are being developed to extract copper from low-grade copper ores. **2 MARKS**
   
   c Using the methods named in **both** parts **a iii** and **a iv**, explain **in detail** whether copper in the ore is reduced or oxidised. Include half equations in your answer to both methods, assuming the method in part **a iii** is carried out on copper(I) sulfide. **6 MARKS**

5 **H** Describe the advantages and disadvantages of using bioleaching to extract copper metal. **6 MARKS**

# Exam-style questions

**01** This question is about the treatment of water. Some of the stages in the treatment of reservoir water are shown in **Figure 1**.

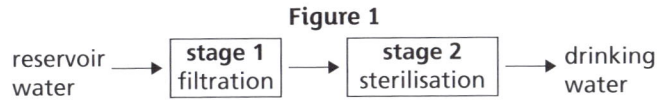

**Figure 1**

reservoir water → stage 1 filtration → stage 2 sterilisation → drinking water

**01.1** What is removed from the reservoir water during **stage 1**?

Choose the correct answer. 1 MARK

- **A** dissolved salts
- **B** microbes
- **C** solids

**01.2** Name one chemical that can be added to sterilise the water in **stage 2**. 1 MARK

**01.3** Explain why it is not correct to describe the drinking water in **Figure 1** as pure. 1 MARK

**01.4** Some countries have limited supplies of fresh water. Instead, they have to treat salty water.

**Figure 2** shows one method of obtaining drinking water from salty water.

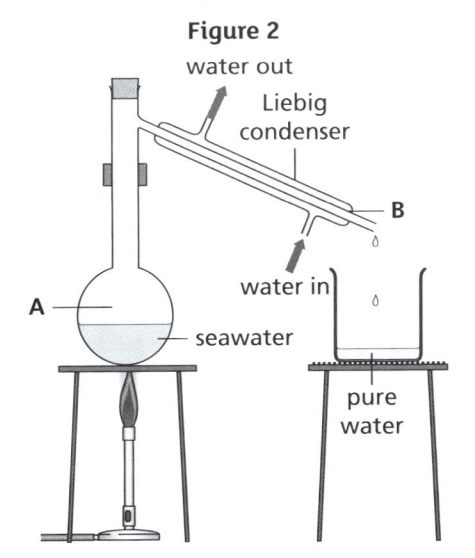

**Figure 2**

Name this technique. 1 MARK

**01.5** Name the change of state that occurs at **A**. 1 MARK

**01.6** Name the change of state that occurs at **B**. 1 MARK

**01.7** This technique is not often used to produce drinking water from salty water. Suggest why. 1 MARK

**01.8** The drinking water produced in **Figure 2** does not contain dissolved solids.

Describe how you could show that this water does not contain dissolved solids without using a chemical test. 2 MARKS

**02** Shopping carrier bags can be made from poly(ethene) that comes from crude oil, or from corn starch that comes from plants that are grown and harvested.

**Table 1** contains information from a Life Cycle Assessment (LCA) comparing the two types of shopping bags.

**Table 1**

| Life cycle stage | Shopping bag made from corn starch | Shopping bag made from poly(ethene) |
|---|---|---|
| raw materials | corn on the cob plants | crude oil |
| manufacturing process | Starch is extracted by reacting the corn with acid at 100 °C. Manufacturing process takes six weeks. | Crude oil is heated to 400 °C and fractionally distilled. Ethene is produced by cracking, which involves heating to 800 °C. Manufacturing process takes less than one day. |
| use during its lifetime | can be reused until the bag splits or breaks will break down after 70 days | can be reused until the bag splits or breaks will not break down |
| disposal | can be disposed of in compost or in landfill biodegradable can be recycled | landfill, non-biodegradable difficult to recycle, can be disposed of by burning |

Use the information in **Table 1**, and your own knowledge, to compare the advantages and disadvantages of the two types of carrier bags. 6 MARKS

C12 The Earth's resources

173

# Paper 1 questions

**01** A molecule of methane is shown in **Figure 1**.

**Figure 1**

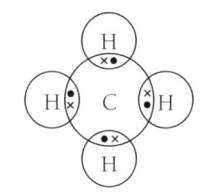

**01.1** What is the chemical formula of methane?

Select the correct answer.

- **A** C$_4$H
- **B** CH$_4$
- **C** C4H

1 MARK

**01.2** In **Figure 1**, what does •× represent?

Select the correct answer.

- **A** a pair of electrons
- **B** a pair of neutrons
- **C** a pair of protons

1 MARK

**01.3** What particles are present in the nucleus of a carbon atom?

Select the correct answer.

- **A** neutrons and electrons
- **B** protons and electrons
- **C** protons and neutrons

1 MARK

**Figure 2** shows another way of representing a molecule of methane.

**Figure 2**

**01.4** What type of bond is represented by each line?

Select the correct answer.

- **A** covalent bond
- **B** ionic bond
- **C** metallic bond

1 MARK

**01.5** The bonds in methane are very strong but methane has a low boiling point.

Why does methane have a low boiling point?

Select the correct answer.

- **A** methane has a giant structure
- **B** methane has only four bonds per molecule that need to be broken
- **C** methane has weak intermolecular forces between its molecules

1 MARK

**02** This question is about the Periodic Table.

**02.1** An early version of the Periodic Table was published by a scientist. The scientist left gaps. Give **one** reason why the scientist left gaps in this Periodic Table.

1 MARK

**02.2** Which scientist published this early Periodic Table?

Tick (✓) **one** box.

Bohr ☐
Chadwick ☐
Mendeleev ☐

1 MARK

**02.3** The modern Periodic Table is different to the early Periodic Table.

One extra group of elements has been added.

What is the name of the extra group of elements in the modern Periodic Table?

Tick (✓) **one** box.

alkali metals ☐
halogens ☐
noble gases ☐

1 MARK

**02.4** Why do the elements in Group 1 of the modern Periodic Table have similar chemical properties?

Tick (✓) **one** box.

the elements all form negative ions ☐
the elements all have one electron in the outer shell ☐
the elements all have the same number of shells ☐

1 MARK

**02.5** **Table 1** shows the melting points of the first five elements going down Group 1.

| Element | Melting point in °C |
|---|---|
| lithium | 181 |
| sodium | 98 |
| potassium | X |
| rubidium | 39 |
| caesium | 29 |

**Table 1**

Predict the value of **X**.      X = _____ °C

1 MARK

174

**Paper 1 questions**

**02.6** Give **one** observation you would see when a small piece of potassium is added to water. 
1 MARK

**02.7** **Table 2** shows information about the first five elements going down Group 7.
Complete **Table 2**. 
2 MARKS

| Element | State at 150°C | Symbol | Formula of the compound with hydrogen |
|---|---|---|---|
| fluorine | gas | F | HF |
| chlorine |  | Cl | HCl |
| bromine | gas | Br | HBr |
| iodine | liquid | I | HI |
| astatine | solid | At |  |

**Table 2**

**02.8** The elements in Group 7 consist of molecules. What is the formula of a molecule of bromine?
Tick (✓) **one** box.
Br ☐
$Br_2$ ☐
$Br^2$ ☐
2Br ☐
1 MARK
AQA, 2022

**03** This question is about electrolysis. Molten sodium chloride is electrolysed in an industrial process to produce sodium. **Figure 3** shows a simplified version of the electrolysis setup.

**Figure 3**

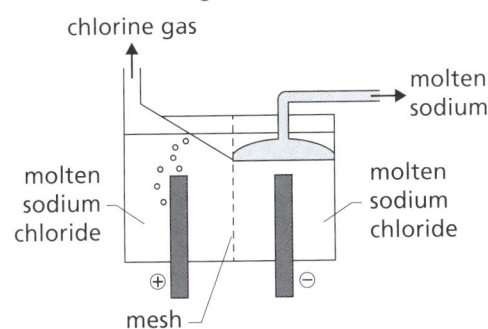

chlorine gas
molten sodium
molten sodium chloride
molten sodium chloride
mesh

**03.1** Which is the correct half equation for the production of sodium?
Tick (✓) **one** box.
Na + e⁻ ⟶ Na⁺ ☐
Na ⟶ Na⁺ + e⁻ ☐
Na⁺ + e⁻ ⟶ Na ☐
Na⁺ ⟶ Na + e⁻ ☐
1 MARK

**03.2** A mesh is used to keep the products of the electrolysis apart. Suggest **one** reason why the products of the electrolysis must be kept apart.
1 MARK

**03.3** Which type of particle passes through the mesh in the electrolysis of molten sodium chloride?
Tick (✓) **one** box.
atom ☐
electron ☐
ion ☐
molecule ☐
1 MARK

Aqueous sodium chloride solution is electrolysed in a different industrial process.
Two gases and an alkaline solution are produced.
Which **two** ions are present in aqueous sodium chloride solution in addition to sodium ions and chloride ions? 
2 MARKS

**03.4** Name the alkaline solution produced.
1 MARK

**03.5** Explain how the alkaline solution is produced. You should refer to the processes at the electrodes.
3 MARKS
AQA, 2022

**04** This question is about metals.

**04.1** **Table 3** shows information about four substances.

|   | Melting point in °C | Boiling point in °C | Does it conduct electricity in the solid state? | Does it conduct electricity in the liquid state? |
|---|---|---|---|---|
| A | −117 | 79 | no | no |
| B | 801 | 1413 | no | yes |
| C | 1535 | 2750 | yes | yes |
| D | 1610 | 2230 | no | no |

**Table 3**

Which substance could be a metal?
Tick (✓) **one** box.
A ☐
B ☐
C ☐
D ☐
1 MARK

**04.2** Explain why alloys are harder than pure metals.
3 MARKS

175

**04.3** A student wants to compare the reactivity of an unknown metal, **Q**, with that of zinc. Both metals are more reactive than silver.

The student is provided with:
- silver nitrate solution
- metal **Q** powder
- zinc powder
- a thermometer
- normal laboratory equipment.

No other chemicals are available.

Describe a method the student could use to compare the reactivity of metal **Q** with that of zinc. Your method should give valid results.

**4 MARKS**

*AQA, 2021*

**05** Some students were investigating the rate at which carbon dioxide gas is produced when metal carbonates react with an acid.

One student reacted 1.00 g of calcium carbonate with 50 cm³, an excess, of dilute hydrochloric acid.

The apparatus used is shown in **Figure 4**.

**Figure 4**

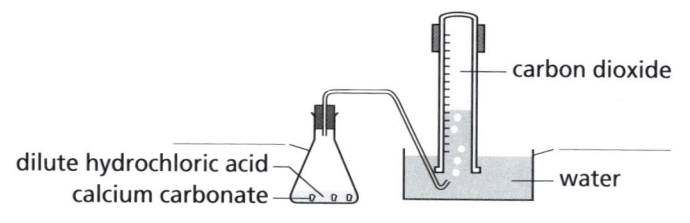

dilute hydrochloric acid
calcium carbonate
carbon dioxide
water

**05.1** Complete the **two** labels for the apparatus on the diagram.

**1 MARK**

**05.2** The student measured the volume of gas collected every 30 seconds.

**Table 4** shows the student's results.

| Time in seconds | Volume of carbon dioxide collected in cm³ |
|---|---|
| 30 | 104 |
| 60 |  |
| 90 | 198 |
| 120 | 221 |
| 150 | 232 |
| 180 | 238 |
| 210 | 240 |
| 240 | 240 |

**Table 4**

**Figure 5** shows what the student saw at 60 seconds.

**Figure 5**

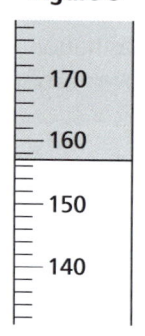

170
160
150
140

What is the volume of gas collected?

**1 MARK**

**05.3** Why did the volume of gas stop changing after 210 seconds?

**1 MARK**

**05.4** **H** Another student placed a conical flask containing 1.00 g of a Group 1 carbonate ($M_2CO_3$) on a balance.

He then added 50 cm³, an excess, of dilute hydrochloric acid to the flask and measured the mass of carbon dioxide given off.

The equation for the reaction is:

$$M_2CO_3 + 2HCl \rightarrow 2MCl + H_2O + CO_2$$

The final mass of carbon dioxide given off was 0.32 g.

Calculate the amount, in moles, of carbon dioxide in 0.32 g carbon dioxide.

Relative atomic masses, $A_r$: C = 12; O = 16.

**2 MARKS**

**05.5** **H** How many moles of the metal carbonate are needed to make this number of moles of carbon dioxide?

**1 MARK**

**05.6** **H** The mass of metal carbonate used was 1.00 g.

Use this information, and your answer to **05.5**, to calculate the relative formula mass $M_r$ of the metal carbonate.

If you could not answer **05.5**, use 0.009 43 as the number of moles of metal carbonate. This is not the answer to **05.5**.

**1 MARK**

176

**05.7** **H** Use your answer to **05.6** to calculate the relative atomic mass $A_r$ of the metal in the metal carbonate ($M_2CO_3$) and so identify the Group 1 metal in the metal carbonate.

If you could not answer **05.6**, use 230 as the relative formula mass of the metal carbonate. This is not the answer to **05.6**.

Remember, you must show your working. **3 MARKS**

**05.8** **H** Two other students repeated the experiment in **05.4**.

When the first student did the experiment some acid sprayed out of the flask as the metal carbonate reacted.

Explain the effect this mistake would have on the calculated relative atomic mass of the metal. **3 MARKS**

**05.9** **H** The second student used 100 cm³ of dilute hydrochloric acid instead of 50 cm³.

Explain the effect, if any, this mistake would have on the calculated relative atomic mass of the metal. **3 MARKS**

*AQA, 2014*

**06** **H** Ethane reacts with bromine at room temperature in sunlight.

The reaction is shown below in **Figure 6**.

**Figure 6**

H-C(H)(H)-C(H)(H)-H + Br—Br ⟶ H-C(H)(H)-C(H)(H)-Br + H—Br

**06.1** Suggest why this reaction will not take place at room temperature in the dark. **1 MARK**

**06.2** The bond energies are presented in **Table 5**.

| Bond | Bond energy in kJ/mol |
|---|---|
| C—C | 347 |
| C—H | 413 |
| Br—Br | 193 |
| C—Br | 290 |
| H—Br | 366 |

**Table 5**

Show that the energy transferred to the surroundings by the reaction is 50 kJ/mol. **3 MARKS**

**06.3** Copy and complete the reaction profile. Show arrows to label the activation energy $E_a$ and the energy transferred to the surroundings.

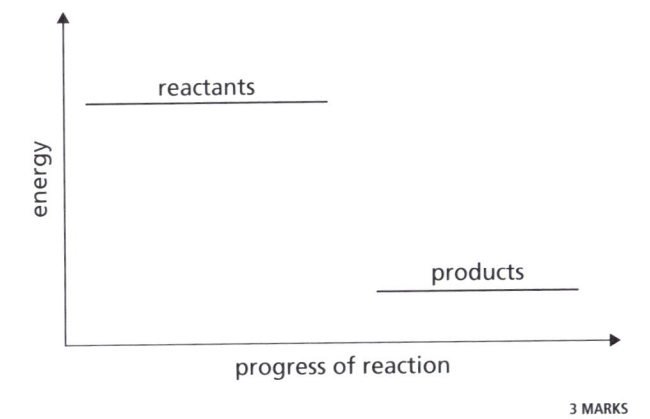

[Reaction profile diagram: energy vs progress of reaction, showing reactants at higher energy level and products at lower energy level]

**3 MARKS**

177

# Paper 2 questions

**01** This question is about gases in the Earth's atmosphere.

**01.1** Complete **Table 1** to show the current composition of the Earth's atmosphere.

Table 1

| Percentage of the gas in the Earth's atmosphere | Name of gas |
|---|---|
| 79 | |
| 20 | |
| 1 | carbon dioxide, water vapour, and noble gases |

2 MARKS

Three billion years ago the temperature on Earth was much higher, as were the percentages of carbon dioxide and water vapour in the atmosphere.

**01.2** Explain why the percentage of water vapour decreased. 2 MARKS

**01.3** Give **two** processes that caused the percentage of carbon dioxide to decrease. 2 MARKS

**02** This question is about materials used to make food plates. Food plates are made from paper, polymers or ceramics.

**Table 2** shows information about plates of the same diameter made from each of these materials.

Table 2

| | Food plate material | | |
|---|---|---|---|
| | Paper | Polymers | Ceramics |
| raw material | wood | crude oil | mined clay |
| number packaged in 10 cm³ cardboard box | 500 | 100 | 50 |
| average number of times used | 1 | 400 | 1000 |
| biodegradable? | yes | no | no |
| recyclable? | yes | yes | no |

**02.1** **Table 2** does not show information about energy usage. Suggest **two** pieces of information about energy usage which would help to produce a complete life cycle assessment (LCA) for the three food plate materials. 2 MARKS

**02.2** Evaluate the use of these materials for making food plates. You should use features of life cycle assessments (LCAs). Use **Table 2**. 4 MARKS

**02.3** Describe how ceramic food plates are produced from clay. 2 MARKS

AQA, 2020

**03** This question is about paper chromatography. A food colouring contains a dye.

**03.1** Plan an investigation to determine the $R_f$ value for the dye in this food colouring.

$$R_f = \frac{\text{distance moved by substance}}{\text{distance moved by solvent}}$$

Your plan should include the use of:
- a beaker
- a solvent
- chromatography paper.

6 MARKS

**03.2** Two students investigated a dye in a food colouring using paper chromatography. Each student did the investigation differently. The $R_f$ values they determined for the **same** dye were different. How did the students' investigations differ?

Tick (✓) **one** box.

length of paper used ☐
period of time used ☐
size of beaker used ☐
solvent used ☐

1 MARK

Figure 1

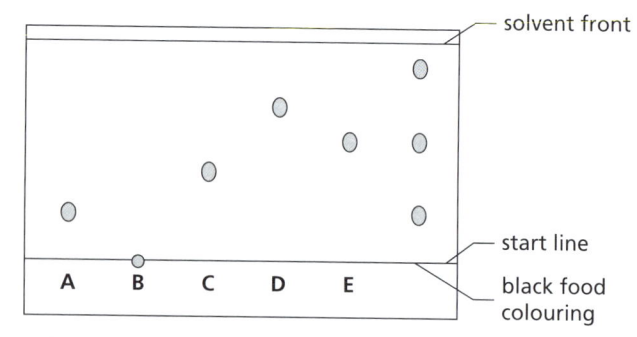

[Figure 1 shows a chromatography diagram with solvent front at top, start line at bottom with black food colouring at start, and spots A, B, C, D, E at various heights.]

**03.3** What do the results in **Figure 1** tell you about the composition of the black food colouring? 2 MARKS

**03.4** Paper chromatography involves a stationary phase. What is the stationary phase in paper chromatography?

Tick (✓) **one** box.

beaker ☐
dye ☐
paper ☐
solvent ☐

1 MARK

# Paper 2 questions

**04** Hydrogen gas is produced by the reaction of methane and steam.

**04.1** **Figure 2** represents a molecule of hydrogen.

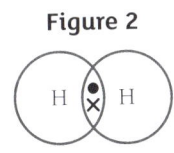

**Figure 2**

What type of bond joins the atoms of hydrogen?

Tick (✓) **one** box.

A ☐ covalent
B ☐ metallic
C ☐ ionic
**1 MARK**

**04.2** A catalyst is used in the reaction.

Choose the correct answer to complete the sentence.

| A catalyst | increases the rate of reaction. |
| | increases the temperature. |
| | increases the yield of a reaction. |

**1 MARK**

**04.3** The equation for the reaction of methane and steam is:

$$CH_4(g) + H_2O(g) \rightleftharpoons CO(g) + 3H_2(g)$$

What is meant by the symbol $\rightleftharpoons$? **1 MARK**

**04.4** Ⓗ Lowering the pressure reduces the rate of reaction.

Explain why, in terms of particles. **2 MARKS**

**04.5** Ⓗ The graph shows the yield of hydrogen at different temperatures. The forward reaction is endothermic. How does **Figure 3** show that the forward reaction is endothermic? **1 MARK**

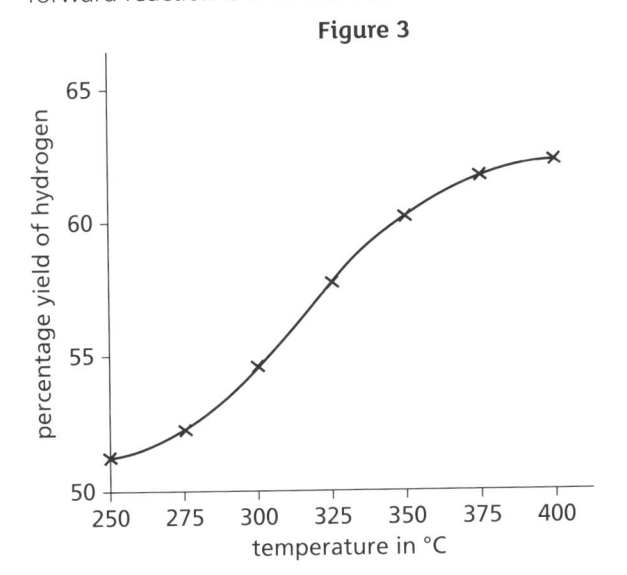

**Figure 3**

**04.6** Ⓗ Why is a higher yield produced if the reaction is repeated at a lower pressure? **1 MARK**

**05** **Figure 4** shows how crude oil can be separated into fractions **A**, **B**, **C**, **D**, **E**, and **F**.

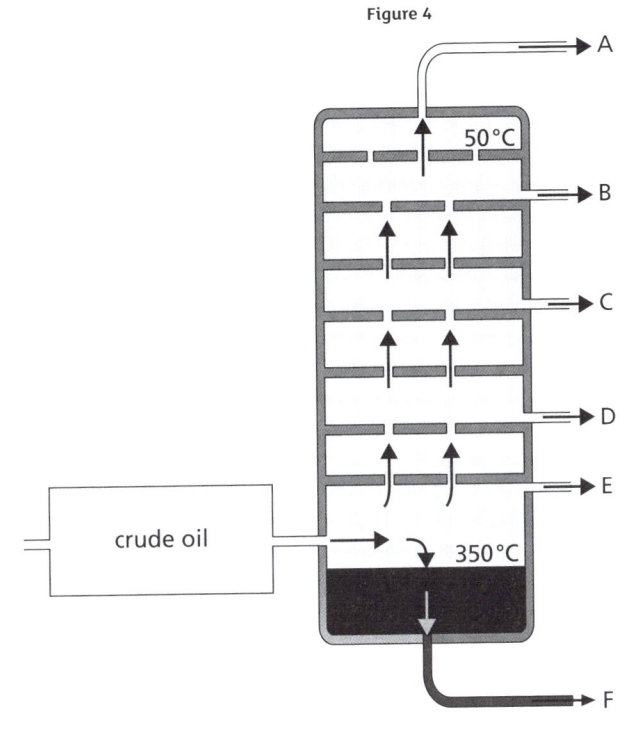

**Figure 4**

**05.1** Which fraction contains hydrocarbons with the lowest boiling point? **1 MARK**

**05.2** Which fraction contains hydrocarbons with the longest carbon chains? **1 MARK**

**05.3** Fractions **B**, **C**, **D**, and **E** are liquids at room temperature. Which fraction contains the hydrocarbons that are the most flammable? **1 MARK**

**05.4** Which fraction **B**, **C**, **D**, or **E** would be the most viscous? **1 MARK**

**05.5** Hydrocarbon **V** was cracked to form four different hydrocarbons: **W**, **X**, **Y**, and **Z**.

The equation for the cracking process is shown below.

| V | | W | | X | | Y | | Z |
| $C_{28}H_{58}$ | → | $C_{14}H_{30}$ | + | $C_9H_{18}$ | + | $C_2H_4$ | + | $C_3H_6$ |

Describe the conditions for cracking. **2 MARKS**

**05.6** Give the general formula for hydrocarbon **V**. **1 MARK**

**05.7** Hydrocarbon **W** and hydrocarbon **X** are both colourless liquids. Describe a chemical test and the result of the test to identify hydrocarbon **X**. **2 MARKS**

179

# Maths skills for Chemistry

## MS1 Arithmetic and numerical computation

### Learning objectives

After this topic, you should know how to:
- recognise and use expressions in decimal form
- recognise and use expressions in standard form
- use ratios, fractions, and percentages
- make estimates of the results of simple calculations.

How big is an atom? How many atoms are in 12 g of carbon? What is the size of a nanoparticle?

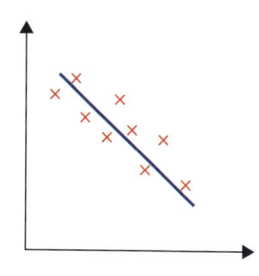

▲ **Figure 1** Looking for patterns in data

▲ **Figure 2** There are $6.02 \times 10^{23}$ atoms in this 12 g of carbon

Scientists use maths all the time – when collecting data, looking for patterns, and making conclusions. This chapter includes the maths you need for your GCSE Combined Science: Trilogy course. The rest of the book gives you many opportunities to practise using maths when it is needed as you learn about chemistry.

▲ **Figure 3** If you use a pH meter to measure the pH of a solution, your reading could be a decimal number

## 1a Decimal form

There will always be a whole number of atoms in a molecule, and a whole number of protons, neutrons, or electrons in an atom.

However, when you make measurements in science the numbers may *not* be whole numbers but numbers *in between* whole numbers. These are numbers in decimal form, for example, the volume of acid used in an experiment could be 22.35 cm$^3$, or the mass of a powder could be 8.7 g.

The value of each digit in a number is called its place value. For example, in the number 4512.345:

| thousands | hundreds | tens | units | • | tenths | hundredths | thousandths |
|---|---|---|---|---|---|---|---|
| 4 | 5 | 1 | 2 | • | 3 | 4 | 5 |

## 1b Standard form

Place values can help you to understand the size of a number; however, some numbers in science are too large or too small to understand when they are written as ordinary numbers. For example, the number of atoms, ions, or molecules in a mole of substance, 602 000 000 000 000 000 000 000, or the diameter of the nucleus of a hydrogen atom, 0.000 000 000 000 001 75 m.

# Maths skills for Chemistry

**Standard form** is used to show very large or very small numbers more easily.

In standard form, a number is written as $A \times 10^n$.

- $A$ is a decimal number between 1 and 10 (but not including 10), for example, 6.02 or 1.75.
- $n$ is a whole number. The power of ten can be positive or negative, for example, $10^{23}$ or $10^{-15}$.

This gives you a number in standard form, for example, $6.02 \times 10^{23}$/mol or $1.75 \times 10^{-15}$.

▲ **Figure 4** What do 18 g of water, 108 g of gold, and 4 g of helium have in common? They all have $6.02 \times 10^{23}$ number of particles

Table 1 explains how you convert numbers to standard form.

**Table 1** How to convert numbers into standard form

| The number | The number in standard form | What you did to get to the decimal number | ...so the power of ten is... | What the *sign* of the power of ten tells you |
|---|---|---|---|---|
| 1000 m | $1.0 \times 10^3$ m | you moved the digits 3 places to the *left* to get the decimal number | +3 | the positive power shows the number is *greater* than one |
| 0.01 s | $1.0 \times 10^{-2}$ s | you moved the digits 2 places to the *right* to get the decimal number | −2 | the negative power shows the number is *less* than one |

When carrying out multiplications or divisions using standard form, you should add or subtract the powers of ten to work out roughly what you expect the answer to be. This will help you to avoid mistakes.

## Multiplying numbers in standard form

You can use a scientific calculator to calculate with numbers written in standard form. You should work out which button you need to use on your own calculator (it could be EE, EXP, 10^x, or ×10^x).

> **Study tip**
>
> Always remember to add any relevant units, for example, metres (written as 'm').

> **Synoptic link**
>
> To see how chemists use numbers in standard form, see Topic C1.7.

> **Study tip**
>
> Check that you understand the power of ten, and the sign of the power.

▲ **Figure 5** You can use a scientific calculator to do calculations involving standard form

181

# MS1 Arithmetic and numerical computation

▲ **Figure 6** Airships were common before the 1940s when a series of high-profile accidents occurred and their use was surpassed by aeroplanes

## Maths

### Worked example 1

The Avogadro constant $N_a$ tells you how many particles are in a mole of any particles. Its value is $6.02 \times 10^{23}$ per mol.

Calculate how many atoms of helium there are in an airship containing about $2.58 \times 10^4$ moles of helium gas.

### Solution

**Step 1:** Write down the formula for the number of atoms.
number of atoms = $N$ (/mol) × number of moles (mol)

**Step 2:** Substitute numbers into the formula for number of atoms.
number of atoms of helium = $(6.02 \times 10^{23}/\text{mol}) \times (2.58 \times 10^4 \text{mol})$
= **$1.55 \times 10^{28}$ atoms** in standard form

## 1c Ratios, fractions, and percentages

### Ratios

A **ratio** compares two quantities. A ratio of 2 : 4 of carbon atoms to oxygen atoms means that for every two carbon atoms, there are four oxygen atoms.

You can describe the number of carbon atoms in relation to the number of oxygen atoms using many different ratios, for example, 2 : 4, 1 : 2, and 0.5 : 1. All of the ratios are equivalent – they mean the same thing.

You can simplify a ratio so that both numbers are the lowest whole numbers possible.

▲ **Figure 7** You should always add acid to water. Mixing acid and water is an exothermic process. If you add water to acid so much energy can be transferred that boiling acid splashes out of the mixing vessel

## Maths

### Worked example 2

A student mixed 15 cm³ of acid with 90 cm³ of water. Calculate the simplest ratio of the volume of acid to the volume of water.

### Solution

**Step 1:** Write down the ratio of *acid : water*.
**Step 2:** Both 15 and 90 have a common factor, 5.
Divide both numbers by 5.
**Step 3:** Both 3 and 18 have a common factor, 3.
Divide both numbers by 3.

$$\begin{array}{c} 15 : 90 \\ \div 5 \downarrow \quad \downarrow \div 5 \\ 3 : 18 \\ \div 3 \downarrow \quad \downarrow \div 3 \\ 1 : 6 \end{array}$$

To get the simplest form of the ratio, you have divided by 15 (i.e., 3×5), which is the highest common factor of 15 and 90.

## Synoptic link

To see examples of how chemists use ratios, look at Topic C8.2.

### Fractions

A fraction is a part of a whole.

$\dfrac{1}{3}$ ⟶ The numerator tells you how many parts of the whole you have.
⟶ The denominator tells you how many equal parts the whole has been divided into.

# Maths skills for Chemistry

To convert a fraction into a decimal, divide the numerator by the denominator.

$\frac{1}{3} = 1 \div 3 = 0.33333\ldots = 0.\dot{3}$ (the dot shows that the number 3 recurs, or repeats over and over again).

To convert a decimal to a fraction, use the place value of the digits, then simplify. For example, the smallest place value in 0.045 is a thousandth, so $0.045 = \frac{45}{1000}$. This can be simplified to $\frac{9}{200}$.

## Maths

### Worked example 3

A student has a 25 g sample of sodium chloride. Calculate the mass of $\frac{2}{5}$ of this sample.

### Solution

$\frac{2}{5}$ of 25 g is the same as $\frac{2}{5} \times 25$ g, so:

**Step 1:** Divide the total mass of the sample by the denominator.

$25\,\text{g} \div 5 = 5\,\text{g}$

**Step 2:** Multiply by the numerator.

$5\,\text{g} \times 2 = \mathbf{10\,g}$

▲ **Figure 8** One square of this chocolate bar represents $\frac{1}{24}$. A column of four squares represents $\frac{4}{24}$, which can be simplified to $\frac{1}{6}$

### Study tip

Place values were introduced in Maths Skills MS1a.

## Percentages

A percentage is a number expressed as a fraction of 100, for example:

$77\% = \frac{77}{100} = 0.77$

## Maths

### Worked example 4

A student found that a 7.5 g sample of limestone contained 7.2 g of calcium carbonate.

Calculate the percentage by mass of calcium carbonate in the sample.

### Solution

**Step 1:** Calculate the fraction of calcium carbonate in the sample.

$\frac{\text{mass of calcium carbonate}}{\text{mass of limestone}} = \frac{7.2\,\text{g}}{7.5\,\text{g}}$

**Step 2:** Convert the fraction to a decimal.

$\frac{7.2}{7.5} = 7.2 \div 7.5 = 0.96$

**Step 3:** Multiply the decimal by 100%.

$0.96 \times 100\% = \mathbf{96\%}$

▲ **Figure 9** One of the biggest areas of limestone in the UK is in the Yorkshire Dales National Park

183

# MS1 Arithmetic and numerical computation

You may also need to calculate a percentage of a quantity.

## Maths

### Worked example 5

3.2 tonnes of limestone are put into a lime kiln. After an hour, 25% of this was converted into lime. How many tonnes of limestone were converted into lime?

### Solution

**Step 1:** Convert the percentage of limestone to a decimal.

$$25\% = \frac{25}{100} = 0.25$$

**Step 2:** Multiply by the total mass of limestone.

$0.25 \times 3.2$ tonnes = **0.8 tonnes**

▲ **Figure 10** Old lime kilns are a common sight in the Yorkshire Dales

Finally, you may need to calculate a percentage increase or decrease in a quantity from its original value.

## Maths

### Worked example 6

A student heats a 4.75 g sample of copper (II) carbonate. The mass decreases to 3.04 g. Calculate the percentage change in mass.

### Solution

**Step 1:** Calculate the decrease in mass.
4.75 g − 3.04 g = 1.71 g

**Step 2:** Divide the decrease in mass by the original mass.

$$\frac{1.71\,g}{4.75\,g} = 0.36$$

**Step 3:** Convert the decimal to a percentage.
$0.36 \times 100\%$ = **36%**

Remember that in this case the answer is a percentage *decrease*.

## 1d Estimating the result of a calculation

When you use your calculator to work out the answer to a calculation you can sometimes press the wrong button and get the wrong answer. The best way to make sure that your answer is correct is to estimate the answer in your head first.

▲ **Figure 11** Copper(II) carbonate

## Synoptic links

You can find examples of how chemists use percentages in Topic C11.2.

**Maths skills for Chemistry**

## Maths

### Worked example 7

A reaction produces gas at a constant rate of 34 cm³/min. Find the volume of gas produced after eight minutes. Estimate the answer and then calculate it.

### Solution

**Step 1:** Round each number up or down to get a whole number multiple of 10.

34 cm³/min is about 30 cm³/min

8 min is about 10 min

**Step 2:** Multiply the numbers in your head.

30 cm³/min × 10 min = 300 cm³

**Step 3:** Do the calculation and check it is close to your estimate.

Volume = 34 cm³/min × 8 min = **272 cm³**

This is quite close to 300 so it is probably correct.

Notice that you could do other things with the numbers:

$34 + 8 = 42$

$\dfrac{34}{8} = 4.3$

$34 - 8 = 26$

Not one of these answers is close to 300. If you got any of these answers you would know that you needed to repeat the calculation.

## Summary questions

1. If the mass of 1 mole of chlorine atoms is 35.5 g, calculate the mass of 6.0 moles of chlorine atoms. **1 MARK**

2. **a** The concentration of a dilute acid is 0.000 038 g/dm³. Express this concentration in standard form. **1 MARK**

   **b** A metal ore can be processed at a plant at a rate of about $5 \times 10^4$ tonnes per year. If this rate is maintained, how long will it be before $1.6 \times 10^6$ tonnes will be used up? **1 MARK**

3. **a** What is the simplest ratio of masses (sulfur : oxygen) in a mixture that contains 48 g of oxygen and 144 g of sulfur? **1 MARK**

   **b** A 300 tonne batch of bauxite was found to contain 60% aluminium oxide. What mass of aluminium oxide is in the batch? **1 MARK**

   **c** The approximate percentage of nitrogen gas in the air is 80%. Express this percentage as a fraction. **1 MARK**

185

# MS2 Handling data

## Learning objectives

*After this topic, you should know how to:*

- use an appropriate number of significant figures
- find arithmetic means
- construct and interpret frequency tables and bar charts
- make order of magnitude calculations.

▲ **Figure 1** In 2009, the UK consumed 1 611 000 barrels (four significant figures) or $1.6 \times 10^6$ (two significant figures) of oil per day

## Synoptic links

To find out how to use this type of calculation, you can find examples in Topics C8.1 and C8.2. There are also many examples of applying significant figures in the calculations in Chapter 4.

## 2a Significant figures

Numbers are rounded when it is not appropriate to give an answer that is too precise.

When rounding to **significant figures (s.f.)**, count from the first non-zero digit.

These masses each have three significant figures. The significant figures are underlined in each case.

<u>153</u> g        0.<u>153</u> g        0.00<u>153</u> g

Table 1 shows some more examples of measurements given to different numbers of significant figures.

**Table 1** The number of significant figures – the significant figures in each case are underlined. Notice that zeros at the end of decimal numbers are significant – see the last example in the table.

| Number | 0.0<u>5</u> s | <u>5.1</u> nm | 0.<u>775</u> g/s | <u>23.50</u> cm³ |
|---|---|---|---|---|
| Number of significant figures | 1 | 2 | 3 | 4 |

In general, you should give your answer to the same number of significant figures as the piece of data in the question that has the lowest number of significant figures.

Remember that rounding to significant figures is *not* the same as rounding to decimal places. When rounding to decimal places, count the number of digits that follow the decimal point. For example, 0.00153 has three significant figures but five decimal places.

### Maths

**Worked example 1**

Calculate the mean rate of a reaction that gives off 25 cm³ of gas in 7.85 seconds.

**Solution**

**Step 1:** Write down what you know.

volume of gas given off = 25 cm³     (2 s.f.)
time = 7.85 s     (3 s.f.)

You should give your answer to 2 s.f.

**Step 2:** Write down the equation that links the quantities you know and the quantity you want to find.

$$\text{mean rate of reaction (cm}^3\text{/s)} = \frac{\text{amount of product formed (cm}^3\text{)}}{\text{time } t \text{ (s)}}$$

**Step 3:** Substitute values into the equation.

$$\text{speed} = \frac{25 \text{ cm}^3}{7.85 \text{ s}}$$

$$= 3.184713376 \text{ cm}^3\text{/s}$$

$$= \mathbf{3.2 \text{ cm}^3\text{/s}} \text{ to 2 s.f.}$$

186

## 2b Arithmetic means

### How to calculate the mean
To calculate the **mean** (or average) of a series of values:
- add together all the values in the series to get a total
- divide the total by the number of values in the data series.

You will often need to do this with your sets of repeat readings when conducting investigations. This helps you to obtain more accurate data from sets of repeat readings where you have some random measurement errors.

> **Maths**
>
> **Worked example 2**
> A student measured the time to collect $20.0\,cm^3$ of hydrogen gas from the reaction of magnesium ribbon in excess dilute sulfuric acid.
>
> Their results were as follows:
>
> 18.7 s    19.5 s    18.5 s    19.2 s
>
> Calculate the mean time to collect $20.0\,cm^3$ of the gas.
>
> **Solution**
>
> **Step 1:** Add together the recorded values.
>
> 18.7 s + 19.5 s + 18.5 s + 19.2 s = 75.9 s
>
> **Step 2:** Then divide by the number of recorded values (in this case, 4 times were recorded).
>
> $\frac{75.9\,s}{4}$ = **18.9 s** (3 s.f.)
>
> The mean time to collect $20.0\,cm^3$ of hydrogen gas was 18.9 s. (3 s.f.)

▲ **Figure 2** When measuring a volume, you should repeat the measurements, then take a mean of your results

## 2c Frequency tables and bar charts

### Frequency tables and bar charts
The word **data** describes observations and measurements that are made during experiments or research.

**Qualitative data** is non-numerical data, such as colours or elements. For example, the chemical elements can be divided into the categories metals, metalloids, and non-metals.

The frequency table (Table 2) shows the number of metal, non-metals, or metalloids in the first 20 elements.

**Table 2** A frequency table for the number of metals, non-metals, and metalloids in the first 20 elements

| Type of element | Frequency |
|---|---|
| metal | 7 |
| non-metal | 11 |
| metalloid | 2 |

The height of the bars in the bar chart (Figure 3) represent the frequency of each category.

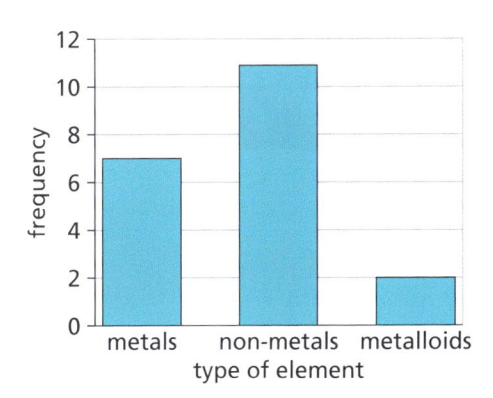

▲ **Figure 3** Number of metals, non-metals, and metalloids in the first 20 elements

**Maths skills for Chemistry**

187

## MS2 Handling data

> **Study tip**
>
> When drawing a bar chart with discrete data, remember to leave a gap between each bar.
>
> When drawing a bar chart with continuous data, do *not* leave a gap between each bar.

**Quantitative data** is numerical measurements.

**Discrete data** can only take exact whole number (integer) values (usually collected by counting).

**Continuous data** can take any value (usually collected by measuring), such as mass, volume, or density.

The frequency table (Table 3) shows the density of the first 20 elements. Density cannot be measured exactly, so the measurements are grouped into intervals.

**Table 3** A frequency table for the density of the first 20 elements

| Density $d$ in g/cm³ | Frequency |
|---|---|
| $0 < d < 1$ | 6 |
| $1 \leq d < 2$ | 8 |
| $2 \leq d < 3$ | 5 |
| $3 \leq d < 4$ | 1 |

There are no gaps between the bars when the data is continuous (Figure 4).

## 2d Estimates and order of magnitude

Being able to make a rough estimate is helpful. It can help you to check that a calculation is correct by knowing roughly what you expect the answer to be. A simple estimate is an **order of magnitude** estimate, which is an estimate to the nearest power of 10.

For example, to the nearest power of 10, you are probably 1 m tall and can run 10 m/s.

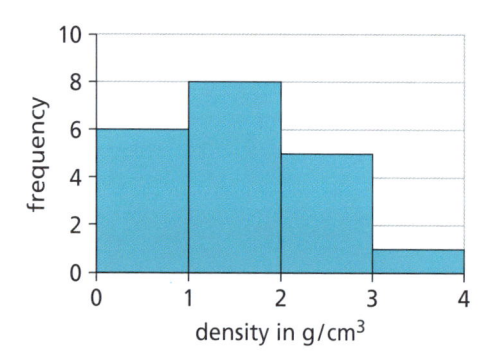

▲ **Figure 4** Density of the first 20 elements

▲ **Figure 5** Orders of magnitude can be useful but take care with them. Your height to the nearest power of 10 is probably 1 m but the average height of a 15-year-old boy is 1.7 m and a 15-year-old girl is 1.6 m. Similarly, to the nearest power of 10 you can run 10 m/s, but the mean speed of the eight finalists of the men's 100-metre sprint in the 2008 Beijing Olympics was 9.92 m/s – a lot faster than most of us can actually run

You, your desk, and your chair are all of the order of 1 m tall. The diameter of a molecule is of the order of $1 \times 10^{-9}$ m, or 1 nanometre.

# Maths skills for Chemistry

## Maths

### Worked example 3

If the size of a molecule is of the order $1 \times 10^{-9}$ m, and the size of a nanoparticle is of the order $1 \times 10^{-8}$ m, estimate how the nanoparticle's size compares with the size of the molecule to the nearest order of magnitude.

### Solution

**Step 1:** Divide the order of magnitude of the nanoparticles by the order of magnitude of the molecule.

$$\frac{1 \times 10^{-8}}{1 \times 10^{-9}} = 10$$

**Step 2:** Interpret the answer to the calculation.

The nanoparticle is one order of magnitude ($10^1$) larger than the molecule.

## Synoptic links

You can practise making orders of magnitude calculations in Topics C5.8 and C12.1.

## Summary questions

1. How many significant numbers are the following numbers quoted to?
   a. 33.0 **1 MARK**
   b. 0.02 **1 MARK**
   c. 250 **1 MARK**
   d. 13.35 **1 MARK**
   e. 0.225 **1 MARK**
   f. $3 \times 10^5$ **1 MARK**
   g. $1.673 \times 10^{-6}$ **1 MARK**
   h. $6.02 \times 10^{23}$ **1 MARK**

2. a. A student timed how long it took for a pencil mark on a piece of paper under a conical flask took to disappear as a precipitate formed in the flask. They repeated the experiment three times and obtained the following results:

   1st test: 184 s   2nd test: 203 s   3rd test: 196 s

   Calculate the mean time taken for the pencil mark to disappear, giving your answer to the appropriate number of significant figures. **2 MARKS**

3. A student tested how long it took to collect 10 cm³ of oxygen gas when four different metal oxides (labelled as **A** to **D**) were added to catalyse the breakdown of identical solutions of hydrogen peroxide. The student wrote the results as follows:
   **A** took 18 seconds; **B** took 27 seconds; **C** took 12 seconds; **D** took 35 seconds

   a. What type of variable is 'name of metal oxide' – qualitative or quantitative? **1 MARK**
   b. Draw a table and record the student's results in it. **2 MARKS**
   c. Display the results graphically. **4 MARKS**

4. a. Some estimates state that our current supplies of coal will run out in about 300 years. How many orders of magnitude is this estimate made to? **1 MARK**
   b. Describe how you would estimate the answer to a calculation involving numbers expressed in standard form. Use the case of an annual usage of a metal ore of $1.6 \times 10^8$ tonnes/year, the estimated reserves of the metal ore of $7.5 \times 10^{10}$ tonnes, and the calculation of how long the metal ore will last at the current rate of usage. **3 MARKS**

# MS3 Algebra

## Learning objectives

After this topic, you should know how to:

- understand and use the symbols: =, <, <<, >>, >, ∝, ~
- change the subject of an equation
- substitute numerical values into algebraic equations using appropriate units for quantities.

## 3a Mathematical symbols

You have used lots of different symbols in maths, such as +, −, ×, ÷. There are other symbols that you might meet in chemistry. These are shown in Table 1.

**Table 1** The symbols you will meet whilst studying chemistry

| Symbol | Meaning | Example |
|---|---|---|
| = | equal to | 2 g/s×2 s = 4 g |
| < | is less than | the mean diameter of an atom < the mean diameter of a nanoparticle |
| << | is very much less than | the diameter of an atom << the diameter of a round-bottom flask |
| >> | is very much bigger than | the number of atoms in a polymer molecule >> the number of atoms in a hydrogen molecule |
| > | is greater than | the pH of an alkali > 7 |
| ∝ | is proportional to | pressure of a gas ∝ its concentration |
| ~ | is approximately equal to | 272 cm$^3$ ~ 300 cm$^3$ |

▲ **Figure 1** The diameter of a round bottom flask is very much bigger than the diameter of even the biggest atom

## 3b Changing the subject of an equation

An equation shows the relationship between two or more variables. You can change an equation to make *any* of the variables become the subject of the equation.

To change the subject of an equation, you can do an opposite (inverse) operation to both sides of the equation to get the variable that you want on its own.

This means that:

- subtracting is the opposite of adding (and adding is the opposite of subtracting)
- dividing is the opposite of multiplying (and multiplying is the opposite of dividing).

### Maths

#### Worked example

Look at the equation for the number of moles of a substance.

$$\text{number of moles } n = \frac{\text{mass } m}{\text{relative atomic mass } A_r}$$

Change the equation to make mass *m* the subject.

#### Solution

**Step 1:** Multiply both sides by the relative atomic mass $A_r$.

$$n \times A_r = \frac{m}{A_r} \times A_r$$

190

**Step 2:** Cancel out any repeating variables.
The two $A_r$ variables on the right-hand side of the equation can cancel out.

$$n \times A_r = \frac{m}{\cancel{A_r}} \times \cancel{A_r}$$

This gives the final equation:

$$m = n \times A_r$$

> **Synoptic link**
>
> You can see examples of changing the subject of equations in the chemical calculations in Chapter 4.

## 3c Quantities and units

### SI units

When you take a measurement in science you need to include a number *and* a unit. When you do a calculation your answer should also include both a number *and* a unit. There are some special cases where the units cancel but usually they do not.

Everyone doing science, including you, needs to use the **SI system of units**.

Table 2 shows some of the quantities that you will use, along with their units.

**Table 2** Some quantities, and their units, you will meet during GCSE Combined Science: Trilogy course

| Quantity | Base unit |
| --- | --- |
| time | second, s |
| temperature | kelvin, K |
| amount of substance | mole, mol |
| energy | joule, J |
| pressure | pascal, Pa |
| electric potential difference | volt, V |

▲ **Figure 2** Measurements should have units. 3 is not a measurement, but 3 cm³ is

For example, 1.5 seconds is a *measurement*. The number 1.5 is not a measurement because it does not have a unit.

Some quantities that you *calculate* do not have a unit because they are relative values, for example, relative atomic mass.

### Metric prefixes

You can use metric prefixes to show large or small multiples of a particular unit. Adding a prefix to a unit means putting a letter in front of the unit. It shows you that you should multiply your value by a particular power of 10 for it to be shown in an SI unit.

For example, 3 kilometres = 3 km = $3 \times 10^3$ m. To convert the unit from metres to kilometres, a 'k' is put in front of the 'm'.

Most of the prefixes that you will use in science involve multiples of $10^3$. However, when dealing with volumes in chemistry you will often deal with decimetres cubed (dm³), where a decimetre (dm) is one tenth of a metre (or $1 \times 10^{-1}$ m).

# MS3 Algebra

> **Synoptic links**
>
> You can see examples of changing between metres and nanometres in Topic C1.7, and conversions between cm³ and dm³ in Topic C4.4.

**Table 3** Common prefixes you will use with your units

| Prefix | Symbol | Multiplying factor |
|--------|--------|--------------------|
| giga   | G      | $10^9$             |
| mega   | M      | $10^6$             |
| kilo   | k      | $10^3$             |
| deci   | d      | $10^{-1}$          |
| centi  | c      | $10^{-2}$          |
| milli  | m      | $10^{-3}$          |
| micro  | μ      | $10^{-6}$          |
| nano   | n      | $10^{-9}$          |

## Converting between units

It is helpful to use standard form when you are converting between units. To do this, it is best to consider how many of the 'smaller' units are contained within one of the 'bigger' units. For example:

- there are 1 000 000 000 nm in 1 m. So, $1\,\text{nm} = \dfrac{1}{1\,000\,000\,000}\,\text{m}$
  $= 1 \times 10^{-9}\,\text{m}$

- there are 1000 cm³ in 1 dm³. So, $1\,\text{dm}^3 = 1000\,\text{cm}^3$
  $= 1 \times 10^3\,\text{cm}^3$

> **Summary questions**
>
> 1. How would you read the following expressions as a sentence?
>    a. the pH of an acid < 7 *1 MARK*
>    b. rate of reaction ∝ the concentration of reactant **A** *1 MARK*
>    c. 22 dm³ ~ 24 dm³ *1 MARK*
>
> 2. Here is an equation chemists use to calculate the 'atom economy' of a reaction:
>
>    $$\text{percentage atom economy} = \frac{\text{relative formula mass of desired product} \times 100}{\text{sum of relative formula masses of all reactants}}$$
>
>    a. Rearrange the equation above to make its subject the 'relative formula mass of the desired product' in the equation. *1 MARK*
>    b. Rearrange the equation above to make its subject the 'sum of the relative formula masses of all the reactants' in the equation. *1 MARK*
>
> 3. a. Express 58 nm in metres (m), using standard form. *1 MARK*
>    b. Express 25.6 dm³ (decimetres cubed) in cm³, using standard form. *1 MARK*

Maths skills for Chemistry

# MS4 Graphs

During your GCSE Combined Science: Trilogy course you will collect data in different types of experiments or investigations. In investigations, the data is collected from a practical where you have changed *one* independent variable and measured its effect on a dependent variable.

## 4a Collecting data by changing a variable

In many investigations you change one variable (the independent variable) and measure the effect on another variable (the dependent variable). In a fair test, the other variables are kept constant.

For example, you can vary the concentration of sodium chloride in water (independent variable) and measure the effect on the temperature of the boiling point (dependent variable).

A scatter graph (Figure 1) lets you show the relationship between two numerical values.

- The independent variable is plotted on the $x$-axis (horizontal axis).
- The dependent variable is plotted on the $y$-axis (vertical axis).

The **line of best fit** is a line that goes roughly through the middle of all the points on the scatter graph. The line of best fit is drawn so that the points are evenly distributed on either side of the line.

If the gradient of the line of best fit is:

- **positive** it means as the independent variable *increases* the dependent variable *increases*
- **negative** it means as the independent variable *increases* the dependent variable *decreases*
- **zero** it means changing the independent variable has no effect on the dependent variable.

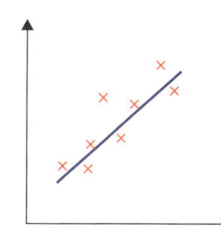

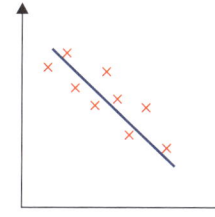

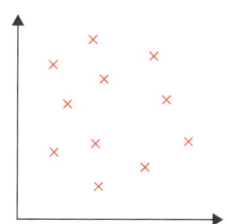

You say that the relationship between the variables is positive or negative, or that there is no relationship.

For example:

- as you increase the concentration of a reactant, the rate of reaction increases
- as you increase the temperature of water, the time it takes sugar to dissolve decreases.

### Learning objectives

After this topic, you should know how to:
- translate information between graphical and numeric form
- explain that $y = mx + c$ represents a linear relationship
- plot two variables from experimental or other data
- determine the slope and intercept of a linear graph
- draw and use the slope of a tangent to a curve as a measure of rate of change.

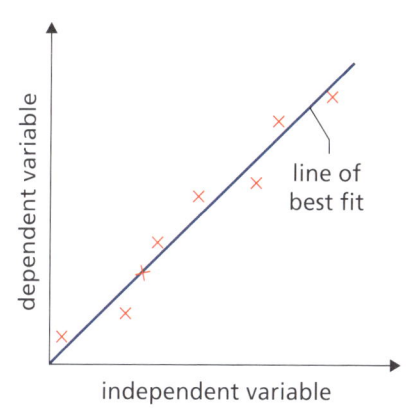

▲ Figure 1 A scatter graph

### Study tip

Use a transparent ruler to help you draw a straight line of best fit so you make sure that there are the same number of points on either side of the line.

# MS4 Graphs

The presence of a relationship does not always mean that changing the independent variable *causes* the change in the dependent variable. In order to claim a causal relationship, you must use science to predict or explain *why* changing one variable affects the other.

## 4b Graphs and equations

If you are changing one variable and measuring another you are trying to find out about the relationship between them. A straight line graph tells you about the mathematical relationship between variables but there are other things that you can calculate from a graph.

### Straight line graphs

The equation of a straight line is $y = mx + c$, where $m$ is the **gradient** and $c$ is the point on the *y*-axis where the graph intercepts, called the *y*-intercept.

Straight line graphs that go through the origin (0,0) are special. For these graphs, *y* is directly proportional to *x*, and $y = mx$. If two quantities are directly proportional, as one quantity increases, the other quantity increases by the same proportion.

In science, plotting a graph usually means plotting the points then drawing a line of best fit.

When you describe the relationship between two *physical* quantities, you should think about the reason why the graph might (or might not) go through (0,0).

For example, if you are measuring the volume of a gas produced in a reaction over time, when the time = 0 s (at the start of the reaction), the volume of gas produced at that point will be obviously be 0 cm$^3$.

However, if you are measuring the mass of reactants over time, in a reaction that gives off a gas, at time = 0 s, the *y*-intercept will not be zero but the starting mass of the reactants.

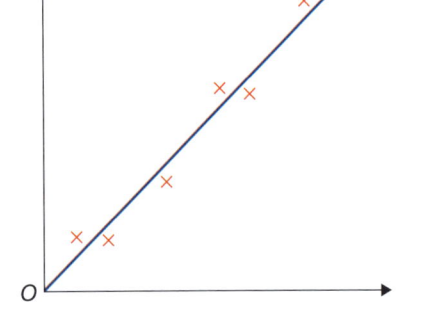

▲ **Figure 2** A line of best fit that passes through the origin

## 4c Plotting data

When you draw a graph you choose a scale for each axis.

- The scale on the *x*-axis should be the *same* all the way along the *x*-axis but it can be *different* to the scale on the *y*-axis.
- Similarly, the scale on the *y*-axis should be the *same* all the way along the *y*-axis but it can be *different* to the scale on the *x*-axis.
- Each axis should have a label and a unit, such as 'time in s'.

## 4d Determining the gradient of a straight line

When you are studying rates of reaction you might need to calculate a gradient from a graph of either:

- the amount of reactant as it decreases with time, or
- the amount of product as it increases with time.

For all graphs where the quantity on the *x*-axis is time, the gradient will tell you the *rate of change* of the quantity on the *y*-axis with time.

The gradient is calculated using the equation:

$$\text{gradient} = \frac{\text{change in } y}{\text{change in } x}$$

**Maths skills for Chemistry**

## 4e Using tangents

The graphs that you investigate may be curved lines.

To find the rate of reaction at a point **T** on the curve:

- Draw a tangent to the curve. The line should pass through point **T** and have the same slope as the curve at that point.
- Make a right-angled triangle with your line as the hypotenuse. Make sure that the triangle is large enough for you to calculate sensible changes in values.
- Use the triangle to read off the *change in y* and *the change in x*.
- Calculate gradient = $\dfrac{\text{change in } y}{\text{change in } x}$

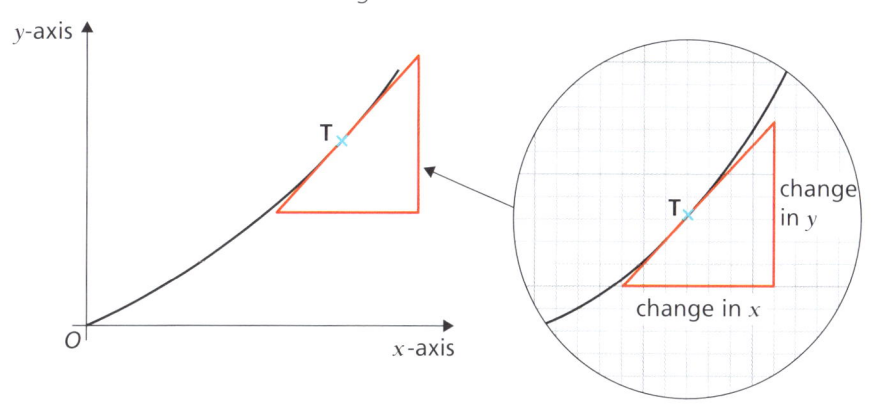

▲ **Figure 3** You find the gradient by drawing a tangent

> **Synoptic link**
>
> For a worked example of how to calculate the initial rate of a reaction from a line graph, see Topic C8.4.

### Summary questions

1. Sketch a line graph, labelling the *x*- and *y*-axes, that shows:
   a. a positive, constant gradient that passes through the origin (0,0) **1 MARK**
   b. a negative gradient – the gradient decreases as *x* increases. **1 MARK**
2. a. Write the general equation that describes a straight line on a graph, using the letters *y*, *x*, *m*, and *c*. **1 MARK**
   b. Identify what letters *m* and *c* represent on the straight line graph. **2 MARKS**
   c. Write the general equation that describes a straight line on a graph that passes through the origin (0,0). **1 MARK**
3. Calculate the gradient of the line at 30 seconds. **4 MARKS**

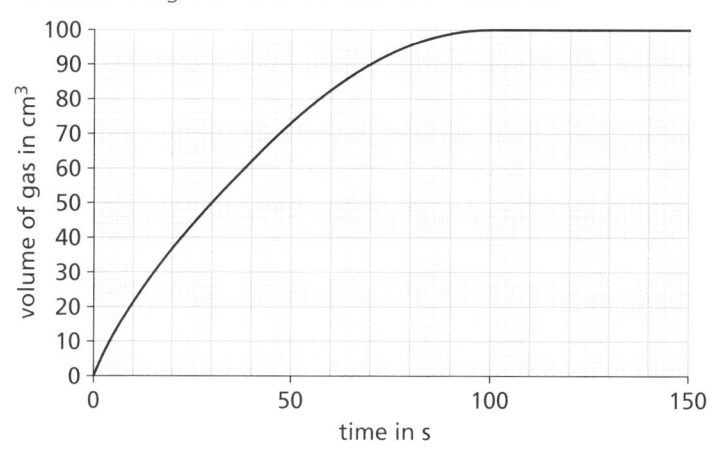

195

# MS5 Geometry and trigonometry

### Learning objectives

*After this topic, you should know how to:*

- visualise and represent 2D and 3D forms including 2D representations of 3D objects
- calculate areas of rectangles, and surface areas and volumes of cubes.

### Synoptic links

For some examples of the 2D and 3D representations of structures and molecules, see Chapter 3.

## 5a Shapes and structures

An important part of chemistry is visualising and representing the shapes and structures of elements and compounds. Throughout this book you will see 2D representations and models of the 3D shapes that make up all substances. Although you are not be expected to reproduce the more complex structural diagrams, you should be able to interpret what given structures represent.

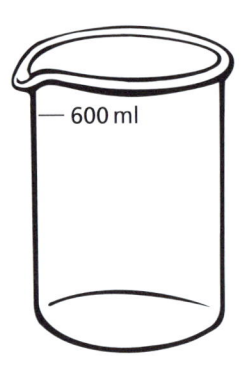

▲ **Figure 1** When drawing an experimental setup, a cross-section diagram is used instead of a diagram that shows the perspective

## 5b Area, surface area, and volumes

### Surface area

You should remember the formulae for the area of rectangles and triangles.

- area of a rectangle = base ($b$)×height ($h$)
- area of a triangle = $\frac{1}{2}$×base ($b$)×height ($h$)

The surface area of a 3D object is equal to the total surface area of all its faces. In a cuboid, the areas of any two opposite faces are equal. This allows you to calculate the surface area of the cuboid without having to draw a net.

### Maths

#### Worked example 1
A tiny grain of salt is a cuboid, measuring 15 μm×20 μm×80 μm. Calculate its surface area.

#### Solution
**Step 1:** Calculate the area of each face.

area of face 1 = 15 μm×20 μm = 300 μm²
area of face 2 = 15 μm×80 μm = 1200 μm²
area of face 3 = 20 μm×80 μm = 1600 μm²

**Step 2:** Calculate the total area of the three different faces.

area = 300 μm² + 1200 μm² + 1600 μm² = 3100 μm²

**Step 3:** Multiply the answer to **Step 2** by 2 because the opposite sides of a cuboid have equal areas.

total surface area = 2×3100 μm² = **6200 μm²**

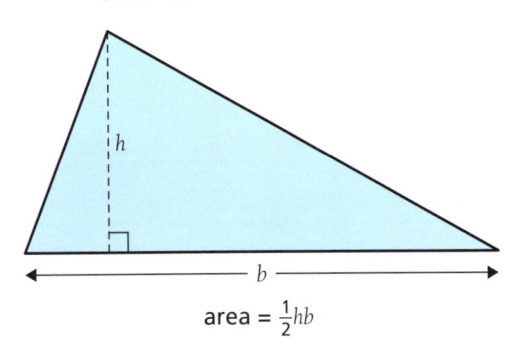

area = $hb$

area = $\frac{1}{2}hb$

▲ **Figure 2** Calculating the area of a rectangle and a triangle

Maths skills for Chemistry

## Volumes

Use this expression to calculate the volume of a cuboid:

volume of cuboid = length ($l$)×width ($w$)×height ($h$)

You can calculate the volume in different units depending on the units of length, width, and height.

### Maths

#### Worked example 2

Calculate the volume of a ceramic block of length 15 cm, width of 6 cm and depth of 1.5 cm, expressing your answer in $cm^3$ and $m^3$.

#### Solution

**Step 1:** Calculate the volume using the equation.

volume = length×width×height
= 15 cm×6 cm×1.5 cm
= 135 $cm^3$
= 140 $cm^3$ (2 s.f.)

**Step 2:** Convert the measurements to metres.

length = 0.15 m
width = 0.06 m
height = 0.015 m

**Step 3:** Use the equation to calculate the volume.

volume = length×width×height
= 0.15 m×0.06 m×0.015 m
= 0.000135 $m^3$
= **0.00014 $m^3$** (2 s.f.)

▲ **Figure 3** What is the surface area of a grain of salt?

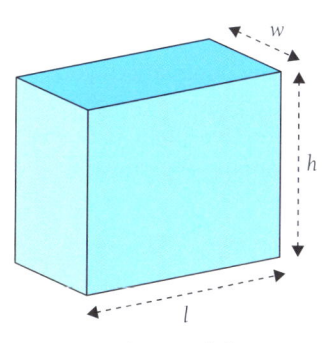

volume = $l$×$h$×$w$

▲ **Figure 4** Calculating the volume of a cuboid

### Synoptic links

For chemists, the concept of surface area to volume ratio (SA:V) is important when explaining the effect of particle size on the rate of a reaction; see Topic C8.2.

## Summary questions

1 Look at the 3D model of methane, $CH_4$, in Figure 5.
   a Use the 3D model to draw a 2D ball and stick model of methane. **1 MARK**
   b Draw a 3D model of methane. Find out and use the actual H—C—H bond angles in $CH_4$ in your answer. **2 MARKS**
2 A nanoparticle is made that has a cubic shape of side 20 nm.
   a Calculate the surface area of the nanoparticle cube, in $nm^2$. **1 MARK**
   b Calculate the volume of the nanoparticle cube, in $nm^3$. **1 MARK**
   c Calculate the surface area to volume ratio of the nanoparticle cube. The unit will be 'per nm' (/nm). **1 MARK**

▲ **Figure 5** A 3D model of methane

197

# Working scientifically

▲ **Figure 1** All around you, everyday, there are many observations you can make. Studying science can give you the understanding to explain and make predictions about some of what you observe

## WS1 Development of scientific thinking

Science works for us all day, every day. Working as a scientist you will have knowledge of the world around you, particularly about the subject you are working with. You will observe the world around you. An enquiring mind will then lead you to start asking questions about what you have observed.

Science usually moves forward by slow steady steps. Each small step is important in its own way. It builds on the body of knowledge that we already have. In this book you can find out about:

- how scientific methods and theories change over time (Topics C1.5, C2.1, and C11.1)
- the models that help us to understand theories (Chapter 3)
- the limitations of science, and the personal, social, economic, ethical, and environmental issues that arise (Topics C9.3, C11.3, C12.1, C12.5, and C12.6)
- the importance of peer review in publishing scientific results (Topic C12.5)
- evaluating risks in practical work and in technological applications (Topics C12.6 and WS2).

The rest of this section will help you to work scientifically when planning, carrying out, analysing, and evaluating your own investigations.

## WS2 Experimental skills and strategies

### Deciding what to measure

**Variables** are quantities that change or can be changed. It helps to know about the following two types of variable when investigating many scientific questions:

A **categoric variable** is one that is best described by a label, usually a word. For example, the type of metal used in an experiment is a categoric variable.

A **continuous variable** is one that you measure, so its value could be any number. For example, temperature, as measured by a thermometer or temperature sensor, is a continuous variable. Continuous variables have values (called quantities). These are found by taking measurements and SI units such as grams (g), metres (m), and joules (J) should be used.

### Making your data repeatable and reproducible

When you are designing an investigation you must make sure that you, and others, can trust the data you plan to collect. You should ensure that each measurement is **repeatable**. You can do this by getting consistent sets of repeat measurements and taking their mean. You can also have more confidence in your data if similar results are obtained by different investigators using different equipment, making your measurements **reproducible**.

> **Study tip**
>
> **Deciding what to measure**
>
> There are more types of variable but knowing about categoric and continuous variables will help you to make sense of scientific investigations. Understanding these variables will help you to decide for yourself how to plan fair tests and how to display your results. This in turn will improve your conclusions and evaluations.

**Working scientifically**

You must also make sure you are measuring the actual thing you want to measure. If you don't, your data can't be used to answer your original question. This seems very obvious, but it is not always easy to set up. You need to make sure that you have controlled as many other variables as you can. Then no one can say that your investigation, and hence the data you collect and any conclusions drawn from the data, is not **valid**.

### How might an independent variable be linked to a dependent variable?

- The **independent variable** is the one you choose to vary in your investigation.
- The **dependent variable** is used to judge the effect of varying the independent variable.

These variables may be linked together. If there is a pattern to be seen (e.g., as one thing gets bigger the other also gets bigger), it may be that:

- changing one has caused the other to change
- the two are related (there is a correlation between them), but one is not necessarily the cause of the other.

## Starting an investigation

Scientists use observations to ask questions. You can only ask useful questions if you know something about the observed event. You will not have all of the answers, but you will know enough to start asking the correct questions.

When you are designing an investigation you have to observe carefully which variables are likely to have an effect.

An investigation starts with a question and is followed by a **prediction**, and backed up by scientific reasoning. This forms a **hypothesis** that can be tested against the results of your investigation. You, as the scientist, predict that there is a **relationship** between two variables.

You should think about carrying out a preliminary investigation to find the most suitable **range** and interval for the independent variable.

### Making your investigation safe

Remember that when you design your investigation, you must:
- look for any potential **hazards**
- decide how you will reduce any **risk**.

You will need to:
- write down your plan
- make a risk assessment
- make a prediction and hypothesis
- draw a blank table ready for the results.

> **Study tip**
>
> Observations, measurements, and predictions backed up by creative thinking and good scientific knowledge can lead to a hypothesis.

▲ **Figure 2** Safety precautions should be appropriate for the risk. Chlorine gas is toxic but you do not need to wear a gas mask when only a small amount of chlorine gas is produced in an investigation carried out in a well-ventilated laboratory or fume cupboard

▲ **Figure 3** Imagine you wanted to investigate the effect pollution from a chemical factory has on nearby plants. You should choose a control group that is far away enough from the chemical plant to not be affected by the pollution, but close enough to be still experiencing similar environmental conditions

### Study tip

Trial runs will tell you a lot about how your investigation might work out. They should get you to ask yourself:

- Do I have the correct conditions?
- Have I chosen a sensible range?
- Have I got sufficient readings that are close enough together? The minimum number of points to draw a line graph is generally taken as five.
- Will I need to repeat my readings?

### Study tip

Just because your results show precision it does not mean your results are accurate.

Imagine you carry out an investigation into the energy value of a type of fuel. You get readings of the amount of energy transferred from the burning fuel to the surroundings that are all about the same. This means that your data will have precision, but it doesn't mean that they are necessarily accurate.

## Different types of investigations

A **fair test** is one in which only the independent variable affects the dependent variable. All other variables are controlled and kept constant.

This is easy to set up in the laboratory, but almost impossible in fieldwork. Investigations in the environment are not that simple and easy to control. There are complex variables that are changing constantly.

So how can we set up the fieldwork investigations? The best you can do is to make sure that all of the many variables change in much the same way, except for the one you are investigating. For example, if you are monitoring the effects of pollution on plants, they should all be experiencing the same weather, together – even if it is constantly changing.

If you are investigating two variables in a large population then you will need to do a survey. Again, it is impossible to control all of the variables. For example, imagine scientists investigating the effect of a new drug on diabetes. They would have to choose people of the same age and same family history to test. Remember that the larger the sample size tested, the more valid the results will be.

**Control groups** are used in these investigations to try to make sure that you are measuring the variable that you intend to measure. When investigating the effects of a new drug, the control group will be given a placebo. The control group think they are taking a drug but the placebo does not contain the drug. This way you can control the variable of 'thinking that the drug is working', and separate out the effect of the actual drug.

## Designing an investigation

### Accuracy

Your investigation must provide **accurate** data. Accurate data is essential if your results are going to have any meaning.

### How do you know if you have accurate data?

It is very difficult to be certain. *Accurate results are very close to the true value*. However, it is not always possible to know what the true value is.

Sometimes you can calculate a theoretical value and check it against the experimental evidence. Close agreement between these two values could indicate accurate data.

You can draw a graph of your results and see how close each result is to the line of best fit.

Try repeating your measurements and check the spread or range within sets of repeated data. Large differences in a repeated measurement suggest inaccuracy. Or try again with a different measuring instrument and see if you get the same readings.

### Precision

Your investigation must provide data with sufficient **precision** (i.e., *close agreement within sets of repeat measurements*). If it doesn't then you will not be able to make a valid conclusion.

## Working scientifically

**Precision versus accuracy**

Imagine measuring the temperature after a set time when a fuel is used to heat a fixed volume of water. Two students repeated this experiment, four times each. Their results are marked on the thermometer scales in Figure 4:

- a **precise** set of results is grouped closely together
- an accurate set of results will have a mean (average) close to the true value

### How do you get precise, repeatable data?

You have to repeat your tests as often as necessary to improve repeatability.

You have to repeat your tests in exactly the same way each time.

You should use measuring instruments that have the appropriate scale divisions needed for a particular investigation. Smaller scale divisions have better *resolution*.

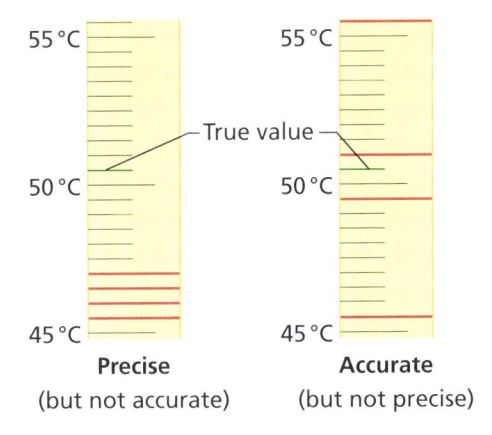

▲ **Figure 4** The green line shows the true value and the pink lines show the readings two different groups of students measured. Precise results are not necessarily accurate results

## Making measurements

### Using measuring instruments

There will always be some degree of uncertainty in any measurements made (WS3). You cannot expect perfect results. When you choose an instrument you need to know that it will give you the accuracy that you want (i.e., it will give you a true reading). You also need to know how to use an instrument properly.

Some instruments have smaller scale divisions than others. Instruments that measure the same thing, such as mass, can have different resolutions. The resolution of an instrument refers to the smallest change in a value that can be detected (e.g., a ruler with centimetre increments compared to a ruler with millimetre increments). Choosing an instrument with an inappropriate resolution can cause you to miss important data or make silly conclusions.

But selecting measuring instruments with high resolution might not be appropriate in some cases where the degree of uncertainty in a measurement is high, for example, judging when an 'X' under a conical flask disappears (Topic C8.1). In this case, a stopwatch measuring to one hundredths of a second is not going to improve the accuracy of the data collected.

▲ **Figure 5** Despite the fact that a stopwatch has a high resolution, it is not always the most appropriate instrument to use for measuring time

## WS3 Analysis and evaluation

### Errors

Even when an instrument is used correctly, the results can still show differences. Results will differ because of a *random error*. This can be a result of poor measurements being made. It could also be due to not carrying out the method consistently in each test. Random errors are minimised by taking the mean of precise repeat readings, looking out for any *outliers* (measurements that differ significantly from the others within a set of repeats) to check again, or omit from calculations of the mean.

201

The error may be a systematic error. This means that the method or measurement was carried out consistently incorrectly so that an error was being repeated. An example could be a balance that is not set at zero correctly. Systematic errors will be consistently above, or below, the accurate value.

## Presenting data

### Tables
Tables are really good for recording your results quickly and clearly as you are carrying out an investigation. You should design your table before you start your investigation.

### The range of the data
Pick out the maximum and the minimum values and you have the **range**. You should always quote these two numbers when asked for a range. For example, the range is between the lowest value in a data set, and the highest value. *Don't forget to include the units.*

### The mean of the data
Add up all of the measurements and divide by how many there are. As seen in WS2, you can ignore outliers in a set of repeat readings when calculating the mean, if found to be the result of poor measurement.

### Bar charts
If you have a categoric independent variable and a continuous dependent variable then you should use a bar chart.

### Line graphs
If you have a continuous independent variable and a continuous dependent variable then use a **line graph**.

### Scatter graphs
These are used in much the same way as a line graph, but you might not expect to be able to draw such a clear line of best fit. For example, to find out if the melting point of an element is related to its density you might draw a scatter graph of your results.

## Using data to draw conclusions

### Identifying patterns and relationships
Now you have a bar chart or a line graph of your results you can begin looking for patterns. You must have an open mind at this point.

Firstly, there could still be some anomalous results. You might not have picked these out earlier. How do you spot an anomaly? It must be a significant distance away from the pattern, not just within normal variation.

A line of best fit will help to identify any anomalies at this stage. Ask yourself – 'do the anomalies represent something important or were they just a mistake?'.

▲ Figure 6 How you record your results will depend upon the type of measurements you are taking

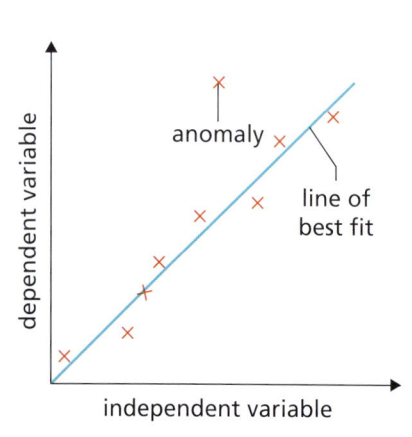

▲ Figure 7 A line of best fit can help to identify anomalies

202

Secondly, remember a line of best fit can be a straight line or it can be a curve – you have to decide from your results.

The line of best fit will also lead you into thinking what the relationship is between your two variables. You need to consider whether the points you have plotted show a linear relationship. If so, you can draw a straight line of best fit on your graph (with as many points above the line as below it, producing a 'mean' line). Then consider if this line has a positive or negative gradient.

A **directly proportional** relationship is shown by a positive straight line that goes through the origin (0, 0).

Your results might also show a curved line of best fit. These can be predictable, complex, or very complex. Carrying out more tests with a smaller interval near the area where a line changes its gradient will help reduce the error in drawing the line (in this case a curve) of best fit.

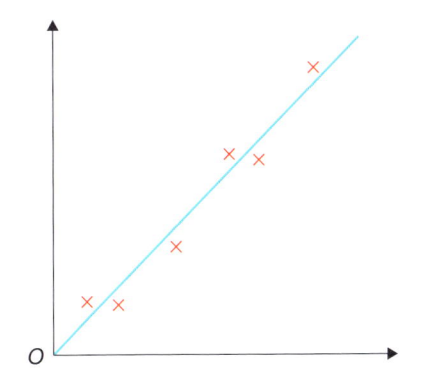

▲ **Figure 8** When a straight line of best fit goes through the origin (0, 0) the relationship between the variables is **directly proportional**

## Drawing conclusions

Your graphs are designed to show the relationship between your two chosen variables. You need to consider what that relationship means for your conclusion. You must also take into account the repeatability and the reproducibility of the data you are considering.

You will continue to have an open mind about your conclusion.

You will have made a prediction. This could be supported by your results, it might not be supported, or it could be partly supported. It might suggest some other hypothesis to you.

You must be willing to think carefully about your results. Remember it is quite rare for a set of results to completely support a prediction or be completely repeatable.

Look for possible links between variables, remembering that a positive relationship does not always mean a causal link between the two variables.

Your conclusion must go no further than the evidence that you have. Any patterns you spot are only strictly valid in the range of values you tested. Further tests are needed to check whether the pattern continues beyond this range.

The purpose of the prediction was to test a hypothesis. The hypothesis can:

- be supported
- be refuted
- lead to another hypothesis.

You have to decide which it is on the evidence available.

# Working scientifically

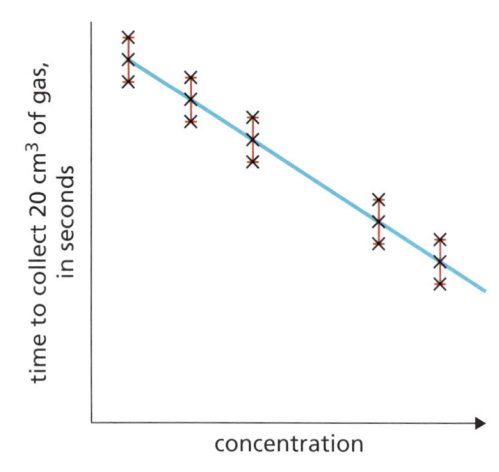

▲ **Figure 9** Indicating levels of uncertainty by plotting all the measurements taken. These are all the measurements of a group that chose five different concentrations to test and repeated each test three times

## Making estimates of uncertainty

You can use the range of a set of repeat measurements about their mean to estimate the degree of **uncertainty** in the data collected.

For example, in a test that looked at the effect of concentration on the rate of reaction between calcium carbonate and acid, a student got these results:

40 $cm^3$ of acid and 10 $cm^3$ of water gave off 20 $cm^3$ of carbon dioxide in 45 s (1st attempt), 49 s (2nd attempt), 44 s (3rd attempt) and 48 s (4th attempt).

The mean result = (45 + 49 + 44 + 48) ÷ 4 = 46.5 s

The range of the repeats is 44 s to 49 s = 5 s

So, a reasonable estimate of the uncertainty in the mean value would be half of the range.

In this case, we could say the time taken was 46.5 s plus or minus ±2.5 s.

You can include a final column in your table of results to record the 'estimated uncertainty' in your mean measurements.

The level of uncertainty can also be shown when plotting your results on a graph (Figure 9).

As well as this, there will be some uncertainty associated with readings from any measuring instrument. You can usually take this as:

- half the smallest scale division. For example, 0.05 $cm^3$ for each burette reading, or
- on a digital instrument, half the last figure shown on its display. For example, on a balance reading to 0.01 g the uncertainty would be ±0.005 g.

## Anomalous results

**Anomalies** (or outliers) are results that are clearly out of line compared with others. They are not those that are due to the natural variation that you get from any measurement. Anomalous results should be looked at carefully. There might be a very interesting reason why they are so different.

If anomalies can be identified while you are doing an investigation, then it is best to repeat that part of the investigation. If you find that an anomaly is due to poor measurement, then it should be ignored.

## Evaluation

If you are still uncertain about a conclusion, it might be down to the repeatability, reproducibility, and uncertainty in your measurements. You could check reproducibility by: looking for other similar work on the Internet or from others in your class; getting somebody else, using different equipment, to redo your investigation (this occurs in peer review of data presented in articles in scientific journals); or trying an alternative method to see if it results in you reaching the same conclusion.

When suggesting improvements that could be made in your investigation, always give your reasoning.

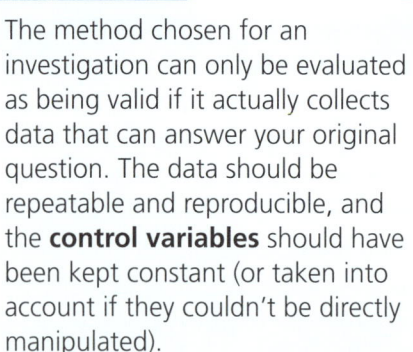

> **Study tip**
>
> The method chosen for an investigation can only be evaluated as being valid if it actually collects data that can answer your original question. The data should be repeatable and reproducible, and the **control variables** should have been kept constant (or taken into account if they couldn't be directly manipulated).

> **Synoptic link**
>
> See the Maths Skills section to learn how to use SI units, prefixes, and powers of ten for orders of magnitude, significant figures, and scientific quantities.

# Glossary

**Accurate** A measurement is considered accurate if it is judged to be close to the true value.

**Acid** When dissolved in water, its solution has a pH value less than 7. Acids are proton (H⁺ ion) donors.

**Activation energy** The minimum energy needed for a reaction to take place.

**Alkali** Its solution has a pH value more than 7.

**Alkali metal** Elements in Group 1 of the Periodic Table.

**Alkane** Saturated hydrocarbon with the general formula $C_nH_{2n+2}$, for example, methane, ethane, and propane.

**Alkene** Type of hydrocarbon. Its general formula is $C_nH_{2n}$, for example, ethene, $C_2H_4$.

**Alloy** A mixture of two or more elements, at least one of which is a metal.

**Anhydrous** Describes a substance that does not contain water.

**Anode** The positive electrode in electrolysis.

**Anomalies** Results that do not match the pattern seen in the other data collected or are well outside the range of other repeat readings (outliers).

**Aqueous solution** The mixture made by adding a soluble substance to water.

**Atmosphere** The relatively thin layer of gases that surround planet Earth.

**Atom** The smallest part of an element that can still be recognised as that element.

**Atomic number** The number of protons (which equals the number of electrons) in an atom. It is sometimes called the proton number.

**Avogadro constant** The number of atoms, molecules, or ions in a mole of any substance (i.e., $6.02 \times 10^{23}$ per mol).

**Balanced symbol equation** A symbol equation in which there are equal numbers of each type of atom on either side of the equation.

**Base** The oxide, hydroxide, or carbonate of a metal that will react with an acid, forming a salt as one of the products. (If a base dissolves in water it is called an alkali.) Bases are proton (H⁺ ion) acceptors.

**Biofuel** Fuel made from animal or plant products.

**Bioleaching** The process of extracting metals from ores using microorganisms.

**Blast furnace** The huge reaction vessels used in industry to extract iron from its ore.

**Bond energy** The energy required to break a specific chemical bond.

**Burette** A long glass tube with a tap at one end and markings to show volumes of liquid; used to add precisely known volumes of liquids to a solution in a conical flask below it.

**Carbon footprint** The total amount of carbon dioxide and other greenhouse gases emitted over the full life cycle of a product, service, or event.

**Catalyst** A substance that speeds up a chemical reaction by providing a different pathway for the reaction that has a lower activation energy. The catalyst is chemically unchanged at the end of the reaction.

**Categoric variable** Categoric variables have values that are labels. For example types of material.

**Cathode** The negative electrode in electrolysis.

**Ceramics** Materials made by heating clay, or other compounds, to high temperatures (called firing) to make hard, but often brittle, materials, which make excellent electrical insulators.

**Chromatography** The process whereby small amounts of dissolved substances are separated by running a solvent along a material such as absorbent paper.

**Climate change** The change in global weather patterns caused by excess levels of greenhouse gases in the atmosphere.

**Closed system** A system in which no matter enters or leaves.

**Collision theory** An explanation of chemical reactions in terms of reacting particles colliding with sufficient energy for a reaction to take place.

**Composites** Materials made of two or more different materials, containing a matrix or binder surrounding and binding together fibres or fragments of another material which acts as the reinforcement.

**Compound** A substance made when two or more elements are chemically bonded together.

**Concentration** The amount of substance dissolved in 1 cubic decimetre ($dm^3$) of solution.

**Continuous variable** Can have values (called a quantity) that can be given by measurement (for example, mass, volume, temperature, etc.).

**Control group** If an experiment is to determine the effect of changing a single variable, a control is often set up in which the independent variable is not changed, thus enabling a comparison to be made. If the investigation is of the survey type a control group is usually established to serve the same purpose.

**Control variable** A variable which may, in addition to the independent variable, affect the outcome of the investigation and therefore has to be kept constant or at least monitored.

**Covalent bond** The bond between two atoms that share one or more pairs of electrons.

**Covalent bonding** The attraction between two atoms that share one or more pairs of electrons.

**Cracking** The reaction used in the oil industry to break down large hydrocarbons into smaller, more useful ones.

**Data** Information, either qualitative or quantitative, that has been collected.

**Delocalised electron** Bonding electron that is no longer associated with any one particular atom.

**Dependent variable** The variable for which the value is measured for each and every change in the independent variable.

**Directly proportional** A relationship that, when drawn on a line graph, shows a positive linear relationship that passes through the origin.

**Discrete data** Data that can only take certain values.

**Displacement reaction** A reaction in which a more reactive element takes the place of a less reactive element in one of its compounds or in solution.

**Displayed formulae** A chemical formula that shows the arrangement of all the bonds and atoms in an organic molecule, using the chemical symbols of atoms and lines to represent bonds.

**Distillation** Separation of a liquid from a mixture by evaporation followed by condensation.
**Dot and cross diagram** A drawing to show only the arrangement of the outer shell electrons of the atoms or ions in a substance.
**Double bond** A covalent bond made by the sharing of two pairs of electrons.

**Electrolysis** The breakdown of a substance containing ions by electricity.
**Electrolyte** A liquid, containing free-moving ions, which is broken down by electricity in the process of electrolysis.
**Electron** A tiny particle with a negative charge. Electrons orbit the nucleus of atoms or ions in shells.
**Electronic structure** A set of numbers to show the arrangement of electrons in their shells (or energy levels).
**Element** A substance made up of only one type of atom. An element cannot be broken down chemically into any simpler substance.
**Endothermic** A reaction that takes in energy from the surroundings.
**Equilibrium** The point in a reversible reaction at which the forward and backward rates of reaction are the same. Therefore, the amounts of substances present in the reacting mixture remain constant.
**Exothermic** A reaction that transfers energy to the surroundings.

**Fair test** A fair test is one in which only the independent variable has been allowed to affect the dependent variable.
**Filtration** The technique used to separate substances that are insoluble in a particular solvent from those that are soluble.
**Flammable** Easily ignited and capable of burning rapidly.
**Formulation** A mixture that has been designed as a useful product.
**Fraction** Hydrocarbons with similar boiling points separated from crude oil.
**Fractional distillation** A way to separate liquids from a mixture of liquids by boiling off the substances at different temperatures, then condensing and collecting the liquids.
**Fullerene** Form of the element carbon that can exist as large cage-like structures, based on hexagonal rings of carbon atoms.

**General formula** A chemical formula that applies to all the related compounds in a class of organic compounds, such as 'the alkanes'.
**Giant covalent structure** A huge 3D network of covalently bonded atoms.
**Giant ionic lattice** A huge 3D network of atoms or ions.
**Gradient** A measure of the slope of a straight line on a graph.
**Group** All the elements in the columns (labelled 1 to 7 and 0) in the Periodic Table.

**Half equation** An equation that describes reduction (gain of electrons) or oxidation (loss of electrons).
**Halogens** The elements found in Group 7 of the Periodic Table.
**Hazard** A hazard is something (e.g., an object, a property of a substance, or an activity) that can cause harm.
**Hydrated** Describes a substance that contains water in its crystals.
**Hydrocarbon** A compound containing only hydrogen and carbon.
**Hypothesis** A proposal intended to explain certain facts or observations.

**Incomplete combustion** When a fuel burns in insufficient oxygen, producing carbon monoxide as a toxic product.
**Independent variable** The variable for which values are changed or selected by the investigator.
**Inert** Unreactive.
**Intermolecular forces** The attraction between the individual molecules in a covalently bonded substance.
**Ion** A charged particle produced by the loss or gain of electrons.
**Ionic bonding** The electrostatic force of attraction between positively and negatively charged ions.
**Ionic equation** An equation that shows only those ions or atoms that change in a chemical reaction.
**Isotope** Atoms that have the same number of protons but different number of neutrons, i.e., they have the same atomic number but different mass numbers.

**Law of conservation of mass** The total mass of the products formed in a reaction is equal to the total mass of the reactants.
**Le Châtelier's Principle** When a change in conditions is introduced to a system at equilibrium, the position of equilibrium shifts so as to cancel out the change.

**Life cycle assessment (LCA)** Carried out to assess the environmental impact of products, processes or services at different stages in their life cycle.
**Limiting reactant** The reactant that is used up first in a reaction.
**Line graph** Used when both variables are continuous. The line should normally be a line of best fit, and may be straight or a smooth curve.
**Line of best fit** A straight line that represents the general trend of data. An equal number of data points should be above and below the line of best fit.

**Mass number** The number of protons plus neutrons in the nucleus of an atom.
**Mean** The arithmetical average of a series of numbers.
**Mixture** When some elements or compounds are mixed together and intermingle but do not react together (i.e., no new substance is made). A mixture is not a pure substance.
**Mole** The amount of substance in the relative atomic or formula mass of a substance in grams.
**Molecule** A particle made up of two or more atoms, held together by covalent bonds.

**Neutral** A solution with a pH value of 7 which is neither acidic nor alkaline. Alternatively, something that carries no overall electrical charge.
**Neutralisation** The chemical reaction of an acid with a base in which a salt and water are formed. If the base is a carbonate or hydrogencarbonate, carbon dioxide is also produced in the reaction.
**Neutron** A dense particle found in the nucleus of an atom. It is electrically neutral, carrying no charge.
**Noble gases** The very unreactive gases found in Group 0 of the Periodic Table. Their atoms have very stable electronic structures.
**Non-renewable** Something which cannot be replaced once it is used up.
**Nucleus** (of an atom) The very small and dense central part of an atom that contains protons and neutrons.

**Order of magnitude** A comparison of the size of values. Two values are the same order of magnitude if their difference in size is small in comparison to other values being compared.

# Glossary

**Ore** Ore is rock which contains enough metal to make it economically worthwhile to extract the metal.
**Oxidation** A reaction in which oxygen is added to a substance or electrons are lost.

**Particle theory** A model to explain the movement and arrangement of particles in a substance.
**Particulate** Small solid particle given off from motor vehicles as a result of incomplete combustion of their fuel.
**Periodic Table** An arrangement of elements in the order of their atomic numbers, forming groups and periods.
**pH** A number which shows how strongly acidic or alkaline a solution is.
**Pipette** A glass tube used to measure accurate volumes of liquids.
**Polymer** A substance made from very large molecules made up of many repeating units.
**Precipitate** An insoluble solid formed by a reaction taking place in solution.
**Precise** A precise measurement is one in which there is very little spread about the mean value. Precision depends only on the extent of random errors – it gives no indication of how close results are to the true (accurate) value.
**Prediction** A forecast or statement about the way something will happen in the future.
**Product** A substance made as a result of a chemical reaction.
**Proton** A tiny positive particle found inside the nucleus of an atom.

**Qualitative data** Data that is descriptive or categorical.
**Quantitative data** Data that is numerical or a measurement.

**Range** The maximum and minimum values of the independent or dependent variables.
**Ratio** A way of comparing two or more quantities, showing how many times one is contained within the other.
**Reactant** A substance we start with before a chemical reaction takes place.
**Reaction profile** The relative difference in the energy of reactants and products.
**Reactivity series** A list of elements in order of their reactivity.
**Recycling** The process in which waste materials are processed to be used again.

**Reduction** A reaction in which oxygen is removed or electrons are gained.
**Relationship** The link between the variables that were investigated.
**Relative atomic mass ($A_r$)** The average mass of the atoms of an element compared with carbon-12 (which is given a mass of exactly 12). The average mass must take into account the proportions of the naturally occurring isotopes of the element.
**Relative formula mass ($M_r$)** The total of the relative atomic masses, added up in the ratio shown in the chemical formula, of a substance.
**Repeatable** A measurement is repeatable if the original experimenter repeats the investigation using the same method and equipment and obtains the same or precise results.
**Reproducible** A measurement is reproducible if the investigation is repeated by another person, using different equipment, and the same results are obtained.
**Retention factor ($R_f$)** A measurement from chromatography: it is the distance a spot of substance has been carried above the baseline divided by the distance of the solvent front.
**Reversible reaction** A reaction in which the products can re-form the reactants.
**Risk** The likelihood that a hazard will actually cause harm.
**Rusting** The corrosion of iron.

**Salt** A compound formed when some or all of the hydrogen in an acid is replaced by a metal.
**Saturated hydrocarbon** A hydrocarbon with only single bonds between its carbon atoms. This means that it contains as many hydrogen atoms as possible in each molecule.
**Shell** An area in an atom, around its nucleus, where electrons are found.
**SI system of units** A system of units for physical quantities that are considered the standard units.
**Significant figures (s.f.)** The important digits within a number. All non-zero digits are significant. Zeros may be significant if followed by another non-zero digit.
**Standard form** A way of displaying large and small numbers.
**State symbols** The abbreviations used in balanced symbol equations to show if reactants and products are solid (s), liquid (l), gas (g), or dissolved in water (aq).

**Strong acids** Acids that completely ionise in aqueous solutions.

**Thermal decomposition** The breakdown of a compound by heating it.
**Transition element** Element from the central block of the Periodic Table.

**Universal indicator** A mixture of indicators that can change through a range of colours to show how strongly acidic or alkaline liquids and solutions are.
**Unsaturated hydrocarbon** A hydrocarbon whose molecules contains at least one carbon–carbon double bond.

**Valid** Suitability of the investigative procedure to answer the question being asked.
**Variable** Physical, chemical, or biological quantity or characteristic.
**Viscosity** The resistance of a liquid to flowing or pouring; a liquid's 'thickness'.

**Weak acids** Acids that do not ionise completely in aqueous solutions.
**Word equation** A way of describing what happens in a chemical reaction by showing the names of all reactants and the products they form.

# Index

accuracy 200–204
acidity 80–81
acid rain 79, 156, 157, 168–169, 171
acids 68, 74, 76, 78–83, 87, 96, 114, 115, 144
   amino 142
activation energy 100–101, 110–113, 116
alkali metals 4, 26–27, 30–31, 68, 74
alkalinity 80–81
alkalis 76, 78–81, 96
alkanes 128, 131, 134–135
   general formula of 129
alkenes 134–135
alloys 52–53, 90, 141, 171
aluminium 18, 53, 66–67, 69, 70, 72, 77, 90–91, 160, 168
   recycling of 170–171
aluminium ions 39, 76, 91
aluminium oxide 39, 69, 70, 170
   electrolysis of 90–91
aluminium sulfate 57, 162
amino acids 142 see also chromatogram(s)
ammonia 42–43, 78, 103, 116, 148–149
ammonia gases 119, 150–151
ammonium chloride 119
ammonium nitrate 78, 99
analysis 48, 153, 163
   and evaluation 201–202
   chemical 140–147
   instrumental 138
   quantitative 2
anhydrous copper(II) sulfate 118, 120–121, 132–133, 140, 163
anode(s) 86–93, 145, 167 see also cathode and electrolysis
anomalies 202, 204
aqueous solutions 6–7, 29, 59, 63, 70–71, 80–83, 87–89, 92–93
atmosphere see also climate change; greenhouse gas(es) and pollutants
   Earth's early 148
   evolving 150–151
   oxygen in the 148–149
atomic model 12–13
atomic number(s) 14–19, 23, 25
   base(s) 76–78, 80–81, 93, 156
   Avogadro constant 57, 182

balanced equations(s) 58–61, 103, 115, 117, 124, 132–133
ball and stick model(s) 40, 44, 197
bar chart(s) 187–188, 202
base(s) 76–78, 80–81, 93, 156
battery 47
bauxite 90, 160, 170
biofuels 10, 155, 160
biogas 164–165
bioleaching 167
Bohr, Niels 13
boiling points 8, 34–35, 163, 193
   alkali metals 26–27
   crude oil 131
   giant covalent structures 47
   halogens 28–29
   hydrocarbons 129–131, 134
   ionic compounds 40
   metals 24
   miscible liquids 10–11
   noble gases 24–25
   non-metals 25
   pure substances and mixtures 140–141
   small molecules 44–45
bond breaking 101, 102
bond energy 102–103
bonding 2, 28, 34–55, 66, 87, 106, 139
   covalent 36, 42–44, 47, 129
   in graphite 47–48
   ionic 36–39, 86
   metallic 50–51
bond making 101, 102
bromide
   copper(II) 87
   iron(III) 28
   molten lead 88
   potassium 29
   sodium 77
bromide ions 29, 87, 88
bromine 27–30, 57, 87
bromine molecule 88
buckminsterfullerene 48–49
burette 81, 117, 204

calcium carbonate 6, 79, 96–97, 111, 114–115, 145, 150, 183, 204
calcium chloride 38–39
calcium hydroxide 99, 145, 156
calcium oxide 96, 99, 156

calculations 2, 13, 15, 143, 161, 180, 191, 201
   bond energy 102–103
   chemical 56–65
   estimating the result of 184–185
   involving standard form 181
   of data 169
   order of magnitude 186, 188–189
carbon 14, 17, 24, 46–49, 52, 56–57, 70–71, 73
   'locked into' rocks 150
carbon atom 14, 43, 47–49, 52, 56, 58, 106, 128–130, 134–135, 182
carbon capture and storage 154–155 see also techniques
carbon dioxide gas 76, 79, 91, 113, 114, 150
   testing for 145
carbon footprint 154–155
carbon monoxide 73, 132–133, 156–157
catalyst(s) 49, 98, 101, 110, 114, 117
   biological 116
   hot 134–135
   platinum 28
cathode 86–93, 167 see also anode and electrolysis
ceramic block 197
ceramic wool 135
ceramics 170
Chadwick, James 13
changes of state 34–35
charge
   electrical 15, 40–41, 45, 53
   negative 14, 16, 29, 36, 38, 53
   nuclear 31
   positive 12–14, 16, 30–31, 36, 38, 76
   relative 14–15
   total 39
chemical symbols 4–5, 56
chloride ion(s) 36, 38, 40, 86, 92
chlorine gas 27, 44, 59, 86, 92–93, 123, 199
   testing for 145
chromatograms 11, 142–143
chromatography 8–11, 142–143
climate change 152–156
closed system 122–124
coal 132, 150, 156, 160 see also fossil fuels

# Index

cobalt(II) chloride paper  121, 132–133, 163
collision theory  110–113
combustion  96, 108, 132–133, 156–157
   complete  132–133
   incomplete  132–133, 156–157
combustion reactions  58
composite materials  48–49, 160
compounds
   carbon  128
   chemical  18, 22, 36
   complex  56
   copper  167
   covalent  29, 87 *see also* electrolysis
   insoluble carbonate  150
   ionic  26–29, 38–41, 45, 76, 86–87, 90
   molecular  45
   organic  106, 128, 135
   potassium  89
   pure  142
   toxic organic  165
   unsaturated  134
concentrations  82–83, 89, 93, 110, 190
   calculating  62–63
   of acid  111, 114
   of carbon dioxide  152–153
   of chlorine gas  123
   of reactants  114–115, 122, 124, 193
   oxygen  149
   of sodium chloride  193
conclusions  97, 114–115, 169, 180, 198–204
concrete  160
conductivity  45, 48
   electrical  48–49
   testing  41
conservation of mass  6, 58–59, 60
control groups  200
cooling  9, 35, 66, 97–99, 128, 166
copper  4, 6, 50, 53, 68–73, 87, 89, 168
   extract(ing)  71, 166–167
   recycling  171
copper(II) bromide  87
copper(II) sulfate  70, 77, 118–121, 144, 163, 166–167
copper salts  77, 121
covalent bonding  36, 42–44, 47, 129
cracking  134–135
crude oil  46, 128–135, 150, 160–161
cryolite  90–91
crystallisation  8–9, 74, 98, 118
crystals  40, 76–79, 98, 140, 144–145
   copper(II) sulfate  120–121

metal  50–51
salt  74–75
silver  50
sodium chloride  9, 41
trichloride  123

Dalton, John  12–13, 22
data  180, 186–189, 194, 202–203
delocalised electrons  47–48, 51, 53
density  17, 26, 49, 90, 188, 202
dependent variable  193–194, 199–200, 202
desalination  163
diamond  43, 46–49
dilute acid  68–70, 74–75, 81, 144
displacement reaction(s)  6, 29, 70–71
displayed formulae  129
distillation  8–11, 128–129, 162–163
dot and cross diagram(s)  37, 39, 43–44
double bond(s)  43, 134–135
dynamic equilibrium  122–123

electrolysis  73, 86–89, 145, 170–171
   aluminium oxide  90–91
   aqueous solutions  92–93
   brine  92–93
   metal extraction  166–167
   zinc chloride  87
electronic structures  17–19, 30
   alkali metals  26–27
   halogens  28–29
   ions  36–39
   simple molecules  42–45
electrons  5, 12–13
   charge  12
   covalent bonds  42–44
   delocalised  47–48, 51, 53
   energy levels (shells)  13, 18, 19, 24–30, 38, 43–43, 51
   number in an atom  15–16, 18, 180
   oxidation and reduction  71, 87, 88, 91, 104
   shared pairs  43
   shielding effect  30–31
elements  5, 8, 73, 141 *see also* Periodic Table
   chemical  22–24, 72, 187
   density  17, 26, 49, 90, 188, 202
   structures of  24, 196
   transition  4, 25
endothermic reactions  97–98, 100–101, 103, 120, 125

energy changes  100, 120–121
   activation energy  100–101, 110–113, 116
   bond energy  102–103
   energy transfer  35, 96–98, 101–103, 120–121, 200
   exothermic reactions  96–101, 103, 116, 125
   reversible reactions  120–121
energy levels  2, 13, 18–19, 24–26, 28, 30–31, 38, 42–43, 51, 100
   *see also* shells
energy transfer  35, 96–98, 101–103, 120–121, 2000
   bond breaking and bond making  101
   calculations  102–103
   endothermic reactions  97–98, 100–101, 103, 120, 125
   exothermic reactions  96–101, 103, 116, 125
equilibrium  82, 122–123
   pressure and  124–125
equilibrium mixture  122–124
error(s)  109, 113, 187, 201–203
estimation  169
ethanoic acid  80, 82
ethanol  10, 62, 161
ethene  45, 134–135, 161, 169
evaluation(s)  143, 198, 200–201, 204
evaporation  34–35
exothermic reactions  96–101, 103, 116, 125
equations  2, 15, 28–29, 57–59, 74, 109, 118, 186, 197
   balanced  58–61, 103, 115, 117, 124, 132–133
   balanced chemical  58, 60, 121, 133, 167
   balanced symbol  27, 58, 61, 73, 75, 79, 103, 124, 133
   changing the subject  190–191
   chemical  6–7, 74, 149, 166
   graphs and  194–195
   half  70–71, 75, 88–93, 167
   ionic  70–71, 75, 78
   reversible reaction  124–125
   symbol  6–7, 70
   word  6–7, 27, 73, 75
extraction of metals  70, 72–73, 166–167, 171

fair test(s)  113–114, 193, 198, 200
fertilisers  78, 141, 164–165
filtrate  8

filtration 8, 170
finite resources 128, 160, 161, 166, 171
flammability of hydrocarbons 130
formulae 76, 128–129, 196
formulations 181, 140–141
fossil fuels 116, 132, 150–156, 160–161, 171
   combustion of 157
fractional distillation 10–11, 130–131, 134
frequency of collisions 110–112, 114–116
   see also collision theory
   frequency tables 187–188
fuels 96, 128, 135 see also biofuel
   fossil 116, 132, 150–157, 160–161, 171
   hydrocarbon 132–133, 157
fullerenes 48–49

galvanised steel 50–51
gases 144–145, 152–153
   greenhouse 152–156, 169
   hot 119
   monatomic (single atom) 25
   noble 4, 19, 24–25, 36, 151 see also Periodic Table
   oxygen 6, 26, 60, 89, 91, 117, 144–145, 148
   petroleum 131–132
   reacting 114–115
   testing for 144–145
   unreactive 151
Geiger and Marsden experiment 12–13
giant covalent structures 43, 46–47
giant ionic lattice 40–41
giant ionic structures 40–41
giant metallic structures 51–53
global dimming 157
global warming 153–154, 168, 171
glucose 149–150, 161
gold 4, 12, 25, 69, 72–73, 116, 181
graphene 48–49
graphite 46–49, 86
   bonding in 47
graphs 152–153, 160, 200, 203–204
   cooling curve 35
   line 195, 200, 203
   'pH value' 81
   reaction rate 108–109, 113–115
   scatter 193, 202
   sketch 97
   straight line 194–195
greenhouse gases 152–156, 169

Group 0 (noble gases) 19, 24–25, 36, 38
Group 1 (alkali metals) 18–19, 24, 26–27, 29–31, 36–38, 68, 76, 79
Group 7 (halogens) 24, 28–31, 36–39, 76, 89

Haber process 103
half-equations 70–71, 75, 88–93, 167
halide 29, 89, 93
halogens 4, 28–230, 89, 93
hand warmers 98–99
hazards 69, 199
heating curve 35
hydrocarbons 128–129
   alkanes 129
   alkene molecules 134
   combustion 132–133
   cracking 134–135
   fractional distillation 128–129, 130–131
   properties 130
hydrochloric acid 6, 61, 74, 79–83, 108
   comparing acids 82
   concentrations 114
   dilute 61, 75, 79, 81, 83, 111, 115, 150
   limiting reactant 61
   testing for carbon dioxide gas 145
   testing for chlorine gas 145
hydrogen gas 26–27, 61, 68–69, 75, 89, 92–93, 115, 145, 187
   Haber process 103
   test for 6, 144
hydrogen chloride 42, 58–59, 80, 119
hydrogen ions 70, 74–75, 82–83, 88–89, 92–93
hypothesis 97, 114, 199. 203

impurities 90, 117, 140, 156–157, 162 see also fossil fuels and potable water
incomplete combustion 132–133, 156–157
independent variable 117, 193–194, 199–200, 202
infrared radiation 152 see also greenhouse gases
insoluble base(s) 76–78
instrumental analysis 138
intermolecular forces 44–45, 47, 130 see also fractional distillation and graphite
investigations 8, 187, 193, 198, 200
iodide 29, 117
iodine monochloride 123

ionic bonding 36–39, 86
ionic compounds 26–29, 38–41, 45, 76, 86–87, 90
ionic equation(s) 70–71, 75, 78
ions 16
   negative 16–17, 24, 36, 38, 74, 82, 86–89
   positive 16–17, 24, 36, 38, 53, 68, 70, 75–76, 87–89
iron 25, 52–53, 68–79, 71–74, 90, 116
   extract 171
   oxidation 98
   recycling 170–171
   rusting 108
iron nail 166
isotopes 16–17, 23, 56

lattice 41, 43, 46–47, 51, 53, 87, 120
   3D model 40
Law of conservation of mass 6, 60
leachate 167 see also copper(II) sulfate
Le Châtelier's Principle 123
life cycle assessments (LCA) 168–169
light sensor 109, 129
limestone 79, 114, 150, 156, 160, 183, 184
limewater 132–133, 145
limiting reactants 61
line of best fit 193, 202 see also graph(s)
liquids 6, 12, 25, 34–35, 62, 109
   distillation 128–129
   fractions 131
   immiscible 10
   miscible 10–11
   pure 10
   thick 130–131
   washing-up 141
lithium 16, 19, 30–31, 68, 69
   reaction with water 26–27
litmus paper 118, 145

macromolecules 43 see also diamond
magnesium 60–61, 68–69, 70–71
mass 6, 58–59
   balanced equations 60–61
   reaction mixture 108
mass number 14–16, 17
maths skills 180–197
   algebra 190–192
   arithmetic and numerical computing 180–185
   geometry and trigonometry 196–197
   graphs 193–195

# Index

handling data 186–189
see also calculation(s) and graph(s)
mean 201, 202, 203, 204
measurements 143, 188, 191, 198, 201
melting points 26–27, 34–35, 87
   alkali metals 26
   aluminium oxide 90
   giant covalent structures 46–47
   halogens 28
   ionic compounds 40
   metals 53
   pure substances 140
   simple molecules 44
   transition elements 24–25
Mendeleev, Dmitri 23
metal carbonates 76, 79, 82
metal chlorides 27
metallic bonding 51
metal oxides 68, 73, 76, 80, 150
metal crystals 50–51 see also rusting
metals 4, 5, 15, 39
   alkali 4, 26–27, 30–31, 68, 74
   alkaline earth 4
   alloys 52–53, 90, 171
   bonding in 50–51
   catalysts 116
   displacement reactions 70–71
   extracting/extraction 70, 72–73, 90–91, 166–167, 170–171
   galvanised 50–51
   giant 51–52
   ions 26, 28, 51, 53, 75, 76, 89, 166
   melting and boiling points 26
   non- 4, 5, 16, 24–29, 36–38, 52, 70–73, 76, 187
   reaction with acids 68, 69, 74–75
   reaction with halogens 28–29
   reaction with water 26, 68, 69
   reactivity 26–27, 30, 3, 36, 38, 42–43, 68–70, 72, 74–75
   recycling 170–171
   rusting 50, 98, 108, 170
   salts 29, 74–79
   transition elements/metals 4, 25, 76, 116
methane 42, 44, 96, 129
   in atmosphere 148, 150–151, 152, 154
miscible liquids 10
mixtures 8–11, 128, 140–142
molecular model 44
molecules 4, 25, 30, 56–59, 82, 91, 103, 110, 156, 180, 196

alkane 129, 134
bromine 29, 88
diatomic 28
hollow-shaped 48 see also fullerenes
gas 124
hydrocarbon 130–131, 134–135
hydrogen and oxygen 101 see also bond breaking and bond making
organic 106, 128
protein 116
simple 42–44, 46
water 7, 34, 40–41, 78
moles (mol) 56–57, 60, 61, 103, 124, 133, 182, 190

nanoparticles 49, 111, 180, 189, 190, 197
nanotubes 48 see also fullerenes and graphene
natural gas 96, 132, 150, 156, 160, 165
negative ions 16–17, 24, 38, 74, 82, 86–89
   charges on common 76
   gaining electrons to form 36
neutralisation 78, 80–81
neutralisation reaction 76–77, 78, 96
neutrons 13–17, 23, 56, 180
Newlands, John 22–23
nitrates 74
nitrogen 4, 44, 148–151, 156–157, 169
   fertilisers 78, 141, 164–165
   Haber process 103
nitrogen oxides 156–157 see also pollutants
noble gases 4, 19, 24–26, 28, 36–38, 42, 151
non-metals 4, 5, 16, 26–29, 37, 38, 52, 70–73, 76, 187
   reactive 24–25, 36, 42
non-renewable resources 116, 128
nucleus 5, 14, 16–18, 30–31, 36, 180
   evidence for 12–13

oil 10, 26, 46, 128–135, 140, 150, 156, 160–161, 186 see also crude oil and pollutants
   distillation of 130–131
oil refineries 10, 131, 132, 134
oil-rich nations 163 see also desalination
OILRIG 71, 75, 88
orders of magnitude 83, 160, 188, 204
ores 68, 72, 73, 90, 160, 170, 171 see also bauxite

extracting metals from 166–167 see also phytomining and bioleaching
organic compounds 106, 128, 135
alkenes 134–135
outliers 201, 202, 204
oxidation 68, 71, 75, 88, 98, 132, 157
oxygen gas 6, 26, 60, 89, 91, 117, 144, 148
   testing 144, 145

paint 160 see also renewable resources
paper bags 169 see also life cycle assessments (LCA)
paper chromatography 10–11, 142–143
particle theory/model 34–35
particulates 156–157
Periodic Table 2, 4, 5, 14, 15, 18, 19, 22–27, 30, 36, 56, 76 see also relative atomic mass
   ions and the 38–39
photosynthesis 148–149, 150–151, 153, 155 see also carbon
pH scale 80–81 see also neutralisation
phytomining 167
pipette 143 see also chromatograms
plastic bag 169 see also paper bag
pollution 156, 166, 170, 171, 200
poly(ethene) 168–169, 215, 224
polymers 45, 106, 134, 160–161
poly(propene) 160 see also renewable resources
positive ions 16–17, 24, 38, 53, 68, 70, 75, 87–89
   charges on common 76
   losing electrons to form 36
potable water 162–165
potassium 19, 26–27, 29, 30, 68–69, 72, 76, 89
precipitate 109, 138
precise/precision 113, 187, 200–201
pressure 25, 34, 110, 116, 123–125, 150, 190, 191
   effects of 114–115
   enormous 46 see also diamond
   high 114, 128
   low 12, 114
   reduced 163
products 6–7, 58–60, 78, 86–88, 92–93, 102, 122, 124
   endothermic reactions 96–97, 100, 101, 125
   exothermic reactions 96, 98, 100,

101, 125
  mass calculations 58–59
  measuring 108–109
  rate of reaction 108–109, 117
  reaction profiles 100–101, 116
  reversible reactions 118–119, 120–121
propene 134–135
protein molecules 116
protons 13–18, 23–25, 30–31, 36, 56, 180
purity 2, 140, 162, 163

rate of reaction 106–122, 186, 193, 195, 196
  catalysts 98, 101, 110, 116–117
  collision theory 110–111, 112
  concentration 114–115
  collecting data 108–109, 180
  pressure 114–115
  reversible reactions 118–121
  surface area 110–111
  temperature 112–113
raw materials 68, 160–162, 168–171 see also renewable resources
reactants 60, 69, 71, 76, 102, 111, 116–117, 194 see also moles (mol)
  chemical equations 6–7
  collision theory 110
  concentration of 114–115, 124, 193
  endothermic reactions 96–97, 100–102, 125
  equations and calculations 58–59
  equilibrium 122–123
  exothermic reactions 96, 99–102, 125
  limiting 61
rate of reaction 108–109
reversible reactions 118–119
reaction profile 100–101, 103, 116, 120
reactivity 68, 87
  alkali metals 4, 26–27, 30–31, 68, 74
  within groups 30–31
  halogens 28–29
  order of 29, 68–70
reactivity series 68–72, 74, 87
recycling 165, 168, 170–171
redox reactions 71, 74, 75, 167
reduction 68, 71–73, 75, 88, 155 see also oxidation
relative atomic mass 56–57, 60
relative formula mass 62–63
renewable resources 160, 161
repeatability 201, 203, 204
repeating units 45 see also polymers
reproducibility 203, 204

resources 66, 169
  finite 128, 160, 161, 166, 171
  limited 138, 170
  natural 138, 160–161, 168
  non-renewable 116, 128
renewable 160, 161
  water 162
retention factor (Rf) 142–143
reverse osmosis 163
reversible reactions 82, 118–119
  energy and 120
  energy changes in 121
  equilibrium 122–123, 124–125
risks 93, 154,155, 199
  evaluation of 198
rusting 50, 98, 108, 170
Rutherford, Ernest 13

salts 8–9, 38, 59, 69, 93, 98
  acids, metals, and 74–75
  copper 77, 121
  displacement reactions 70
  formulae of 76
  halogens 29
  making 77, 78–79
  potable water 162–163
  reversible reactions 118
surface area 196–197
salt solution 8–9, 74, 162
salt water 164
saturated hydrocarbons 129, 134–135 see also unsaturated hydrocarbons
self-heating can 99
separation 90
  crude oil 130
  fractional distillation 10–11, 130
  mixtures 8–9
  paper chromatography 10–11
sewage treatment 164–165
  shell electrons 44, 47
  shell 13, 18–19, 51, 150 see also energy levels
  inner 30–31
  outer 19, 24, 27, 31, 37, 42–44, 47, 75
  outermost 18–19, 24–26, 28, 30–31, 37–39
shielding effect 30–31
significant figures 56–57, 111, 133, 186, 204
silicon 18, 46
silicon dioxide (silica) 46
silver 4, 25, 26, 69, 70, 72, 74
silver crystals 50

silver nitrate 50, 70,
simple molecules 42–44, 46
sludge 164–165, 167
smelting 166–167,171
sodium 5, 14, 16, 27, 31, 66, 92, 183, 193
  alkali metals 26
  electron shell diagram 18
  ions 36, 37, 38, 40
  Periodic table 19, 30
  reacting masses 59
  reactivity series 68–69, 72
sodium chloride 27, 28, 37, 41, 44, 45, 63, 92
  common salt 98
  bleach 93
sodium chloride crystals 8–9
sodium hydroxide 6, 19, 26, 59, 62, 63, 80, 92
  acid + alkali 78
  bleach 93
  insoluble bases 76–77
  oven cleaner 81
sodium hydroxide solution 76, 78, 90, 81, 92–93
solids 6, 7, 9, 12, 24, 27, 41, 109, 131
  hydrocarbons 134
  properties of 34–35
  surface area 110
  treating the sewage sludge 164–165
  water safe to drink 163
soluble base 81
solutions 40, 71, 81, 97, 98, 112, 115, 167
  acidic 83, 118
  alkaline 68, 80, 118
  aqueous 6, 7, 29, 82, 83, 87–89, 92–93
  colourless 27
  concentration of 62, 110, 114
  reacting 78
  sulfate 71
  thinking of 154–155
solvents 8–11, 162
spectator ions 91, 120
spectroscopy 190–191
standard form 16, 246–248
starch 172–173
states of matter 36–37
state symbols 6
steel 191, 216–217, 223
stoichiometry 66
strong acids 98–99
structural formulae 161
structures 42–43, 45–55, 57–61
sugars 47, 172–173

212

# Index

sulfates  90–91, 189
sulfur dioxide  71, 202
surface area  57, 130–131, 136, 262
sustainability  70–71, 207
symbol equations  6, 64–67
techniques  68, 108, 142, 163
  carbon capture and storage  154–155
  extract copper  167
  life cycle assessment (LCA) 168–169
  separation  8–11
temperature  10
  low  26, 116,
  high  41, 46, 116, 134–135, 156, 157, 165, 166, 171 *see also* catalysts, cracking, pollutants *and* sludge
  room  4, 9, 25, 41, 45, 74, 112, 121, 31
testing
  a prediction  22
  conductivity  41
  for carbon dioxide gas  145
  for chlorine gas  145
  for gases  132, 144–145
  for hydrogen gas  144
  for oxygen gas  144
theories  2, 148, 198
  collision  110–113
  particle  34–35
  'plum-pudding'  12
thermal decomposition  119, 134, 166
thermal decomposition reactions  96, 134
thermal energy  46, 47, 49, 52, 53
Thomson, J.J.  12–13
transition elements  4, 25
tungsten  73

uncertainty  161, 169, 201, 204
  making estimates of  204
universal indicator  26, 80, 81
unsaturated hydrocarbons  135

variables  200, 203
  control  204
  dependent  200, 202
  independent  199, 200, 202
viscosity  130, 131
volume  34, 62, 78, 81, 114, 115, 117, 197, 201
  continuous data  188
  decimal form  180
  estimating the result  185
  increasing  109
  large  154, 163

metric prefixes  191
ratios  182
significant figures  186
straight line graphs  194
surface area  196
surface area to  49, 110, 111, 116, 197

washing-up liquids  141 *see also* formulations
water vapour  148, 149, 152 *see also* greenhouse gases
weak acids  82–83,
working scientifically  198–204

zinc  50, 69–75, 86, 87, 90, 144, 171
zinc chloride  77, 86
zinc crystals  50

# Appendix 1: the Periodic Table

| Group 1 Alkali metals | 2 | | | | | | | | | | | | 3 | 4 | 5 | 6 | 7 Halogens | 0/8 Noble gases |
|---|---|---|---|---|---|---|---|---|---|---|---|---|---|---|---|---|---|---|
| | | | | | | 1 H hydrogen 1 | | | | | | | | | | | | 4 He helium 2 |
| 7 Li lithium 3 | 9 Be beryllium 4 | | | | | | | | | | | | 11 B boron 5 | 12 C carbon 6 | 14 N nitrogen 7 | 16 O oxygen 8 | 19 F flourine 9 | 20 Ne neon 10 |
| 23 Na sodium 11 | 24 Mg magnesium 12 | | | | | | | | | | | | 27 Al aluminium 13 | 28 Si silicon 14 | 31 P phosphorus 15 | 32 S sulfur 16 | 35.5 Cl chlorine 17 | 40 Ar argon 18 |
| 39 K potassium 19 | 40 Ca calcium 20 | 45 Sc scandium 21 | 48 Ti titanium 22 | 51 V vanadium 23 | 52 Cr chromium 24 | 55 Mn manganese 25 | 56 Fe iron 26 | 59 Co cobalt 27 | 59 Ni nickel 28 | 63.5 Cu copper 29 | 65 Zn zinc 30 | | 70 Ga gallium 31 | 73 Ge germanium 32 | 75 As arsenic 33 | 79 Se selenium 34 | 80 Br bromine 35 | 84 Kr krypton 36 |
| 85.5 Rb rubidium 37 | 88 Sr strontium 38 | 89 Y yttrium 39 | 91 Zr zirconium 40 | 93 Nb niobium 41 | 96 Mo molybdenum 42 | (98) Tc technetium 43 | 101 Ru ruthenium 44 | 103 Rh rhodium 45 | 106 Pd palladium 46 | 108 Ag silver 47 | 112 Cd cadmium 48 | | 115 In indium 49 | 119 Sn tin 50 | 122 Sb antimony 51 | 128 Te tellurium 52 | 127 I iodine 53 | 131 Xe xenon 54 |
| 133 Cs caesium 55 | 137 Ba barium 56 | 139 La* lanthanum 57 | 178.5 Hf hafnium 72 | 181 Ta tantalum 73 | 184 W tungsten 74 | 186 Re rhenium 75 | 190 Os osmium 76 | 192 Ir iridium 77 | 195 Pt platinum 78 | 197 Au gold 79 | 201 Hg mercury 80 | | 204 Tl thallium 81 | 207 Pb lead 82 | 209 Bi bismuth 83 | 210 Po polonium 84 | (210) At astatine 85 | 222 Rn radon 86 |
| (223) Fr francium 87 | (226) Ra radium 88 | (227) Ac# actinium 89 | (261) Rf rutherfordium 104 | (262) Db dubnium 105 | (266) Sg seaborgium 106 | (264) Bh bohrium 107 | (277) Hs hassium 108 | (268) Mt meitnerium 109 | (271) Ds darmstadtium 110 | (272) Rg roentgenium 111 | (285) Cn copernicium 112 | | (286) Nh nihonium 113 | (289) Fl flerovium 114 | (289) Mc moscovium 115 | (293) Lv livermorium 116 | (294) Ts tennessine 117 | (294) Og oganesson 118 |

*58–71 Lanthanides

| 140 Ce cerium 58 | 141 Pr praseodymium 59 | 144 Nd neodymium 60 | (145) Pm promethium 61 | 150 Sm samarium 62 | 152 Eu europium 63 | 157 Gd gadolinium 64 | 159 Tb terbium 65 | 163 Dy dysprosium 66 | 165 Ho holmium 67 | 167 Er erbium 68 | 169 Tm thulium 69 | 173 Yb ytterbium 70 | 175 Lu lutetium 71 |

#90–103 Actinides

| 232 Th thorium 90 | 231 Pa protactinium 91 | 238 U uranium 92 | 237 Np neptunium 93 | 239 Pu plutonium 94 | 243 Am americium 95 | 247 Cm curium 96 | 247 Bk berkelium 97 | 252 Cf californium 98 | (252) Es einsteinium 99 | (257) Fm fermium 100 | (258) Md mendelevium 101 | (259) No nobelium 102 | (260) Lr lawrencium 103 |

Key: relative atomic mass / chemical symbol / name / atomic (proton) number

Periods 2–7

# OXFORD
UNIVERSITY PRESS

Great Clarendon Street, Oxford, OX2 6DP, United Kingdom

Oxford University Press is a department of the University of Oxford. It furthers the University's objective of excellence in research, scholarship, and education by publishing worldwide. Oxford is a registered trade mark of Oxford University Press in the UK and in certain other countries.

© Lawrie Ryan 2024

The moral rights of the author have been asserted

First published in 2024

All rights reserved. No part of this publication may be reproduced, stored in a retrieval system, or transmitted, used for text and data mining, or used for training artificial intelligence, in any form or by any means, without the prior permission in writing of Oxford University Press, or as expressly permitted by law, by licence or under terms agreed with the appropriate reprographics rights organization. Enquiries concerning reproduction outside the scope of the above should be sent to the Rights Department, Oxford University Press, at the address above.

You must not circulate this work in any other form and you must impose this same condition on any acquirer

British Library Cataloguing in Publication Data
Data available

978 1 38 205143 9

10 9 8 7 6 5 4 3 2 1

The manufacturing process conforms to the environmental regulations of the country of origin.

Printed in the United Kingdom by Bell and Bain Ltd, Glasgow.

**Acknowledgements**

The publisher and authors would like to thank the following for permission to use photographs and other copyright material:

**Cover:** Sua Balac/closer&closer. **Photos: viii:** Daboost / Shutterstock, Jantakon / Shutterstock; **p2:** Kateryna Kon / Shutterstock; **p2(inset):** art_of_sun / Shutterstock; **p4:** Brostock / Shutterstock; **p8:** Pixelspieler / Shutterstock; **p22(l):** SHEILA TERRY / SCIENCE PHOTO LIBRARY; **p22(r):** The Picture Art Collection / Alamy Stock Photo; **p23(t), 80(b):** SCIENCE PHOTO LIBRARY; **p23(b):** Olga Popova / Shutterstock; **p26, 62, 74, 98, 119, 180(t):** MARTYN F. CHILLMAID / SCIENCE PHOTO LIBRARY; **p27:** TREVOR CLIFFORD PHOTOGRAPHY / SCIENCE PHOTO LIBRARY; **p42:** Oleg Znamenskiy / Shutterstock; **p43:** JOEL AREM / SCIENCE PHOTO LIBRARY; **p44, 197(b):** Michael J Thompson / Shutterstock; **p46, 181(m):** Africa Studio / Shutterstock; **p49:** Ambelrip / Shutterstock; **p50, 96(l):** Lawrie Ryan; **p52:** Bloomberg / Contributor / Getty; **p53(t):** kozzi / 123RF; **p53(b):** jk1887 / 123RF; **p66:** iamlukyeee / Shutterstock; **p66(inset):** Anwarul Kabir Photo / Shutterstock; **p68(t):** tr3gi / 123RF; **p68(m):** dell640 / 123RF; **p68(b):** XXLPhoto / Shutterstock; **p72(t):** Nordroden / Shutterstock; **p72(b):** Jose Luis Stephens / Shutterstock; **p78:** Nigel Cattlin / Alamy Stock Photo; **p79:** R.M. Nunes / Getty; **p80(t):** Claire Dobson; **p90:** Attl Tibor / Shutterstock; **p93(t):** Studioshots / Alamy Stock Photo; **p93(l):** Elenathewise / 123RF; **p93(r):** anocha89 / 123RF; **p96(r):** Christopher Wood / Shutterstock; **p97:** claire norman / Shutterstock; **p99:** Praisaeng / Shutterstock; **p106:** Gary L Jones / Shutterstock; **p106(inset):** Mariyka Herman / Shutterstock; **p110:** emzet70 / Shutterstock; **p112(t):** mavo / Shutterstock; **p112(b):** EcoPrint / Shutterstock; **p113:** MaraZe / Shutterstock; **p116(t):** Inna Reznik / Shutterstock; **p116(b):** adam88x / 123RF; **p118, 182(b):** ANDREW LAMBERT PHOTOGRAPHY / SCIENCE PHOTO LIBRARY; **p120, 140:** MARTYN F. CHILLMAID / SCIENCE PHOTO LIBRARY; **p121:** SCIENCE PHOTO LIBRARY; **p128:** Alf Ribeiro / Shutterstock; **p131:** tomas1111 / 123RF; **p132:** yocamon / 123RF; **p133:** tonlammerts / 123RF; **p134:** jaochainoi / 123RF; **p138:** PAUL D STEWART / SCIENCE PHOTO LIBRARY; **p138(inset):** kskaz / Shutterstock; **p141:** alexraths / 123RF; **p143, 184(b):** ANDREW LAMBERT PHOTOGRAPHY / SCIENCE PHOTO LIBRARY; **p148(t):** vulkanette / 123RF; **p148(b):** NASA / SCIENCE PHOTO LIBRARY; **p149(l):** Ikonya / Shutterstock; **p149(r):** gunnarassmy / 123RF; **p150:** gunarex / 123RF; **p154:** Leighton Collins / Shutterstock; **p155:** OLOS / Shutterstock; **p156(t):** martin33 / 123RF; **p156(b):** gemphoto / Shutterstock; **p157:** pixelthat / 123RF; **p160:** John Cancalosi / Alamy Stock Photo; **p161:** Zigmunds Dizgalvis / Shutterstock; **p164:** anticainen / 123RF; **p165:** Sigur / Shutterstock; **p166:** alicenerr / 123RF; **p168:** rmorijn / 123RF; **p169:** volff / 123RF; **p170:** KtD / Shutterstock; **p171(t):** Don Paulson / Alamy Stock Photo; **p171(b):** Kodda / Shutterstock; **p172:** avLitrato / 123RF; **p180(b):** photong / Shutterstock; **p181(l):** Efired / Shutterstock; **p181(r):** Shahril KHMD / Shutterstock; **p181(b):** Becris / Shutterstock; **p182(t):** Everett Collection / Shutterstock; **p183(t):** mphoto / Shutterstock; **p183(b):** Anthony Brown / Alamy Stock Photo; **p184(t):** Andrew Fletcher / Shutterstock; **p186:** Kagai19927 / Shutterstock; **p187:** massawfoto / Shutterstock; **p188(l):** SpeedKingz / Shutterstock; **p188(r):** Pete Niesen / Shutterstock; **p190:** Imagesmith / Shutterstock; **p191:** YanLev Alexey / Shutterstock; **p197(t):** runi / Shutterstock; **p198:** Annto / Shutterstock; **p199:** Kletr / Shutterstock; **p200:** Alexei Novikov / Shutterstock; **p201:** hxdbzxy / Shutterstock; **p202:** R&R PhotoStudio / Brent Parker Jones.

Artwork by Q2A Media, Aptara Inc., Phoenix Photosetting, Erwin Haya, Wearset Ltd., Peter Bull Art Studio, HL Studios, Mike Hall, and Oxford University Press.

Although we have made every effort to trace and contact all copyright holders before publication this has not been possible in all cases. If notified, the publisher will rectify any errors or omissions at the earliest opportunity.

Links to third party websites are provided by Oxford in good faith and for information only. Oxford disclaims any responsibility for the materials contained in any third party website referenced in this work.

FSC MIX Paper | Supporting responsible forestry
FSC® C007785